22 95

The Holocaust
and the Liberal Imagination

The Holocaust
and the
Liberal Imagination

A Social and Cultural History

Tony Kushner

BLACKWELL
Oxford UK & Cambridge USA

First published 1994

Blackwell Publishers, the publishing imprint of
Basil Blackwell Ltd
108 Cowley Road
Oxford OX4 1JF, UK

Basil Blackwell Inc.
238 Main Street
Cambridge, Massachusetts 02142, USA

British Library Cataloguing in Publication Data
A CIP catalogue record for this book is available from the British Library

Library of Congress Cataloging-in-Publication Data
Kushner, Tony (Antony Robin Jeremy)
The Holocaust and the liberal imagination: a social and cultural history/Tony Kushner.
p. cm.
Includes bibliographic references and index.
ISBN 0–631–19482–7. — ISBN 0–631–19483–5 (pbk.)
1. Holocaust, Jewish (1939–1945)—Influence. 2. Liberalism—Great Britain—History—20th century. 3. Liberalism—United States—History—20th century. 4. Political culture—Great Britain—History—20th century. 5. Political culture—United States—History—20th century. 6. Great Britain—Social conditions—20th century. 7. United States—Social conditions—1933–1945.
I. Title.
D804.3.K87 1994
940.53'18—dc20   93–49879
CIP

Typeset in 10 on 12pt Times by
Paul Stringer, Oxford
Printed in Great Britain by
T. J. Press (Padstow) Ltd, Cornwall

This book is printed on acid-free paper

*To Eleanor Rathbone who knew, cared and acted
and to Jack Kushner, for a life free of the threat and
co-presence of genocide*

Contents

Part III: The Post-War World

Preface

A short note is necessary to explain the purpose and scope of this book. *The Holocaust and the Liberal Imagination* attempts to explain and not to condemn the responses and reactions of the democratic world to the attempted destruction of European Jewry. There is a growth industry of academic and general books on the Allies or 'free world' and the Holocaust which concentrate on state policies and international diplomacy. This work will not ignore 'high politics' or bureaucratic procedures but will attempt a more inclusive approach. It will concentrate on the impact of the Holocaust on ordinary people in the democracies and will examine the actions of the nation-states in the light of popular responses. The disciplines of social, cultural, gender and labour history, previously marginalized in Holocaust studies, will be employed to add a different dimension to the existing literature.

The book will focus particularly on Britain and the Holocaust. Nonetheless, its approach will be comparative, especially with regard to the United States of America, thus allowing consideration of mono-cultural and plurally defined liberal democratic societies. *The Holocaust and the Liberal Imagination* also adopts a secular chronology covering the 60-year period from the Nazi rise to power to the present day. Ultimately this study argues that the Holocaust, both at the time and subsequently, is not simply German, Jewish or Continental history but is an integral yet neglected part of the experience of many countries away from the killing fields. It is consequently as much a contribution to Anglo-American social and cultural history as it is an account of the Holocaust.

Acknowledgements

I was vaguely aware growing up in Manchester during the 1960s and 1970s that my Jewish family (which included a physically disabled mother and deaf-blind brother) would not have stood much chance in Nazi Germany. Looking back it surprises me how little reference was made to the Holocaust, either at school or in Jewish activities. The subject was close to taboo status. I am thus particularly grateful to the late Department of Economic and Social History at the University of Sheffield – the first centre for the study of minority issues and racism within the British historical establishment – for opening up areas that I knew to be important. Members of that department, especially Colin Holmes, encouraged me to continue as a postgraduate which I did, initially at the University of Connecticut. I should like to take the opportunity, rather belatedly, of thanking the History Department at Storrs, Connecticut, for an excellent year which convinced me that I wanted to become a professional historian. Bruce Stave and Bill Hoglund deserve particular praise for strengthening my interest in minority studies and introducing me to American history.

The work for this book has been carried out in my tenure as Parkes Fellow (and more recently as Marcus Sieff Lecturer) in Jewish/non-Jewish Relations in the Department of History, University of Southampton. I should like to thank all at the University and those outside it who have supported the Parkes Library and activities linked to it. James Parkes himself in the late 1920s was first encouraged to embark on his practical and academic work on the issue of antisemitism by the generosity of the Sieff family. I am delighted and honoured to occupy a position which continues that link. James Parkes features throughout this book in his devoted work on behalf of European Jewry. As this bloody century comes to an end there is a desperate need for people of Parkes' stature and integrity.

I should like to acknowledge the help and encouragement of Bernard Naylor, University of Southampton Librarian, Gordon Higginson, Vice Chancellor of the University of Southampton and Raymond Plant, Chair of the Parkes Library Committee, during a crucial period, and, more recently, Henry Ettinghausen for recognizing the worth of the Parkes Library and archive.

All in the History Department at Southampton deserve my thanks. Alastair Duke, Brian Golding, John Oldfield and Tessa Webber are owed a tremendous debt for keeping my department supportive and humane in these days of attrition and government tactics of divide and rule. Paul Smith, Kevin Sharpe and John Rule gave early encouragement to this project and the Arts Faculty helped its completion with small but important research grants. Undergraduate students, especially on my third year Special Subject, have always provided a challenge and a stimulus. Joanne Reilly, a postgraduate at Southampton working on the liberation of Belsen, deserves particular mention.

Friends and colleagues took precious time and care to look at draft chapters. I would like to thank Martin Alexander, Ken Lunn, John Oldfield, Colin Richmond, Greg Walker and Bill Williams for their helpful comments and encouragement. My work owes much to discussions with those in Britain who are opening up the subject of the Holocaust, including Richard Bolchover, David Cesarani, Andy Charlesworth, Bryan Cheyette, Ben Helfgott, Colin Holmes, Louise London, Andrea Reiter, Colin Richmond, Bill Williams and Isabel Wollaston. David Sorkin, editor of the 'Jewish Society and Culture' series at Blackwell backed this project from the start and provided invaluable comments on the manuscript. Simon Prosser at Blackwell has been equally supportive and helpful, as has my copy-editor, Paul Stringer. Thanks also to Sybil Lunn for her work on the index.

Librarians and archivists have been helpful to me in Britain, the United States and Israel. I would like to single out in particular those at the Parkes Library – Geoff Hampson, Wendy Buckle and, more recently, Jenny Ruthven – who have provided excellent support and good humour. I am also indebted to Chris Woolgar, an outstanding archivist who has transformed the state of Jewish records in recent years. Others on his team, including Karen Robson, have been a model of efficiency and helpfulness. Paul Bogey, Oron Stone, Joan Chapman and Nick Graffy have also gone beyond the call of duty within the University Library staff. The staff at the Wiener Library deserve particular praise as do all at the Mass-Observation Archive, University of Sussex, especially Dorothy Sheridan and Joyce Eldridge. Thanks also to those at the Central Zionist Archives, Jerusalem, and Dennis Rohrbaugh at the Research Foundation for Jewish Immigration, New York, for most enjoyable and productive overseas visits. Richard Storey at the Modern Records Centre,

University of Warwick, Richard Samways at the Greater London Record Office, Simone Mace at the Rothschild archive, David Massel at the Board of Deputies of British Jews and Jean Ayton at Manchester Central Reference Library have always taken a particular interest in my work. Bill Williams, Don Rainger and Catherine Rew have made returning to the Manchester Jewish Museum a pleasure, as has Rickie Burman at the London Museum of Jewish Life. I must also express my gratitude to the archivists and librarians at the British Library, British Library of Political and Economic Science, Imperial War Museum, National Labour Museum, Public Record Office, Southampton Central Reference Library, Universities of Hull, Liverpool, Manchester and Sheffield, and Yad Vashem Institute. I would like to take this opportunity of thanking the trustees at the Mass-Observation Archive, the Research Foundation for Jewish Immigration and the Rothschild archive for permission to quote material in their archives. The editors of the journals *Immigrants and Minorities* and *Holocaust and Genocide Studies* gave encouragement by publishing my earlier work on this project.

It is a great pleasure to acknowledge the role of friends and relatives in the completion of this book. The Cavaliers have provided a welcome distraction and prove that it is still possible to *enjoy* sport. Old friends from Cheadle deserve particular mention as do more 'recent' ones from the States, including fellow writer Anne Rimbey. At Southampton I have cherished the friendship of all my colleagues, especially the captain of the Cavaliers, Nick Kingwell. Greg Walker, Colin Richmond, Bill Williams, Richard Bolchover, Ken Lunn, Bryan Cheyette and David Cesarani have combined academic support with keeping me relatively sane. Lastly my family: in my first monograph which was published in 1989 I thanked them for their support and added that 'Maybe one day I will get a *real job*!'. The remark was partly misunderstood by academic friends who thought it referred to my then temporary status. I am now 'permanent' at Southampton but fear that my family still do not see it as 'real' work. It is, however, their love that has kept me going. My mother on hearing of my routine for writing this book commented that it sounded 'just like a proper writer'. For showing me the importance of tolerance and the necessity of pluralism throughout my life I can forgive her this slip.

Finally, my wife Mag has provided friendship and love throughout. Our son Jack arrived at the last stages of this work and provided a welcome sense of perspective amidst all the copy-editing and proof-reading.

Tony Kushner

Introduction:
The Holocaust in Global Perspective and as Social History

The study of the destruction of European Jewry during World War II has now become a hotbed of activity. Its spectacular growth in recent years has led to the covering of much new ground and the focusing on issues and dimensions previously unconsidered. It is hardly surprising, however, that the attempt to broaden and deepen the territory explored has led to an uneven development: at times, the pursuit of new angles has simply distorted rather than clarified our understanding. This is perhaps most clearly evidenced in the study of the Allies and the Holocaust:

No country was as consistent and as callous in its actions aimed at sealing escape routes to those who tried to flee for their lives as was Great Britain. And no country had as many individuals in decision-making positions and as many government offices involved in that undertaking. Next to the Germans, who as the designers of the Final Solution and its executioners are in a category of their own, the British carry the heaviest guilt for that abomination, that collapse of human morality, the Holocaust.[1]

Of all the countries who must take the blame for refusing to save the Jews, the most culpable is undoubtedly Britain . . . the depraved German Nazis were not alone in their murdering – they had accessories all over the world.[2]

It would be easy to dismiss such nonsense as the crude ravings of amateur historians. Unfortunately these views have gained popular credence, especially among sections of the Jewish world. Despite the obvious pitfalls and the potential for distortion when considering the liberal democracies and their responses to the Holocaust (the remarks of an irate British official in 1946 should perhaps here always be kept in mind: 'His Majesty's Government were not responsible for countless Jewish deaths and suffering. The Nazis were responsible.'[3]), it is still a crucial area of study. First, the Holocaust was a global event and it was not only the perpetrators and victims who were connected to it. Second, both at state level and in society as a whole, the events and their aftermath made an impact even in countries physically unconnected to the implementation of mass murder. Two such countries were the liberal democracies of Britain and the United States, whose experience forms the focus of this book (with particular attention given to the former nation). The Holocaust, I will argue, is very much a part of their histories. But before scrutinizing this specific aspect, it is important to chart how the histories and representations of the Holocaust have developed.

I

During the war itself, the foundations for the study of what was to become known as the Holocaust, or, alternatively, the *Churban* or *Shoah*, were well established.[4] On the Continent the 'Oneg Shabbat' archive was established in Poland as early as October 1939 by Jewish historians because, in the words of its founder, Emmanuel Ringelblum, 'it was so important to dwell on every event as it happened, lest it be forgotten'.[5] In the Soviet Union, the Jewish Anti-Fascist Committee performed a similar function. From a project started in 1943, its members outlined the enormity of the destruction of East European Jewry in harrowing detail.[6] In the West, the Centre de Documentation Juive Contemporaine was established in Paris during 1943 as part of the resistance movement. Away from the Jewish graveyard of Europe, YIVO (the Yiddish Scientific Institute) documented the fate of European Jewry from the safety of New York, having transferred from Vilna in 1939.[7] Similarly the Wiener Library had moved to London from the Netherlands just before the outbreak of the war and was, by 1945, already an internationally recognized centre for the study of Nazism in general and the persecution of the Jews in particular.[8] It is true that not all the evidence collected in the war was immediately available. Little of the Soviet material was released as the Jewish Anti-Fascist Committee was liquidated by Stalin in the post-war years. The Oneg Shabbat archive was not recovered for several years after 1945 and some records were ruined, others never found. Yet after the war the material gathered as evidence for the Nuremberg War Crimes Tribunals and the testimony of the accused added a rich vein of relevant material.[9] Despite the availability of a wide range of evidence, however, it was to be several decades after 1945 before the Holocaust became established not only as an academic subject, but also in more popular cultural representations. Put boldly, before the 1960s at the earliest, the Holocaust as a self-enclosed entity had not yet entered into the general consciousness or memory of the Western world.

The combination of relative neglect followed by intensive interest has produced some bizarre results. Nevertheless, it has been suggested that the Holocaust 'is now a thoroughly mature area of academic study . . . [with] the guidelines of its numerous and often fierce debates . . . clearly marked out.'[10] One sign of that maturity has been the production of 'the first major work synthesizing and summarizing the findings of research historians on the history of the Holocaust' by Michael Marrus in 1987. In this work Marrus was clear about his aims: 'to integrate the history of the Holocaust into the general stream of historical consciousness'.[11] It would be naive to assume, however, that the early neglect followed by later intensive concern have cancelled each other out by yielding a new, balanced synthesis. The point can be illustrated by the place of the victim in representations of the Holocaust.

The first major historians of the Holocaust, Leon Poliakov in France and Gerald Reitlinger in England, were in close agreement that the voice of the Jews themselves would be used sparingly in their narratives. Both researched their works in the late 1940s and published them in the early 1950s. Poliakov in his *Breviare de la haine* (1951) stated that 'wherever possible, to forestall objections, we have quoted the executioners rather than the victims'. In similar vein, Reitlinger in his *The Final Solution* (1953) commented that although caution was needed for all sources, it was 'particularly' necessary when approaching survivor accounts.[12] Indeed the two surveys relied heavily on the Nuremberg Trial materials and largely ignored the significant number of published survivor testimonies available by the end of the 1940s. Both Poliakov and Reitlinger were aware of the incredulity of their audience (the former, in his introduction, commented on 'the appearance of publications in which doubt is cast on the number of Jewish victims and on a great many other things', and thereby highlighted the disturbingly deep roots of Holocaust denial). 'Authenticity' was thus required and it was assumed that evidence from the victim was somehow less persuasive and objective; it was somehow softer than material emanating from the persecutor. It has been suggested with regard to concentration camp memoirs that

Even though a great number of these texts were produced immediately after the author's release from camp and thus can be expected to give an authentic record of the writer's experience, historians generally do not trust them when looking for evidence of the historical truth of the camps.[13]

A recent and generally sophisticated analysis of German public responses to antisemitism in the Nazi era has suggested that many testimonies 'hardly constitut[e] firm historical evidence'. The author instead favours the intelligence material gathered by the Nazis themselves to 'the recollections of German Jews . . . [which] should in most cases be used simply to illustrate or add colour to an account based on less subjective sources – allowing us to feel the pulse of events by adding atmosphere to *the historian's detached and analytical reconstruction*' (my emphasis).[14] Reitlinger, in particular, revealed two tendencies that pervaded the historical profession in the post-war world. The first was the concentration on dominant men in the study of the past. A form of machismo was at work, shown in the preference for perpetrator evidence and a concentration on the 'hard' world of the male mass murderers. As Joan Ringelheim suggests, 'Gender may seem to be invisible in Holocaust literature (whether scholarly or otherwise); in fact, its role awaits disclosure'. There has been, for example, little work carried out on the experience of women during the Holocaust.[15] The second is equally revealing with regard to the level of intellectual snobbery and self-imposed limitations of many historians after 1945: 'The hardy survivors . . . were seldom educated men'. Reitlinger added that 'impressions recorded from the receiving end give a new twist to the often oblique language of German bureaucracy and they are necessary to complete the story'.[16] The victim in the early Holocaust histories emerges almost as an afterthought and as an interesting but not essential element in the story. The approach reached its apex with the still definitive account of the killing process, Raul Hilberg's monumental *The Destruction of the European Jews*. Hilberg announced unapologetically that his was 'not a book about the Jews. It is a book about the people who destroyed the Jews. Not much will be read here about the victims. The focus is placed on the perpetrators.' Indeed, the sentiments expressed in the late 1950s by Ball-Kaduri of the Yad Vashem Institute (which set up a testimony department in 1954) that 'the daily life of the Jews, their feelings and reactions, and the numerous acts of resistance carried out by the Jewish community, have come to us from memoirs and accounts given by eye-witnesses' made little impact for several decades.[17]

Thirty years later there are still important Holocaust books being written in which the Jewish experience is relayed only through the testimony of their murderers. In response to this limiting approach, Martin Gilbert produced his epic account, *The Holocaust: The Jewish Tragedy* (1986). The book employs a detailed chronology and is, in the author's words,

an attempt to draw on the nearest of the witnesses, those closest to the destruction, and through their testimony to tell something of the suffering of those who perished, and are forever silent.[18]

In the quarter century between the first histories of the Holocaust and the work of Martin Gilbert, a mass of printed survivor material (in addition to the discovery of fresh contemporary testimony from the war years) became available to scholars. Oral history, and more recently video interviews, have added layer upon layer to our knowledge of the Holocaust from the perspective of the persecuted.[19] There can be no excuse now, in view of the readily available documentation, for the voice of the victim not to be heard. But a dilemma remains. The sheer volume of personal testimonies confronts the historian with the problem of providing coherence. It has been suggested that the task of the historian is to generalize, yet the very nature of victim testimony almost denies such a possibility. Lawrence Langer, in his powerful analysis of survivor video testimony, has stressed how 'the Holocaust has a different beginning for each witness'.[20] This problematic chronology reveals not only the geographical complexity of the Holocaust, but also the varying speeds at which the persecution occurred, reflecting changes in the pattern of the war, local circumstances, power struggles within the Nazi hierarchy and the responses of the Jews themselves. The dilemma facing historians of the Holocaust is that they now have to face the choice of incorporating material that is both voluminous *and* idiosyncratic or, alternatively, of ignoring it. The latter strategy brings with it the false conclusions reached by some early Holocaust historians, namely that the Jews were merely passive victims of genocide. While ultimately the Jews themselves were unable to stop the destruction process, it is clear now that their complex and varied responses to persecution have to be given serious consideration to gain an understanding of the overall picture.[21] Moreover, ignoring the experiences of the Jews, although allowing coherence, also runs the risk of replicating the image given by their persecutors – the victims becoming a faceless mass, lacking any human dignity. The inclusion of the victims on both a collective and individual level greatly broadens the scope of the study of the Holocaust but it also poses questions about basic premises of the subject, including its chronology and geography.

With regard to the latter, it is perhaps not surprising that in the immediate aftermath of World War II, the Holocaust was seen as a Nazi crime and, therefore, solely the responsibility of the German nation. Countries in the West such as France and Holland had no desire to be reminded of their role in the execution of the 'Final Solution'. Instead, in the difficult post-war period, attempts to bolster national self-prestige were made and resistance to Nazism was emphasized. It was perhaps not surprising that there were few who wished to undergo a searching re-examination of possible collaboration in the war. Thus the first major historical work on Holland and the destruction of Dutch Jewry was not published until the 1960s and was greeted with unease and some animosity by a society that had been embarrassed and even hostile to the returning survivors after 1945.[22] One indication of the lack of concern relating to the Holocaust in Holland was the initial difficulty in finding a publisher for the diaries of Anne Frank in the late 1940s. As the historians of the Anne Frank House Museum put it: 'There was little interest . . . during the first post-war year in reminders of that black period. It was time to look forward, not backward, and sights were set on the future and the rebuilding of the Netherlands.' Remarkably, a decade later, when the book had already become an international best-seller and been transported onto screen and stage, the Anne Frank House in Amsterdam was very close to being demolished to make way for new office developments.[23] In France the process of self-scrutiny of the Vichy years was even longer in coming. Henry Rousso stresses that after the war 'The return of victims from the Nazi concentration camps was the event most quickly effaced from memory'. It is significant that it was Robert Paxton and Michael Marrus, two leading historians from North America, who pioneered the detailed investigation into Vichy and the Jews in a book published as late as 1981. Paxton and Marrus's work was essential in highlighting that a totally Germanocentric approach to the implementation of the Holocaust distorted the reality and disguised the complexity of the decision-making process. As they pointed out:

It has been customary to assume that what befell the Jews of France during the German occupation, beginning with discriminatory legislation in 1940 and culminating with the death of many thousands of French and foreign Jews between 1942 and 1944, was largely the work of nazi zealots who imposed their views on a defeated country. That seemed the only possible explanation for so apparently abrupt a change of climate in June 1940 . . . [yet] when we began . . . to look closely at the measures taken against Jews in France during the German occupation, we found that the French had much more leeway than was commonly supposed, and that victor and vanquished had interacted much more intricately than we had expected.[24]

For the first years of the occupation, Vichy's own agenda concerning the Jews was of greater importance than the German input with regard to the implementation of antisemitism. Moreover, 'Vichy anti-Jewish policy was . . . not only autonomous from German policy; it was a rival to it. Vichy struggled with the occupying authority in an attempt to assert its own sovereignty in anti-Jewish matters.' The timing, scope and direction of the Holocaust in France cannot be understood without recognizing the input of Vichy.[25]

In post-war Eastern Europe the rapid onset of Stalinization in areas previously overrun by the Nazis precluded the discussion of the ethnic particularism of the Jewish fate. In the crude anti-fascism of the post-war years, Jews were submerged as victims under their national origins. Thus, until very recently, the Auschwitz Museum which has been visited by nearly 20 million people since the war, 'described the identity of the victims merely as "people" – men, women, and children, of twenty-eight different nations, alongside which Jews were just one nationality'.[26] Discussion of the involvement of local populations in areas of the Soviet Union such as Lithuania, Latvia, Estonia the Ukraine and Belorussia in the destruction of the Jews was impossible. The release now of archival material from the former Soviet Union is making clear that such local involvement was not only important in the process of destruction; it was also critically significant in determining the timing of the mass murders in the east. At times, as Dina Porat has illustrated with regard to Lithuanian involvement in the *Einsatzgruppen* forces, the Nazis were concerned lest local enthusiasm for butchering the Jews interfered with their own sovereignty in the area.[27] Indeed, Martin Broszat, the German historian and a leading proponent of the functionalist interpretation of the Holocaust (that the destruction of European Jewry, like many aspects of Nazi policy, emerged from confusion, competition and constant improvisation rather than from a clear plan), went so far as to argue that the decision to embark upon the 'Final Solution' came out of local, but spontaneous, actions.[28] Providing an alternative model, Christopher Browning, with specific reference to the Holocaust in Serbia but arguing more generally, has suggested 'it was not pressure from above for deportation that caused local leaders to kill; rather, it was pressure from below for deportation that caused the central authorities to provide the means to kill locally'. Thus in Serbia between 1941 and 1942 'Berlin sent SS and Foreign Office representatives to Belgrade to urge a "local solution" to the Jewish question. They discovered upon arrival that their pressure was unnecessary, for a local solution was already underway.'[29] The debate between Broszat and Browning about the direction of causality did not preclude general agreement between the two that the 'study of events at the local level also enriches our understanding of the decision-making process at the center'. Again, the scope, but also the complexity, of the study of the Holocaust has expanded rapidly.[30]

Linked to the early concentration on Germany, and the exclusion of the involvement of other countries, was the fixation on the Nazi elite and its responsibility for the Holocaust. Based on the material from the post-war trials, 'The initial representation of the Holocaust perpetrators was that of criminal minds, infected with racism and antisemitism, carrying out criminal policies through criminal organizations.'[31] There was a concentration on Hitler to the exclusion of others in the Nazi elite in addition to a macabre interest in the psychopathic behaviour of those involved in mass murder, including the demonization of figures such as Rudolf Höss, commandant of Auschwitz or Joseph Kramer, 'The Beast of Belsen'.[32] Some comfort could be found in the idea that those involved were somehow abnormal, social and psychological misfits. In addition there was commercial potential in the selling of the Nazi crimes as horror stories with sado-masochistic and pornographic potential. The work of social psychologists, many themselves refugees from Nazism, summarized in *The Authoritarian Personality*, tended to confirm the existence of an abnormal minority, prone to prejudice and involvement in intolerant organizations.[33] In fact it was not until the 1970s that this work was challenged (most notably by Stanley Milgram[34], who showed that individuals could engage in extreme behaviour towards one another not through abnormal personality traits but because of pressures emanating from authority and collective conformity). Historians were slower to change their 'Hitlercentric' approach, but Christopher Browning has been a pioneer in stressing that

> Now the time has come to go beyond the ideology and policymaking of the Nazi leaders and the initiatives and organizing of the 'banal' bureaucrats who made implementation of the Final Solution possible. Ultimately the Holocaust took place because at the most basic level individual human beings killed other human beings. And they did so in large numbers over an extended period of time. They became 'professional killers'.[35]

Through such a 'normalizing' approach, Browning has illustrated not only how the Holocaust was implemented by 'ordinary men', but also the importance of grass-roots involvement (including those involved with day-to-day technical matters in the mechanics of mass murder), in the decision-making process. He thus quite rightly demands a study of 'the emergence of the Final Solution by looking both from the top down and from the bottom up'.[36]

The German editors of a recent collection of 'contemporary texts . . . and the minutes of interrogations in which the murderers, accomplices and onlookers give an unembellished account to their interrogators of how the mass murder of the Jews was organized and carried out to the bitter end' were at pains to show that those involved 'were perfectly ordinary people'. Indeed, their photographs 'do not portray fanatics foaming at the mouth as they commit murder, nor do they show beasts who arouse our disgust, but perpetrators (spurred on by spectators) performing their "work" and who, afterwards, exhausted but satisfied, enjoyed a few beers in their free time'. The volume, while continuing the tradition of perpetrator-focused Holocaust studies, does enable a clear insight into 'Daily life during the Holocaust'.[37] Moreover, it reveals the ease with which the killing fitted into a seemingly normal everyday pattern. The work, by also including the testimony of bystanders, highlights, contrary to popular perceptions which have since grown up, that the Holocaust did not occur in a hermetically sealed and 'hidden' world, but was part of the daily life of hundreds of thousands of onlookers or what Elmer Luchterhand has called 'co-presents'. Phrases such as 'Planet Auschwitz' and '*l'univers concentrationnaire*', while useful in stressing the different moral world in camp life, are also dangerous in giving the impression that what went on inside the camps was unknown to all but the perpetrators and the victims.[38] As Gordon Horwitz suggests: 'We think of the concentration camp as an isolated realm'. Such an image was maintained for a long time, reflecting both the elitist approach with regard to the study of the Holocaust and the unsurprising hesitance of bystanders to speak out. Those who lived near to the sites of mass destruction were simply ignored at the end of the war and for decades after. 'Every camp, however,' we have been reminded, 'had civilian communities in the immediate vicinity, yet to date remarkably few persons have returned to the sites of destruction to attempt the delicate task of examining the camps within this context.'[39]

The genius of Lanzmann's epic film *Shoah* or Horwitz's study of 'Living Outside the Gates of Mauthausen' is that they expose, through the contemporary nature of their work, how the Holocaust occurred in real places and was observed in all its complexity and horror as part of everyday life. As more material is released from the former Soviet archives, it becomes clearer that the Holocaust occurred in hundreds of sites, many of them previously unknown to historians. In turn, the number of contemporary witnesses also has to be revised upwards.[40]

The concentration on the Nazi elite also camouflaged for many years the knowledge, responses and reactions of the German population to the persecution and then murder of the Jews. At first it was assumed that there was public support for the antisemitic policies pursued by the Nazis. So strong were such postulations that no attempt was made to verify such assumptions or examine the relationship between the state and the populace on the Jewish question.[41] Nevertheless, from the 1960s a new generation of historians emerged, German and non-German, who questioned the reality of the all-powerful Nazi state. Soon the issue of popular antisemitism was addressed and, since the 1970s, a series of studies has appeared on the subject and a debate has developed between those who suggest German indifference to the Jewish fate during the 1930s and those who allege actual support for the Nazi's antisemitic programme.[42] Both sides of the debate have tended to isolate popular responses towards the Jews and antisemitism from other contexts. The relative importance of Jewish issues and its significance in everyday matters becomes hard to establish when based on the generalized and often distorted reports emanating from the Nazis or, less frequently, their ideological opponents.

In contrast, David Bankier's work, partially based on the same sources but supplemented by more local material and contemporary observations from Germans, German Jews and foreign witnesses, provides a more dynamic analysis. He relates responses to changes in the public mood and support for Nazism and the leadership in general. Bankier provides one of the most negative assessments of German attitudes towards the Jews, concluding that 'Nazi antisemitism was successful not because the German population changed course and suddenly became devotees of racial theory: it was effective because large sectors of German society were predisposed to be antisemitic'.[43] His pessimistic analysis can be questioned, especially his dismissing of most *opposition* to manifestations of antisemitism as being selfish in origin and ultimately unconcerned with the fate of the Jews themselves. Nevertheless, the strength of Bankier's approach lies in his contextualization of the subject matter. He shows how the German people could not avoid contact with Jewish issues and how their silence during the persecution and ultimate destruction of the Jews did not imply lack of knowledge or interest. Indeed, whereas previous studies such as those by Kershaw, Stokes, Steinert and Gordon had tended to suggest that the German public was not aware of the 'Final Solution' in the war or was so involved with day-to-day problems to be indifferent to such matters, Bankier highlights the reverse.[44] Letters from East Europe, the open deportation of German Jewry and Allied propaganda provided constant information. The issue was simply too central to Nazism to be avoided. Bankier again provides a damning analysis of popular German responses, stressing selfish fear of reprisals rather than humanitarian concern as the motivation for any disapproval of mass murder. Bankier's work is provocative but it has shown the essential need to relate, even in the Nazi dictatorship, high-level decision making on the persecution of the Jews to public opinion. In turn he has made clear the importance of such matters on an everyday level to the German population not only from 1933 to 1939 but also for the years of the war. This has become crucial given the attempt of sections of German society to emphasize the continuity and normality of ordinary life in the Nazi era and thereby to play down the significance of the persecution of the Jews.

Edgar Reitz's epic television film *Heimat* (1984) was made as a conscious response to the rejection of German guilt emanating from the Holocaust. It was intended to restore self-prestige and the precious memory of the overall sweep of German history for its people. Written as a gut response to the American series *Holocaust*, which caused great intergenerational tensions in West Germany, it is hardly surprising that *Heimat*, designed to heal such wounds, hardly mentioned the destruction of the Jews. Issues of memory and national identity were also at the heart of the *Historikerstreit*, or historians' debate, which developed just two years after Reitz's immensely popular film. After his film, which charts the life in a German village in the Hunsruck between 1919 and 1982, Reitz received more than 10,000 letters 'recalling memories of that time, often in the language and the framework of the film'.[45] Similarly, conservatives in the *Historikerstreit* made a plea, in Mary Nolan's words, 'to normalize the study of Nazism, to empathize with the little man, and to recognize that many aspects of the Third Reich, including its most horrendous acts, were not unique'. Those on the right, she adds,

challenged social historians to speak less glibly about the 'normality' of everyday life in Nazi Germany, to inquire about the penetration of politics into everyday life. . . . The centrality of the Holocaust to the *Historikerstreit* serves as a deserved reprimand to Left historians who have ignored anti-Semitism, racism, and the Final Solution.[46]

What is needed for the German case are studies building on the work of David Bankier, but ones that less readily dismiss the potential of the testimony of ordinary people and the findings of local studies relating the experience of the Jewish minority in villages, towns and cities in the Nazi era.[47]

II

So far it has been illustrated how post-war perceptions of the Holocaust have broadened and moved from a Hitlercentric perpetrator focus to one incorporating the role of 'ordinary people' in its execution, the involvement of non-Germans in the occupied or Nazi-influenced countries, the impact on the Jews themselves and the presence of bystanders across the Continent in all the processes of destruction. Nevertheless, in all these areas, despite the challenge offered by scholars as diverse as Browning, Hartman, Horwitz and Bankier and the contribution of Claude Lanzmann, a top-down approach to the study of the Holocaust still dominates. If this is true of well-established areas such as the implementation of the 'Final Solution', it is even more particularly the case in the relatively new area of 'free world'/Allied responses to the persecution and destruction of European Jewry.

The issue of the destruction of European Jewry was one of the least controversial in the Nuremberg Trials. Tensions between the former Allies, especially between the United States and the USSR, created immense difficulties for those involved, but the 'crimes against humanity' represented by the murder of the Jews were straightforward. They were a clear-cut if not major feature of the trials and a way of proving the guilt of some of the Nazi perpetrators.[48] It is hardly surprising that the early trial material did not deal with the role of the former Allies in the persecution of the Jews. The shock experienced by both British and American society when concentration camps such as Belsen and Buchenwald were liberated in the spring of 1945 (although neither, as we shall see, were initially linked to the Jewish tragedy) merely emphasized the huge gap that divided free countries and those responsible for such atrocities. It was the Nazis who were on trial, not humanity as a whole.[49]

It is true that material was freely available from the war which did allow one to question the policies towards European Jewry pursued by both British and American governments. In Britain, publicists such as Eleanor Rathbone and Victor Gollancz had published pamphlets exposing the fate of the Jews and the inaction of the British government. In the United States, Henry Morgenthau, Secretary of State to the Treasury and a leading force in the creation of the War Refugee Board in 1944, published, as early as 1947, extracts of his diary highlighting similar apathy and even antipathy in high-level official American government circles.[50] The destruction of European Jewry, as will be stressed throughout this book, was not a secret history known only to the Allies during the war. It was reported *and* discussed. But neither Britain nor America, nor indeed other English speaking countries, were, in the difficult immediate post-war years, ready for a radical reappraisal of their roles in the war – roles that had already become mythologized. Each of the former Allied, Axis and occupied nations had their own reasons for neglecting their connection to the Jewish disaster in the war. Gerald Reitlinger, who, as we have seen, published the first major survey of the Holocaust, is an interesting example of such tendencies in Britain. The son of a prominent Jewish banker, he was educated at the exclusive Westminster School and Christ Church, Oxford. Reitlinger became famous for his country house parties in Kent and Sussex, 'which earned him the title of "The Squire"'.[51] In Reitlinger's *The Final Solution* the history of Belsen and its liberation by British soldiers (in fact the only major camp liberated by Britain) was stressed. The patriotic motif was further highlighted when he dealt (in just two paragraphs) with the British and American governments' responses to the Holocaust in the war. He was happier acknowledging the American State Department's 'positive obstruction' of rescue measures in the war than he was acknowledging 'the apparently evasive attitude of the British Foreign Office'. Consequently he concluded that

Mr Henry Morgenthau . . . has rather unfairly attributed a large measure of this delay [in helping Romanian Jews to escape through transfer payments] to the excessive cautiousness of the British Government. But the Nuremberg prosecution were later to unearth a correspondence which showed plainly that the obstacle was Ribbentrop and the German Foreign Office'.[52]

In 1967, Reitlinger published a second edition of his by now classic work. Although much of the text remained unchanged, he did alter his response to Morgenthau's critique of the Foreign Office by adding that its caution was 'Doubtless . . . a sufficient obstacle', and slightly modifying his earlier analysis of this issue by adding that 'the greatest [rather than the only] obstacles were Ribbentrop and the German Foreign Office'.[53]

The minor changes made by Reitlinger reflected a broader significance, moving beyond the specific subject of Rumanian Jewry in 1943. In the 1960s, consideration of the Allied responses to the Holocaust started to develop. That this had made only a limited impact in Britain is shown by the lack of space given to the subject by Reitlinger in 1967 (still just two paragraphs in over 500 pages of text) and the modest nature of the changes he had made. Nevertheless, the relevance of British policies in the war was no longer denied.

As with many areas linked to the study and representation of, and popular responses to, the Holocaust, the Eichmann Trial (1961–2) had made a major impact. The complexity as well as the horror of the Holocaust was to some extent clarified by the trial in Jerusalem. The pathetic figure of Eichmann (Arendt's 'banality of evil') itself highlighted the fact that the atrocities had been carried out by 'ordinary people' and not inhuman 'monsters'.[54] The focus was still on the immediate perpetrators, the Nazi hierarchy, but other issues, including the negotiations over Hungarian Jewry in 1944 (which involved the British government) and the Allies' failure to bomb Auschwitz in the same year, were raised. These were not necessarily fresh allegations, but it was the first time such issues, which directly connected the Allied governments to the events of the Holocaust, were given international and popular prominence. As the Israeli newspaper *Davar* put it at the height of the Eichmann trial:

The Allies' lack of concern about the fate of European Jewry has now been demonstrated. They uttered profuse expressions of sorrow about the savage murder of the Jews, but did not do anything practical to save them.[55]

Other factors were at work, including the availability of government documentation and the involvement of a critical school of refugees and survivors anxious to analyse all aspects of the Holocaust. In Britain it included the policies of the countries which had given the refugees asylum. Their work was disseminated in limited circulation publications such as the journal of the Association of Jewish Refugees, *Information*, the *Wiener Library Bulletin* and the cultural forum, *The Jewish Quarterly*.[56]

Other work on Britain and the Holocaust was carried out in Israel at the Yad Vashem Institute. Yad Vashem was formally instituted by the Israeli government in 1953 and became the world's leading centre for the study and research of the Holocaust by the end of that decade. From this base came Andrew Sharf's *The British Press & Jews Under Nazi Rule*, the first book to explore the issue of Allied knowledge of the destruction of the Jews. Apart from its pioneering quality and its raising of the issue of the psychological evasion of unpleasant truth, Sharf's work is revealing in the reception given to it by one of its sponsors, the Institute of Race Relations (London). Its director, Philip Mason, suggested that 'To the Institute of Race Relations the interest of this book lies not so much in any light it may throw on anti-Semitism as on the machinery of evasion'. The Institute, at that point dominated by white liberals pursuing an assimilationist stance with regard to Britain's black populations, so as to 'improve' race relations, was not interested in the Holocaust or any Jewish matters *per se* – '[I]t is therefore more by analogy than directly that we are concerned with their problems'. That this should be the view of the largest semi-official body concerned with issues of race and racism shows the marginalized status of the Holocaust (as well as that of the thousands of refugees and survivors) in Britain as late as the 1960s.[57]

Sharf's work is also enlightening in that it came out of an Israeli milieu in which the legacy of the last years of the Palestine mandate ensured that there was no possible restraint on criticizing British policy in the war and after. The book contained sections on refugee and Palestine policy prompting Mason to comment that 'Dr. Sharf writes as a partisan and from *the British point of view* [my emphasis] is open to the charge of lacking a sense of proportion; the waging of a major war is essentially a matter of planning what one can do against what one would like to do'. The area of Britain and the Holocaust was thus still too sensitive a subject to explore in the 1960s. It challenged the myths of the British war effort which were still sacrosanct and was not able to be part of the slowly developing idea of multi-culturalism. As Mason put it: 'The Jews are separated from the European population by religion, culture [and] history.'[58] Only outsiders within Britain such as the more culturally and historically conscious refugees/survivors or those from abroad were able to make the connection. The foundations established by Sharf and others were not built upon for well over a decade and remained beyond the concern of 'mainstream' British historians. By the late 1960s, this pattern was in marked contrast to the situation in the United States.

Within a three-year period, starting in 1968, four major books were published on America's refugee and rescue policy towards the Jews of Europe in the Nazi era. Some of these works, in the words of one of the authors writing a decade later, were 'as much cries of pain as they [were] serious history'.[59] They reflected the anguish of a new generation of American Jews (and, in the case of David Wyman, an American Protestant) confronting the immensity of the Holocaust. Importantly, however, their passion and, at times anger, revealed the authors' self-confidence, demonstrated in their criticism of American icons such as Franklin Roosevelt and the myths of America as a haven for the oppressed (as well as the American Jewish leadership in the war). It is clear that a sea-change in attitudes had taken place. Well after World War II, there was reluctance in the Jewish community to research the issue of American antisemitism: Jews did not feel secure enough at home to undertake such a dangerous project.[60] By the 1960s, however, public manifestations and organized forms of antisemitism had declined in the United States. Moreover, the decade of black consciousness encouraged more open expression of ethnic identity among American Jewry as did the pride emerging from Israeli success in the 1967 war. In addition, the works on America and the Holocaust reflected the newly available government sources on the subject. On a cultural and ideological level the United States witnessed a new generation coming to terms with the events of World War II and confronting issues such as the marginal status of ethnic and racial minorities in a supposedly open society, black civil rights and the Vietnam War.[61]

The work produced was of uneven quality. Arthur Morse's *While Six Million Died* – 'the untold and shocking account of the apathy shown, and the deliberate obstructions placed by the USA and Britain in the way of attempts to save the Jewish people from Hitler's "final solution"'[62] – was the work of a journalist. Morse, nevertheless, opened up important areas of study and his popular approach sparked public debate in ways that more academic works could not. Some of the works, including Morse's, were marred by their accusatory nature, 'resembl[ing] prosecutors' briefs before the court of public opinion'. By contrast, Henry Feingold wished his *The Politics of Rescue* 'to move beyond the moral aspect to examine the political context in which America's response was conceived'.[63] The search for context was indeed neglected and replaced by an indictment of American government, public opinion or the American Jewish community. The only common theme was the relative importance of domestic antisemitism in explaining the paucity of the American response. But using the prism of 'antisemitism' to view the strengths and weaknesses of American refugee and rescue policy was likely to distort the view. First, it tended to ignore other factors and thereby added to the accusatory (or, occasionally, the defensive) quality of the early works. Second, 'antisemitism' and its variants were rarely defined. The emotion-laden term did not help to stimulate constructive debate. Public discussions and perceptions of the issues involving the subject of America (or the Allies in general) and the Holocaust tended to lack sophistication or subtlety. Claims of total American indifference owing to antisemitism were easy to make but hardly did justice to the complexity of the issues involved. The study of the Holocaust had been opened up by the study of the Allied response, but the anger and guilt present in some of the early works led to distortion of the new angle.

Fortunately, much of the work subsequently produced was of a high academic quality in the United States and by the mid-1980s a mature historiography developed. Refugee and rescue policy in the Nazi era was at least now placed in a political context.[64] In the United Kingdom and its 'white' colonies, such as Australia, New Zealand and Canada, debate was slower in developing. In Britain itself the restraints outlined earlier continued to operate until the early 1970s. The first major academic work on Britain and refugees from Nazism in the pre-war era, published in 1973, was, significantly, written by an American (A. J. Sherman) and sponsored by the Institute of Jewish Affairs, itself funded by the international World Jewish Congress and an organization closely involved, as we will see, in such questions during the war itself. The Institute also sponsored research continuing the story through to World War II (for example, Bernard Wasserstein's *Britain and the Jews of Europe*, published in 1979). Two years later Martin Gilbert's *Auschwitz and the Allies* was published. However, these books remained isolated.[65] They generated very little specific debate and were not incorporated in the study of Britain during the Nazi era. In short, the historiography remained undeveloped and the works lacked a context in which to operate (other than surveys of the Allied response to the Holocaust, in which they were assumed to be the final word on the British response). Furthermore, the television film version of *Auschwitz and the Allies* was firmly in the accusatory camp. Public debate thus remained crudely constructed. Only recently has a constructive critique of the work of Sherman, Wasserstein and Gilbert been offered.[66]

A similar pattern developed in Canada, Australia and New Zealand. There, the first major works were published in 1983, 1985 and 1988 respectively.[67] All three countries had operated fiercely restrictive and selective immigration policies which continued after 1945 against Jewish displaced persons from Europe. That little was published on such issues before the 1980s reveals the internal restraint operating in such countries. Indeed it was partly examples abroad, such as the works on British and American policies, that prompted the new studies. Even then there was a heated response to these critical studies and the development, as in the United States, of revisionist attitudes which questioned the role of antisemitism in government refugee policy and were generally less critical of the Allies.[68]

In roughly a quarter of a century, therefore, a specific area of Holocaust studies has developed, namely that of the responses and attitudes of the liberal democracies to the persecution of the Jews. A greater sophistication has evolved including the consideration of the role of bureaucracies and bureaucrats and the placing of refugee and rescue policy in broader contexts (such as other internal and external political debates). One feature unites the great majority of this work – be it academic or popular, damning or not, American, British, Australian, New Zealand and Canadian – this being its elitist, top-down approach. It is largely based on government records (often only recently made available) or the high diplomatic activities of Jewish organizations. Public opinion is not necessarily ignored, but is viewed in a limited, two-dimensional way, through opinion polls or second-hand reports, and rarely from records generated from below. In short, Allied responses to the Holocaust have been studied as political or diplomatic issues but not as social history. The examination of free world/Allied responses, after decades of neglect, has now become integrated into Holocaust studies, even if they continue to be ignored by 'general' historians. In the process this new dimension on the subject has incorporated some of the limitations and biases of the area as a whole.

The implications of the top-down approach are serious. Although it might be assumed that government debates and decisions alone are the crucial factors in determining free world/Allied responses, high-level decisions were not taken and cannot be understood without reference to popular opinion, especially in the liberal democratic countries. Michael Marrus has rightly pointed out with regard to bystanders to the Holocaust that there is a tendency 'to condemn, rather than to explain'. In contrast he stresses how essential it is 'to give contemporaries a fair hearing'.[69] In some of the more recent literature, such a process is beginning to occur with regard to leading statesman and civil servants. The more objective approach has yet to percolate through to those outside government or high diplomatic circles. As a result, concepts such as 'public opinion', 'pressure from below' and the like are treated rather crudely. In particular, there is a tendency to assume automatically popular antipathy towards the entry of Jewish refugees without examining the often complex roots of both collective and individual responses to the issue. Therefore, the relationship between public opinion and government responses to the crisis of European Jewry in liberal democratic countries such as the United States and Britain has yet to be studied with any sophistication. The net result has been the imposition of limitations by those who only study 'history from above' in an area where such an approach is clearly unsatisfactory.[70]

In the American case, scholars such as David Wyman and Saul Friedman have argued that politicians and government officials were influenced by hostile, anti-Jewish feeling from the public. Others, such as Henry Feingold, are less concerned with pressure from below and concentrate on the internal debate within the American government. There seems to be tacit agreement, however, that influential or not, the vast majority of the public was hostile to anything other than a token entry of Jewish refugees to America. In the British case, even less work has been done (partly because of the relative absence of opinion poll material) on popular responses to refugee and rescue policy.[71] There is a great danger, largely realized, that public opinion is dealt with in an essentially patronizing manner. No real attempt has been made to look at the responses of interest or pressure groups to the Jewish crisis from their own perspective, leading almost inevitably to the tendency to condemn rather than to explain. Outright hostility (or, more rarely, sympathy) is easier to chart than what is the more normal and complicated response, ambivalence and ambiguity. The role of organizations (Jewish, Christian and secular) have been generally marginalized in the formation of state refugee and rescue policies. Where considered, full justice has rarely been given to the complexity of their responses.

The now dominant approach also excludes the relationship between the 'ordinary' individual in the liberal democracies and the Holocaust. Concentration on high-level decision making can lead to the assumption that the persecution of the Jews in the Nazi era had no bearing on the lives of ordinary people in countries such as the United States and Britain. It will be argued throughout this book that this is far from the case. Even when silence was the dominant response, the persecution of the Jews was still part of the consciousness of those remote, both physically and morally, from the destruction of the Jews in Europe. The Holocaust was not just part of the history of Nazi-controlled Europe – it impinged, even on the level of everyday life, on the individual and collective histories of Allied nations. By limiting consideration of the response to governments and high diplomacy, important aspects of individual and national histories and memories have been ignored. In summation, research on the liberal democracies has significantly broadened the geographical and political scope of the history of the Holocaust. Much of the work has been carried out, however, as if the maturing of recent disciplines and approaches of gender studies, labour history, social history, cultural studies and even immigrant and minority studies had not occurred.

III

The chapters in this study will attempt, 'to connect everyday life and high politics, and to rethink each in the light of the other'.[72] They are designed as social history, not in the sense of some of its earlier practitioners 'as the history of a people with the politics left out', but moving to what Eric Hobsbawm describes as 'the History of Society'.[73] It is, in E. P. Thompson's words, the pursuit of history

in its totality, that is . . . not as another 'sectoral' history – as economic, political, intellectual history, as history of labour, or as 'social history' defined as yet another sector – but as a total history of society, in which all other sectoral histories are convened.[74]

Beyond such broadly defined social history, this work is an attempt to explore the reactions of liberal societies when confronted with an *illiberal* phenomenon – the isolation of a minority and the eventual murder of six million of its members. In the liberal *Weltanschauung*, all stages of the Nazi persecution of the Jews, from early discrimination to outlawing, expulsion and murder, were anathema. They were an assault on one of the basic tenets of liberalism, the liberty of the individual. Essential to liberalism, especially in its British and American forms, was the concept of toleration. As Susan Mendus suggests,

Although other political ideologies may find a place for the value of toleration, it is in liberalism that that place is most exalted. Moreover, it is the liberal tradition which has most robustly defended toleration as a good in itself, not a mere pragmatic device or prudential expedient.[75]

It was clear, from the start, that the Nazi regime was *intolerant* towards its Jewish minority. For many, the removal of essential freedoms for groups such as the Jews, trades unions, socialists and Christians was sufficient indictment of the Nazi regime. Religious and political liberty were essential to the liberal faith. Nevertheless, the responses to Nazi antisemitism from the liberal democracies was more complicated than might be assumed. Some were baffled by the cause of the persecution of the Jews or suggested that the stories were exaggerated; others blamed the Jews themselves. Rather than representing a break from the liberal frontage and a slip away from toleration, it will be argued that such responses were a vital part of the liberal ideology itself. Toleration, especially towards racial and religious minorities, is often viewed as the antidote to expressions of violence and discrimination. Racism, for example, is often seen as due to 'the limits of liberalism', its imperfect extension across all sectors of society.[76] More recently, however, particularly in Britain through the work of scholars engaged in study of Afro-Caribbean and Jewish minorities, it is the *limitations of toleration itself* which have come under scrutiny. In a case study of late Victorian Manchester, a city that prided itself on the strength of its liberal traditions, Bill Williams has argued that 'Jews were validated not on the grounds of their Jewish identity, but on the basis of their conformity to the values and manners of bourgeois English society'. Williams concludes that such conditional acceptance ('the informal mechanisms of liberal toleration') 'remain[s] the quintessential means by which British society accommodates ethnic minorities: the central driving force of British racism'. This study will suggest that it is often the *strength* of liberalism and toleration rather than its weakness that explains the complex nature of democratic responses towards the persecution of the Jews.

Along with a commitment to toleration and liberty, belief in human progress has been a crucial component of liberalism. Lionel Trilling in his *The Liberal Imagination* has argued that

As [liberalism] carries out its active and positive ends it unconsciously limits its view of the world to what it can deal with, and it unconsciously tends to develop theories and principles, particularly in relation to the nature of the human mind, that justify its limitations.

The Holocaust, along with the use of other twentieth-century technology for destructive purposes, fundamentally challenges the belief in progress. One solution to this liberal dilemma is to make Auschwitz 'Not our patch'. George Steiner has argued that in the case of British culture and the Holocaust, the 'abstention from public and private encounter tells of a continuum of sanity, of liberal imagining, in British politics'. *The Holocaust and the Liberal Imagination* will explore how nineteenth-century concepts of rationality dealt with perhaps the most irrational event in human history.[77]

At the heart of such issues concerning the nature of liberalism is the confrontation with difference. The Holocaust was truly an international event, yet it took place and was observed by a vast array of nation states. In countries such as Britain and America, which will be the focus of this study, the domination of a liberal ethos needs to be placed alongside issues of national identity. The cultural frameworks of 'Britishness' (or, more frequently, 'Englishness') and 'Americanness' determined reactions and responses of these countries to the persecution of the Jews. The acceptance of diversity and the terms upon which 'difference' was accommodated were of central importance in British and American confrontations with the Jewish crisis. They were of equal significance as the commitment to liberty in these liberal democracies' ideology and cultural self-image.[78]

In one of the pioneering studies of America and the Holocaust, Henry Feingold suggests that 'The villain of the piece, in the last analysis, may not be the State Department or even certain officials but the nature of the nation-state itself'.[79] In Britain and America it is true that what was perceived as national self-interest often impeded any attempts to offer help to the Jews. In both countries, however, there was a genuine belief in government circles and beyond that their national reputations as places of asylum and for fighting intolerance had been maintained throughout the Nazi era. Indeed, on occasions measures were taken expressly to maintain such liberal images.[80] Sometimes they were tokenist but they should not be summarily dismissed. National exclusivity and the lack of commitment to diversity explains much of the ease with which the Holocaust was carried out in Nazi-occupied or influenced countries. There were times, however, where national self-prestige, rather than a commitment to the Jews *per se*, led to dramatic acts of rescue and relief. The cases of Italy and Denmark, perhaps the most important in terms of saving the Jews in the war, were the result of Italian and Danish self-esteem rather than philosemitism or opposition to antisemitism (both countries had restrictive immigration policies aimed at the Jewish refugees in the 1930s and the former had implemented antisemitic laws in 1938 more for internal reasons than pressure from the Nazis).[81] National identities and their interplay with the dominant liberal ideologies determined the responses of countries such as Britain and America to the Holocaust.

IV

This book will follow a 'straightforward' chronology, starting with the 1930s, moving to World War II and finally dealing with responses to the Holocaust from 1945 to the present. The adoption of such a framework does not imply, it must be stressed, any support for the idea of a straight path development of the Holocaust. There is a danger in works which attempt in Claude Lanzmann's words to oversimplify the Holocaust through the distorting means of history and chronology:

starting in 1933, with the Nazi rise to power – or even before, by exposing the various currents of nineteenth century German antisemitism . . . they attempt to lead us, year by year, stage by stage, almost harmoniously, so to speak, to the extermination.

Lanzmann stresses that 'between the conditions that allowed the extermination and the extermination itself – the *fact* of extermination – there is a discontinuity, a gap, a leap, an abyss'.[82]

In contrast, Martin Gilbert has stressed that 'chronology is the key to understanding everything'. It is a philosophy that Gilbert has followed closely in his major works on the Holocaust, employing, at times, an almost day-by-day approach.[83] Gilbert is not alone in tackling the Holocaust in its totality through developmental chronology: indeed, his strategy represents the norm. Thus Leni Yahil's textbook on the subject (originally published in Hebrew in 1987), which is by far the most inclusive in terms of areas covered and synthesis of recent research, covers the story in three chunks: 1932 to 1939, 1939 to spring 1941, and from spring 1941 until the end of the war. Yahil's work represents a tremendous achievement in that she has

tried to interweave the broad circumstances created by the times; the intentions and actions of the Nazis toward the Jews; the condition, fortunes, and behavior of the Jewish communities from the eve of the period of persecution until its end; the nature of the relations between the Jews and the peoples among whom they lived; the attitude of the world's nations to the Jewish problem before and during World War II; and the response and endeavors of the Jews in the free world.[84]

For the first and second chronological parts of the book, Yahil separates 'the aims and actions of the Germans from those of the Jews',[85] yet the work's very strength in terms of its inclusiveness creates dilemmas in its use of chronology. The Holocaust incorporates many different chronologies, such as those of its high-level perpetrators, its implementors, its victims, opponents and bystanders, of regions and nation states. With regard to the specific area of Allied responses in the war, knowledge and perceptions of the destruction process varied from country to country and between state and public. It must be stated clearly, for example, that both Britain and the United States had unique chronologies when confronting the persecution of the Jews in the war, ones that do not necessarily directly (or at times even indirectly) correspond to the actual events in Europe. Attempts to strait-jacket all the varied and conflicting chronologies into a simplifying pattern carry immense dangers.

In their *A World in Turmoil: An Integrated Chronology of the Holocaust and World War II*, Hershel and Abraham Edelheit confront the problem of the day-by-day approach: 'Since any number of events may conceivably have occurred on a single day, all such events have been cited as independent entries with the most important cited first.'[86] Thus on 19 May 1943 we learn that the Warsaw ghetto uprising occurred and a little later in the text that the Anglo-American Refugee Conference at Bermuda opened. Both, particularly on the symbolic level, have special significance in the history of the Holocaust. Students of the Allied response have been quick to point out the bitter irony of this coincidence. The immense bravery of the Jewish fighters working almost entirely without outside assistance has been contrasted with the apparently feeble efforts towards rescue of the Jews made by the two great Allies from the luxury of this exclusive island. The juxtaposition has, of course, great poignancy, yet it brings with it the temptation to criticize the American and British politicians and bureaucrats *directly* in the light of the tragic ghetto battle.[87] Those at Bermuda can be accused of many shortcomings, but events in the Warsaw ghetto in April 1943 were beyond their control. The chronological approach brings with it the risks always inherent in the use of hindsight. In this particular example, it is crucial to understand how contemporaries at the Bermuda conference understood events. The Allied statesmen brought with them a powerful domestic agenda, part of which, however, reflected the way they had confronted and assimilated the available information concerning Nazi antisemitism since 1933 or at least the start of the war. By separating out different Holocaust chronologies there is a greater possibility of understanding why contemporaries acted as they did. In the process one can avoid the blanket and often undifferentiated accusations which can accompany this rightly emotive subject (bearing in mind, of course, that to understand is not *necessarily* to condone).[88]

The chronological divisions employed in this study are thus specifically applicable to its subject matter – Britain and to a lesser extent America – and their confrontation with the Holocaust, rather than the process of extermination itself. In both countries, for example, knowledge either at a state or a popular level of what had occurred to the Jews of Europe was not simply out of date, it was also distorted and confused.[89] Indeed, the unravelling of the complex events would take many decades on both sides of the Atlantic and is still, as the century draws to a close, to be completed. As Lanzmann concludes, 'The chronological account that begins with the [anti-Jewish] boycott in April 1933 and leads us *naturally* into the gas chambers at Auschwitz or Treblinka is not, strictly speaking, false but rather dismally flat and one-dimensional.'[90]

The first section of this book examines the period from the Nazi rise to power to the outbreak of World War II. In these years, Nazi antisemitism was open and widely reported across the world. Its most blatant act, the

Nazi-termed *Kristallnacht* in November 1938, received immense publicity outside Germany. Moreover, the liberal democracies became directly connected to the antisemitic policies of the Third Reich through the reception or rejection of Jewish refugees. There was thus, on the surface, a greater synchronism between Nazi policies and knowledge of them outside Germany in the period from 1933 to 1939 than at any other stage of the Holocaust. Nevertheless, the manner in which news concerning anti-Jewish legislation, expulsions and violence became assimilated in free world countries was, despite the clarity of information available, still complicated, reflecting the importance of domestic ideologies. The first chapter explores the situation in the country perhaps least affected by antisemitism of a political nature, Britain, and makes comparisons with the reactions and responses in other liberal democracies.

From this general introduction to the period from 1933 to the outbreak of war, this section moves on to a more specific study of responses to the persecution of the Jews, that of the labour movement in the free world. Michael Marrus has highlighted how

Refugees, one might argue, always arrive at the wrong time. Seldom has this been more true than with those fleeing Nazism in the 1930s. Throughout Western Europe, where most anti-Nazis were headed, economic depression conditioned attitudes toward immigration. . . . Impatient by definition, refugees ran into a wall of restrictions hastily erected in Western European countries in the early 1930s. For those contemplating flight, the problem was not so much the inability to enter countries of refuge as it was securing permanent residence rights. Governments were reluctant to consider refugees as anything but visitors, soon to pass through their countries on their way to somewhere else. Jobs were the crucial factor.[91]

Given the centrality of such issues, it is remarkable that no sustained or detailed research has been carried out on the reactions and responses of the labour movement in countries such as Britain or America, either at an organized or informal level, to the European Jewish crisis in the 1930s. It is again a reflection of the dominant high-level approach adopted by Holocaust historians. The second chapter will analyse the importance of economic as against humanitarian arguments within the labour world when facing a refugee influx. It will, however, place both within a wider ideological framework, namely, the question of national identity in the labour world. Indeed, full justice to the complex but highly influential responses adopted by the labour movement cannot be achieved unless issues as wide-ranging and apparently unconnected as the influence of Keynesian ideas and the place of internationalism are considered. Ultimately such responses cannot be confined to consideration of the economic depression or 'antisemitism', but relate to concepts of 'Englishness', 'Dutchness' 'Americanness' and so on in the respective labour movements.

One area still awaiting detailed investigation in the history of the Holocaust is the question of women, or of gender in general. Only recently has research been carried out on the role of women as persecutors in National Socialism or, alternatively, as victims of the concentration and death camp structures. And even less consideration has been given to women as victims of the other killing processes in the Holocaust.[92] Like many areas of male-dominated history, women's experience has been ignored. It has also taken time for those within the specific area of women's history to confront a tradition of racism, including, in the Holocaust, its genocidal form.[93] Work on women and the Holocaust is still at a nascent stage and it is not surprising that the gender aspects of both the Nazis' antisemitic policies and the refugee policies of the liberal democracies have yet to be systematically explored. In the occupation of domestic service, legislation implemented in Nazi Germany in the 1930s and the requirements of some countries in the free world coincided. In Britain and Holland especially, the acceptance of tens of thousands of Jewish women as domestics enabled them to put on the appearance of relatively liberal immigration policies and was a crucial feature of escaping from Greater Germany. Only through an explanation which incorporates issues of gender, the role of middle-class women and the power of trade unions can such policies be understood properly. While again economic considerations played a major role, underlying questions of assimilation permeated the domestic servant refugee policy. In such processes, the largely female domestics were not passive figures and their experiences as refugees will be considered in depth.

The start of World War II marked a dramatic transformation in the responses to Nazi antisemitism. Although officially the Nazi regime was still anxious to export its 'Jewish problem', Britain, Commonwealth countries and the United States formally ended their limited refugee policies of the 1930s. As the war progressed and the persecution of the Jews intensified, understanding, if not knowledge, of what was occurring in Europe declined. In Britain and the Commonwealth (from September 1939) and the United States (from December 1941), the war was experienced through individual national frameworks. It was from these exclusive constructions (and, at times, their mutual inter-relationship) that the persecution of the Jews would be confronted. It led, at times, to the total marginalization of the destruction process by Britain and America. The fourth chapter outlines the ideological background through which state and society in these liberal democracies perceived the most illiberal event in modern history.

From this general setting, the next two chapters examine in detail the relationship between public opinion and Allied government policies with regard to the Jews of Europe. What was the response of the churches, the Jewish community, the labour movement and other secular bodies to the Jewish crisis? How did such organizations respond to grass roots opinion? And how, in turn, did the government respond to popular pressure? The work that has been carried out tends to view public opinion only through governmental records. Here, such material is combined with the records of the popular bodies themselves, including the diaries of ordinary people. In particular, the archives of the social survey organization, Mass-Observation, will be utilized. Mass-Observation was founded in 1937 and carried out intensive investigations into British social life until 1950. As well as its projects on everyday life, some 500 Mass-Observers kept diaries during or after World War II.[94] Only through an inclusive approach using such records can the impact of the Holocaust on Allied society be analysed and an understanding be reached of these liberal democracies and their policies towards the Jews of Europe. Chapter 5 covers the period up to the Allied Declaration in December 1942 when it will be argued public knowledge of the fate of European Jewry peaked. Chapter 6 continues the story up to the end of the war. It analyses the strange paradox of why great British public sympathy towards the Jews of Europe failed to liberalize British policies and why, conversely, almost the reverse was true in the United States. Questions of ethnic pluralism and universalism in all these issues will be at the forefront of the discussion. It will also be argued that the term 'indifference', perhaps the one most frequently employed to describe Allied responses to the Holocaust, is, when examined in detail, totally inappropriate. Although the actions taken by state and public in the Allied nations were, inevitably, inadequate to the immense needs of European Jewry, 'indifference' does not do justice to the complexity of such responses. Sympathy, antipathy and, most frequently, ambivalence were present, but all represented a confrontation and interaction with the Jewish disaster: not the lack of interest that 'indifference' suggests. To say, for example, that neither British nor American society cared whether European Jewry was destroyed or not does a serious injustice to both war societies, just as glib assertions that the war was fought by the Allies to save the Jews distorts the reality in the other direction.[95]

The final extended chapter moves from the end of the war to the present. It reflects the fact that although the killing process was essentially confined to the war, the Holocaust did not simply 'end' with the liberations of the camps or the close of hostilities. This was most clearly the case with the survivors who could not simply be expected to forget the horrors of the war. As Lawrence Langer suggests, the memory of their experiences remains with them with exceptional clarity decades after the war.[96] It is also now recognized that the impact has not simply been left on one generation but has been passed on to the children of survivors. The needs of survivors and their children were for a long time neglected and still do not receive the attention they deserve.[97] Yet in dealing with the 'presentness' of the Holocaust we need also to consider its broader impact outside those immediately affected. Speaking as an American Jew, Sander Gilman has written that 'Most Jews here and abroad of my father's generation and mine still need the *Shoah* not to be a past event; we need it to be a part of our daily reality.' Although some orthodox Jews are unhappy with this situation, the Holocaust is an essential part of modern Jewish identity. For Jews in the late twentieth century, the Holocaust is simply not 'Yesterday's racism'.[98]

The Holocaust, however, is far too large an event for its impact to be felt only in the Jewish community. Every country has had its own way of remembering and forgetting the destruction of the Jews. In each case, national identity and self-image play a central role. Thus in the Auschwitz Museum and elsewhere in Poland until very recently, 'The mass murder of Jews becomes significant in Polish memory only insofar as it is perceived as precursor to the Poles' own, unfulfilled genocide.'[99] In the Polish and other East European examples, ideology also played a central role, often obscuring the specific Jewish aspect of Nazi atrocities. In the West, however, questions of national identity and memory of the war in conjunction with the prevailing *liberal* ideology also closely shaped perceptions of the Holocaust. Different patterns of Holocaust remembrance have emerged in Germany, countries previously occupied or influenced by the Nazis, and the former Allied nations. Even in the last category, there was great divergence between Britain and the United States in their memories of the Holocaust. This final chapter explores the ideological underpinnings of these national post-war confrontations with the Holocaust.

V

Survivors such as Elie Wiesel and Saul Friedlander have put great stress on the dangers inherent in making the Holocaust 'accessible' to the general public in an age of mass media. Wiesel in particular has criticized fictionalized, televised and film versions of the Holocaust where viewers 'get a little history, a heavy dose of sentimentality and suspense, a little eroticism, a few daring sex scenes, a dash of theological rumination about the silence of God and there it is: let kitsch rule in the land of kitsch, where, at the expense of truth, what counts is ratings and facile success'. Wiesel calls, therefore, for greater silence but he also stresses that 'no one can retell Auschwitz after Auschwitz. The truth of Auschwitz remains hidden in its ashes.'[100] Friedlander has added that he sees a potentially

insoluble paradox when facing the extermination of the Jews of Europe: on the one hand, the memory of these victims is more present than ever in our historical consciousness; on the other hand, both the representation of the events and their interpretation are facing limits which may well be inherent in the very nature of this crime.[101]

Both these leading intellectuals rightly point out the dangers of trivialization and the limitations of understanding and representation when confronting the Holocaust. Wiesel, particularly, however, also tends at times to mystify the Holocaust by refusing to consider any popularization or compromise in re-telling the event. Yehuda Bauer has responded to what he sees as a potential danger in responses to the Holocaust, coming mainly from literary and theo-logical works, by stressing that 'In order to avoid mystification, we must . . . probe the historical background'.[102] In similar vein, Claude Lanzmann has said of *Shoah* that

My film is a counter-myth – that is, an investigation into the Holocaust's present. At the very least it is an investigation into the scars left by a past on places and on people's minds that are still so fresh and unhealed that this past gives the strange impression of being outside of time.[103]

This book, by focusing on 'free world' and Allied responses (and especially those on a popular level), is an attempt to continue the process of historicizing and demystifying the Holocaust. It concludes by examining the options of the state and the individual within liberal democracies in the modern world when confronted with the mass genocide of others. Rather than belittling its import-ance, focusing on the involvement of 'ordinary people', even in the remoteness of the liberal democratic world, will, I hope, emphasize the extraordinary nature and complexity of this unsurpassed crime against humanity. For surely the Holocaust must be seen as global and universal both in its implementation and its impact.

Part I

1933 to 1939

1
Liberal Culture and the Nazi Persecution of the Jews, 1933 to 1939

In an important classroom Holocaust education initiative, seven 'key concepts' are identified in the process of 'Exploring Allied Responses to the "Final Solution"': Prejudice, Indifference, Realpolitik, Racism, Mass Media, Anti-semitism and Isolationism'.[1] The choosing of these particular concepts represents not the weakness of the project (which is up to date and well thought out) as much as the state of contemporary literature in the particular area of the Allies and the Holocaust. There is, for example, comparatively little attention given to those who were sympathetic to the plight of the Jews and took action in the free world on their behalf.[2] More critically the stress on negative concepts such as 'prejudice', 'antisemitism' and 'indifference' in the Allied camp overlooks the complexity of responses which emerged in the Nazi era. As we will see, there were indeed individuals in countries such as Britain and the United States who devoted themselves in an unreservedly positive way to the fate of the Jews. Conversely, there were also some in the liberal democracies who remained uncritical of the Nazi regime, including its anti-semitic policies. Although both 'camps', it must be emphasized, were numerically small, if not insignificant, their importance rested in their ability to offer for consideration a clear, though obviously contrasting, agenda for the state and society. The views of the vast majority of the population are, however, harder to categorize. They represented an amalgam of antipodes: of sympathy and antipathy towards the Jews, and of surprise/anger and lack of concern over Nazi antisemitism. Responses and attitudes varied from person to person, and, importantly, within the same individual according to time and circumstance. A further crucial consideration was the national context in which such reactions were framed.

No systematic attempt has been made to analyse the reaction of ordinary people in the democratic world to the Nazi persecution of the Jews. The range of responses appears to defeat any attempt to generalize and even studies as specific as that on 'British Enthusiasts for Nazi Germany' confront the reader with chapters entitled, for instance, 'Diverse Individuals'. Moreover, as Martin Gilbert has suggested, there is no clear link between personal relations with Jews in the liberal democracies and attitudes to the Nazi persecution of the Jews.[3] It must be suggested that the historiography's undeveloped and confused nature relates to the insufficient consideration given to ideological and cultural factors. In countries as diverse as Holland, France, the United States and Australia, antisemitic/anti-immigrant organizations in the 1930s have been scrutinized with regard to the Jewish refugee crisis.[4] These movements were, however, often isolated in society and remote from political power. In contrast, we know relatively little about the dominant liberal culture in the democratic world and its response to Nazi antisemitism. The ambiguities of liberalism, it will be argued, working within individual national frameworks, were of crucial importance in determining popular and state reactions to the crisis of European Jewry in the 1930s.

Opposition to religious/racial intolerance combined with an ambivalent attitude towards Jewish *difference* in the liberal nations. This was true even in France, the Western country outside the Nazi sphere of influence possessing the strongest tradition and experience of domestic antisemitism. Here it was, as Vicki Caron suggests, the ambivalence of the *liberal* camp, and its eventual abandonment of the Jewish cause, that ultimately hindered the entry of Jewish refugees at the time of greatest need in the last year before war.[5] One of the French corner-stones of liberalism, the commitment to absolute right of asylum, gave way to a harsh and discriminatory restrictionism. Yet the closing of French doors was also carried out in the name of liberalism and the change had occurred within the space of less than a decade. In Britain the process operated almost in the reverse sequence to that of France. Although in theory retaining some commitment to the right of asylum, the 1919 Aliens Act in Britain stopped almost all immigration. Restrictionist policies were largely maintained through the first five years of the Nazi regime and then were loosened at the same point that France and many other countries effectively closed their doors.

This chapter is not an attempt to re-examine the bureaucratic history of British or other immigration control procedures – these have been excellently covered elsewhere. Nor will it draw up a league table of relative generosity towards Jewish refugees between various 'free world' countries – a device which contains the inherent danger of condemning rather than explaining and, in the process, losing sight of local contexts. Instead, it will analyse more generally how a liberal democratic culture and ideology, perhaps expressed no more clearly than in Britain and the United States, confronted the Nazi persecution of the Jews in peacetime.[6]

I

Although the level of immigration differed enormously, the British and American governments exhibited many similarities in controlling entry of foreigners after World War I. Both countries had instituted minor controls before 1914 which had made only a limited impact on the number of immigrants arriving. The intense nationalism, exclusivity and intolerance of British and American societies during World War I (in addition to the massive increase in state intervention) provided the stimulus for post-war immigration control. Nevertheless, subtle differences between the two countries emerged after 1918 which would have implications for those trying to escape from the Third Reich in the following decade. Immigration control in the United States through the quota systems imposed in 1921 and especially 1924 was heavily biased against Eastern and Southern Europeans. Such racialization of control was reinforced by the paranoia of the post-war 'red scare' aimed particularly at East European Jews. American immigration control of the 1920s was not absolute, but it was heavily informed by an ever-narrowing and racialized definition of Americanness and a powerful anti-communist impulse. Control in Britain came earlier and was far more exclusionary. The 1919 Aliens Act was aimed at controlling the activities of aliens in Britain and ensuring that 'undesirable' foreigners, such as East European Jews, Germans and Chinese, were, in general, kept out of the country. It was supplemented by Aliens Orders of 1920 and 1925, which aimed specifically to remove and restrict the entry of black seamen.[7] Such pieces of legislation should not be seen only as devices to stop economic competition against British workers; they also relate to a country which was increasingly narrowing its own national identity and deciding who could and could not become an 'Englishman'. Deportation, the fear of deportation and difficulty in becoming naturalized were common features of the alien experience in Britain after 1918.[8] Furthermore, in most years throughout the 1920s, more aliens left the country than were granted the right to enter. A bias against aliens with alleged radical sympathies was present in all these state actions. A senior figure in the Home Office Aliens Department told a Jewish communal worker in 1919 that the British government 'were making enquiries with regard to Bolshevism, and they found that so many Jews were mixed up with it, that they had decided to keep them out'. Nevertheless, the anti-communist hysteria in the United States which continued throughout the Nazi era was far more

profound than in Britain. In both countries, therefore, a clear pattern of immigration control had emerged before the Nazi rise to power. As the Home
Secretary, Sir William Joynson-Hicks, put it in 1925, referring to less than a
thousand Jewish transmigrants stranded in Britain due to American immigration quotas: 'They are the class of people who come from the east of Europe
that we do not want, and America does not want them either'.

With the Nazi rise to power and the possibility of an influx of Jewish
refugees, the British Home Secretary, Sir John Gilmour, was at pains early
in 1933 to emphasize the continuity of existing legislation against aliens.
Stressing what was to be a vital theme of refugee policy across the English-
speaking world throughout the Nazi era, Gilmour commented to the House
of Commons that each case of German Jews seeking entry would be 'judged
on its merits'. By April 1933 the prominent liberal humanitarian Norman
Angell was privately complaining of 'the difficulty German Jews have in
getting into England' despite the sympathetic noises being made.[9]

There is a dual significance to Gilmour's remark. First, it reflected the
continuation of immigration restriction in most but not all liberal democracies
before and after the Nazi rise to power. In countries such as the United States,
Canada, Australia, South Africa and New Zealand, it involved the persistence
of policies which had a strong racial or ethnocentric basis. Only certain types
of immigrants were welcome, especially those of white Anglo-Saxon origin.
Escape in the first years of Nazism would be hard, except to countries which,
for economic and ideological reasons, still retained the vestiges of open-door
immigration policies. This was particularly true of France and Holland which
also had the attraction of their proximity to Germany.[10] Second, Gilmour
reflected the strong commitment to individualism and opposition to treating
the Jews as a collective entity. Jews should be treated as individuals and be
judged (in this case as prospective immigrants) accordingly. Their ability to
be assimilated into the national culture was the key factor in such considerations. Antisemitism was seen as the unacceptable price that would have to
be paid for allowing in refugees who would not be able to adjust to the
'English' way of life. The fear of antisemitism and of the dilution of national
identity were thus factors of great importance in determining refugee policies
in the 1930s. Such issues need to be given serious attention and should be
put on an equal footing to the more obvious economic considerations in a
decade of international recession. Indeed, as will emerge in the two following
chapters, questions of economics, culture and ideology were closely combined
and, in many instances, are impossible to disentangle. It was not only refugee
policy that was shaped by the nature of liberalism. The whole question of the
persecution of the Jews in Nazi Germany was also viewed through the same
prism in the free world. Reactions to Nazi antisemitism in the democracies
can only be understood by analysing both the strengths and the limitations of

liberalism when faced with the challenge of an intolerant and ultimately genocidal state.[11]

Andrew Sharf has suggested that 'from the beginning to the end, few facts of Nazi anti-Semitism were left unstated by the British press'.[12] His comments have particular validity for the 1930s and could be extended to include the newspapers of the United States and most other democracies. A common perception (and one stated with great clarity by the historian A. J. P. Taylor with regard to the British case) is that 'Englishmen of all classes and of all parties were offended by the Nazi treatment of the Jews. . . . [It] did more than anything else to turn English moral feeling against Germany, and this moral feeling in turn made English people less reluctant to go to war'.[13] There are two problems with Taylor's analysis. The first relates to level and intensity of information available in the liberal democracies. The second concerns the ideological and cultural restraints through which the information would be transmitted and received.

The quality British press had reported the activities of the Nazi movement throughout the 1920s. It gave the Nazi movement particular attention from the 1930 elections in Germany (although until 1933 it has been suggested that 'little was said' about its antisemitism). With the Nazi takeover, interest inevitably broadened and popular newspapers followed the qualities in charting the progress of the new regime.[14] Papers such as the *Manchester Guardian*, *The Times* and the *Daily Telegraph* benefited from their past coverage of the Nazi movement and were thus less bewildered by the appearance of political antisemitism. Generally they gave a thorough and consistent account of the early attacks on German Jewry but outside these papers there was less success in reporting Nazi antisemitism. Incredulity (such as that expressed by the *Baptist Times*, which commented that it was 'difficult to discover a motive for this strange return to the policy of the Dark Ages in twentieth century Germany') led to incoherent and uneven reporting in much of the popular and parochial British press. As early as May 1933, one assiduous follower of the media commented that 'The papers generally are dropping the Jewish persecution in Germany'.[15]

In May 1933, Eleanor Rathbone, MP for the Combined Universities, commented that the revelations on Nazi antisemitism in the *Manchester Guardian* (the newspaper in Britain, and beyond, which was to provide perhaps the most outstanding coverage of the persecution of the Jews from 1933 to 1945) were

invaluable. But unfortunately, everybody does not, though everybody should, read the 'Manchester Guardian'. The little that appears on the subject in most journals is quite insufficient to bring home to their readers the real significance of these events. The general public, jaded with horrors and pre-occupied with its own distresses, only knows vaguely that the German Government is persecuting the German Jews, feels sorry about it, and turns to its own affairs.[16]

A British visitor to Germany in its first months under the Nazi regime wrote to Rathbone that he was depressed not only about what he had seen, especially with regard to racial persecution, 'but also at the . . . lack of knowledge of Germany in England, not least in the House of Commons'. His latter comments were not far off the mark. Although the issue was not totally avoided, there was no full debate of the Nazi persecution of the Jews in the Commons in 1933. Ultimately the desire to avoid upsetting future relations with Germany was paramount. One historian has gone as far to describe a 'conspiracy of silence' over the subject in parliament in the first year of Nazi rule.[17]

The unevenness of reporting and the lack of any lead given by the state was bound to limit comprehension of the seriousness of Nazi antisemitism in the liberal democracies. Such limitations were to be recurring themes throughout the Nazi era, and only once, in December 1942, was this pattern to be broken in Britain, the United States and elsewhere. It is, however, essential to understand that the available information would be channelled through domestic ideological considerations that were (just as much as the quantity and quality of information received) to hinder understanding of the Jewish plight.[18]

It has been suggested with regard to the British response to early Nazi attacks on the Jews that 'The liberals played down anti-Semitism because they strove desperately to keep their belief in a liberal universe which would behave in a liberal way. Their principles remained, but their theory could not possibly fit these terrible new facts.'[19] It will be necessary to question part of this analysis, for, until the horrors of *Kristallnacht* in November 1938 (and, for some, even beyond), many in countries such as Britain and the United States would use the dominant liberal culture to explain the causes of Nazi antisemitism. In the process of trying to understand the problem, they focused not so much on the Nazis as on the persecuted Jews.

Reference has already been made to the fundamental ambiguity of liberalism in relation to Jewish issues. In the liberal democracies, to attack Jews *as Jews* was anathema, yet many Western cultures held deeply ingrained views of the 'Jew'. Nevertheless, the representation of the Jewish 'other' was essentially bifurcated – the 'good Jew' (for example, the assimilated, honest patriot) was contrasted with the 'bad Jew' (foreign, diseased and subversive). After Jews had been granted political emancipation, it was assumed that antisemitism would, like Jewish exclusivity, wither away.[20] Some tension might persist as some Jews held on to their clannish ways, but it was assumed in Western countries at least that 'the Jewish problem' had been solved. With the rise of the Nazi state, a dilemma arose: how to explain why a modern European country was apparently attacking a *whole* people with a 'total lack of discrimination. The crime is to be a Jew, and for that no professional eminence, no degree of capacity in business, no public service and no private virtue can atone.' In this editorial, the *Daily Telegraph* was showing an understanding of the fact that Nazi antisemitism could not be understood as a rational attack on Jewish misbehaviour. The Nazis had moved from a critique of particular Jews as individuals or as sub-groups behaving badly on to an undifferentiated and total racial attack on a whole community.[21]

Winston Churchill (who had harboured his own fears of the alleged threat posed by international Bolshevik Jews after World War I), was also to question whether the liberal critique of the roots of antisemitism was able to explain Hitler's prejudices. He visited Hitler's friend, Hanfstaengl, in the summer of 1932 and asked

why is your chief so violent about the Jews? I can quite understand being angry with Jews who have done wrong or are against the country, and I understand resisting them if they try to monopolize power in any walk of life; but what is the *sense* [my emphasis] of being against a man simply because of his birth? How can a man help how he is born?[22]

This search for rationality in Nazi antisemitism was to occupy the thoughts of many in the liberal democracies in the first years of Nazi rule. One solution was, despite the virulence of the Nazi assault, to cling to the liberal formula and see German actions as exaggerated, unjust, but understandable reactions to a real Jewish irritant. Before the Nazi rise to power, the London *Observer* tried to explain Hitler's 'unsatisfactory . . . anti-Jewish policy' by suggesting that

It must not be forgotten that the major part of the German Republican Press is in Jewish hands, and that the polemics against Hitler, which verge occasionally on the ridiculous, are dictated by a real and, in some cases, almost hysterical fear, which is entirely personal.[23]

The first year of Nazi rule did not necessarily challenge such perceptions. In Britain, newspapers criticized Nazi excesses but also commented how 'the Jewish predominance in the Press and the theatre imported a purely materialistic aspect of life into Germany which had the effect of debasing the high national ideals which formerly united the German race'. Similarly, in the United States, there was comment on the 'large Jewish element in the financial, commercial, professional and official life of present-day Germany'.[24] There is strong evidence in both countries, as we shall see, that such press opinion carried broad public support. For example, in a poll carried out in April 1938, 48 per cent of the American population thought the persecution of the Jews was partly (and 10 per cent, entirely) the Jews' own fault.[25]

A case study of Sir Horace Rumbold, British Ambassador to Berlin at the time of the Nazi seizure of power, reveals some of the tensions operating within the liberal ideology when directly confronted with the reality of Nazi antisemitism. Rumbold's reactions reveal the interplay of English nationalism with a commitment to liberal principles; a profound understanding of the depths of Hitler's antisemitism yet a continuing adherence to the liberal critique of the Jews. It would be easy to dismiss Rumbold as a reactionary antisemite whose prejudices warped his whole perception of the Jewish plight. This, however, would not do justice to the complexity of his views.

There is no doubt that on a social and cultural level, Rumbold found Jews distasteful. It was part of a profound xenophobia which he carried with him across his worldwide travels. Englishmen, to Rumbold, were simply superior to all other nationalities. They 'always ha[d] a better sense of fair play than a foreigner.'[26] Jews specifically were 'an alien race' who in Europe had engaged in intrigue, profiteering and Bolshevism. When arriving in Berlin, he wrote that it was a fine city, 'the only fly in the ointment [being] the number of Jews in the place. One cannot get away from them.' Such views appear reminiscent of sections of *Mein Kampf*, but Rumbold, as his biographer suggests, was appalled by Nazi antisemitism and 'never deflected from his view that Nazism was evil'.[27]

Rumbold was to express his views on Nazi antisemitism in two important memoranda sent to the Foreign Secretary, Sir John Simon, in late March and early April 1933. He was aware from the start of the regime that Nazi anti-semitism was to be taken most seriously: 'The Jewish community in [Germany] are faced with a much more serious danger than mere bodily maltreatment or petty persecution.' From his experience of studying Hitler's speeches and a close reading of *Mein Kampf*, Rumbold realized that Hitler subscribed 'to the most violent anti-semitic principles'; his antisemitism went beyond ra-tionality. *Mein Kampf* 'teem[ed] with contradictions and misconceptions,' but Hitler's antisemitism was total and essential to his world view. Hitler, Rumbold realized, was obsessed with the 'Jewish peril'.[28]

Although his commitment to English nationalism and strong antisocialist views put Rumbold firmly in the conservative camp, his attitudes towards the Jews and Nazi antisemitism owed much to liberal ideology. First, Rumbold objected to Nazi antisemitism because it was indiscriminate and therefore could not be contained within an individualistic framework. As he wrote to his son, he could not accept Nazism because he was 'a convinced believer in the liberty of the subject'.[29] Yet in explaining Nazi antisemitism, Rumbold emphasized two factors: the first was Hitler's irrational hatred; the second was the role played by the Jews in German society. Rumbold, as was the case with so many others, accepted uncritically that Jews had a monopoly over many professions – finance, the arts and newspapers – in pre-Nazi Ger-many. In this sense to him there *was* a Jewish irritant. It was, in his mind, further exacerbated by the presence and activities of East European Jewish immigrants after 1918 in Germany when 'a most undesirable type of Hebrew reached the larger cities'. Rumbold was careful to distinguish between these Russian and Galician Jews, with their profiteering and Bolshevism, and the 'good' German Jews who were 'industrious and valuable'. The tragedy of Germany was that the 'bad' Jews had created the atmosphere for antisemitism to flourish. With such an impetus given to Hitler, 'the best elements in the Jewish community will now have to suffer and are suffering for the sins of the worst'.[30]

Rumbold, despite his strong ethnocentrism, which at times verged on racial determinism, could not accept the total racial ideology of Hitler. On the one hand, the British Ambassador was unwilling to challenge his own views that Jews were frequently an irritant in society and were thus often responsible for creating antisemitism. On the other, he thought the Nazis' indiscriminate attack on the Jews was barbaric – further convincing Rumbold of the superiority of the English people.

Even some of those sympathetic to the Nazi regime struggled to come to terms with its antisemitism. Ernest Tennant was a merchant banker who had, through his business, established close ties with Germany. He was prominent in Britain during the 1930s in developing friendship between the two countries and formed the Anglo-German Fellowship in 1935. Unlike Rumbold, Tennant remained an admirer of the Nazi regime and supported cooperation with Germany as late as the summer of 1939. Nevertheless, his critique of Nazi antisemitism was remarkably similar to that of Rumbold. In 1933 he commented that 'over the Jewish question it is not fair to lay the entire blame on Herr Hitler. A section of the Jews are also to blame.' The problem largely resulted from the Galician and Polish Jews who 'would create a Jewish problem wherever they go'.[31] By 1934 Tennant acknowledged that

Hitler's handling of the Jewish question has . . . been his greatest mistake. That he was justified in reducing the Jewish control in certain trades and professions even the best Jews in Germany themselves admit, but it should have been done in a very different way. There was no *need* [my emphasis] to insult the whole Jewish race which is what he has done.[32]

Ultimately Tennant articulated a classic liberal ideology on the Jews, writing to his Chairman at the Fellowship, Lord Mount Temple, that 'the tragedy of the Jew in Germany is that he will not be assimilated'. Some Jews were an irritant, but it did not excuse the 'deplorable . . . cruel and vulgar anti-Jewish campaign' of Streicher and others.[33] Similarly, Lord Dawson of Penn, the King's physician, was another admirer of Nazi Germany and a believer in the idea that Jews had obtained a stranglehold on defeated Germany. Nevertheless, he felt that the Nazis could displace the excessive power of the Jews without cruelty, they could make their regulations prospective and not turn to ruin people in established positions because they cannot show a long 'aryan' ancestry.[34]

There was thus a wide range of opinion which could accept neither the extremism of Nazi antisemitism nor the irrelevance of Jewish activities in the stimulation of such hostility. In October 1933 the *Manchester Guardian* was pushed to address the problems associated with the idea that the Jews had somehow earned their misfortune:

We have heard repeatedly in our own columns of the 'other side': of the undue preponderance of Jews in the professions, of the many foreign Jews who flocked in after the war, of the Jews involved in this and that 'scandal'. Were it all true, which it is not, how would it justify the relentless grinding down of the Jewish race, which lives in Germany . . . in misery and terror?[35]

The difficulty in the democratic countries was explaining the *ferocity* of Nazi antisemitism within a liberal framework. Widespread adherence to the theory of 'well-earned' antisemitism made it hard to comprehend what was happening in Germany. In the resultant confusion, few in the liberal democracies were willing to challenge their own views on what was seen as 'the Jewish question'. Recognizing this dilemma, Jewish organizations embarked on a futile attempt to solve the question of whether or not Nazi antisemitism was justified. A series of pamphlets was produced by bodies such as the Board of Deputies of British Jews and the Anglo-Jewish Association. Tables of statistics were employed to show the limited Jewish role in all aspects of German society including the press, government, industry and the cinema. Particular attention was paid to the issue of East European post-war Jewish immigrants and attempts were made to play down their numbers. In short, a liberal discourse was used to explain an illiberal phenomenon. Working against deeply ingrained cultural assumptions of the subversive Jewish financier, alien or radical, prevalent in the Western world, it is hardly surprising that the impact of such defensive literature was minimal. Moreover, the debate focused on the agenda raised by those trying to explain away the Nazis' actions, rather than addressing the collective and individual tragedies of German Jewry and the horrors of Nazi antisemitism.[36]

The less complicated (though equally problematic) strategy utilized to justify Nazi antisemitism was to deny its existence or to claim it had suffered from exaggeration. This was a practice particularly employed by sympathizers of the Nazi regime, the 'Fellow travellers of the Right', but it was by no means limited to this group. Indeed, in the United States, Deborah Lipstadt has commented how significant sections of the mainstream press were sceptical about the stories of Nazi antisemitism. She concludes that, by early in the

Nazi rule, 'a pattern had emerged which would characterize the reaction of the press as well as the public to the entire Nazi persecution. Americans did not doubt that things were difficult for the Jews but seemed reluctant to believe that they were as bad as reporters on the scene claimed.'[37]

Those with ideological affinities to the Nazi movement, such as native Fascist organizations in the liberal democracies, had clear motives in trying to play down what appeared to be the most unsavoury aspects of the new German regime. Yet admirers and defenders of the Nazis could be found during the 1930s in much wider circles. There were those who felt an affinity to the Germans as a people, those who felt an uneasy conscience about the 'harshness' of the Versailles peace terms and many more who wished to avoid the bloodshed of another world war. The existence of Nazi antisemitism thus became a major problem, particularly for those arguing the moral case for an appeasement or isolationist policy. Given the ease of international communications, even within the limitations imposed by the Nazi state, it would seem difficult to deny the reality and extent of Nazi antisemitism. There were, however, several factors that could be utilized to minimize its significance. First, the largely discredited atrocity stories of World War I and the blatant nationalistic manipulation of the press in the conflict led to a popular distrust of all official and journalistic information after 1918. This scepticism was widespread and international. Second, there was a specific discourse about Jews that came into play. The popular image of Jewish power within the liberal world contrasted strongly with the representation of Jews as innocent and defenceless victims. In turn the idea of Jewish power could be channelled into the theory of 'well-earned' antisemitism.

All these tendencies were evident in the work of some of the key British journalists of the 1930s. George Ward Price, Beverly Nichols and Douglas Reed all stressed the specific Jewish problem in Germany which to a lesser or greater extent in their minds justified state legislative action. They denied the extent of Nazi antisemitism and explained that it had been manipulated out of all proportion by influential Jews in the world's media. G. E. O. Knight, literary editor of *Books and Authors*, wrote in 1933 that he saw 'no murder of Jews' in Germany and that 'mountains had been made out of molehills'.[38] Ernest Tennant wrote the following year of the 'abominable lies about Germany[,] some spread by refugees'. Jews interfering with the British press and Jewish politicians were 'able to keep our Cabinet Ministers continually supplied with anti-German propaganda'.[39] Nichols noted in September 1936 that 'the excesses have been wildly exaggerated' and Ward Price commented in 1937 that reporting of Nazi antisemitism had been prone to 'gross and reckless accusations'.[40] Knight, Tennant, Nichols and Ward Price were, until 1939 at least, firmly in the appeasement camp. In a category all of his own was Douglas Reed, *The Times* correspondent in Berlin until 1938 when his virulent anti-appeasement views lost him his job. In that year he shot to international fame with his bestselling *Insanity Fair* which predicted the *Anschluss*. Reed believed in a remarkable conspiracy theory in which he claimed Hitler and the Nazis were controlled by the Jews; rather than combating Germany's real Jewish problem, Hitler's antisemitism was 'a hollow bluff'.[41]

It would be easy to dismiss the significance of these writers, but it should be remembered that Reed was perhaps the most widely read non-fiction author in Britain before the war and Ward Price has been described as 'the outstanding special correspondent of the 1930s'.[42] Rather than *create doubt* about the veracity and scope of Nazi antisemitism, such authors and journalists in Britain, the United States and elsewhere merely *confirmed* popular scepticism. It was based partly on a distrust of 'atrocity stories' and partly on a distrust of the Jews themselves. It is important to stress that few in the liberal democracies supported the world view of Nazis at home and abroad that the Jews were a unified malevolent force intent on obtaining power. In fact ambivalent attitudes towards Jews, reflecting the dominant liberal ideology, were the norm. The minority who were totally opposed to the Jews were mirrored, however, by a small number of people (Jews and non-Jews, religious and secular) who were drawn out of sympathy to the nightmare world of the persecuted in the Third Reich.

II

In 1933, outside the Anglo-Jewish community there was no one in Britain more moved by the fate of the Jews and other victims of the Nazis than Eleanor Rathbone. She was aware that in democratic countries suffering their own problems of unemployment and poverty there was every reason for people to ignore the sufferings of the Jews and others in a foreign country. Rathbone was anxious from the start of the Nazi regime to point out the *universal* significance of the persecutions, but she realized she had to do so from an insular British position. She thus commented in frustration as early as May 1933 that the general public

does not realise that this matter is most intimately our own affair, that the Jews and Socialists and pacifists of Germany are merely providing at once the emotional outlet, the practising-ground, and the excuse for a mood of hatred and an intention of revenge which are really directed against Germany's late enemies, including ourselves.[43]

In fact Rathbone found the whole idea of Nazism vile. Its treatment of minorities, of political opponents and of women were all repugnant to her deeply held and highly progressive liberal principles. She started from a perspective of helping the Jews by defending 'the general claim of humanity'. Beyond this she rejected the Nazis' racism and instead, generations ahead of her time, praised the enriching impact of immigration and racial diversity which she saw to be one of Britain's best features. Yet Rathbone's direct appeal to the interest of a narrow British nationalism revealed the problems of those in the liberal democracies trying to alert the world to the fate of the Jews.[44]

In the summer of 1935 physical violence against Jews erupted across Nazi Germany and in November the Nuremberg Laws, which effectively separated the Jews from the rest of society, were instituted. The persecution of the Jews was again headline news in the democracies. There were some in Britain, such as Colonel Meinerzhargen, an ex-War Office official, who accepted the need for such legislation believing that 'the German has a perfect right to treat the Jew as an alien and deny him German citizenship. He even has a right to expel him from Germany, but it must be done decently and with justice.'[45] It must be suggested that in the liberal democracies such views were extreme. There may have been a tendency to see Jews as somehow 'un-British', 'un-French', 'un-American' and so on, but there was little demand for any legislation to that effect, certainly towards those born in these countries. Yet the persecution of the Jews, however much disapproved, was not seen as a problem for the democracies. Until 1938 at least, liberal democratic societies managed to live with the persecution of the Jews in other countries without much discomfort, even though this rarely implied support for the Nazis' antisemitic policies. Indeed many were content to accept that such matters were the internal affair of another sovereign state.

Shortly after the Nuremberg Laws and the antisemitic riots in the summer of 1935 which preceded them, an organizer of Anglo-German youth summer camps wrote in anger to Eleanor Rathbone. Rathbone had taken part in a demonstration in London against Nazi activities which prompted the following highly revealing response from the camp leader:

Liberal opinion of all shades in this country is naturally unsympathetic to so undemocratic a system as the National-socialist regime, and would oppose its introduction here. The treatment of the Jews is still more directly contrary to English principles, and all Englishmen alike feel a corresponding sympathy with the oppressed minority, but I submit to you most emphatically . . . that it is no way our business to attempt to interfere with the internal affairs of Germany.

Rathbone replied that she could not

agree that the persecution of vast numbers of people on the grounds of their race, politics or religion does not concern all humane people and I have come to the conclusion that the best and most effective way of registering our disapproval is by avoiding visits to and trading with Germany.[46]

As a total believer in the freedom of the individual, Rathbone also felt it was the role of the individual to do all that was possible to isolate those who perpetuated cruelties against minorities and to aid the victims of oppression. If they did not, they themselves bore some responsibility for evils committed. As she wrote early in 1936 to one of the main Anglo-German travel agents with regard to the forthcoming Olympics, British travellers to the games would 'encourage a belief in Germany that British people are ready to condone or to disbelieve in the atrocities of the German Government, to accept its protection and to add to its revenues by trading with it'.[47]

It has been suggested that in the United States in the 1930s 'some scores or perhaps even hundreds of Christian personalities were found, who did . . . a great deal for the refugees'.[48] In Britain before *Kristallnacht* the same was probably true. There were those such as Rathbone, the writer Storm Jameson, the clergyman James Parkes and the politician Harold Nicolson who were inextricably drawn into the plight of the Jews in the 1930s. In so doing they encountered a world of suffering, of constant tension and the fight against the bureaucracies of the nation state – Fascist and liberal democratic. The pressures and the nightmare world of those trying to escape were clearly revealed in a letter from Prague written by a British worker for the Czech Refugee Trust in April 1933:

My work has always been very heavy and has involved much interviewing etc. On an average . . . 500–600 people come to my office each morning and the difficulties of working have been greatly added to in the last month. Many people who have permits [for Britain] . . . a) have had no passports, b) have been unable to approach the Gestapo for an ausreise, or c) have ausreise which expire long before the authorities here get around to giving the visa! So many people in *odd* hours – very odd ones – chasing around in taxis trying to locate these. Addresses change daily and it is very difficult to keep pace with the number of obstacles which arise. Speaking of these, the obstacle created by the [British] P[assport] C[ontrol] O[ffice] here are almost greater than those created by the Gestapo. The former has proven absolutely unbearable, refusing visas on cards sans lists (even though it must be admitted that no one could have a card without being on some list); making obstructions over small mistakes in cards, refusing to recognize the possibility of a name being spelt differently on a passport than on a card or on a H[ome] O[ffice] list – and sending back passports not visaed time after time. It is hard to cope with this in the face of present political difficulties which anyone in this part of the world can see are increasing daily. We have not much time left here. . . . The people form queues before the Passport office from 4 and 5 a.m. on; some of these people go time after time for as many as 8 or 10 days, and never succeed in getting near enough attention for a visa. The P.C. office is hopelessly understaffed and badly staffed; and it is of no use to continue to give at your end permits which do not materialize at this end.

To these exceptional individuals, there was no choice but to be involved in this larger, painful world. After hearing of atrocities committed against Austrian Jews, Harold Nicolson remarked: 'I am glad I am in a position to do something, however slight to help. I simply could not just remain idle and do nothing.' Similarly Storm Jameson noted that she refused

to regret the energy spent writing polemics against war and Fascism. Still less the energy given to helping a few, too few, men and women to escape the hell of German concentration camps, and then to keep them alive . . . I could not have held aloof.[49]

The impact on the physical and mental health of individuals engaging in such work was large. In 1939 the commentator Louis Adamic attempted to communicate to the American public the difficulties facing one particular body (the National Coordinating Committee for Aid to Refugees and Emigrants Coming From Germany):

To get a feeling and understanding of it, one has to spend a day in the Coordinating Committee's offices and watch the faces of the refugees as they come in or stand in lines; see the harassed, overworked staff; listen in on transatlantic telephone calls, and read such cables as the following which come in daily: 'My husband in concentration camp. If you cannot help him and me, in God's name take out our young children'.

The involvement and influence of some of these activists in both Britain and the United States was made possible by access to privileged society – government circles, the media and the intelligentsia. Nevertheless, they chose to bond themselves to the fate of people who by nationality, ethnicity and religion had no connection other than a common humanity. The case of the churches in Britain and the United States in the 1930s highlights the isolation of the activists from the majority of contemporary figures.

Although paying tribute to the work of some personalities, Haim Genizi concludes that the vast majority of American Christians remained apathetic to the fate of refugees, non-Jewish and particularly Jewish. In Britain it has been suggested that the domination of 'liberal optimism' in theological debate and practice meant that many Christians 'were ill-prepared for the revelations of Nazi evils'.[50] In conjunction with a Christian discourse that blamed the Jews (because of the crucifixion) for their own continuing persecution, there was, as with other sections of society, a failure to understand the origins of Nazi antisemitism. Although an extreme case, Arthur Headlam, Bishop of Gloucester and Chairman of the Church of England Council on Foreign Relations throughout the Nazi era, illustrated such tendencies. Headlam, like many others in Britain during the 1930s, blamed Jewish behaviour for the rise of Nazi antisemitism, suggesting that '[The Jews] are not altogether a pleasant element in . . . German life'.[51] Conversely, Bishop Bell of Chichester (who campaigned particularly on behalf of non-Aryan refugees), Bishop Henson of Durham and Reverend James Parkes, who were all vocal and frequent in their denunciations of Nazi antisemitism, were essentially outsiders in the Church of England. Parkes was to devote his life to exposing the Christian origins of antisemitism, but, as he later wrote, to do so in the 1930s and 1940s was to embark on 'a lonely job'. Many Christians did become involved in the Jewish crisis after the pogrom of November 1938, but before then their leaders, with the above and a few other notable exceptions, had not embraced the importance and centrality of the issue.[52]

In contrast, the Jews in the liberal democracies (as well as other groups persecuted in the Third Reich such as socialists and trade unionists) were drawn more blatantly into the reality of this nightmare world. The labour movement's attack on Nazism was almost unanimous and trade unionists in both Britain and the United States kept up a solid boycott of Germany, avoiding the sort of contact condemned by Eleanor Rathbone. The question of helping refugees from Nazism was, however, more complex. As will be shown in the following chapter, its response was essentially ambivalent as humanitarian sympathy and economic self-interest, international solidarity and ethnic prejudice all intertwined.[53] Similar ambiguity existed within the Jewish communities of the democracies.

In almost identical moves, the Jews of Britain and of Holland in the first months of the Nazi regime came into an agreement with their respective governments. Jewish refugees would be looked after by their co-religionists and would not become a charge on the state.[54] Such offers represented conditional generosity on behalf of the established Jewish communities. On the positive side, they allowed a flexibility in state immigration policy that certainly in the British case would have been otherwise difficult to achieve. Nevertheless, such policies placed distinct limitations on the numbers who could enter as refugees. Neither the Jewish minorities nor their states wanted a large influx of foreign Jews who they feared would stimulate native antisemitism. For the Jewish communities of the liberal democracies, international ties and solidarity would ensure some communal response to their brethren in Nazi Germany. Ultimately, however, they would respond essentially, as with the rest of society, through an agenda set by domestic concerns.

For the Jews in a whole range of liberal democracies in the 1930s, both on an organized and popular level, perhaps the greatest concern was the rise of antisemitism and Fascism on a global level. Developments in Eastern Europe, particularly in Poland (as well as Germany), suggested that antisemitism, rather than being the exception in some reactionary countries, was becoming the rule. Domestic manifestations of antisemitism in countries such as Britain and the United States thus assumed a very large significance in the lives of the Jewish minorities.[55] As a result, the perceived freedom of action to help the persecuted Jews of Europe was diminished. A defensive strategy towards allowing in refugees (particularly by making sure only the 'right kind' were given permission to enter) and controlling the actions of those who had escaped thus became the standard policy of Jewish communities across the liberal democracies. There were important dissenting voices demanding freer entry, but they tended to come from individuals and organizations located away from the power structures of the Jewish establishments such as the 'left', some Zionists and very orthodox groupings.[56]

On a popular basis, the fear of antisemitism (as well as the real problems that confronted Jews economically and socially in the 1930s) also affected responses and reactions to the Jews of Nazi Germany. For one, the persecution of the Jews abroad increased Jewish insecurity and sense of isolation. For another, Jews such as those in Britain remained remote from the full horror of what was happening on the Continent. This duality is expressed well in the memoirs of a North East London Jew, Morris Beckman, who was a teenager in the 1930s. Beckman relates how

In all honesty, despite the Mosley blackshirts and the bad news from Nazi-occupied territory, we Jews were still leading enjoyable study and sports-filled lives. [The *Kristallnacht* pogrom] brought home to us as nothing up to then what a dangerous world it had become for Jews. [Nevertheless,] normality was the order of the day.[57]

A small but significant number of Jews in the liberal democracies devoted themselves to the plight of the persecuted Jews. Some had been involved in such work before and ensured that there was a great deal of continuity of policy. Others emerged from the ranks of East European Jewish refugees from the turn of the century, as did Jewish women previously marginalized by religious and secular organizational structures. Much of the refugee and rescue work was carried out on a voluntary basis. The limitations and biases of the refugee organizations' policies, which were imposed by the restraints of their ideology (particularly their general desire not to upset their governments, in addition to their fear of unleashing domestic antisemitism) and their semi- or non-professional status, cannot be ignored. Such bodies, particularly in Britain, were highly influential in the state's decision-making process. It must be emphasized, however, that the stress placed on their staff as individuals was immense. They faced confronting the impact of Nazi antisemitism on ordinary people on a daily basis and their organizations had insufficient resources to cope with the immensity of the problem, particularly in the 18 months before war. As was the case with their Christian and secular counterparts, physical and mental breakdowns were not uncommon among Jewish workers for the refugees from Nazism.[58]

It must be emphasized that the pro-refugee activists were in a small if vocal minority. Until 1938 only a tiny section of the public in countries such as Britain and the United States had come into meaningful contact with the Jewish crisis either at home or abroad. The number of refugees allowed into the liberal democracies was small, press coverage of the persecutions was, on the whole, patchy and, of crucial importance, governments were unwilling to stress the issue in international diplomacy for fear of upsetting good relations with the Nazi leadership. In Britain this was taken to particularly absurd levels in the case of film censorship in the 1930s, when it was 'clear that no overtly anti-Nazi film would be permitted'. This was true of films attacking (even indirectly) Nazi antisemitism. No offence was to be given to Germany nor any stimulation given to antisemitism at home by the stressing of Jewish themes. One script, *The Exiles*, was to be rejected unless 'the producers carry out their intention of not making the country identifiable in any way'. Liberal objections to 'difference' were also revealed when the censor suggested that 'the exiles themselves are not made to look unmistakable Jews'. The same tendency was evident in a more sympathetic way in Michael Tippett's opera *Child of Our Time* which was written shortly after the November 1938 pogrom. Tippett purposefully avoided mentioning the Jews in this work so as to give his work a universal quality limited neither to a particular time nor a particular victim.[59] The situation in the United States was only slightly less severe. Some important anti-Nazi films were released but they often only hinted at the specific fate of the Jews. There were also the influential *March of Time* news documentaries in this area.[60] It still remains that in the first five years of Nazi rule, the amount of information available to ordinary people in the democracies about the Jewish plight was essentially limited. Along with the important ideological and cultural restraints already outlined, it must be suggested that while most people were aware that the Jews were being treated badly by the Nazi regime, their understanding of the situation did not go much further. For a while, at least, this was to change with the *Kristallnacht* pogrom which so horrified Tippett and so many others in the democracies.

III

Samuel Rich, a minor communal figure in the Anglo-Jewish community and an individual involved in refugee affairs, wrote in his diary two days after the November 1938 pogrom and sickened by the fresh news that German Jewry would be further penalized:

[it was the] end of German Jewry[,] a huge communal fine! – life in concentration camps *to be paid for*, no Jew to enter any theatre, concert, public place whatever. Jews to pay to rebuild what was burnt to Goring's orders – no compensation for any riot damage – My God! – And all the world *permits* it! *It's not their business!* They will find that it *is* their business, when it is too late.

Three days later Rich added to his diary: 'Placards tell of concerted action to help German Jews. . . . Perhaps they are beginning to see it is not a *Jewish* question!'[61] The isolation of those trying to communicate the plight of the Jews in a culturally exclusive atmosphere and the later realization that they might have succeeded in opening up the question are exposed by these two quotations. It has been suggested with regard to Britain and the German Jews in 1933 that 'The examination and solution of these questions [such as the alleviation of antisemitism inside the Nazi state and allowing in Jewish refugees] was not, fortunately, left entirely to the government. . . . Nevertheless, the final course of action had to be determined by the authorities.'[62] Five years later these questions reappeared across the liberal democracies. Should more refugees be let in? Should official protests be offered? These issues have been examined before, but the relationship between state and public in the liberal democracies has not received the attention it deserves.

Kristallnacht, with its brutal murders of scores of Jews and wholesale destruction of Jewish property, was carried out in the full glare of world publicity: 'The Nazis made very little attempt to conceal any evidence of the pogrom'.[63] The violence, death and destruction received front-page treatment across the liberal democracies. Banner headlines and powerful photographic images of burning synagogues ensured that the event would be seen as a special occurrence. Ordinary people in the liberal democracies were given the chance to confront, for the first time, the immensity of the Jewish plight. It has been suggested that 'nobody, of course, defended the pogrom'. This, as will emerge, was not absolutely true, but any minor qualifications do not detract from the fact that there was widespread revulsion on a popular level in all the liberal democratic countries.[64]

The horror expressed was largely spontaneous and deeply felt. From Bradford, Yorkshire, came a petition from 'twenty-three ordinary people':

We, the undersigned, whilst sincerely wishing to gain and hold the friendship of the German people, wish to express our horror and indignation at the treatment meted out by those at present in authority in Germany, to thousands of innocent and helpless people simply because they happen to belong to the Jewish race.

We feel that British public opinion is overwhelmingly with us in this expression of disgust and ask that the British Government will use strong, speedy and effective measures to make this point of view known to the leaders of the German nation.[65]

Cuthbert Headlam, previously a leading Conservative figure in the pro-appeasement camp, wrote in his diary that

It really is too appalling that such brutalities should go on in the 20th century. I don't see how we can go on trying to come to terms with a Government capable of such atrocious injustice and cruelty. Public opinion in England simply won't stand it.

Indeed the first opinion poll carried out in Britain on Jewish issues, shortly after the pogrom, confirmed Headlam's views. Seventy-three per cent of the sample believed that the persecution of the Jews was an obstacle to good understanding between Britain and Germany.[66] The British government thought otherwise. Warnings that the pogrom was about to occur from Wilfred Israel, who had close contacts with both countries, were ignored and no official protest was launched after the violence.[67] *Kristallnacht*, coming so soon after the Munich agreement, shattered any moral arguments left in defence of appeasement, but British foreign policy continued regardless. Elsewhere, the United States recalled its Ambassador to Germany, Hugh Wilson. After much deliberation, President Roosevelt released a press statement stating that he himself 'could scarcely believe that such things could occur in a twentieth century civilization'. Taken as a whole, however, the issue was not pursued by the democracies for long or with much vigour. In terms of *governmental* protests, as Lionel Kochan concludes, 'Humanitarian sympathies yielded to *raison d'état*'.[68]

If the events of *Kristallnacht*, however horrific, were ultimately seen by all the democracies as the concern of another nation state and not their own responsibility, there was still great diversity in refugee policies in the crucial months after the international conference at Evian in July 1938. The range of responses is all the more striking given the unanimity emerging from the Evian conference. The conference came from an initiative of President Roosevelt. He was motivated partly by genuine humanitarian concern but his main aim was more cynical: he wished to maintain the United States' liberal reputation while shifting the responsibility of the refugee crisis onto the international community. In fact a tacit agreement was reached between Britain and the United States in which the latter agreed not to criticize the former's Jewish quotas for Palestine and the former agreed not to push the issue of the latter's restrictive and discriminatory immigration laws.[69]

It would be wrong to dismiss totally the Evian conference as a cruel facade, even if the progress made in liberalizing immigration restrictions was limited. Apart from some mainly empty promises from Latin American countries, it was clear from the conference that no major power was willing to state publicly that it would open its doors more widely to Jewish refugees. The British government response in official statements was particularly marked by a limited and cautious approach to rescue. It is therefore surprising that shortly after in what was the last 12 months before the war it was Britain that was to play the leading role among the democracies in attempting to solve the refugee crisis. From *Kristallnacht* to the start of the war, more than 40 per cent of the Jews who escaped Nazi-controlled Europe found refuge in Britain.[70] In bold contrast to the policies pursued by France, previously the most important receiving society outside the United States, Britain liberalized its immigration policies in a significant way. In Canada, Australia, Holland and the United States, only a very minor easing of restrictions occurred after *Kristallnacht*, but their collective impact was nothing like as impressive as that of Britain.[71]

British 'generosity' post-*Anschluss*, and particularly post-*Kristallnacht*, needs to be put into context. First, the possible link to a parallel closing of the doors of Palestine should not be dismissed. Guilt at the appeasement of Arab unrest and the further move away from the remnants of the Balfour declaration encouraged, in recompense, greater flexibility in immigration policy at home. Similarly, unease at the implication of the Munich agreement had its counterpart in an explicit British government-sponsored scheme to help rescue Czech refugees. Second, the liberalization of entry policy in 1938 was made easier by the fact that so few had been allowed entry to Britain before that year. Developments in France and, to a lesser extent, Holland, followed a reverse pattern. Lastly, most of the 40–50,000 allowed in after the *Anschluss*, and particularly after *Kristallnacht*, came to Britain on temporary transit visas.[72] Despite these important qualifications, it remains that Britain became the major centre of rescue for Nazi-persecuted Jews in the desperate months before war. Elsewhere in the democracies, economic fears and the worry over stimulating domestic antisemitism stopped any significant liberalization of policy and in France at least immigration control actually increased. Such concerns over the spread of antisemitism were also expressed most vocally in Britain by senior government figures, but they were overruled by the Prime Minister, Neville Chamberlain.[73]

In the United States, Canada, Australia and Britain there were public demands post-*Kristallnacht* for their governments to open their doors to persecuted Jews.[74] The contrast between the responses of the American and British governments to such pressure is striking. In the United States, the Wagner-Rogers Bill to bring 20,000 refugee children, despite its support from a range of religious and secular bodies, was never implemented. There were those such as Clarence Pickett, director of the Non-Sectarian Committee for German Refugee Children, who stressed that

When you get concerned about children you do not look at their race or color so much, but you want the children taken care of, and if children in Germany are neglected then we are participants in that neglect, and that is a bad example for our children over here.

Ultimately, however, Roosevelt's government did not wish to stir up potential anti-alienist/antisemitic feeling in the United States and, therefore, it strove to appease the restrictionist lobby in Congress.[75] In Holland after *Kristallnacht* a limited scheme to help children to escape and move on to other countries was implemented. Britain, following this lead and aware that its liberal reputation was at stake, created the child refugee movement. It was born out of an amalgam of state concern and a popular outcry to do something to help the Jews of Nazi Europe. One person, whose family was involved in the rescue of a four-year-old from Vienna, recalled that action was essential: 'Hitler's regime in Germany tormented me'. Nearly 10,000 children, between 80 and 90 per cent of whom were Jewish, were allowed in to Britain before the outbreak of war in what was, with its size and scope, a unique scheme of rescue.[76]

The limitations of this scheme, 'The Price of Humanity', (and of others, such as that for domestic servants) should not be overlooked. The children came on temporary visas and were therefore not an immediate or long-term economic threat to British workers and the British government insisted that they would not in any way become a charge on taxpayers. Moreover, most of the children came alone and ultimately many would never see their parents again. Some were treated coolly and even with brutality. One former refugee remembers 'the taunts of "Your own don't want you, so we took you in". They received payment for our keep. I did the work . . . handing in my wages intact, as did my brother at fourteen.' Overall, however, it should be recalled that the numbers involved in this scheme were by no means tokenist. Most were taken in by non-Jewish families and thus the numbers of Britons drawn directly into the European Jewish tragedy expanded into the thousands, even if some still remained clueless about the reasons behind the emigrations.[77] With some initial lead by the state, an involvement was made possible in the fate of people connected only by a common humanity. Small refugee committees were set up across Britain in these months. Margareta Burkill, a central figure in the Cambridge Refugee Committee, recalls that after *Kristallnacht*, there was 'a sort of electric current, every little town, every village in England said: "We must save the children"'. Jewish bodies were established in all the major conurbations, but there and in smaller settlement areas, Christians and particularly non-conformist groups such as the Quakers, played an important role in organizing rescue and relief. By September 1939, 50–60,000 refugees from Nazism were present in Britain; and, in the Refugee Children's Movement alone, there were 12 regional and 65 area committees in the country. In the United States a similar process operated in the formation of local refugee committees. As a former activist recalled: 'it was a small number of people in each city who got the thing rolling. But they did a superb job.'

The November 1938 pogrom had thus shaken liberal assumptions about the persecution of the Jews in Greater Germany. But would it lead to a fundamental reassessment of the plight of the Jews as a whole?[78]

IV

It might be assumed that the events of *Kristallnacht* and the presence of a significant number of refugees in the democratic countries would have increased popular understanding of the nature of Nazi antisemitism. In Britain the contrast has been pointed out between the initial shock of hearing about the November 1938 pogrom and the 'particularly striking . . . speed with which the first impressions appear to have faded'. Similarly in the United States it has been suggested that, 'Unfortunately, far too many people soon forgot the incident'.[79] A leading reporter claimed as early as February 1939 that 'there are those in England and in America who shrug complacent shoulders and who say: "Oh things can't be as bad as we hear"'. Another observer in Britain commented at the same time that 'indignation towards German [antisemitic] methods had cooled off considerably'.[80]

A remarkable cultural product of this return to treating Nazi Germany normally can be found in a British textbook, *Brush Up Your German*, published by Dent, one of the leading educational presses, and written by J. B. C. Grundy, head of Modern Languages at the elite Shrewsbury School. Grundy had produced a similar volume in 1931 but found no difficulty in adjusting to the new regime. The book was completed post-*Kristallnacht* yet managed to display on its front cover a sketch of a storm-trooper. The representation is more akin to a boy-scout than the main participant in an open and bloody pogrom. The textbook does not deny a Nazi animus towards Jews, but makes light of the subject. Instead, Grundy revealed much admiration for the Nazi regime. Any criticism is of a gentle nature and represents more a sense of British superiority over the Germans than a fundamental attack on Nazism. Finally the reader, having learnt of the efficiency of the new state, is confronted in a Nazi glossary with useful phrases such as '*die Rassenschande*, racial shame (e.g. of marriage with Jew)' and '*jüdisch-marxistisch*, Jewish and Marxist, hostile, bad', showing an accommodation with the racist state that appears effortless. Writing from the comfort of one of England's leading public schools, just months after the open state-sponsored violence and murder of *Kristallnacht*, Grundy could say of the main character of his book, that 'as he comes across the new institutions of the Third Reich, he begins to realize that they are not all humbug. If others will follow him in this the author will be more than content.'[81]

Few attempts have been made to analyse this extraordinary adjustment made in the liberal world to the horrors of the Nazi pogrom. Sander Diamond suggests that 'other events took precedence – national defense and concern over the deterioration of European conditions – and the plight of the Jews became a matter of lesser importance'.[82] Considerations of national issues and the failure of the Jewish disaster to fit into such concerns were clearly of great significance. After the initial tentative protests, the major political figures in the democracies did not publicly return to the plight of the Jews again in peacetime. It was hard, therefore, for ordinary people to make the connection with a persecuted minority in another land. There were, after all, major problems at home in 1939.

A year after the pogrom, a London journalist met with a refugee friend, 'G', to help translate an article written by another Austrian exile for an English paper. The comments of the journalist to her friend are worth quoting to illustrate the problem of placing *Kristallnacht* in an English national context:

I told her that it was not explicit enough – the writer would say 'On this day . . .' and I would say 'which day?' and G. would reply 'The day of the pogrom . . .'. Then I'd have to say 'Which pogrom? When?' 'The pogrom on the anniversary of the Munich putsch.' 'Which day was that?' I tried to point out to her – which she saw immediately – that although all these events were so overwhelmingly important to the man who had lived through them, to people in England they were foreign history, and that life had been flowing on at the same time in England . . . their eyes had not been fixed entirely on Austria.[83]

The importance of parochialism alone does not explain, however, the genuine uncertainty in ordinary people's minds in the democracies, so soon after the November pogrom, about the real nature of Nazi antisemitism. The abandonment of the issue as a matter of international concern by democratic governments partly accounts for some confusion among the public. Nevertheless, we must return again to the domination of a liberal ideology (and its tenacity) in order to comprehend more fully the swift fading of popular memory in the democratic nation states with regard to *Kristallnacht*.

Blanche Dugdale, a leading British non-Jewish Zionist, was unsurprised by the scale of the pogrom. Having followed the Nazis' antisemitism closely, *Kristallnacht* seemed to her a continuation and culmination of the movement's barbarity if not its ultimate potential.[84] Elsewhere in Britain, few had taken in the importance of antisemitism in the programme and ideology of the Third Reich. Instead attempts were made to understand the pogrom within a liberal framework in which a rational motivation for the violence was sought. Not surprisingly, confusion and incredulity emerged. To the MP 'Chips' Channon, the pogrom was 'unnecessary' and to the Earl of Crawford there was 'so little cause for it whereas if anything of the kind took place here one would know that the Jews contribute much too high a proportion of the criminal classes'. Similarly, the Prime Minister, Neville Chamberlain, pondered: 'No doubt Jews aren't a lovable people; I don't care about them myself; but that is not sufficient to explain the Pogrom.' Channon, Crawford and Chamberlain all harboured a dislike of Jews on a social level and believed that Jews constituted some degree of nuisance in the world. Yet the level of this Jewish 'irritant' could not explain the violence of the Nazi response.[85]

The ease with which memories of *Kristallnacht* dimmed in the democratic world was thus the result of a combination of factors. Other domestic and international worries and a failure to connect them to the fate of the Jews were of fundamental importance. The strength of liberal idealism in which such events should not have occurred needs also to be considered. Yet the failure of the liberal imagination to acknowledge the unthinkable has to be placed alongside other aspects of the liberal discourse on Jewish issues. In a post-emancipatory society antisemitism was deemed, ultimately, to be the fault of the Jews. *Kristallnacht* briefly threatened to challenge such an analysis, therefore the easiest solution was to forget about the pogrom. By early 1939 a detailed investigation into British attitudes found the 'very ordinary' response that 'the Jews really bring it all on themselves'. A schoolmaster suggested that Jewish sufferings were 'the bird coming home to roost' and added that the Jews should 'cure themselves [of their exclusivity] first before they ask for sympathy'. One school survey of 11 to 12-year-olds found comments that British Jews were left alone 'because *they* [my emphasis] have not done wrong'. Another sample of 17-year-olds found only two out of 30 agreed with Hitler's antisemitic methods, but found that most were still distrustful of the Jews in general.[86]

A few, mainly in the fascist and pacifist camps, went further and actually denied that the persecutions had occurred. After the pogrom, the British Union of Fascists' *Action* reminded its readers of 'such blatantly untrue stories as that of the corpse factory during the [First World] War' and added that the present stories were part of 'World Jewry's War Plots'. Similar comments could be found in the columns of *Peace News* as late as August 1939.[87] Total denial of the veracity of the atrocities was, at this stage, mainly limited to extremists, but a more general distrust of the Jews in the liberal democratic societies enabled scepticism about the scale of the Jewish disaster to have wider credence. It was a feature which would continue and intensify during the war in countries such as Britain and the United States. The experience of Jewish refugees in both countries before the war indicates the importance of such tendencies in the form of everyday life.

V

Rather than representing, as A. J. P. Taylor suggested, 'walking propaganda against the Nazis', refugees often found the task of explaining their position very frustrating.[88] The Hallgarten family, refugees from Germany, were frequently asked 'What have you really done that you had to leave your country?'; 'What criminal act have you done?' Friedal Hallgarten adds that 'many people were absolutely without understanding'. Ludwig Guttmann was medical director of the Jewish hospital in Breslau. He escaped to Britain in 1939 and first settled in Oxford. There he met F. A. Lindemann, professor of experimental philosophy, friend and later advisor to Churchill and a long-standing anti-Nazi. Lindemann was anxious to hear of Guttmann's experiences, but when he was told

of the burning books, the condition of people admitted to my hospital after interrogation by the Gestapo, broken in body and spirit, and of the events of Kristallnacht, he somewhat sneeringly interrupted me, saying 'You must not tell me atrocity legends'.[89]

Similarly, Myra Baram, a refugee who came to Britain as a governess, was told that her brother could not have been put in a concentration camp *simply* because he was Jewish. It was for such reasons that the Central Office for Refugees put out a pamphlet in 1939 stressing that refugees 'through no fault of their own, have been placed in the most embarrassing of all circumstances'. The situation in the United States was little different. The psychologist, Bruno Bettelheim, recalled his reception in American society after his release from Dachau and Buchenwald in 1939:

I was anxious to force on the awareness of as many people as possible what was going on in Nazi Germany. . . . But I met with little success. At that time, nothing was known in the U.S. about the camps, and my story was met with utter disbelief . . . people did not wish to believe Germans could do such horrendous things. I was accused of being carried away by my hatred of the Nazis, of engaging in paranoid distortions. I was warned not to spread such lies.

Similarly, Walter Bieringer, a refugee worker in Boston, was faced with incredulity when he attempted to explain the situation of the Jews to American Masonic lodges: 'they were so unbelieving about what was happening'.[90]

The treatment of refugees (children and adults) varied immensely in British and American society. Some were treated by both Jews and non-Jews with love, kindness and a real understanding of their terrible plight. Attempts were made by these exceptional individuals to compensate the refugees for the horrors and hardships they had encountered in Nazi Europe. A former child refugee in Britain recalls her hosts as simply marvellous [people] – if standards of human decency and ordinary down-to-earth kindness are the measurements by which we judge them. These relatively simple people did not allow their traditional doubt about Jews or their current hate of Germans to deter them from taking into their modest home us foreign-speaking and strangely dressed youngsters.

Another recalls her English headmistress who 'would allow me to spend time in her room where she talked and encouraged me and said healing things like "We'll show Hitler that he can't do things like that!".'[91] Furthermore, few in Britain were totally opposed to the entry of refugees (just 26 per cent according to a poll carried out in July 1939) and there was an absence of any popular violence or mass movement against the newcomers.[92] The majority of the population, however, remained ambivalent about the refugee presence. There was suspicion of the refugees for economic reasons, but also out of a common distrust of them on more general, cultural grounds. Such tendencies were referred to most honestly in his diary a few days after *Kristallnacht* by Cuthbert Headlam:

I had a call from Professor R[,] thrusting articles upon me. I wonder whether he is genuine gentleman or merely posing as a military expert? One always rather distrusts German Jews who are expelled from Germany – one ought not to, especially today, but one has an instinctive suspicion of them.

The unease was also recorded privately by Virginia Woolf, adding to her diary at a time of some personal frustration in February 1939: 'Innumerable refugees to add to the tangle. There – I've recorded them when I said I wouldn't.'[93]

The response of the refugee organizations at this point was to make the refugee presence as invisible as was possible in British society. On one level it could be achieved by submerging many, especially women, into the 'downstairs' world of domestic service. As will be shown, up to 20,000 refugees would join this occupation. Several thousand were also kept outside the public eye through the Richborough (or Kitchener) refugee camp in Kent.[94] For other refugees still at large, the policy was to camouflage their activities. Speaking German in public was frowned upon and the main refugee bodies in Britain, based at Bloomsbury House (the Central Office for Refugees), concentrated their attention on anglicizing the refugees with all possible speed. The refugees who were under the control of such organizations soon learnt the message. An article in the *Kitchener Camp Review*, on 'One Refugee's Advice to the Other', concluded: 'behave like the English people. Do not dress conspicuously, do not speak loudly, be polite, smile and be thankful. Once more, BE ENGLISH!' The results were clear: one refugee recalls that he 'had to become more English than the English, play cricket, drink in pubs. I always felt I was acting a part.' Another remembers his brother becoming 'almost hyper-English, he had a passion for cricket'.[95] The importance of learning to play by 'English' rules (and particularly those of the national game) in the lives of refugees in Britain was crucial. As we will see later, only refugees saved through the Chief Rabbi's Emergency Committee were able to reject freely such expected behaviour patterns in Britain – although, even then, it was much to the disquiet of liberal opinion inside the Jewish community.[96]

In the United States during the 1930s, the pressure on immigrants to assimilate totally was less powerful than in Britain. Nevertheless, a programme of dispersal away from New York and a general policy of retraining refugees for inconspicuous jobs was undertaken by American Jewish agencies. Fear of domestic antisemitism was again a motivating factor behind such policies. 'The New York Jewish question is a great problem, and is understood as such by Americans. Anyone who goes to New York helps to aggravate this problem,' refugees were warned in 1938. Largely unsuccessful attempts were made to persuade the refugees to 'Go West young man!'. A former worker for the refugees outlined the reasons for such dispersal policies: 'they would become Americanized more quickly, they wouldn't all stick together, as they did in New York'. Nevertheless, although the significance of this factor should not be exaggerated, the nature of Americanization had changed compared to the 1920s. There was a greater acceptance of ethnic pluralism in American society and the concept of what it meant to become an American had become more flexible. Moreover, 'Racism and xenophobia survived, but their relative acceptance declined.' Nativism did not disappear, however, and it continued to flourish on anti-radicalist sentiment and the threat of the 'enemy within'. Furthermore, restrictionists were vocal and influential inside and outside of Congress. Yet although there was still seen to be a need for the refugees to 'Americanize', there was also a growing recognition and acceptance of diversity among the American people. Writing of the problems of 'de-Germanization', a refugee wrote in 1939:

If by purifying the European heritage one becomes an American, we Germans, retrained in English language and American history, have been led a straight and promising way. Indeed, if we can stand the strain, pass the test, and live long enough, we may hope that something will still become to us and will enable us to repay, from our purified European tradition, our debt to America.

A former refugee recalls the situation in Pittsburgh where people 'saw us as Germans first, and Jews second, and Americans third'. In Britain there were no such 'mainstream' models of ethnic plurality. Refugees, even after decades in the country, felt that they could become British, but never 'English'.[97] Furthermore there was little acceptance that the country had traditions of immigration in which the refugees could be viewed and of which they could feel part. Campaigners such as Eleanor Rathbone, who from within the liberal tradition supported the idea of a Britain past, present and future that was diverse, worked in an isolated intellectual and cultural atmosphere.

VI

To summarize: the antisemitism of the Third Reich in the pre-war period was carried out openly. Information about its extent was accessible to the liberal democratic world, but cultural and ideological factors acted as a barrier to the full assimilation of the available evidence. On a governmental level, factors of international diplomacy, defined in an exclusive manner, ensured that the specific fate of the Jews as a minority group (rather than as individuals) would rarely receive particular attention. Officials, even at the Evian conference, publicly avoided mentioning *Jewish* refugees as such.[98] The refugees who managed to escape to the liberal democracies were under immense pressure to assimilate. This factor, in conjunction with the failure to understand why the refugees had been forced to leave and a general cultural antipathy to foreigners/Jews, meant that the presence of tens of thousands of refugees only slowly changed public awareness of the real nature of Nazi antisemitism before the war. National and international problems in the liberal democratic countries also hindered comprehension. Domestic concerns predominated and these were rarely connected to the fate of the Jews. On the rare occasions when the persecution of the Jews did become prominent at home, widespread public sympathy in the democracies was evident. Its potential was briefly illustrated in Britain just after *Kristallnacht* when, with state encouragement, the British public responded by helping to rescue nearly 10,000 through the *Kindertransporte* scheme. Public demands for such action in other countries were not satisfied. Even in Britain, however, the government was reluctant to continue the lead given over the rescue of refugee children. The persecution of the Jews in Nazi Europe was not a major, or even a minor, issue in liberal democratic policy-making in 1939. It thus became hard for the campaigners on behalf of the persecuted Jews to maintain public interest in the subject. Despite their isolation, campaigners such as Eleanor Rathbone had achieved much throughout the 1930s, particularly in the rescuing of individual or small groups of refugees. Nevertheless, they rarely succeeded in their broader aim of bonding the peoples of each particular liberal democratic nation state with the persecuted Jews abroad. Dorothy Thompson, in many ways Eleanor Rathbone's counterpart in the United States, was convinced that efforts should be made to help Jews escape and improve the lot of those staying:

The attempt must be made, if only as a testimony to the vitality of our faith in the democratic principles which we profess to live by. On those principles our institutions are founded, and with them are integrated the fundamental concepts of our civilization. Therefore, the attempt must be made not out of pity for the exiles, actual and potential, but as a reaffirmation of our own beliefs, lest they become hollow dogmas to which, eventually, not even lip service will be given anywhere.

Instead the liberal democracies in the 1930s followed more insular policies determined by *realpolitik*. The only restraining factor which stopped total inaction on behalf of the persecuted Jews was a desire to preserve liberal reputations and a fear of appearing mean in international circles. The democracies engaged in humanitarian one-upmanship while restraining their help to the Jews within increasingly narrow bounds.

This chapter has set the background in which the liberal democracies responded and reacted to the illiberal persecution of the Jews in the Third Reich. We now move to consideration of the refugee crisis during the 1930s through a consideration of the British and American labour movements. In a decade of massive unemployment and job insecurity, the policies pursued by trades unions and others in the labour world would be of crucial importance in the implementation of liberal democratic refugee policies. In the opinion poll carried out in Britain during July 1939, of the 70 per cent in favour of allowing refugees the right to enter, 84 per cent still believed they should do so 'with restrictions designed to safeguard British workers and taxpayers'.[99] Was this to be a question purely of economics, or would other cultural and ideological factors come into play?

2
Their Brothers' and Sisters' Keepers?: The Nazi Persecution of the Jews and the Labour Movement

In the words of Humbert Wolfe, a senior Whitehall official, British government practice was, at least until 1938, 'not to vary the aliens administration in favour of or against the refugees'. There was to be no refugee policy as such, only a continuation of immigration control procedures which had developed before the Nazi rise to power. Wolfe, however, by juxtaposing the terms 'alien' and 'refugee', was acknowledging the dilemma in state policy. He also pointed out in 1935 that there had been 'very little criticism of such assistance as has been given to refugees in this country'. It was hardly surprising, however, because 'the numbers admitted have been very small as compared with those admitted to other countries'.[1] But treating the refugees simply as problematic immigrants became difficult when placed alongside any kind of commitment to an asylum policy. Nevertheless, government restrictionism could be vindicated on moral and practical grounds as designed to protect the national interest, especially at the level of economics. With continuing high levels of unemployment throughout the 1930s and the misery of mass poverty throughout the Western world, it was not difficult to justify the use of immigration policies designed to protect the jobs and conditions of workers in the democracies. Consciences could be further salved by a tokenist rescue of prominent individuals.

The role of the organized labour movement in the creation of such policies should not be minimized. Individual and national trades unions not only on the whole supported restrictionist measures, they also encouraged and were often instrumental in their implementation. In October 1939 Sir Herbert Emerson, the director of the Inter-Governmental Committee on Refugees (one of the few vaguely positive results of the Evian conference), looked back on the limited progress made in opening the doors of the 'free world' to the persecuted Jews:

Before the war the problem of refugees in countries of temporary refuge was a serious one. It was an embarrassment to the Government concerned, it was viewed with suspicion by organized labor, and, although much of this suspicion was founded on false economics, it none the less increased the danger of anti-semitism.

That astute observer of the world scene, George Orwell, went further in 1940, concluding that 'In the years before the war it was largely trade-union opposition that prevented a big influx of German Jewish refugees'.[2] As we will see, neither the comments of Emerson nor Orwell can be dismissed lightly. The lack of subsequent consideration given to the vital role played by the labour movement in liberal democratic policy-making with regard to the Nazi persecution of the Jews is indeed a serious omission.[3] But the problems facing the organized labour world should also not be ignored. In labour circles, the moral dilemma in confronting the crisis of those attempting to escape from Nazism were even greater than they were for governments in the liberal democracies. Nationalism and internationalism, idealism and prejudice were all exposed in the labour movement. It led to responses which on the surface now *appear* confused and contradictory (if not, at times, hypocritical), but in reality expose the conflicting contemporary pressures operating on organized labour.

In the language of the 1930s, those trying to flee from the Third Reich to the liberal democracies were regarded alternatively as 'aliens', 'refugees', 'political refugees', 'foreigners', 'foreign workers', 'exiles from Nazi persecution', 'Jews', 'persecuted Jews', 'foreign Jews' and many other similar combinations. None of these terms on its own was directly value-loaded (as, say, compared to the antisemitic phraseology of the British Union of Fascists and its ugly references to 'refuJews', or 'the riff-raff of half the world' as one American union leader indelicately put it), yet their surface neutrality disguises the varying images and discourses associated with each particular label.[4] It is, for example, hardly surprising that those escaping from Nazism were likely to receive more sympathetic treatment as 'refugees' than as 'aliens' or 'foreigners'. It is less obvious that in the 1930s 'political refugees' would be better placed than 'Jewish refugees' or that in many Western countries 'alien' was often associated automatically with 'Jew' (a term that itself carried negative associations). Indeed, the intricate and sometimes intractable difficulties of the labour movement in the democracies in this area were often 'solved' by skipping from one category to another. They could call for strict immigration control against aliens while simultaneously appearing sympathetic to the entry of refugees from Nazism even if the 'aliens' and the 'refugees' were, in reality, the same people. In the British case particularly, although much of the debate in the labour movement blatantly concerned Jewish refugees, the word 'Jew' was studiously avoided. Unravelling such responses is thus a complex operation. The task is not made easier by the understandable contemporary desire, stressed by William Gillies, Secretary of the Trades Union Congress (TUC) International Department in 1938, 'to refute assertions which have been made . . . that the British and International Labour and Trade Union movements have not been as sympathetic as they should be'. Self-delusions of generosity in the labour world were powerful, and it was a rare moment of honesty when the TUC General Council stated in 1938 its anxiety 'that some practical expression be given to the sympathy which is generally felt' on the refugee question.[5]

I

Historians have focused considerable attention on the agitations at the turn of the century which led to the formal or informal closing of doors to immigrants, many of whom were poor Jews from Eastern Europe. There has been a tendency, as David Feldman suggests with regard to Britain (although his comments have much wider validity), 'to approach the anti-immigration movement as an episode in the history of prejudice or anti-Semitism – an unpleasant spectacle of some fascination but of little significance more generally'. There is a danger, Feldman adds, that in the process 'We have learned little of the intellectual currents, cultural symbols, and political visions which rendered opposition to immigration meaningful for those who took this position'.[6] One could add that in the late nineteenth and early twentieth century, opposition to immigration was not the only response of the labour movement. International solidarity with foreign workers and the potential of the newcomers as trade unionists (as well as a need to listen to the immigrant voice) led to responses towards immigration which were complex, ambivalent and rarely totally restrictionist. As Kenneth Lunn concludes, 'labour responses towards immigrants . . . have too often been defined . . . by a simplistic notion of overt hostility'.[7]

The situation had changed markedly after World War I, especially in the United States. The nationalism generated by the war, and economic dislocation after it, pushed the American Federation of Labor (AFL) away from any pretence of internationalism (marked particularly by its virulent anti-communism) and firmly into the restrictionist camp. As John Higham argues, economic arguments alone do not explain why the AFL moved to become one of the major supporters of the 1924 Johnson-Reed Act (which set limited immigration quotas heavily biased against 'non-Nordic' nationals): 'Immigration, it believed, had exceeded the nation's capacity to unify and Americanize. This explicit appeal to national homogeneity had not graced official AFL declarations before the war period.' At first its leader Samuel Gompers was reluctant to embrace the discriminatory clauses, but by 1924 he openly 'embraced the idea that European immigration endangered America's racial foundations'.[8]

In Britain, control through the Aliens Restriction Act of 1919 came sooner and was more draconian. Support for this measure came mainly from conservative forces but there was little meaningful opposition from the left/liberal world. Radicals such as Josiah Wedgwood, later one of the main campaigners on behalf of the persecuted Jews, demanded the end of control on humanitarian grounds as well as the need to maintain the freedom of the individual and freedom of movement. Further on the left, John Scurr called for the loosening of restriction, again for humane reasons but also to show international solidarity. In an atmosphere of increasing insularity and commitment to 'Englishness', such pleas were rejected by the Conservatives (who were not averse to playing an aliens card at election time) and the two insecure Labour minority governments of 1924 and 1929–31.[9] In February 1930, after less than a year of the second of these governments, the Labour Party Research Department addressed itself to the 'almost absolute powers' possessed by the Home Secretary with regard to right to entry and deportation of immigrants. It feared that Parliament would not stand for any relaxation of alien restriction but called for limited flexibility with regard to political/religious asylum. If an individual had genuine fear of persecution abroad, permission to land ought to be granted but only if 'he can show that he is not likely to be chargeable to public funds'. Such a philosophy (including its potential gender bias) was at the basis of the British labour movement's responses to the refugee crisis throughout the 1930s.[10]

In Britain, the near-consensus across the political divide on the need for immigration control, and the strange combination of right-wing populist and labour support for restrictive and discriminatory measures in the United States, had drastically changed the situation from the pre-1914 world. Nationalism and the pursuit of 'Englishness' or '100 per cent Americanism' created an atmosphere during the 1920s in which a group of just 1,000 Russian Jews could find themselves rejected by an American quota system and left stateless in an English camp for the better half of a decade.[11] Michael Marrus has suggested that refugees from Nazism 'ran into a wall of restrictions hastily erected in Western European countries in the early 1930s'. In actual fact, many of these barriers had been constructed earlier in response to, or in fear of, the agitation of native workers. Indeed, the problem for many in the labour world after 1933 was how to respond in a meaningful way to the victims of

Nazism in the face of the immigration gates they had already supported closing.[12]

It must be stressed that in the European liberal democracies and the United States, those in the labour movement had little difficulty in condemning the Nazi movement and all that it stood for. The outlawing of trade unions and of socialist organizations in Nazi Germany (following on from such measures in fascist Italy) ensured a swift and unanimous condemnation from those on the right as well as the left in the labour world. In Britain, labourite pragmatists such as Walter Citrine (General Secretary of the TUC throughout the Nazi era) and Ernest Bevin (General Secretary of the Transport and General Workers Union, the biggest in Europe), dominated trade union politics throughout the 1930s. Both were united in their hatred of communism but shared a common view of the dangers of fascism. Citrine produced a powerful study of the pernicious impact of the latter in 1933, entitled 'Dictatorship and the Trade Union Movement', and Bevin told the Labour Party Conference in 1936: 'Which is the first institution that victorious Fascism wipes out? It is the trade union movement.'[13]

In 1933, with the TUC playing a leading role, the International Federation of Trades Unions set up an emergency fund for victims of Nazism. Hugh Gaitskell, the future Labour leader, was despatched to Europe to distribute aid and help people to escape. France, Holland, Britain and the United States would play an important role in providing refuge for socialist and trade union leaders persecuted under the fascist regimes. The impetus for the rescue and often the payment of their upkeep came from within the labour movements of the liberal democracies. Even in countries which operated very restrictive immigration policies in the early years of the Third Reich (such as Britain and the United States), governments showed remarkable flexibility in allowing such victims of Nazism the right to enter. Although the numbers involved were never high, the case of political refugees does indicate government sensitivity to trade union pressure in the area of immigration.[14]

Some of those helped through the International Solidarity Fund were Jewish. The historian Max Beer came to Britain in 1933 after the first antisemitic purges and received some assistance so that he could continue his researches at the British Library. It was emphasized, however, that the help was given 'for the sake of the work he has done for the Socialist Movement in Europe, and in particular, as the first historian of our own British Socialist Movement'.[15] The internationalist, but labour movement-specific, concern illustrated in such relief did not, however, stop general condemnation of the Nazi movement's racial and religious intolerance. Nevertheless, consideration of the persecution of the Jews varied in intensity. The subject did not receive particular attention in the TUC until 1934, whereas in October 1933 the Executive Council of the AFL at its annual convention was anxious to connect the terror and brutality shown against leaders of the German trades union movement 'with the inauguration of a campaign of Jewish persecution unparalleled in modern history'. While the TUC was, by reasons of geography as well as outlook, closer to the events in the fascist countries, the AFL devoted more time in the 1930s to the antisemitism of the Nazi regime, certainly in its first few years, than its British counterpart.[16] The reasons behind this difference in approach can be explained partly by the ethnic diversity of the organized American labour movement, even within the elitist AFL. The sentiments of its Executive Council report in 1933 would have been hard to transfer to a British situation in which consideration of ethnic plurality was not an issue:

The utter destruction of the independent trade union movement of Germany by those now in control of the German government has been equalled only by the ruthless persecution of Germany's Jewish population. Persecution of this kind arouses intense feeling among the membership of organized labor. Our great movement rests upon the broad principle of racial tolerance and of no discrimination because of creed or nationality. Our great organized labor movement is engaged in the noble work of blending into a common brotherhood all working people, without regard to creed, color or nationality. We abhor racial persecution and we protest vigorously against the persecution of the Jewish people of Germany.

In the same report, however, the AFL Executive Committee stressed its opposition to a Bill in Congress which wished to remove the prohibition on immigrants who might become public charges. It also objected to attempts to restore the right of free entry for those fleeing racial or political persecution. The AFL's response was blunt:

There is not a country in the world where there is not religious or political persecutions and if the old law was restored many thousands would be permitted to come into the country.

We must strive in every way possible to prevent any modification of the immigration laws. There has never been a time when restricted immigration is more necessary than now.[17]

The economic roots of such restrictionism (between 12 and 15 million Americans were unemployed in 1933) are not hard to detect. But other less blatant factors were also in operation. In spite of its lip service to a 'common brotherhood', the racialized world view of the AFL that had developed during the 1920s continued into the 'devil's decade'. In 1932, William Green, the AFL President, stressed that immigration was not only an economic question, it brought with it 'a serious task of assimilation'. Further immigration would harm American society. The following year, Green stated with regard to the nationalistic ex-servicemen's American Legion that 'In the protection of

America from being over-run by an immigration quota that would be injurious, not only to the immigrants, but to ourselves, we stand together'.[18]

The greatest concern of the AFL was over oriental immigration. In 1934 pressure from AFL led to the exclusion of Filipino immigrants to the United States. Paul Scharrenberg of the California State Federation of Labor proudly announced in his welcoming speech to the AFL delegates in its 1934 annual conference that

for the first time in the history of the American labor movement we can say that we have made a clean sweep. No more Orientals can come to our state and nation, and that is due entirely to the loyal and unswerving support of the American Federation of Labor.[19]

Did, however, such racial protectionism on behalf of the AFL also include potential Jewish refugees from Nazism? The answer is not straightforward. On one level, the blatant racism exposed in the AFL's opposition to the entry of oriental immigrants and the discrimination openly practised by many of its constituent unions was not present in consideration of Jewish refugees.[20] The horror expressed repeatedly by the AFL leadership about the persecution faced by the Jews in Germany was genuine. In its Nazi form, racial discrimination was abhorred. Nevertheless, on the level of its general cultural and national outlook, it cannot be said that the AFL regarded Jewish immigrants (or Jewish workers as a whole) as necessarily unproblematic. The AFL's commitment to 100 per cent American patriotism and its concomitant hatred of alien communism created a suspicion of Jewish labor leaders on the left. It was exposed unpleasantly in 1935/6, at a time of great rivalry and bitterness within the American labor movement. At this point the Congress of Industrial Organizations (CIO) was created by labor leaders dissatisfied by the failure of the AFL to expand rapidly away from its basis in 'craft' membership. Some of the unions which broke away from the AFL did indeed have Jewish leaders and many Jewish members, such as Sidney Hillman's Amalgamated Clothing Workers' Union of America, David Dubinsky's International Ladies Garment Workers' Union and M. Zaritsky's United Hatters, Cap and Millinery Workers' International Union. Nevertheless, it was a gross exaggeration to state, as the AFL's Vice-President Woll suggested, that the CIO was 'composed largely of Jewish workers'. Woll accused them of ingratitude as the AFL had earlier taken 'them by the hand when there were few hands willing to greet them' even though these Jewish immigrants had preached old world theories 'alien to our own beliefs and doctrines'.[21] Moreover, the AFL repeatedly stressed its opposition to the CIO on the grounds that it was opposed to 'every ism except Americanism, and the American people'. Its equal hatred of 'Communism and Nazism' ensured policies that were ambivalent on Jewish issues.[22]

Nazi antisemitism was constantly attacked by the AFL, but loosening immigration control for its victims brought with it not only economic risks but also the possibility of bringing in immigrants who were seen as hard to assimilate and generally undesirable.

In 1934 and 1935, representatives of the International Ladies' Garment Workers' Union proposed resolutions to the annual AFL conference, calling on the organization to 'extend every possible aid to facilitate the entry of fugitives from Nazi and fascist terror on account of trade union activity or racial or religious affiliation'. The AFL responded sympathetically but ultimately stated that it could not support the resolution which 'would run counter to the immigration laws now in existence as a result of the activities of the American Federation of Labor'. It was a policy that was maintained until the latter stages of World War II.[23]

Several strategies were adopted by the AFL as an alternative to changing the nature of the United States' discriminatory immigration laws. First, great stress was put on the American movement boycotting German goods and services which the AFL pledged would continue

until the German government recognizes the right of the working people of Germany to organize into bona fide, independent trade unions of their own choosing, and until Germany ceases its repressive policy of persecution of Jewish people.

The AFL's backing and leading role in the boycott campaign was ideologically sincere. When calling for the boycott, President Green spoke with great passion, outlining the nature of Nazism, the horror of its persecutions and the impact on the groups and individuals affected.[24] However, the boycott complemented the more general restrictionist policies pursued by the AFL in the 1930s. It would help pressure the Nazis to change their ways and might ultimately transform the regime into a more acceptable government. At the same time, it must be added, the boycott helped to remove competition from American workers.[25]

The boycott was of no direct benefit to those trying to escape persecution and in the area of rescue and relief the AFL adopted a policy similar to the TUC. Appeals were launched asking American workers to contribute to a fund for victims of Nazism. In 1934 the Jewish Labor Committee was formed in New York to confront the problems posed to Jewish workers by the Third Reich and later the right-wing regimes of Eastern Europe. Most of the major Jewish unions and socialist groupings were represented, covering several hundred thousand workers of the American Jewish labour force. Through joint appeals with the AFL, the American government was persuaded to let several hundred prominent Jewish labour figures from Europe enter the United States. Away from such case-specific work, it has been stressed that after 1935 'there is no record of any effort on the part of either the Jewish Labor Committee or any of its affiliates to pressure the AFL to modify its position on immigration'. The selection of suitable immigrants matched the immigration policies pursued by the American government throughout the Nazi era – ones which were supported by the AFL at least until 1942.[26]

The third strategy employed by the AFL, particularly in the late 1930s, was to back increased Jewish immigration to Palestine. Again genuine sympathy for the plight of the Jews combined with a more cynical desire to keep the refugees out of the United States.[27] Taken together, the AFL's responses show outrage at Nazi antisemitism mixed with the need to protect what was seen as self-interest. Economic concerns were crucial in the formation of all the strategies adopted by the AFL, but so was the centrality of its identification with 'Americanism'. The AFL's interpretation of this concept joined loathing of Nazi racial persecution with fears of alien subversion undermining the American scene.

II

In Britain the domination of domestic considerations equally and perhaps even more blatantly limited consideration of the persecutions in Nazi Germany. As in the United States, definitive unemployment figures are unavailable – only 60 per cent of the British workforce was insured and therefore entitled to state benefit. It has been estimated that only in one year between 1930 and 1938 did unemployment fall below 10 per cent. Unemployment reached a peak of 3.4 million in 1932 and was rising again in 1938, reaching another high of 2.16 million.[28] As in the United States, the later 1920s was a period of general retreat in organized labour's significance, especially in Britain after the failure of the 1926 General Strike. Citrine and Bevin provided cautious leadership in the 1930s: recognizing the TUC's limited bargaining power, they followed policies aimed at maintaining levels of employment, pay and status. There was at this time a crisis in ideology in the labour movement shown by the limitations of the second Labour government, in power during 1929-31. Committed in principle to the coming of socialism, there was little sympathy for capitalist-style state intervention in running the economy. Keynesian ideas were thus rejected and the labour movement as a whole was committed to protectionist economic policies.[29]

In the United States, the quota system, though it discriminated against Jewish refugees, did allow some limited possibilities of escape. Britain in contrast, apart from encouraging a few distinguished individuals, scientists and industrialists to emigrate to Britain from Germany after 1933 pursued a closed-door policy. For 'ordinary' people, entry depended on being granted a work permit. These would only be granted if it could be proved that a British subject would not be displaced or 'would [not] otherwise be to the prejudice of British employment'. There was no desire on the government's behalf to upset the labour movement. In 1938 the Ministry of Labour acknowledged that 'In view of the prevailing volume of unemployment and to safeguard the interests of British workers the admission of newcomers is closely restricted.'[30]

As the 1930s progressed, some within the British labour movement realized that the help offered to refugees was increasingly inadequate to their needs. In 1935 the National Council of Labour reported with regard to its International Solidarity Fund that 'The funds so generously contributed a year or two ago are now almost exhausted'. The Fund was faced with the problem of what should happen to those rescued. Such individuals were 'some of their country's finest sons and daughters who have been brought to their present plight because they believed in and worked for freedom'. If the refugees returned to the country of their birth they would face 'certain imprisonment or even death'. No action was taken on the report and those few refugees who had escaped to Britain through the help of the labour movement were left to survive on petty charity.[31]

A year later the British labour movement received a plea from the Labour and Socialist International in Brussels for the rights of refugees to earn a living. It stressed the absurdity of admitting refugees 'who are nearly always without means, and then to forbid them to practice any occupation'. The Brussels report added (with some optimism given organized labour's restrictionism) 'History shows that the work of political immigrants has in the long run been nearly always a source of wealth for countries which have welcomed them'. Again no change of policy was forthcoming from the British labour movement either in easing restrictions with regard to the right to enter or to undertake work.[32]

The refugee policy of the British labour movement thus operated within very narrow restraints. Those few individuals supported were limited to political refugees (and therefore not Jews as such) whose life in Britain was generally insecure and poverty stricken. Lilli Palmer, the actress, recalled refugee life in London as 'tough, news from Germany terrible, money short, work permits . . . the central problem'.[33] It was thus with no great joy that Walter Citrine reported the situation to the TUC in 1937. The International Committee was still giving out weekly allowances to the political refugees but, as Citrine realized, this only reinforced their feelings of helplessness: 'What would you feel like if you had been three or four years away from your own country, existing on a pittance?' Having made the direct connection between the world of British workers and that of the refugees he further enquired

What is the outlook for these people, even in Great Britain? They cannot take jobs unless it is proved overwhelmingly – and it does require some proof – that there is no earthly chance of their displacing British labour in any circumstances; and I have many times regretted that we were not able in our Trade Union Movement to be perhaps a little more generous in respect of providing opportunities for such people to obtain employment in this country.[34]

Until the Evian conference in July 1938 the British labour movement made no concessions on refugee matters. Excluding help given to international bodies (which was relatively substantial), the TUC had granted just £6,350 to individual Austrian and German refugees compared to the $46,000 collected in the United States for similar purposes in 1933 alone. When in 1938 J. W. Stephenson, the fraternal delegate from the TUC at the AFL annual conference, praised the American labour movement's help to victims of fascism, it was more a comment on the poverty of the British response than a reflection of American generosity.[35]

Walter Citrine campaigned for some gentle modifications to British refugee policies and these were achieved within strict limits in the second half of 1938. The General Council of the TUC agreed to the easing of restrictions for refugees able to set up new businesses in 'special areas', with an additional token entry of doctors, dentists and students. More importantly in numerical terms, nurses, domestic servants and land workers trained for skilled agricultural work might be allowed to enter Britain. The General Council stressed that the number admitted each year was to be limited and the relevant trade union would have to give its approval.[36] The responses of the trade unions in all these areas will be examined in detail. As will emerge, it was in the occupations in which trade union influence was weakest or non-existent – domestic service and nursing – that entry to Britain was most generous. It is a detail that reflects the importance of organized labour in determining refugee policy during the 1930s.

In his work on the labour movement and immigration, Kenneth Lunn has stressed the essential need to understand 'how particular responses come to be articulated at particular moments'. It should thus be remembered that one of the cruellest coincidences for the Jews in the Third Reich was that 1938, the point at which many finally realized escape was their only chance for survival, was also a time when unemployment had risen again in many Western countries (to over two million in Britain and 11 million in the United States).[37] Although there was some growth in the economy through re-armament, union outlooks across the liberal democracies were conditioned by the fear of even greater unemployment. As we will see, there were still important differences between unions in their responses towards refugees – even when they faced similar economic problems. Unemployment was by no means the sole determinant of their reactions to allowing in victims of Nazism. Nevertheless, the rigidity of the general TUC line in 1938 highlights Marrus's maxim that refugees 'always arrive at the wrong time'.[38]

In the United States, leaders of both the AFL and CIO voiced their disgust at the violence of *Kristallnacht*. Indeed the first CIO convention took place four days after the pogrom and President John Lewis stressed that his organization stood

for the protection of the privileges of all Americans, whether they be gentiles or Jews or any creed or religion. . . . We stand appalled at what we witness in Europe. Whose heart can fail to become anguished as he reads in the daily press of the terrible abuses and atrocities and indignities and brutalities that are now being inflicted by the German government and some of the German people on the Jews of that nation? [It was] one of the most appalling events in history.

Lewis called on the American State Department to 'make emphatic representations to the German government, protesting the actions of that government in permitting these atrocities to be inflicted on the Jewish people'. If it did so 'the twenty million members of the CIO and their dependants will support the government'. The CIO made no direct call on the American government to liberalize its immigration laws, although it should not be assumed from this that there was a consensus on this issue with the AFL.[39]

In 1938 the AFL reiterated its policy 'to oppose any immigration legislation that [would] be injurious to the welfare of the wage earners of the United States'. William Green reconfirmed his opposition to any legislation which might bring in communist agitators and competing workmen. Moreover, much bitterness was voiced about the CIO's attempt to naturalize Filipino seamen, which the AFL saw as an alibi 'to modify our present effective exclusion laws'. Asiatic exclusion was a fundamental part of the AFL's ideology. Such blatant racism was keenly rejected by the CIO with its stress on internationalism and its greater interest in immigrant workers. The biographer of one of the leading figures in the CIO, Sidney Hillman, comments that 'in its approach to politics, the CIO . . . adopted the standpoint of the working class as a whole – or at least some fair approximation of it – while the AFL self-consciously pursued the political interests of a fragment, one often openly exclusionist, racist, and nativist'. Unlike the AFL, the CIO refused to campaign on the issue of general immigration control, even if its commitment to the unemployed of the United States meant it could not fight for liberalization of the quota laws.[40]

The AFL was an active supporter of several Bills passing through the Senate in 1939 which demanded an ending of all immigration quotas. It was aware that 'At no time in our history has there been such demand for the opening of our doors to the peoples of the world'. But despite the appeals to 'justice and liberty' it was essential, because of 'domestic, economic, and political conditions', to approach the subject 'in the light of cold practical facts'. These were essentially unemployment at ten million and also the 'serious task of assimilation' involved with an immigrant influx. Paul Scharrenberg, one of the legal experts of the AFL and, as we have seen, a leading campaigner for total Asiatic exclusion, told a US Senate hearing in March 1939 that he 'heartily favored' ending all immigration to the United States for several years. The AFL thus supported restrictive immigration policies that were both general and specific. Asiatics were its most serious concern but alien subversives were not far behind in its list of non-desirables.[41]

There was a genuine dilemma for the AFL when it confronted Nazi persecution of Jews. On the one hand, it believed in responding to the Jewish crisis, even if it was to be within the existing immigration control structure. On the other hand, it desired ever firmer restrictionism and its concerns about assimilation and subversion could work against the entry of refugees from Nazism. The AFL hence tried to balance a strong immigration policy with a weak commitment to helping refugees. Unsurprisingly, the AFL found that its influence was to be felt on the side of control. Thus before the Evian conference in 1938, William Green offered the American government AFL support in helping with the refugee crisis, but it was to be on the basis that nothing be done to change the quota system, effectively paralysing any attempts to provide asylum.[42] A year later, however, both the AFL and CIO gave unconditional approval to the Wagner Bill which proposed the entry of 20,000 German refugee children under the age of 14 on a strictly non-quota basis.[43]

Saul Friedman has argued that 'If the Wagner Bill was carried along by the eloquence of its supporters, it was doomed by the ambivalence of others'. Friedman adds that 'the well meaning representatives of America's largest labor unions did more harm than good when they testified before congressional committees'. This criticism, particularly of the AFL, is understandable in the light of the complex views of American organized labor on immigration issues. Nevertheless, Friedman misunderstands their position when he describes labour's response as 'ambivalent' on the German children issue.[44] To both the CIO and the AFL, the Wagner Bill was isolated as a purely refugee question and was therefore divorced from the more general question of immigration. The fact that its recipients would be young children and therefore no immediate threat to American workers helped its leaders to make the distinction. It is crucial, if justice is to be done to these bodies, to understand that their support for the Wagner Bill was genuine. Their stance was important for their own self-image in the light of Nazi persecutions. In the hearings, however, restrictionists managed in the case of the AFL to show how its past opposition to any loosening of immigration control conflicted with its present stance on refugee children.[45] It was the AFL's ambivalence on immigration in general, rather than any question of the sincerity of its support for the Wagner Bill, which was exposed in the hearings. The CIO had no such track record of restrictionism; conservatives managed to smear the organization as pro-communist and therefore un-American. The support of millions of American union members was thus ignored and, instead, the nativist views of organizations such as the American Legion and the Daughters of the American Revolution won the day.[46]

The particular failure of the Wagner Bill most certainly cannot be placed at the door of organized labour. More generally, however, it must be suggested that immigration laws could not have been liberalized to help the refugees from Nazism without the support of the AFL. On this issue, its fundamental ambivalence on the question (a result of a genuine sympathy to the victims of persecution conflicting with economic concerns and commitment to 100 per cent Americanism) meant the AFL could not accept other than a token influx of refugees from Nazism. Yet such was its horror of the evils of Nazism that it was willing to accept the 20,000 German children as a humanitarian gesture. The CIO had even less qualms in accepting the Wagner Bill, but the constant pressure to prove its Americanism ultimately limited its effectiveness on this and other refugee questions.[47] Although few in the American labour movement went as far as the representative of the Wyoming State Federation of Labor in describing immigrants as 'the smuggler, the dope peddler, the gangster, the grafter, the highwayman, the murderer and the kidnapper', there was greater agreement with his comments that 'undesirable aliens displace American working men and women, contributing in large measure to the unemployment situation and the menace of impending revolution'. Ultimately refugees from Nazism were viewed with sympathy but their image as problematic immigrants was one that the American labour movement, with few exceptions, was unable to overcome.[48]

III

By 1939 there were some in the British labour movement who were willing to challenge the dominant restrictionism. Most prominent was the Oxford economist, Roy Harrod, once a liberal but by the late 1930s a prominent member of the Labour party. In an article in the *Manchester Guardian*, further elaborated in a private memorandum addressed to the leaders of the labour movement, Harrod stressed that

The population of this country is declining and needs supplementing by immigration. Further unemployment is not increased merely by the addition to the numbers of the population. The increase in numbers involves in practice an increase in the demand both for consumption goods and for capital equipment. This increase in turn gives rise to an increase in the volume of employment.[49]

Harrod was one of the leading proponents of Keynesian economics in the 1930s. His argument for allowing in more immigrants was thus based both on humanitarian and underconsumptionist macro-economic arguments.

To Harrod, there were only two issues that had to be confronted in achieving a more generous refugee policy. First, the argument that immigration 'always . . . puts "Englishmen out of jobs"' had to be overcome. Harrod believed that 'Economically this has been shown to be false. The problem is how to make the point clear to the Trade Unions and similar organisations.' Second, once 'the main need to "put across" the economic truths' had been achieved, it was necessary to address the issue of 'anti-alien prejudice'. Hostility was

easily aroused and require[d] to be counter-acted by accurate and convincing publicity.

Organized labour has tended all too often to take a short-sighted and sectional view of the problem. It thus mistakenly gives tacit approval to doctrines of nationalism and even racialism. Its task in the present situation should be to review the problem dispassionately and on economic as well as sympathetic grounds give more favourable reception to plans of absorption and settlement.

Harrod showed tremendous confidence in the ability of Britain 'to assimilate a certain proportion of alien population without substantial disturbance to our political and social equilibrium or to our sense of national solidarity'. He stressed that

In view of our flexible institutions, our national characteristic of toleration, the ease with which we maintain relations with our own Jewish elements and with Irish immigrants who often come over with strong Irish-Nationalist sentiment, there does not appear to be much danger that a reasonable proportion of continental immigrants would cause disruption.[50]

Two senior officials in the labour movement, A. L. Scott and William Gillies, Secretary of the International Department of the Labour party, discussed the document in the summer of 1939. Doubt was cast on Harrod's economic arguments, showing the continued failure of Keynesian ideas to take hold in the Labour party. The argument that 'immigration [was] beneficial to a country' was also rejected. Scott assumed that he did 'not see the slightest prospect . . . of the TUC endorsing these views. The Unions would certainly reject them.' Because of this likelihood, Harrod's memorandum was not discussed any further in the Labour party and Scott saw 'very little prospect of the Labour Movement getting a clear policy on the refugee question'. Was Harrod being unduly optimistic?[51]

In July 1939 the bureaucrats in the Labour party refused to take action on Harrod's suggestion that the alien laws should be reformed. Such a move 'might have political reverberations' and would also upset the trade union movement. Ironically at exactly this same point the chairman of the TUC was making his own initiative. In the 1938 annual congress, Citrine stated that it was impossible as a general principle to say to the government that 'We are against refugees coming into this country'. He also acknowledged that it was necessary 'to safeguard the interests of our people'.[52] By the summer of 1939, he was aware that because of the last consideration little had been done by the labour movement to help the increasingly desperate plight of those in Europe. He also realized that the position of those who had escaped to Britain through the International Solidarity Fund had now become intolerable:

The refugees cannot become a charge on public funds yet they cannot be allowed to starve, nor could one tolerate any suggestion of their deportation, which would mean ending their days in a concentration camp or prison, or perhaps facing the firing squad.

The alternative method of assistance which suggests itself is to find employment for them. Among these refugees there are many skilled trade unionists who could be usefully employed in industry.

Citrine thus wrote to all his affiliated unions, 'acting in the hope that there may be opportunities in your trade for the absorption of some of these refugees'. The Secretaries of the unions were asked to reply if they would: (1) agree to the government modifying the ban on refugee employment; (2) cooperate with such a scheme; and (3) offer employment to refugees within their own employment sphere. The survey allows, at the level of the individual union hierarchy, a detailed quantitative and qualitative analysis of the British labour movement and the refugee crisis in the 1930s. It also makes clear 'The dangers of generalizing about a single, unified, working-class or labour response'.[53]

Of some 217 TUC-affiliated organizations, 45 replied, representing just over 20 per cent of the unions, but 65 per cent of all trade union members. The TUC's analysis of 42 of these replies was that 15 were opposed to any relaxation of government restrictions on refugee employment, 'the vast majority on account of unemployment and short time', 14 agreed in principle but saw no scope for employment in their particular trade, 11 agreed to help if opportunities arose and two were unable to provide any answer. In summarizing the responses, the TUC stressed the centrality of employment concerns. These were indeed recurring themes. Other factors become evident, however, from a more detailed investigation of the survey.[54]

Only 27 of the 45 replies directly answered whether they would favour an approach to the government to modify the refugee employment ban. The request required no direct commitment on behalf of individual unions and therefore the high figure of 70 per cent wanting some relaxation on restrictions is partly explained. Nevertheless, much genuine concern was expressed, such as that of Walter Nellies (National Union of Shale Miners and Oil Workers), who was 'quite in favour' as 'We have every sympathy with the object you have in view and hope something tangible may be accomplished to relieve the plight of the refugees'. Only half of those responding positively to this question were willing to provide help themselves, however. Nellies added that, in his specific trade, 'until full employment is found for all, [I] am afraid our cooperation could not be expected'.[55]

There was greater consistency among those opposed to the proposed changes in employment restrictions, with 80 per cent responding negatively to all three questions. The Medical Practitioners' Union was the bluntest, stating that its Executive Committee was 'opposed to the employment of refugees in this country' and 'would not cooperate in any scheme for the provision of work for refugees'. The Secretary added that his 'Union had persistently and consistently opposed permission being granted to refugee doctors to practise in this country'. Of ten negative answers, only one gave an altruistic reason for opposing relaxation of the restrictions.[56]

Two-thirds of those responding stressed that they could not cooperate with the proposed action and 70 per cent replied negatively to the possibility of offering employment to refugees in the union's area of interest. Many of the union responses were at pains to stress that such opposition was morally justified, however difficult the situation of the refugees. Rupert Kneale (Society of Lithographic Artists, Designers and Process Workers) put the case in what he described as a 'candid answer':

The Trade Unions Movements' International sympathies are in advance of, and in conflict with, its protective policies and conservative instincts. To give relief is easy [in fact, the survey had been carried out because sources of funding for refugees were drying up]; to find work for aliens, in any numbers, is more than our Executive Committee dare attempt.

Our consciences in this great human problem can be comfortably placated as we have an 8% unemployment problem; there are hundreds of British boys who would be glad to enter the trade if there was room for them . . . and no foreigner must be allowed to deprive them of any opportunities.[57]

In similar vein, the National Union of Dyers, Bleachers and Textile Workers stated that 'Whilst recognising that sympathy alone is small comfort . . . apart from expressing sympathy, [we] can offer no practical aid. . . . During the past six months the unemployed and underemployed in the Wool Trade industry have averaged 5.5% and 7.5% respectively.' The Monotype Casters and Type-founders Society, with 10 per cent of its membership unemployed, also offered sympathy but were 'unable to assist in this matter'.[58]

It could be argued that those proposing positive schemes, however limited, were able to do so because of the greater buoyancy in their trades. Thus the Association of Women Clerks and Secretaries believed that 'a limited number of skilled translators could probably be absorbed without difficulty, always providing that [union] rates are maintained' and the National Laundry Workers indicated that their trade was 'one of the best for female service and the percentage of unemployment is low in the winter and labour is scarce during the summer'. The Operative Spinners and Twinners' response was positive owing to 'a great shortage of juvenile labour in the cotton industry'. Moreover, both the Amalgamated Engineering Union and the National Union of Blast-furnacemen, Ore Miners, Coke Workers and Kindred Trades pointed to the boom in their industries as a result of re-armament and were thus happy to consider the introduction of suitable refugees.[59]

On the surface, therefore, it would appear that economic factors, with both continuing unemployment and uneven growth, explains both the restrictionism and opportunities offered by the British trade union movement to refugees from Nazism. Nevertheless, a closer analysis of both the language and statistics used by the unions reveals the underlying ideological and cultural consider-ations also at work. First, unemployment and the fear of unemployment was a relative consideration. Rates of unemployment from five through to 50 per cent were used to justify the unions' inability to help. Yet unemployment was not absent in the trades of those unions responding positively. Whereas many unions stated categorically that they would not consider the refugees unless there was zero unemployment in their trades, some, such as the Association of Women Clerks, the National Laundry Workers and the National Union of Agricultural Workers, were willing to consider helping the refugees *despite* some of their members being without jobs. Unemployment rates in these unions were no different to those in unions who had opposed changing the restrictions regarding work permits. The more positive responses reflected not only greater international solidarity, but also a more favourable way of viewing the prospect of refugee employment. It was evident in the response of the representative of the Wheelwrights and Coachmakers in the 1938 Congress who rejected the dominant anti-alienism and stressed his own (Huguenot) immigrant origins: 'If it were not for the fact that this country in the past had opened its arms to refugees from various countries we would not have skilled industries such as the weaving industry here.'[60]

The second point concerns the unions' use of language. Some, while op-posed to modification of refugee employment rules, still employed terminology such as 'these unfortunate exiles' or offered 'utmost sympathy for those who are driven to this country through victimisation on account of trade union or political activities'. There was, however, a pervasive tendency to see the refugees as a threat to British labour. As Ernest Bevin, blunt as ever, put it: 'the Council are unfortunately placed in the position of making a choice between the refugees and our own countrymen, and on that basis they must, of course, choose the latter'.[61] Four unions actually went further and used the presence of 'aliens' in their trade to justify hostility to the entry of further foreign labour. The Association of Cine-Technicians called for the deporting of foreign workers and concluded that to obtain its goal 'To build up a British film industry it is essential that every key position shall be filled by British subjects'. It is thus significant that the groups of trade unions most hostile to refugee employment, such as the furnishing and boot and shoe industries, had a long tradition of anti-alienism. Foreign labour was seen as a threat to employment, wage levels and conditions of work.[62]

On the positive side, those anxious to help emphasized humanitarian concern, ideological affinity to the victims *and* the potential of the refugees. Opportunities should be created for them so that their skills and experiences could be utilized for the good of all. This point of view contrasted starkly with the response of trade unions such as the General and Municipal Workers or the Boot and Shoe Operatives, which saw only harmful consequences, even in the case of the refugee industrialists. Rather than welcoming these entrepreneurs as the providers of tens of thousands of jobs in the depressed areas, the representatives of these unions stressed how refugee industrialists were abusing British hospitality, 'flouting every custom and tradition which obtains in this country, and which has been won by the British workers'. They were 'coming into the drawing room of our business with dirty feet and dirty money'. Such 'little Englanderism', with its connotations of an alien invasion was not isolated – a resolution condemning the activities of refugee firms was actually carried at the 1938 Congress. The refugee question was not just one of economics. At issue, too, was the matter of national identity. As the representative of the General and Municipal Workers queried: 'Do we want in this homogeneous country our little U.S.A.s, our little Germanys, our little Italys, or even our little Czechoslavakias?' But was this also a question of rejecting Jewishness?[63]

On only two occasions in the union responses was any explicit mention made of whether the refugees were Jewish or not. This partly reflected the survey itself which highlighted the political and trade union background of the refugees in Britain. The lack of specific attention given to 'racial/religious' refugees was, as we have seen, a feature of the British labour response, particularly in comparison to the United States. In fact, the vast majority of refugees from Nazism in Britain were Jewish but to stress this might have brought a less sympathetic response. The reply of the National Union of Boot and Shoe Operatives indicates that such fears were not unfounded. Despite the 'race blind' approach of the survey, its Secretary, Chester, wrote to Citrine objecting to the proposed scheme because 'the majority who would benefit by the regulations would not be refugees, but Jews who cannot be placed under such a category'. The other clear mention of Jews came from Ernest Bevin, outlining the specific scheme undertaken by his own union in conjunction with the National Union of Agricultural Workers to place German Jewish refugees on the land. The two references do not neutralize one another, nor should they be seen as isolated.[64]

The sentiments of Chester's union were present in the responses of other unions, even if they were not stated so explicitly. The National Union of Glovers complained that the state of its industry had 'been very bad' as a result of firms employing 'foreign immigrants' and thereby creating unfair competition. The Society of Goldsmiths, Jewellers and Kindred Trades would have been happy to swap the permits granted to aliens for refugees and similarly the Association of Cine-Technicians would accept refugees if it resulted 'in a deportation of other foreign technicians whom we consider are not essential to the British film industry and who are actually displacing British labour'. It must be emphasized that in all these cases, such 'aliens' would have been largely a mixture of Jews from Central and Eastern Europe and the political refugees, with whom they wanted to replace them, generally non-Jewish.[65] Lingering anti-alienism from the turn of the century thus affected some labour responses towards *Jewish* refugees from the Third Reich. In the case of the medical union, as will shortly emerge, this anti-alienism possessed an explicitly racist antisemitic motivation.

The last ideological factor that further complicated the union response was that of gender. Up to 60 per cent of the refugees from Nazism were female and an even higher percentage of the work permits granted were to women. The TUC, like the AFL, had made only limited efforts to recruit and incorporate women. The marginal status of female workers meant that both the state and the unions were less worried about the threat posed by women refugees. In nursing there was no union to consult and the new domestic workers' union had little muscle. Several unions followed the Power Loom Carpet Weavers, who saw 'a possibility for a limited number of females, but not males'. Women's jobs were seen to be less important and thus greater risks could be taken. The same process occurred in the United States in the 1930s if on a more informal level. Those in organizations trying to help the refugees found it very difficult to place men in work. The leader of the Boston Committee for Refugees recalled how they received 'no help from the labor unions'. Refugee households in both Britain and the United States became dependent on the money brought in by wives, many of whom had never worked before. It led to an enormous loss of male status and many men found themselves 'all at sea'. Male-dominated unions were successful in excluding refugees from work on both sides of the Atlantic. It was left to the only explicitly female trade union, the Association of Women Clerks and Secretaries, to table one of the most practical and generous offers concerning refugee employment in Britain.[66]

A pattern thus emerges of a complex series of responses in which economics combined with factors such as anti-alienism and internationalism, humanitarianism and antisemitism, and were channelled through gender considerations in determining the help that could be offered by individual parts of the British labour movement. The range of choices available to the trade unions on the refugee question is further revealed by considering the responses of three important case studies. In the first occupation, agricultural work, limited opportunities became available to the refugees. In the second, the medical world, virtually no help was offered at all and in the third, domestic service, refugees were granted almost free access to jobs.

IV

While in general the occupations of agricultural work, medicine and domestic service were worlds apart in the late 1930s, in several ways their experiences coincided. First, although there was unsatisfied demand for labour in all three areas, unemployment still persisted. Second, each occupation had problems of status, pay and conditions of work. Lastly, all three were weakly unionized. The unions associated with these occupations used economic arguments to explain their hostility to refugee labour. Yet the contrast in work permits granted in the 1930s is stark: 1–2,000 refugees were allowed to work on the land; fewer than 100 refugee doctors were allowed to practise in Britain; but up to 20,000 refugees were given work permits to become domestic servants. The peculiarities and background of each case merit detailed consideration.

The golden days of agricultural workers had long since past and, in the period following World War I, their influence was strictly limited. Nevertheless, there was a slow revival in the 1930s as agricultural prices recovered and by 1939 membership of the National Union of Agricultural Workers stood at 45,000. The Secretary of the union was Bill Holmes, a militant socialist and member of the Independent Labour Party. The most important influence in the union, however, was its more insular President, Edwin Gooch. Gooch was responsible for taking his union away from the Labour party and towards a limited concern with pay and conditions of work. Gooch favoured a policy of agricultural protectionism and, revealing the sharp contrast to the class-conscious Holmes, became President of the Norfolk Chamber of Agriculture in 1935.[67]

Not surprisingly, it was the internationalist Holmes rather than the protectionist Gooch who took an unprompted and positive interest in the refugee problem. The Zionist *Halutz* movement in Nazi Germany had been providing agricultural training for Jewish youngsters prior to emigration to Palestine. *Kristallnacht* and the mass imprisonments in the concentration camps after it wrought havoc with these schemes. As one of its limited proposals for rescue after the pogrom, the British government decided to allow in a 'certain number of young persons from Germany . . . to be trained [in agriculture] for emigration'. In January 1939 the Executive Committee of the Agricultural Workers met to discuss a plan drawn up by the German Jewish Aid Committee. This was to allow at any one time up to 1,000 'fully qualified Jewish farm workers [who] could only be employed in those districts where there were no qualified English agricultural workers registered as unemployed'. These Jewish workers were to receive the district minimum wage. In addition, up to 500 *unqualified* youngsters were to be placed on farms with the employer paying appropriate board and lodging. Holmes, who had been attending meetings of the refugee 'Co-Ordinating Agricultural Committee', proposed support of the scheme which was adopted by his Executive.[68]

The value of this rescue package should not be dismissed. It was particularly important after *Kristallnacht* in helping those whose training centres in Germany were destroyed or closed. Many were now in prisons or camps and could only be released if an offer was made to place them abroad. Its limitations are clear: just 1,350 German and Austrian Jews succeeded in coming to Britain through the scheme at a cost to the refugee organizations of £200,000. As Holmes wrote to reassure his colleagues in February 1939, 'if the whole total are absorbed it will not average more than thirty per county at any one time'. Yet Holmes and his union made an effort to be cooperative. When asked just before the war whether they would clear a bottleneck due to problems of re-emigration and accept 500 of these refugees as permanent employees, the union agreed. It believed the refugee crisis was 'a terrible problem' and suggested that 'something more practical than sympathy should be accorded these refugees'.[69] There were objections to the refugee presence from within the union. Concern about refugee concentration was aired in the Executive Committee and its journal issued a 'Warning' to members in June 1939:

Young men are to be called up. . . . There is a risk – against which the Union must take precautions – that these young men will *not* want to return to the farms because conditions have become worse in their absence. The effect of covering farms with boys from the towns, women . . ., old men fit only for 'reserve', Irishmen (exempt from conscription), refugees, conscientious objectors . . . will be to make it more than ever difficult to maintain and improve the standards of conditions for land labour which have slowly built up by trade unionism.[70]

Elements of the union were thus capable of seeing refugees (and many others) only in a negative light. Yet thanks to the efforts of Holmes and many individuals on a local level, protectionism did not win the day and over a thousand refugees were rescued on agricultural permits in 1939. It reflected a tightly restrained generosity in which the government, the refugee bodies, the union, the farmers and farm workers cooperated. It was not a huge scheme of rescue, but it did show what could be achieved in an occupation blighted by continuing unemployment and unattractive conditions of work. It is in that light that the response of the Medical Practitioners Union (MPU) must be viewed.

Shock is still expressed at the now famous remarks of Lord Dawson of Penn, President of the Royal College of Surgeons, who told the British government in 1933 that the number of refugee doctors 'who could usefully be absorbed or teach us anything could be counted on the fingers of one hand'. The role of the British Medical Association (BMA) in adding to this restrictionism (and also in placing enormous barriers in the way of medical refugees who had managed to escape and wanted to practise) is similarly familiar. Nevertheless, the contributory role of the MPU in helping to bring about the negative response toward refugee doctors has been neglected. In the process of transforming Dawson's demands for almost total restriction into government policy, the MPU played no small part.[71]

Unlike Dawson, who practised in aristocratic circles, most doctors in interwar Britain were under financial pressures. Many were burdened by debt and there were real economic problems facing those in small practices. Undoubtedly these considerations played a major role in determining the support for the leadership of the MPU in its campaign against the refugees. Nevertheless, the success of its two major leaders in the 1930s – Maurice Bayly and Alfred Welply (its General Secretary) – in injecting both conspiratorial and gutter antisemitism into the MPU strongly suggests the prior existence of hostility towards Jews in the medical world. After the *Anschluss* in 1938 a scheme to rescue 500 Austrian refugee doctors was proposed by the Home Secretary but turned down by the BMA. The number was whittled down to 50, a figure supported by the TUC. In fact Bayly of the MPU had played a major role in the rejection of the first proposal. At the 1938 Congress it became clear that the MPU rejected the possibility of *any* refugees being allowed entry. Welply even claimed that 50 refugees would 'dilute our industry . . . with non-union, non-Socialist labour'. Those refugees already practising in Britain '[did] not play the game'.[72]

The President of the MPU stressed that his opposition to the refugees was economic and his organization was 'neither anti-Semitic nor Fascist'. The evidence suggests the contrary. It has been pointed out that the leadership of the MPU, particularly after Bayly became prominent in 1936, drifted towards support of the British fascist movement. In the same year its journal actually supported Nazi legislation banning marriages between Jew and Gentile. Bayly and Welply were influenced by Social Credit ideology and accepted the existence of an international Jewish conspiracy. Moreover, their opposition to the refugees went beyond economic arguments. In the 1938 Congress debate, a representative of the Wheelwrights and Coachmakers rejected the restrictionist arguments of the MPU:

When we, as trade unionists in our own particular trades, find that there are some foreigners who are not in our trade unions, and who are violating trade union rules, our job is to try to get them into the trade union; and that is the job of the Medical Practitioner's Union.[73]

Yet for the MPU this missed the point. As its journal insisted: 'All men know that there is one race which is never absorbed, a race to which claims of "business" always come before any consideration for those who are unwise enough to give them hospitality.' The MPU's leadership rejected the refugees on racial grounds (in World War II, Welply used its offices to coordinate the activities of the extreme antisemitic organizations in Britain: his close relations with the pro-Nazi MP Captain Ramsay brought about the surveillance of Welply and the MPU by the British security services).[74] While the MPU's membership was less extreme, its response was motivated by a more general antipathy of the British medical world towards Jews. There were important exceptions in this pattern – the limited membership of the Socialist Medical Association did what it could for individual refugees, reflecting its internationalist and political world view. Yet the close agreement of Anderson, the General Secretary of the BMA and a 'violent anti-alien', with what the Home Office referred to as the 'trade union section of the Association' guaranteed that few medical refugees would be allowed entry into Britain and even fewer, before the war, would be allowed to practise. Across the Atlantic the American Medical Association played a similar restrictionist role to the BMA.[75]

In the case of the doctors, the British government refused to challenge what it regarded as their unreasonable restrictionism. Such a middle-class constituency could not be ignored. In the case of the domestic workers' union, such class considerations worked in the opposite direction. Attempts to unionize the domestic workers had a long and not overly successful history. In 1937/8 the TUC, as part of a general effort to bring in occupations in which no worker organizations existed, formed the National Union of Domestic Workers for Britain's 1.3 million servants. Recruitment was slow – in July 1939 membership stood at just 805.[76] The union had decided that it would be 'necessary to have a much larger membership of British workers before it would be practicable to enrol foreign nationals'. This policy, its leadership claimed, expressed the 'view of the overwhelming opinion of the present members'. Of even greater importance to the union was the control of further entry of foreign workers into Britain. Indeed it was one of four major points that its representatives put to the Minister of Labour late in 1938.[77]

At first, the union Secretary, Beatrice Bezzant, believed that no consideration should be given to refugees and she refused to meet representatives of the Refugee Central Coordinating Committee (Bloomsbury House) 'in view of the fact that our members regard the interests of refugees as diametrically opposed to their own'. In December 1938 Bezzant was interviewed by the *Evening Standard*, during which she complained that *refugee* servants were creating problems for British domestic workers. This outburst forced a meeting with Mrs Franklin of the Domestic Bureau section of Bloomsbury House. Bezzant warned Franklin that if refugees undercut British servants it would lead to an anti-alien movement – a trump card to play at a time when the *Jewish Chronicle* was complaining of 'A Contemptible Campaign' of popular papers and others claiming that refugees were taking British jobs. Nevertheless, Bezzant agreed that refugees should be seen as different from 'foreign' domestic servants. As with other unions, the Domestic Workers was willing to consider the substitution of 'socialist refugees . . . if their number could be limited to say 500' for the 'people coming in already'. In reality the latter were actually *Jewish* refugees, as most other German and Austrian servants had returned home due to the deteriorating international situation.[78]

Bezzant and her union did not, unlike the MPU, adopt a totally negative attitude towards the refugees. She eventually joined the Domestic Bureau and offered her advice on the best way of maintaining standards and training the refugee women. Her union still lapsed into thinking of the refugees simply as 'foreign workers' and it launched 'a vigorous protest . . . against the number of proposed [domestic worker] permits' granted by the Home Office throughout 1939. As we shall see in the following chapter, the Home Office in the period before the war was granting up to 1,800 such permits a month. The National Union of Domestic Workers did not support total exclusion – small schemes with a limited flow were acceptable to it – but the more generous measures adopted in 1939 were opposed. The union was suspicious of the refugee influx, not just on grounds of numbers but also because it feared that the quality of these newcomers would bring down pay levels and conditions of work.[79] Its failure to influence government policy reflected its weakness in its own occupation and within the labour movement, not just in its relationship with the government. Faced with equally strident demands from middle-class women's groups to *liberalize* admission policy towards domestics and thus help solve 'the servant problem', the government was never in any doubt about which side it would follow. In the United States, an even greater number of domestic servants remained outside the world of organized labour. Dispersed across the country and divided along racial and ethnic grounds, they were even less able to resist the use of foreign domestic workers than their British counterparts.[80]

V

Rupert Kneale, of the Society of Lithographic Artists, Designers, Engravers and Process Workers, acknowledged that his section of trade had received scores of applications from refugees for work. They had admitted a few and rejected the applications of many. When asked if his union would accept any relaxation of the restrictions on refugee employment he was adamant that they could not. The livelihood of his own people must not be endangered. Kneale was so convinced of this fact that he saw no need to discuss it with his Executive Committee. A similar process operated at a higher, national level in the Labour party with the proposals for a less restrictive refugee and immigration policy made by Roy Harrod.[81] There was an assumption that ordinary trade unionists would naturally oppose an influx of foreign workers, even if they were refugees from Nazi tyranny. In July 1938 the TUC offered a clear statement of its position on the question:

Congress has always expressed its utmost sympathy with the position of political refugees. Its attitude to the admission of intellectuals, scientists, and professional men has always been considerate. But with regard to immigrants of the mechanic, skilled artisan, or agricultural type, it is obvious that the position in which we find ourselves we must be concerned with our own people first, the maintenance of trade union standards, wages, and conditions, and the effect which an alien influx might have on a labour market where there are already a million and [a] half unemployed.

The smooth transition from 'political refugees' to 'immigrants' and finally to 'an alien influx' within the course of one paragraph is indicative of the approach taken by the hierarchies of what were the two most important trade union bodies in the liberal democratic world – the TUC and the AFL. Was it, however, a view that reflected the demands of the ordinary trade union member?[82]

In both Britain and the United States there is some evidence of widespread concern on economic grounds over the impact of a large scale immigrant influx. In August 1938 six labour 'protesters' wrote to the TUC-sponsored *Daily Herald* complaining about its supposed 'Pro-Alien bias. . . . We have seen the work that the Labour Party and the "Daily Herald" have done for the working classes undone and ruined by the influx of aliens . . . We appreciate that often the refugees have committed no crime against the country that harries them; but charity begins at home.' Opinion poll material could be used to bolster such individual testimony and underline the argument that leaders such as Citrine and Green, in following restrictionist policies, were only following the wishes of their membership.[83] Nevertheless, it is essential to point out that in neither Britain nor the United States was the *ordinary* membership of the labour movement allowed to become involved in the decision-making process. In Britain at least, every hostile letter from an 'anti-alien' worker was countered by those sympathetic to the refugee plight. Many, particularly on the left in the labour movements of both countries, saw anti-alienism as a 'crude trick of capitalism' designed to split and divert the attention of the working class away from its real problems. The National Unemployed Workers' Movement stressed that 'assistance to the refugees neither injures British unemployed nor can displace British labour'. It was 'sheer humbug' to pretend 'that the plight of the unemployed is being worsened by the refugees. We wish to make it quite clear that the victims of Fascism abroad and the victims of hunger at home are not enemies.'[84] Such responses were not limited to those with strong ideological motives. Many thousands of ordinary British and American workers contributed small (but significant, given the poverty of the decade) amounts to funds for refugees of fascism, just as they gave generously to campaigns for Republican victims of the Spanish Civil War.[85] Others in the leadership of individual unions, such as Bill Holmes in the Agricultural Workers, made painstaking efforts to help rescue refugees and provide them with a livelihood. The experience of those few refugees able to obtain work suggests that the situation was at least flexible. There was initial tension and lack of understanding, not helped by the near-blanket ban on refugees being allowed to become union members. Nevertheless, in many cases adjustments were soon made by the 'native' workers. As we will see, this process occurred even in domestic service, where the leadership alleged that there had been strong opposition from union members to the refugee presence.[86] Yet no encouragement was given on a national level for those expressing positive sentiments towards refugees, nor any challenge mounted to those adopting an anti-alien position. Roy Harrod called for such a move on the part of organized labour, recognizing the isolation of the Jewish minority in the democracies on this issue:

The Jewish organisations . . . urgently require the assistance of non-Jewish bodies, especially in the task of obtaining public sympathy for the refugees, and in spreading the principles of freedom and humanity.

Ultimately, however, organized labour did not agree with Harrod that they should do so 'not merely on moral grounds but because of its actual benefit to the country as a whole'.[87] In the United States, the leaders of both the AFL and CIO were willing on such moral principles to accept the proposals in the Wagner Bill. In Britain, Walter Citrine was committed for reasons of humanitarianism alone to modify in a small way the restrictions on refugee employment. A limited gesture could be made, even though he knew 'that all refugees are not of a type that we could approve'.[88] But the leadership on both sides of the Atlantic had no desire to go beyond such charitable acts. With the partial exception of the CIO, the hierarchy of the American and British trade union movements believed that the refugees were, in essence, problematic immigrants. As a result, organized labour's economic strategies of the 1930s were generally protectionist and sceptical about Keynesian underconsumptionist arguments. The economic orthodoxy of the labour movement, in conjunction with its long-standing opposition to immigration, limited the impact of humanitarian gestures, as was the case with the AFL in the Wagner Bill debate. The restrictionism of the TUC and the AFL combined economic fears with what was referred to by contemporaries as 'labour nationalism'.[89]

Addressing the AFL in 1940, Walter Citrine pointed out that 'our movements have a very close affinity. Our people are drawn basically from the same stock.' Earlier he had told his own organization that he would make sure that any help given to the refugees 'would have to be made so that the livelihood of our own people is not endangered'. He would 'safeguard the interests of our people'.[90] In the dominant mono-cultural ethos of Britain during the 1930s, 'our people' meant the 'English' workers. It is significant that even in sympathetic treatments of the refugee question in the British labour movement, the word 'Jew' was constantly and carefully avoided. In the United States, hesitantly accepting pluralism after the vicious nativism of the 1920s, even the exclusive AFL was pushed to incorporate a 'Jewish' element in its response to the refugee crisis. It did so mainly because of the pressure and influence of some powerful Jewish unions and labour movements which had combined in 1934 to form the Jewish Labor Committee. In the overall responses of organized labour, however, there was more in common than divided the movements in Britain and the United States with regard to the refugees. Even most Jewish unions, on both sides of the Atlantic, were unwilling to challenge the general restrictionism of their respective national organizations and governments. They pushed and were successful in obtaining permission for individual leaders to be given asylum. They also accepted that reasons of economic and social assimilation precluded any help being given to the Jews of Europe on a bigger scale. Significantly the major exceptions came mainly from non-Zionist groups which rejected Americanization and, instead, stressed the need to continue group particularity. Ironically, given their (at best) ambivalent attitude towards religion, on the refugee question they followed a philosophy similar to very orthodox Jews. It remains the case that within British and American Jewry, both the political left and the religious right were weak within the organizational structures and in their access to government circles.[91]

This chapter has concentrated on the responses of the labour movement in Britain and the United States. Elsewhere in the democracies, similar general patterns with local variations (depending on differing traditions and circumstances) emerged. In Holland, initially a significant receiving society for refugees, trade unions maintained their long-standing opposition to immigrants, but the left as a whole provided support for several thousand political exiles from the Third Reich. France played the most important role as a place of asylum for political refugees in the period up to 1938, but beyond that point anti-alienism within the left helped the process of paving the way for Vichy. In Canada and Australia, union restrictionism on racial grounds continued, but there was nevertheless real horror and desire to do something to help after *Kristallnacht*. As in the United States, such pressure from below was generally ignored by the respective governments.[92]

The labour movement as a whole in the liberal democracies played a vital role in the determination of refugee policy. There was genuine sympathy which led to important initiatives in terms of offering asylum. Generally, however, the help given by organized labour involved individuals or small groups. Refugee policy clashed with a commitment to immigration restrictionism. As the latter contained elements of both economic and cultural nationalism, the assistance that the labour world was willing to offer was very limited. The need to protect 'our people' led to immigration policies which, in the words of Josiah Wedgwood, effectively excluded 'the poor, friendless and the male Jews'.[93] It is thus not surprising that perhaps the most significant act of rescue taken in the critical years before World War II was in the area of female domestic service, a feebly unionized occupation in the male dominated labour movement. It is to the world 'below stairs' that we now must turn.

3

An Alien Occupation: Domestic Service and the Jewish Crisis, 1933 to 1939

One of the more seemingly bizarre aspects of the September 1935 Nuremberg Laws for 'the Protection of German Blood and German Honour' was item 3: 'Jews will not be permitted to employ female citizens of German or kindred blood under 45 years of age as domestic servants'. Operating alongside the more obvious decrees banning marriage and sexual relations between Jews and Germans and the symbolic prohibition of Jews displaying the Reich and national flag, the specific nature of the restriction on Jews employing German domestics stands in curious isolation.[1] Psychoanalysts tend to 'see in this a projection of Hitler's anxieties about his own origins' but, as Lucy Dawidowicz pointed out, fears of the possible 'race defilement' that could take place against the German domestic in the Jewish home were 'commonplace in National Socialist ideology'. Indeed, many complained after September 1935 that the new law did not extend far enough: 'criticism of this clause seems to have been quite widespread. Some considered it should also have included a ban on the employment of German maids by mixed couples, or by a single Jewish woman.'[2]

The reaction to the partial ban on Jews employing Aryan servants suggests that apart from sexual anxieties, status concerns were also crucial in the implementation and impact of the domestic servant clause of the Nuremberg Laws. Rather than a quirky anomaly, item 3 of the Law for the Protection of German Blood and German Honour was designed to reinforce the social as well as the racial stigmatization of 'Jewishness'. Its full importance can only be understood properly if the central role of domestic service in Western bourgeois culture is recognized. The 'servant problem' was present in most Western European countries in the inter-war period. It reflected not only a widespread shortage of servants and practical issues of household management, but also the dilemmas of maintaining class distinctions and of keeping up appearances in an increasingly mass society. From the perspective of employment levels, before 1939, domestic service represented the most common female occupation in Western Europe and the United States. Its predominance in the inter-war female occupational structure reflected the scarcity of other, more lucrative, careers for working-class women in a period of economic dislocation and gender inequality, rather than the attraction of domestic service itself. It was into this complex (if increasingly anachronistic) world of 'mistresses and maids' that many thousands of Jewish women in Nazi Germany were thrown in the process of survival. Class, gender, race, nationality and ethnicity combined in a remarkable pattern that was to reveal the generosity, the selfishness and, most importantly, the ambivalence of the liberal democratic response to the Jewish crisis before World War II.[3]

I

In the period before World War I, the rise of factory and office work provided a welcome alternative to the drudgery, lack of freedom and poor pay of domestic service. In Germany between 1895 and 1907 alone the servant population declined by half. Yet the demand for servants remained unsatisfied as the number of middle-class urban households increased. Britain, in contrast to Germany, experienced a rise in the total number of servants employed in the late Victorian period (although other forms of women's work expanded at a much more spectacular rate). The years of World War I witnessed the intensification of the movement of women away from household employment to the booming munition factories and other areas of the economy suffering the shortage of workers after male mobilization.[4] One observer noted that before 1914 the chief complaint amongst the employing class had been the quality of servants. After 1918 the difficulty was obtaining any servants at all. Nevertheless, the rapid post-war reinstatement of male for female workers, in conjunction with the existence of widespread poverty, forced many women many into service in the inter-war years. In Britain the number of domestic servants increased from 1.1 million in 1921 to 1.3 million in 1931 with the figure continuing to rise until the outbreak of World War II.[5]

So desperate was the need for work and the demand for labour that an international market for servants developed in the nineteenth century. Hundreds of thousands of European women (especially from Ireland and Scandinavia) emigrated to the United States to become servants before 1914. In addition, an intra-European market had been in existence before World War I, but after 1918 it expanded rapidly with the closing of American immigration doors. Germany, and to a larger extent, Austria, where poverty was severe, acted as exporters of servants and Britain and Holland became the main receiving societies. By 1931 some 10 per cent of the 111,000 foreigners gainfully employed in Britain were German and Austrian servants. An even greater number of German and Austrian women, perhaps as many as 100,000, were attracted to Holland. In Britain, in spite of further supplies of women from Ireland and depressed areas such as South Wales, there were still not enough servants to meet demand.[6] The peculiar nature of domestic service is shown by the fact that in a situation of unsatisfied demand and a reluctant supply of labour, conditions of work were little better in the inter-war period than in the nineteenth century. Real wages may have increased slightly (although not in a comparable way to office or factory work), but the hours of work (averaging 12 hours a day, with just half a day off a week) and the status of the occupation had not improved. Lack of alternatives for many of the women partly explains why employers could maintain such poor conditions. Also on the mistress side, notwithstanding the efforts of middle-class feminists to promote domestic service as a profession, few employers were willing to change their attitudes towards servants. This was an issue in which status mattered as much as economics. As mistress and maid inhabited the same household, a strict delineation between the two had to be instituted. The employment of the servant brought not only advantages in terms of domestic help, it also gave prestige to the mistress. A psychologist examining the 'servant problem' in the early 1920s put the situation very bluntly: the mistress class did 'not reckon upon their servants being human beings with feelings similar to their own'. The servants, because of their close proximity to their employers, had to be depersonalized (hence the tendency to employ standard first names regardless of their accuracy). Beyond such callousness, many poorer middle-class households seriously strained their resources in employing domestic help. It was another example of status concerns over-riding financial matters in the servant issue.[7]

Domestic servants, as we have seen, remained poorly organized across the Western world. The marginal status of women in the labour movement, problems of dispersion and limited spare time to campaign, allied with the 'complex mixture of loyalty and hostility which bound servant to servant and servant to employer', made mass unionization, despite the huge numbers involved, next to impossible. Thus the barriers set up against immigrant workers at the request of organized labour rarely affected foreign domestics during the 1920s. In Holland, trade union concern over foreign workers at the end of the decade concentrated on male occupations such as mining and building. Unsatisfied demands for domestics and the refusal of Dutch women to accept 'The derisory nature of the cash wages involved, as well as the social stigma attached to the work' meant that the Dutch government was unwilling to stop the massive free entry of German and Austrian servants. Similarly, in Britain, until 1931, no restrictions were imposed on the use of foreign domestics. But in November of that year, perhaps the worst point of the economic depression, 'in view of the fact that the supply of British domestics was found to be increasing', the Ministry of Labour decided to impose a 'higher standard of compliance' and to issue permits to householders seeking foreign workers.[8]

The new regulations required that wages of no less than £36 *per annum* be offered to the foreign worker and stipulated that each household could employ a maximum of two foreign domestics. As a further concession to concerns that British workers would be displaced, and also reflecting hopes that unemployed men might become servants to the rich, no permits were to be offered to male aliens or to married couples. In addition, arrangements over the employment of *au pairs* were tightened so that they would not be used as a way 'to obtain cheap foreign domestic labour'.[9] These would be the regulations facing Jewish refugees attempting to escape to Britain from the Third Reich as servants. It was not the open-door policy towards foreign domestics that had operated during the 1920s, but it would become one of the few options left to those seeking asylum by the late 1930s.

II

At the turn of the century, young Jewish women, even as immigrants in strange lands, found the prospect of domestic service even less appealing than many of their non-Jewish counterparts. Several explanations can be given for this reluctance to work as servants. The nature of the occupation meant that domestics were taken away from their families. For immigrant groups such as Jews and Italians, the maintenance of close family structures was crucial and thus domestic service was used only as a last resort in times of dire financial hardship. In addition, Jewish immigrant mothers and their daughters viewed domestic service with particular disdain. It was seen as a humiliating occupation lacking all status. As one Jewish mother put it to her daughter who had just become a servant: 'Is that what I have come to America for, that my children should become servants?'. Most Jewish daughters shared this viewpoint. At Ellis Island immigration station in New York a Polish Jewish immigrant was asked in an intelligence test 'How do you wash stairs, from the top or from the bottom?'. Her reply was blunt: 'I don't go to America to wash stairs.' At the same time, middle-class Jewish women shared the common

problem of finding suitable servants. In policies that neatly combined philan-
thropy with self-interest, organizations such as the *Jüdischer Frauenbund* (JFB)
in Germany, the Jewish Women's Congress in the United States and the Jewish
Association for Protection of Girls and Women (and, to a lesser extent, the
Union of Jewish Women) in Britain, all tried to offer poor immigrant young
girls and women the chance to train for or practise domestic service.[10] It was
a strategy particularly aimed at 'fallen women' who were a great embarrassment to the established Jewish communities and seen as a source of generating
antisemitism. Predicting the unease that would be felt at the presence of the
later arrivals from Nazi Germany, pushing these women into service not only
provided the Jewish bourgeoisie with a ready-made supply of a scarce com-
modity. It also offered the chance of making their poorer sisters, in effect,
invisible. But so limited was the attraction of domestic work that many Jewish
women chose instead the independence and greater financial rewards of prostitution or uncertain careers in the sweatshops of London, New York and
elsewhere. In the Western democracies, only a small percentage of Jewish
women were employed as domestics before 1914.[11]

In Germany, the severity of the economic dislocation after 1918 forced a
change of strategy within the JFB. Previously, only working-class and largely
immigrant women were encouraged to become servants. By the 1920s, programmes were expanded to allow women from more 'respectable' backgrounds
to retrain as domestics, if only on a temporary basis, thus helping middle-class
families recover from financial ruin.[12] In Britain, although opportunities for
educated Jewish women were still limited, the Union of Jewish Women did
not consider such desperate measures. Poorer Jewish women, however, continued to work in the classic 'immigrant' occupations, particularly the clothing
trade, and generally avoided domestic service. In the inter-war years, a significant proportion of those of East European origin moved into the lower-
middle and middle classes, left the immigrant areas and settled in suburbia.
These households, in addition to those of their more established co-religionists,
created a demand for servants which could not be satisfied from within the
existing British Jewish community.[13]

A series of factors thus coincided to make domestic service a likely passport
to safety even *before* the Nazis' economic assault on German Jewry. In Britain
and Holland (if not the United States, where there was a large internal supply
of black, and to a lesser extent, poor white female labour),[14] the continuation
of immigration policies after the Nazi rise to power left the entry of foreign
servants essentially unaffected. The British Home Office as early as April
1933 envisaged a demand for permission to work as domestics from German
Jewish women.[15] Its forecast was proved to be accurate. In 1934, of 215
'refugee' cases examined by the Ministry of Labour, most were *au pair*
domestics. Unlike many other occupations, sympathetic treatment was given

by the Ministry of Labour in granting permits. Such employment was 'of a minor character or the post [was] in effect being created in special circumstances'. It was added that 'Jewish women have been allowed to take up posts of a domestic or semi-domestic character . . . in private houses'.[16]

The number using this route of departure in the first years of Nazism was limited. The majority of German Jews did not yet wish to emigrate and the domestic service option was problematic. From the late eighteenth century, the household played a central role in the Jewish search for respectability in German society. In the pursuit of this goal the employment of servants was vital in the upholding of standards and status. The transition from a life with domestic help to one with the possibility of being a servant was a step that many German Jewish women would take some time to accept (and some would never adjust to). In addition, the option was, by nature, a limited one. It applied only to women and the wages hardly allowed for the support of dependents. Initially life as a foreign domestic was essentially limited to single Jewish women.[17]

Slowly, however, the situation changed in Nazi Germany. It has been pointed out by Avraham Barkai that the impact of the early antisemitic economic decrees was more devastating on German Jewry than initial scholarship suggested. The gender impact of these policies was particularly marked. Previously dominated by male incomes, Jewish women were forced into a more prominent economic role to keep their families financially afloat. In spite of the limited efforts of the JFB, in the 1920s just 8.8 per cent of employed German Jewish women worked as domestics.[18] Most servants working in Jewish households were non-Jewish. Indeed there were many complaints from German maids after the 1935 Nuremberg Laws that the legislation had ruined their livelihood and threatened to make them a burden to the public. This legislation further opened up opportunities for Jewish women to work as domestics. To ease the adjustment to this new life, the JFB, which continued to function until closed down by the Nazis in 1938, organized domestic schools. As many 'respectable' Jewish women and their children had previously not been expected to play a role beyond overall management of domestic affairs (and leaving the manual tasks to the servants), the JFB schools provided training in such basics as cooking, sewing and repairs in the home. They enabled, as Marion Kaplan has written, 'Jewish middle-class women and their families to adjust to a lower standard of living'. Moreover, it must be added, it helped to prepare Jewish females (ranging from school-children to women in their forties) for future lives as servants in Germany and beyond.[19]

The class factors in these processes are shown in the fact that Austrian, as opposed to German, Jewish women dominated immigration to Britain as domestic servants. In Austria the economic climate was worse than in Germany and the larger percentage of *ostjuden* in the former country led to a greater flexibility in the approach to escape.[20] Nevertheless, as persecution intensified during the 1930s, the desire grew to emigrate from Germany at all costs. As a consequence, demand for places in the Jewish household schools and classes increased in both Vienna and Berlin.

The numbers emigrating to Britain as domestics show a corresponding rise. In 1935 the number of foreign domestics granted the right to enter with work permits was just over 4,000. A year later the figure doubled and in 1937 reached an annual total of 14,000. Maintaining its 'race blind' approach, no official differentiation was made between Jewish and non-Jewish foreign servants entering Britain. It has been estimated, however, that up to 1938, when the regulations changed, at least 7,000 Jewish women had come to Britain through the Ministry of Labour scheme. Even before entry was further liberalized, domestic service had become by far the most common route into Britain.[21]

III

Knowledge of the possibilities of domestic work in Britain came through classic 'immigrant' sources of information. First, British domestic agencies had already established offices in Europe, reflecting the internationalization of the occupation by time of the the inter-war period. One large company specialized in recruitment from Vienna which helped to facilitate the high number of Jewish and non-Jewish domestics coming to Britain from Austria. Second, there were letters from British friends and relatives pointing out vacancies and sometimes even offering employment. Third, those who had already come to Britain encouraged family and friends to join them. Fourth, Jewish communal organizations provided up-to-date information on the different immigration policies operating throughout the world in journals such as *Jüdische Auswanderung*. They put increasing emphasis on the opportunities available through the British domestic scheme, particularly in the desperate months before the war.[22]

There is a strong contrast between the apparent freedom of entry extended to Jewish women through Ministry of Labour permits and the general cautious approach of the British government, backed by the refugee organizations, to let in only 'the right type of refugee'.[23] The apparent paradox was compounded, although partially explained, in a memorandum prepared by the Refugee Coordinating Committee before the Evian conference in July 1938:

The private organisations hope that [the existing] individualised selective immigration practice will be maintained and that the British delegates to the Conference will state that Great Britain is prepared to act as a country of settlement for refugees selected with reference to their personal and occupational qualifications for absorption in the country, and not merely to act as a country of temporary refuge. They hope that as a logical consequence of this *policy of selective admission* [my emphasis], permits of employment will be given more generously to refugees than to other aliens in order that Great Britain can make a constructive contribution to the solution of the refugee problem by facilitating the rapid re-establishment of a limited number.

They believe that it would assist the Conference and the work of assistance if it could be stated, for instance, that special consideration for admission to settlement would be given for persons coming for domestic service, for nursing, for agricultural work, for initiating new industries etc., and for certain groups such as children, students and scholars.[24]

The thrust of this memorandum is remarkably close to the policy pursued by the British government between the end of the conference (and especially after *Kristallnacht*) and the start of the war. Although the child refugees and many others allowed into Britain in this period came on temporary transit visas, British officials indeed recognized on behalf of British officials that the refugee domestics were in a separate category. As Sir Ernest Holderness, a senior figure in the Home Office hierarchy, put it at the time of the Evian conference:

We know . . . that many of the women who are coming here on Ministry of Labour permits for domestic service are of Jewish origin and once admitted will have to be allowed to stay here. Many of the women are not of the domestic class and we anticipate that they will not be content to remain in domestic service and will probably wish to take up some other occupation.

The Home Office, he added, intended 'to keep them in domestic service for at any rate two or three years'. The flexibility was made possible in this particular case because of the 'large unsatisfied demand' for servants in Britain.[25]

Conservative and extreme right-wing elements had campaigned against 'foreign maids' before the Nazi rise to power, complaining that they were 'throwing Englishwomen on the dole'. Later, the British Union of Fascists suggested that German Jewish domestics were 'exploiters rather than refugees . . . the wages and conditions of English domestic workers [were] in the process of being lowered to accommodate aliens'. Moreover, 'the wholesale importation of foreigners was throwing our own countrywomen out of work.'[26] As we have seen, the fledgling National Union of Domestic Workers also protested against the foreign influx. The British government, normally so sensitive to the complaints of anti-aliens, acknowledged in December 1937 that the increase in foreign servants had led to a 'a number of complaints as to the effects [of] this influx'. Significantly, it added that they had not been 'from any representative body of opinion'. In fact, just two months earlier, the Ministry of Labour had received a resolution from the National Council of Women of Great Britain, a middle-class organization representing two million members, that it was

of [the] opinion that the difficulty of obtaining domestic help tends to restrict [the size and functioning of] families to an extent dangerous to the State, [and] urges the Ministry of Labour to grant permits freely to approved young women of other nationalities.

Facing two different constituencies – one middle-class, highly articulate and powerful, and the other working-class and disparate – it is hardly surprising that, according to one senior Ministry of Labour official at the end of 1937, '. . . the influx can be safely permitted to continue'.[27]

Late in 1938, responsibility for Jewish alien domestics was transferred from the Ministry of Labour to the Home Office. The Ministry was unable to cope with the vastly increased number of women applying for permits after the *Anschluss* and *Kristallnacht*. As part of the changes in the bureaucratic process, the Central Office for Refugees (Bloomsbury House) took on much of the administrative burden on behalf of the Home Office. Bloomsbury House in some ways welcomed this move and recognized that

The work of [its] Domestic Bureau is obviously one of the largest pieces of constructive work for the refugees. It is removing large numbers of women from intolerable conditions and giving them the opportunity of earning their living in one of the main industries in this country in which the demand for labour is vastly bigger than the supply.[28]

Revealing the continuity of its policies, even in the case of domestic servants, the Domestic Bureau added that 'The quality and control of this large number is of very great importance'. Indeed, one reason why Bloomsbury House welcomed the transfer from the Ministry of Labour was that it enabled more 'adequate selection and inspection of candidates'. In the mind of the Domestic Bureau, 'The Ministry granted labour permits to any class of aliens coming to work in this country'. The Ministry required no guarantee that workers were fit for domestic service, 'but only evidence that there was an unsatisfied demand for such service'.[29] In fact the evidence suggests that the administration of control by the Ministry of Labour was far from that suggested by the Domestic Bureau. Rejection was a real possibility. In 1938, of 16,281 applications for domestic worker permits, 15 per cent were turned down. Many factors were involved, particularly the age of the applicants, but in individual cases prejudices against certain types of Jews were part of the process.[30] It should also be added that it is clear that some British officials were unhappy about the permits which *were* granted. Captain Jeffes of the Foreign Office Passport Control, who visited offices across Europe in June 1939, was 'appalled to see the bad type of refugee presenting . . . Ministry of Labour permits . . . who were so filthily dirty both in their person and their clothing that they were utterly unfit to go inside a decent British home'. Such prejudice against the *ostjuden* was also present, as we will see shortly, in the response of the refugee organizations. Another Foreign Office official, Reginald Parkin (also of Passport Control), went further and regretted that the immigration policy of the government was so geared to domestic service that 'the better type of refugees . . . were ruled out at the start'.[31] Jeffes and Parkin, were, however, by the summer of 1939 ruing a policy of entry that had already been successfully liberalized. Indeed, the changes made at the end of 1938 with regard to the entry of refugee domestics represented one of the most important in liberal democratic policy-making after *Kristallnacht*.

First and foremost, the transfer to the Home Office recognized that these Jewish women, while coming to Britain to provide labour, were refugees. More specifically, the regulations of 1931 were slightly relaxed for the refugee domestics. A strictly limited number of domestic permits for married couples were introduced and the age limit lowered from 18 to 16 for refugee girls. Until the start of 1939, entry to Britain depended on having a pre-arranged post to occupy. With the effective transfer of responsibility to Bloomsbury House a new system was implemented. The Domestic Bureau was responsible for issuing green cards which were sent to Jewish/refugee organizations across Europe. If the report from the organization was favourable, the Bureau could then apply for a domestic permit which would normally be granted by the Passport Control Office. The Bureau was allowed to admit up to 400 applicants a week. The stress this created on what was at best a semi-voluntary organization was immense. In the first three weeks of January 1939 alone, 1,400 permits were granted.[32]

Those at Bloomsbury House realized that the Home Office was 'delegating its responsibility in this respect to the Co-ordinating Committee'. The burden of this entrustment weighed heavy with the Domestic Bureau. They were anxious to avoid any government criticism and thus implemented policy accordingly.[33] In March and April 1939, the question of Polish Jewish refugees urgently seeking entry to Britain as domestics was raised. The Domestic Bureau was wary of East European Jews creating problems in Britain and thus decided that it was 'not at present dealing with Polish Jews at all'. It was equally concerned that those seeking domestic employment in Britain should be of suitable quality. Inspection and selection 'should be carried out in Greater Germany and . . . as much training as possible should be done in the country of origin prior to entering Great Britain'. One report presented to the Domestic Bureau went as far as to put 'great stress on the need for setting up a Selection Committee, or Committees, in Germany . . . no expense should be spared'. From May 1939, applicants had to pass a test in the German and

Austrian Jewish domestic training schools before permits were granted by Bloomsbury House.[34]

The pressure that such bureaucratic procedures created on those anxiously trying to escape in 1939 was immense. Bianca Heller recalls the situation in Vienna. When a domestic position in Britain was found after three months of waiting, Heller faced problems obtaining her passport. She queued every night 'for weeks and weeks', aware that she had to get out as soon as possible, as people were 'simply disappearing' under Nazi rule.[35] The procedures also caused grave problems for those implementing policy on behalf of the refugee organizations in Europe. Assembling visas, green cards and permission from the Nazi authorities became a nightmare. Bloomsbury House found itself administering a scheme of rescue which was so massive that it had little chance of operating it successfully, especially with its tiny budget. There were times in 1939 when the operation came close to a standstill. In many ways, however, the bureaucracy created by Bloomsbury House in order to find the 'right type of refugee' (and thereby satisfy the British government), was the price the Jewish refugee organizations were willing to pay. In the mind of Bloomsbury House such policies enabled them to control what they saw as an unstable and potentially dangerous situation at home. Those seeking entry could be monitored for suitability, and the refugees actually reaching Britain as domestics could be closely controlled.[36]

Yet the importance of rescue through domestic service should not be minimized. Between 12,000 and 14,000 Jews (the vast majority women) escaped to Britain as domestics in just eight months, the tragically short period in which the Home Office/Bloomsbury House scheme operated.[37] Two weeks before the war, Norman Bentwich, a leading figure in the refugee organizations in Britain, revisited Vienna. He was shocked at the changes that had taken place since 1938 and the success of the Nazi regime's aim to make Jewish life 'literally unendurable'. 'The one hope for all, young and older,' Bentwich remarked,

is emigration; and the main interest is preparation for emigration. During the year nearly 40,000 have passed through classes of training and retraining, which embrace a thousand different branches of manual or domestic work. There is a class, for example, for bar-mixers, and several for butlers, which are attended by lawyers, doctors and industrialists. The possibility of domestic service in England has been a Godsend.[38]

After *Kristallnacht* it was clear that there was no place for the Jews in Greater Germany. Britain became the major place of refuge and domestic service the chief route to safety.

IV

Jews under Nazi control before the war viewed Britain with mixed emotions. Some had romantic notions of the country, acquired through a reading of its literature and history, or an affection for the strength of British liberal democratic traditions. One refugee recalls how she chose her destination: 'I loved England. It was still in Europe. [I] didn't want to go to America, so stayed and became [a] domestic.'[39] Others saw it, perhaps more realistically, as a country whose urban appearance was unattractive, climate grey and economy depressed. The United States, in contrast, was (as with the *ostjuden* at the turn of the century) seen as the 'goldene medineh [golden land]' for the majority of would-be immigrants.[40] It is clear that for some German and Austrian Jews, coming to Britain on a domestic permit was a last resort. Many who had affidavits for the United States realized after the *Anschluss* and *Kristallnacht* that the situation was now desperate and it was therefore unwise 'to sit waiting for [one's American quota] number to come up'. A minority 'were too proud to take a [domestic job] and so they were left behind'. Several thousand permits granted by Bloomsbury House were left untaken. Bureaucratic muddle partly explains this situation, as does the hope that 'something else would turn up'.[41] Of equal importance was, however, despite its relative generosity, the essential limitation of the domestic scheme. It was geared fundamentally towards single women, but even so, wider family responsibilities stopped many from becoming foreign servants. For those with families (apart from the several hundred couples allowed in under the new regulations after *Kristallnacht*) the scheme was impractical. Lenka Berman, writing from Czechoslovakia to the couple in Scotland who had rescued her son, highlighted the dilemmas facing Jews in the summer of 1939:

Though we have registered in March we were told at the American consulate that it may take years till we may get the possibility of emigrating[,] the quota being overcharged. Therefore we should like to go to England if it were possible, of course it is very difficult to get a permit there. A cousin of ours in London who is herself an Austrian emigrant writes to us that I should be able to receive a permit only if I took the position in a domesticity which I should gladly take . . . But it is much more difficult for my husband as I cannot leave him here until he would get a permit. There may be found a way out by time, we pray to God every day that he may help us. I myself am thirty-three . . . I have attended many special courses [on] cold meat [and] English cookery . . . My father is a physician and because of his age of seventy, he is living now retired with my mother in Brno.

With grandparents to worry about as well, there was no way that such individuals could abandon their dependent close relatives and leave for Britain as domestic servants.[42]

In refugee circles in Britain, the story circulated

about the young lady of wealthy Viennese stock who came downstairs on her first morning [as a domestic] in the house of the English people she believed to be her saviours, at half past ten . . . wearing a blue crepe-de-Chine dressing gown with tassel, looking for her breakfast'.

In reality, most Jewish refugees had a good idea of what to expect as foreign domestic servants – hence the delay in leaving until 'it didn't matter, [and] it [became] a question of life and death'.[43] Some would be well-prepared through the domestic schools in Nazi-controlled areas, but, for many, the rush to get out meant they came with little or no time to prepare. Out of 500 women rescued by the remarkable efforts of the Cambridge Refugee Committee on domestic permits, it was found that only two had suitable experience for their new occupation. Refugees resorted to token efforts in order to impress British consular officials that they were indeed suitable domestic material – including roughening clean and 'very unspoiled hands' or learning to make tea the 'English way' before interviews.[44] The refugees were thus not totally naive about what awaited them in the British home. Nevertheless, they often arrived carrying immense psychological burdens. The situation in Greater Germany was deteriorating rapidly, families were left behind, and preparation for their new lives as servants was at best incomplete. How would British society respond to these strange new arrivals?

V

Once in Britain, the state's role in the lives of the refugee domestics (until the outbreak of war) was minimal. They could change jobs (but not occupations) and only needed to keep the police informed of such moves.[45] Otherwise the treatment of the refugees depended on a closed world made up of their employers, their fellow employees and, of great significance, the refugee organizations in Britain. Bloomsbury House in particular acted as a mediator between both the maid and mistress and the state and public. In the United States, no official scheme existed for the rescue of refugees through domestic service. Nevertheless, many would drift into the occupation through the shortages of any other available work. In the process, as we shall see, the organization 'Selfhelp of Émigrés from Germany' formed in 1936 (later simply Selfhelp) played a major role in helping fellow refugees find work in other people's homes and thus re-establish a base from which to build a life in the United

States.[46] The refugee domestics in Britain also took greater control of their lives, but initially the refugee organizations attempted to dominate the situation.

In the world of British domestic service as a whole, Pam Taylor has written of the decisive role of working-class mothers in pushing their daughters into domestic service in the inter-war period. This was primarily due to economic necessity in this depressed period, but Taylor also points out 'that the place and training of the working-class girl in the home contributed not just to her skills but also to her willingness and obedience in service. There is a sense in which mothers were contributing to the exploitation of their daughters.' In many ways the refugee bodies on a national and local level attempted to emulate the role of the domestic's mother.[47]

Generally the policy of the refugee organizations was to 'see refugees spread more evenly throughout the country, rather than having a vast majority living in the North West districts of London'. Such dispersion policies had been attempted earlier with other immigrant groups arriving in Britain in order to ease integration and avoid local animosity. As long as most of the refugees could be kept out of the cities, and particularly the capital, domestic service offered an ideal solution to the British government and those refugee bodies based at Bloomsbury House. Their aim was to assimilate the refugees as quickly as possible, to make them less distinctive and thus reduce their potential for causing antisemitism. Domestic service was 'a very closed world . . . a world to itself' and through its very insularity the refugee presence could be disguised or made invisible to the outside world.[48] A gender factor was also at work. The Home Office was willing, as a small humanitarian gesture, to accept the entry of up to ten married couples a week. It was a small scheme that was particularly important in rescuing Jewish men interned in the concentration camps after the November 1938 pogrom.[49] Nevertheless, the British government was unhappy about the idea of any significant numbers of male refugees coming in as servants. Women, of whatever class or background, were essentially seen as more assimilable material than men. The Home Office believed that there was a danger with male refugees

that such persons, e.g. doctors or others who would not otherwise be admitted, would obtain visas through this channel and later endeavour to enter other employment.

In addition, employing husbands as gardeners would meet with much opposition and 'would result in the displacement of British labour'.[50] Regulations concerning the entry of such husbands thus had a rigour that was lacking in the case of female domestics. Revealing the obsession with the visibility of the refugees, the Home Office decreed that those married couples allowed in 'must not be established in London or the suburbs' and that 'The husband must not undertake work out of doors, such as that of chauffeur or gardener'.

The bias against male refugees was shown in a Ministry of Labour official's terse remark that men coming in through the married couple domestic scheme (even with the low numbers involved and suitable restrictions) could only be seen as being 'probably . . . less harmful than their admission in most other capacities'.[51]

Dispersion to the countryside (where servant shortages were at their most intense) of single female refugees was thus the ideal solution to the liberal refugee organizations. In contrast, the Chief Rabbi's Emergency Council was more concerned for the domestics' religious welfare which was seen to be in jeopardy away from the centres of Jewish life.[52] The refugees, not surprisingly, were less happy about the country option. As was the case with their non-refugee counterparts, life outside the towns increased isolation in an already limited world. For the refugees in particular, it increased their sense of loneliness in a strange environment. The refugee organizations, in spite of all their efforts, faced a constant movement of their charges back to the cities. At the start of the war, of the 9,000 refugee domestics Bloomsbury House could account for, up to 6,000 were located in London alone. But its dispersion efforts had not been totally in vein, for the Domestic Bureau's card index 'covered practically every town and village in the United Kingdom'.[53]

In the cities several hostels were set up for refugee domestics looking for work. Regulations were harsh, training compulsory and stay, as with Kershaw House in Manchester, limited to six weeks maximum. By such monitoring, the refugee bodies hoped to anglicize their charges and prepare them for their new careers. Above all Bloomsbury House wanted to keep the women in domestic service and away from the public eye, but also to avoid them becoming a further charge on the Jewish community. British Jewry in the last year before the war desperately attempted to keep its 1933 pledge to the British government that the refugees would not become a burden on the state. The commitment was made with the intention of supporting, at most, several thousand refugees – not the tens of thousands present in Britain by 1939. In sheer financial terms, the rescue of refugee domestics was cheap (estimated by Bloomsbury House at 25 shillings (£1.25) a person) and there was no further cost involved if the refugee remained in service.[54] The desire to keep the refugees in the occupation was not, however, simply a matter of economics. Refugee children, many of whom became informal and unpaid servants themselves, were also pushed in the direction of careers as domestics when they embarked on vocational training offered by the refugee organizations. These children, like the adult refugees, were discouraged from thinking of a career in the professions. Filling gaps in the British labour market and the possibility of disguising the refugee presence were more important factors than satisfying the personal aspirations of the refugees. Such policies reflected the insecurity of British Jewry during the 1930s. Looking back, the chairperson of the

Domestic Bureau stated that its policy 'all the time was to keep the refugees employed or at least bedded into the life of the country'. The needs of the refugee domestics were perceived less in the way of emotional support and more in the form of practical training. Bloomsbury House would not be remembered with any affection by former domestics and other refugees.[55]

The attitude of Bloomsbury House was made clear in its leaflet *Mistress and Maid*, a widely-circulated publication aimed at both sides of the household. The leaflet mainly focused on the refugees adapting 'as quickly as possible to your new surroundings'. Nevertheless, it recognized that employers might not be aware of the background of their new servants: 'Many of these girls are trying to forget their terrible experiences before they found shelter in this country'. A local refugee worker recalls that employers were given 'the whole story . . . who the people were, what their background was, and so on'.[56] The Domestic Bureau was not mistaken in its belief that some explanation was needed. The failure of British society to comprehend what was happening to the Jews in Greater Germany outlined earlier was particularly marked in the case of employers and their refugee domestics. Some, in offering refugees posts were motivated only by the desire to help. A former domestic recalls that the couple she worked for 'were quite exceptionally human, cultured, sane and fair. They . . . treated me as though I had been *their* daughter.' One 'refugee housekeeper' wrote to the Society of Friends to see if she could rescue a German Jew through the domestic worker scheme (in spite of her general opposition to employing servants). After a year of employing such a housekeeper she reported that it had been 'a great success'. She remarked that the only disadvantage 'of having a refugee housekeeper is that thence forward one is inescapably aware of the misfortunes of Europe's persecuted minorities'. Placing herself in a distinct minority, however, she added that it was essential to make that connection. To her, employing a German Jewish refugee domestic made it 'impossible to cultivate wilful blindness'. In contrast, the majority of the mistress class found it all too easy to ignore or misunderstand the background of their refugee maids.[57]

It was important to those employing refugee domestics essentially for their labour that 'normal' patterns of service were maintained. Crucial to this process was the absolute division between employer and servant. Class considerations between the worlds of upstairs and downstairs were thus of utmost significance in determining the treatment of refugees. Much to the frustration of women and men who were formerly leading professionals in Berlin and Vienna and employers of servants themselves, they were now cooks, maids and gardeners and treated as such. Margareta Burkill, secretary of one of the biggest provincial refugee committees, in Cambridge, was stunned to find 'that dons' wives could treat somebody who was in every way as good as them in an absolutely terrible manner'.[58] Artificially created class barriers had to be maintained and in most cases attempts to bridge them were frowned upon. The process has been described most eloquently by Lore Segal (née Groszmann), whose parents were formerly of great social standing in Vienna:

And so the Willoughby's had put my parents in their place; the refugees belonged to the class of people who eat in the kitchen, sleep on cheap mattresses, and throw their wives down the stairs in an argument – which goes to show that people have, after all, an innate sense of justice and cannot with equanimity be served by their fellows when these too closely resemble themselves.

It is hardly surprising, therefore,

that there was much Mrs. Willoughby did not know. 'Why didn't you embark in Austria and come direct?' she asked my mother one day. 'Why did you come such an awkward way around?' My father, who had just entered the kitchen, stared in astonishment. 'Do you know we had to wait eleven weeks for you and Groszmann?' said Mrs. Willoughby.

As another refugee domestic recalls, from the perspective of her employers, 'They wanted a help in their homes and it was not easy for them to understand what happened to us in Germany, or that we came from comfortable homes with maids'.[59]

A minority of refugees appear to have been treated with more severity because of their marginal status. In 1945 an official in the Ministry of Labour, reviewing the pre-war procedure of allowing in foreign domestics, referred to a class of employer who could keep neither British nor alien servants. It was, however, 'always possible for them to secure fresh aliens from abroad'. He concluded that it was 'very evident that certain employers regarded domestic servants as an inferior race and treated them accordingly'. The Secretary of the Domestic Bureau had also come 'across undesirable employers who exploit these terrified girls and threaten deportation'. In the September 1938 crisis, the *Manchester Guardian* reported with regard to refugee domestics that 'One hears now of many cases of Austrian girls entreating their British employers not to send them "home"'. Most often this manipulation of the refugee's marginality was in the form of work exploitation, but the other major abuse associated with the servant occupation – sexual harassment from males in the household – was also present in the experience of these Jewish women.[60]

Two extremes thus existed in the treatment of the refugee domestics. A minority were looked after with dignity and respect. At the other end of the spectrum, some were treated with shocking brutality and callousness. The majority, however, were received neutrally. The motives of most employers of refugees were not cynical, but their behaviour towards their servants was consistent with general practices in the occupation: 'anyone who came as a domestic, was treated as a domestic . . . no quarter [was] given'; 'the English people were not interested in our glorious past, but rather took us at face value'. In short, charity in helping rescue the Jewish women was not incompatible with exploitation. It is in that light that the difficult relations that developed in British Jewish households between mistress and maid should be viewed.[61]

The worst treatment of refugees and domestics in general occurred in small lower-middle-class households. It was here that the servants could least be afforded and, ironically, most be expected from them. Many refugees recall that their worst treatment was in Jewish homes. Susie Linton, who had three domestic positions in Jewish households in Manchester before the war, relates how

they certainly took advantage. They certainly didn't treat me like a Jewish refugee, they treated me like a char woman. . . . I was willing to work, but I wasn't brought up to housework and they didn't make allowances.

She had insufficient food, no time off and problems of communication, on top of worrying about the fate of her parents whom she had left behind. A British-born Jewish Mancunian recalls how such experiences were not isolated: local Jews 'made slaves of them, gave them terrible jobs . . . treat[ed] them horribly'.[62]

The explanation for this unhappy relationship between the established Jewish community and the newcomers is to be found in the interrelationship between class and ethnicity. Most of those within British Jewry who came to employ the refugee domestics were of marginal middle-class status. They were largely second-generation Jews of East European origin, unsure of their place in British society and also within the Jewish community. On the one hand, the refugees threatened to disturb what was seen as the fragile equilibrium reached by British Jewry after the earlier traumas of the East European influx. Moreover, the tension between *ostjuden* and the Jews of central Europe (and particularly the snobbery of the latter towards the former) at the turn of the century, threatened to re-emerge.[63] There was now a crucial difference: the tables had been turned in the balance of power. The resentment of those of Eastern European origin about the shabby treatment they had received earlier could now be unleashed. On the other hand, the plight of the Jews in Greater Germany disturbed the conscience of British Jewry. To say the least, the territory of domestic service was perhaps the most unsuitable forum for such conflicts to be resolved.

At the start of 1939, a 'domestic employer' wrote to the *Jewish Chronicle* outlining a scheme to solve the problems which were 'proving daily more unsatisfactory' between British Jewish mistresses and refugee maids. She acknowledged that the 'Jewish women come from the abnormal and terribly tragic conditions abroad'. They could not be blamed for trying to escape from Nazism and

The mental and psychological difficulties of the women refugees who come to work in this country [were] great. Many of them have been arbitrarily torn out of professions in which they were highly successful. Others again have been forced out of comfortable and affluent homes suddenly to undertake unaccustomed tasks of toil. A refugee domestic worker may find herself in an English home where there are daughters of her own age, happily and busily absorbed in their future careers. Her own life has collapsed; and she finds herself in a position in which it would require far more philosophy than most of us can claim to reconcile her to her fate.

The solution was more training for the refugee women so that they can make 'a very real and valuable contribution . . . to British home life'. Ultimately, she concluded that

the Jewish woman domestic worker, grateful as she must be for the home that has been afforded her in her plight, must nevertheless be taught, in a sympathetic manner, the facts of her position and the necessity for her own personal co-operation in making the best of it.[64]

In short, the refugee domestics were being asked to 'become England's *ost-juden*'. For this privilege and the chance to show 'the British people . . . that they are getting something in return for the humanity and justice they are showing', the refugees were asked to express gratitude.[65] From the perspective of many Jewish (and non-Jewish) employers of refugee domestics, the foreign workers were simply there to provide efficient labour and, incidently, to be thankful for the opportunity of doing so. One British Jew, normally sympathetic to the plight of refugees and horrified by the persecutions in Greater Germany, wrote in his diary in the summer of 1939:

Marianne is going next month to a place in London where she's to get £1 a week. So much for German refugee girls – they keep agreements and promises while it suits them, as Hitler does.[66]

The impatience of many employers with refugees who did not satisfy either the unrealistic work requirements or the necessary sense of obligation, reflected not over-callousness but the realities of domestic service in Britain. It was an occupation in which human compassion displayed by employers towards employees was essentially frowned upon. What, however, was the perspective from below stairs?

VI

The uneasy balance between servant and employer, based on an odd mixture of loyalty and disdain, was one likely to be upset by the introduction of refugee domestics. At their peak, foreign domestic workers represented less than 1 per cent of the total British servant workforce. In conjunction with the National Union of Domestic Workers and the refugee organizations, strict conditions for the employment of foreign workers were laid down. Efforts were to be made to employ British labour. If none was available, foreign workers must be paid at least 15 shillings (75p) a week and the girls must be healthy, single and not aged over 45. Yet in spite of the small absolute numbers involved and the firm adherence to the regulations, the National Union received 'complaints from domestic workers . . . of the way in which foreign nationals [were] making the bad conditions in domestic employment even worse'. The foreigners did this, they alleged, by undercutting wage rates and lowering conditions overall. The union decided to carry out an investigation in which it found that of 30 allegations, only one gave proof of Home Office regulations being evaded. In reality, the refugees made little or no impact on wage rates or other aspects of domestic work.[67] But there is no doubt that the refugee presence created unease among other servants. A tiny minority joined the British Union of Fascists to air their grievances against the alien influx, and a greater number protested to their union and insisted that foreign workers be banned from membership. Many more expressed their resentment in terms of day-to-day unpleasantness to refugee fellow servants, adding another layer of jealousy to the tensions below stairs.[68] Nevertheless, adjustments could be made, as was the experience of those connected to the Hampstead Club of the Austrian Domestic Workers. One member, a parlour maid, recalled the unfriendliness of a cook towards her. When asked why, the cook responded: 'You refugees, you come over here and work for 12 to 15 shillings a week, you clean windows and shoes. You make the situation for all the domestic servants worse.' After introducing the cook to the Hampstead Club, they were getting on 'better and better': 'Now she showed some understanding for the Austrian women who had come over here without any knowledge of the conditions and who in their bad situation took jobs.'[69]

The Austrian maid concluded that 'Our English colleagues fully realise that most of the Austrian women who are over here were compelled to leave their homeland and they don't object [to] their getting labour permits.' In terms of the union response such antagonisms took longer to resolve than at the work level. The bogus refugee question provided a distraction, the foreign servants serving as convenient scapegoats (excusing the Domestic Workers' lack of impact more generally). Ironically, the leadership so badly required in the union could have been provided by some of the refugees with strong union backgrounds in Austria. Nevertheless, the union's leader, Beatrice Bezzant, was willing to offer advice to refugees, who reported that 'she is always assisting us in a very friendly way'. It was, however, only in the war that individual refugees were allowed to become union members. It remains the case that most of the refugees would be left to their own resources to struggle for survival in British society.[70]

First experiences for the Jewish women in Britain could be traumatic. While to Eva Freeman, arriving from Berlin in June 1939, 'the minute I put my feet down on the London pavements I felt I [had] landed in paradise', many more refugees experienced homesickness. Some, still in their teens, were leaving home for the first time and had left all their family and friends behind. Not surprisingly, surrounded by strangers and often unable to communicate in English, Britain appeared a bewildering and alienating place. Without sympathy and understanding from employers, fellow servants or friends, life could be very isolated. It was only when she discovered that she was able to listen to German radio that Frances Goldberg, a domestic in Liverpool, 'did not go to bed praying not to wake up in the morning'.[71]

Whether sympathetic or not, employers expected work to be done and, for an initial period, cultural and linguistic differences created difficulties as well as some tragi-comedy. One refugee was sacked after a translation error caused her to serve a polite tea party with dog biscuits (rather than the requested miniature cakes). Making tea and toast the 'English' way was one hurdle to clear; and lighting the fire was, perhaps, the greatest. One 'lady' shouted at her distraught young refugee girl:

You are of no use to us playing the piano or speaking a few languages. Before you came to England you had no idea of how to make a fire. I wish I had not let you come.[72]

Employers expected normal service almost immediately. A group of refugees associated with the Austrian centre recorded their first encounters with the English household: '"You have to get up at 7 o'clock in the morning. I'll wait for you in the kitchen." These were our lady's last words. Very tired from the long journey, we went to bed.' The experiences of Lucy Long – 'the work was entirely unaccustomed and hard for one of my background. I learned fast but worked very slowly' – were typical of most.[73]

Some householders were willing to persevere with their foreign domestics, others quickly gave them the sack. The refugees themselves soon came to realize if they were being unnecessarily exploited and would seek fresh appointments. The Jewish refugee domestics, even more than their British counterparts, were highly mobile. It was not unusual for them to have three or more jobs in the relatively short time that they were in the occupation. It was one form of resistance in an occupation which was, as the refugee collective at the Austrian centre put it, even at its best, 'not a very pleasant one'.[74] In terms of poor food, the cold, lack of freedom and spare time, the refugees faced the same conditions as their British colleagues. Nevertheless, as the refugee domestics own newsletter stated:

most of us are still worse off. Why [is] that? Because we are expelled from our homeland, because we lost our friends, because for some time we lost our home, our mountains, our forests, our lakes.[75]

In particular, the pressure to help family placed an enormous burden on the refugees. These women, despite the immense difficulty of their daily life, attempted to get visas, guarantors or work for relatives on the Continent from a society that was largely unable to understand the urgency of the situation. Some had limited success. Others (such as Hilde Gerrard who needed to raise £200 each for her parents, and eventually realized that her mission was impossible) came close to nervous breakdowns as they faced the race against time and insurmountable obstacles.[76]

Fighting for family outside Britain was one great challenge facing the domestics. Another was trying to keep relatives actually in Britain together. In a reversal of traditional roles, even at 15 shillings a week, the refugee women became chief breadwinners. Often children would be in different parts of the country, rescued through the *Kindertransporte*, and husbands had no source of income. Female refugees in both Britain and the United States showed much greater flexibility and adaptability in this period, particularly through their work in service. By their efforts, families were kept intact.[77] That so much was achieved in this period owed much to the internal resources of the refugees and their collective activities. With the neglect and, at times, the hostility of the trade union movement (and the refugee organizations anxious only to keep these Jewish women in service) it was left, as the refugee domestics' paper stated, 'on us to do as much self-aid as possible'.[78]

In London, the refugee domestics ran their own hostel for women needing temporary help. In addition, two clubs were organized where the refugees met to talk about common troubles and to give each other advice. A self-organized domestic club also met in Liverpool which was 'very important to us as refugees. . . . There we came together and discussed our problems, failures and shared our worries.' Through such contact the refugees could learn of the availability of better positions, share methods of coping with the job and ways of helping relatives abroad.[79]

Domestic servants have often been unfairly portrayed as passive victims of exploitation. Generally forced through economic necessity to keep their jobs, they still managed to keep their self-esteem and integrity by resisting the depersonalizing aspects of the occupation. The same could be said of the refugee domestics, who had even fewer opportunities to change their occupation, but maintained a sense of dignity at a time of extreme difficult physical and mental stress. Little of the literature on Jewish exiles from Nazism in Britain and the United States has focused on what the Association of Jewish Refugees once called the 'ordinary refugee'. There has been a bias towards those who have made major scientific, industrial, academic and cultural 'contributions', but scant attention given to the experiences of the 'humble majority'.[80] Such elitism has brought with it a gender distortion and it is not surprising therefore that the experiences of 20,000 Jewish women who came to Britain as domestics and achieved so much have been ignored. The omission is an important one in terms of the internal history of Jewish refugees from Nazism. It also is a vital feature of the response of the liberal democracies to the Jewish plight in the 1930s and the reactions of ordinary people to this crisis.

VII

Of all the democracies, Britain alone had a specific scheme of rescue for the Jews through domestic service. In Holland of some 1,245 individuals registered with the Dutch Jewish refugee organization in July 1933, only 66 or just over 5 per cent were female servants. The freedom from restrictions on this occupation, the tradition of such immigration in Dutch society and proximity made domestic work a likely avenue of escape from Germany. Nevertheless, Jewish immigration to the Netherlands in the 1930s was heavily male-dominated. Holland was seen, and played an important role, as a first refuge from Germany. It was essentially a staging post for later re-emigration. These factors may explain why many more female refugees would entered Britain as domestics than Holland.[81]

Elsewhere in Europe a few Jewish refugees found casual work in France as domestics. A scheme was also outlined by the Domestic Bureau at Bloomsbury House in July 1939 to send 50 Jewish girls to work in Australia as domestics. The tiny numbers involved only serve to highlight the massive nature of what had taken place in Britain with regard to refugee servants.[82] Indeed the only other country which employed refugee Jews as domestics in any large numbers was the United States. Several thousand refugee women became, if only briefly, servants in American homes.

In the past, female domestics had been one of the largest groups entering American society. Between 1911 and 1915, over 12 per cent of all immigrants entering the United States were servants. By the 1930s, the percentage had halved and the absolute number declined much more dramatically. During and immediately after World War I, a major transformation occurred in American domestic service. Servants 'living in' were now a minority and day workers became the norm. This transformation (which was not mirrored in Britain) corresponded to the greater use of black women as domestics especially in the great northern cities. This reserve army of labour acted as a replacement for white women workers whose availability diminished due to the decline of European immigration after 1918.[83] As was the case in Britain, the number of domestics in the United States increased in the inter-war years but the demand for servants still remained unsatisfied. Refugees, on entering American society, found that one way of surviving economically was to embark on low-level manual work, including domestic service. The role of Selfhelp in this process has been briefly referred to. The attitude of this organization to domestic employment, which was run by refugees for refugees, reveals important differences to the British case. In Britain the refugee women were allowed entry on condition that they stayed in domestic service. The refugee organizations tried to ensure that this fixed occupational status was kept in place for as long as was possible. In the United States, refugees became servants on a more voluntary basis. Moreover, the idea of Selfhelp, which placed hundreds of men and women in positions, was that it was a first step towards economic independence and establishing future careers and lives in the United States. In addition the greater flexibility of American domestic work after 1918, along with its emphasis on day work, benefited the refugees. Selfhelp saw domestic work as a means to an end, rather than the ultimate career of the refugees. One former member of Selfhelp describes how the process operated:

In no time we were able to place men and women as couples or women alone in households. We didn't degrade the people. We told them it would only be temporary, until the husband could find a position. We gave them a very quick briefing on what was expected of them. . . . We [told] people who were good housewives if they [started] in a household that it didn't mean they would be a houseworker forever.[84]

Contemporary American surveys suggest that less than one-third of refugee women initially engaged in paid housework. It is also clear that the time spent in service was far shorter than in Britain. In the United States female refugees were not restricted by the government to this occupation alone. Moreover (and, again in contrast to Britain), American Jewish bodies associated with the refugees, such as the Council of Jewish Women, encouraged refugee women to retrain for other careers. It might be assumed that due to differences in class structure, attitudes toward domestic service would vary between Britain and the United States. Indeed some refugees in the United States were surprised at how 'domestic workers [were] treated [t]here as employees, not as servants'. One 49-year-old woman in San Francisco related how she

came from a background of ease and luxury. I never had to do my own housework, but was surrounded by servants. It was not easy for me to adjust to being a servant myself, but I adjusted to it very quickly. I felt very happy in all my jobs and everybody has treated me in a respectful manner. All my employers have made an effort to make me feel at home and I never had the feeling of being a servant.[85]

Nevertheless, brutal treatment of refugee domestics was not infrequent in the United States and social distinctions between mistress and maid were often maintained. One refugee went to her first job on Park Avenue in New York and 'almost fainted when they told her she had to use the back door'. Similarly to the situation in Britain, refugee women were keen to leave domestic work as soon as an alternative arose. By the outbreak of war in Europe there were few refugees in the United States still employed as servants.

The situation in Britain was only slightly less fluid than that in the United States. In the 1930s class considerations were of probably greater importance in the British treatment of refugee domestics than issues of ethnic/racial/national prejudice which were more important across the Atlantic. In both countries sympathy towards the Jewish women was comparatively rare. There were some in Britain, such as the actress Joyce Grenfell, who decided against having 'a foreigner. . . . There's something a bit un-cosy about a non-Aryan refugee in one's kitchen'. Others were more blatantly 'prejudiced indiscriminately against German-speaking persons.'[86] A minority in Britain actually preferred foreign domestics for cultural reasons or were motivated by sympathy in their employment of a Jewish maid. A journalist in London wrote in her diary in 1939 that the family's German refugee servant was 'damned inefficient'. Her mother insisted on keeping the woman because it was her 'contribution. We must do what we can'. Her mother was unusual in that she shared, in her daughter's words, 'class sympathies' with her foreign domestic, although 'her *English* feelings . . . oppose her to the foreigner'.[87] More normal in Britain before September 1939, was the experience of a domestic in Wimbledon where there was 'a neutrality between householders and servants employed by them, in other words to do with the class structure of society at that time and not to do with being foreign'. In both countries, however, status concerns ensured that the refugee domestics would generally be treated with a lack of respect and understanding of their terrible plight.[88]

After the outbreak of war, the situation changed rapidly in the British case as the refugee domestics faced first widespread sackings and then mass internment as suspect enemy aliens. Before that point, however, the predomination of class factors in Britain worked to the overall advantage of those trying to escape from Nazism. The desire to maintain the lifestyle associated with the employment of servants, as well as a genuine determination to help the Jews, enabled a scheme of rescue without parallel to be implemented at that time. The 20,000 Jewish women were treated in a variety of ways, including the extremes of sympathy and naked exploitation. The dominant response to the refugee domestics was, however, essentially one of ambivalence so, as one ex-servant recalls, 'we were given refuge but no security at all'.[89] Perceived national self-interest (which could include the desire to pursue a humanitarian cause) dominated British and other democratic responses on this and similar issues concerning the Jewish fate from 1933 to September 1939. The national framework was to become even more crucial as the liberal democracies confronted the persecution of the Jews during World War II.

Part II

World War II

4
Liberal Culture and the Contemporary Confrontation with the Destruction of European Jewry

The writer and former Austrian refugee Jakov Lind relates his encounters in London with left-liberal American exiles from McCarthyism in the 1950s:

As a new face in the group . . . I soon had a small audience crowded around me asking questions in sweet voices about my experiences in Holland and Germany during the war. I talked far too much, of course, but only while talking did I realize, and this maybe for the first time, that to those who were not there – and most of them had not even been in England which suffered the Blitz and rationing and similar misery – the truly unspeakable events will always remain unbelievable. (Did they really deport small sick children and old dying people from Amsterdam? And you really saw that with your own eyes?) Yes, that and a lot more than that. It all was fairly incredible and that too made sense.

In her study *The Holocaust in American Film*, Judith Doneson suggests that during World War II itself 'the Holocaust played little if any role in the lives of most Americans, Jew or gentile'. She adds that it was only the Allied films, newsreels and reports of the concentration camps liberated in spring 1945 'that brought the reality of the Holocaust to the attention of the [American] public'. This chapter will question the chronology of knowledge and understanding suggested by Doneson and will also analyse whether geography and war experience brought British as opposed to the American society any closer to 'the reality of the Holocaust'.[1]

World War II remains a focal point in British national memory and identity. It is 'that over-riding moment of national dignity and worth'. The later entry into the conflict of the United States and subsequent conflict in Vietnam has made World War II more problematic and less central to American mythology. Revealing imperial arrogance, and thereby neatly avoiding the contribution of its colonies, since 1945 the image has grown up of 'Britain Alone, fighting for democracy and freedom against totalitarianism'.[2] Nevertheless, there is a hesitant recognition of the role played by the United States in the anti-Nazi conflict. In his speech to the Conservative party conference in 1992 at a time when the relationship between Britain and Europe loomed large, the British Prime Minister referred to the

blood ties over many generations with our friends in America. We in this Party will preserve and strengthen our special relationship with the United States. It is long standing.

Tested in many battles. Reinforced by ties of kinship, language and shared values. Britain and America have stood side by side many times in many theatres of war against tyranny and oppression. And we always will.[3]

It is important to stress, however, that the mythologies that have surrounded Britain and the United States in relationship to World War II have not simply been created after the event. They began in the conflict itself and since then have been amended and augmented. As Angus Calder suggests, the war was constructed from below and above, especially during the blitz, as one 'of British or English moral pre-eminence, buttressed by British unity'. In the United States: 'The onset of World War II further stimulated the effort to honor figures from an American rather than an ethnic past. . . . The tolerance for ethnic symbols of any kind was abruptly suspended.'[4]

In June 1942, the United States' *Government Information Manual for the Motion Picture Industry* stressed the need to 'emphasize that this country is a melting pot'. It added that there were 'still groups in this country who are thinking only in terms of their particular group. Some citizens have not been made aware of the fact that this is a people's war, not a group war.' Using an example from the 'Cleveland Cultural Gardens Federation', John Bodnar reveals how this process operated in the 'development of the All-American Garden'. The Federation wished to show that in war the '"nationality groups" had an even greater right to be known as "100 percent Americans" because they had come . . . to escape "obnoxious things in foreign governments"'.[5] The war in both British and American societies would be interpreted and experienced through a combination of nationalism and belief in the superiority of liberal democracy to 'foreign' dictatorships. On an ideological level, it must be stressed, neither of the major partners in the Allies went to war with any clear ideological, as distinct from military, objectives. The fight against Nazism/the Axis and for democracy would remain loosely defined throughout the conflict. It was thus within these nationalistic, but liberal-inspired, frameworks that British and American society and culture confronted the attempted genocide of European Jewry during World War II.

I

It has been emphasized that the Nazi persecution of the Jews during the 1930s occurred quite openly and was reported accurately, if unevenly, throughout the Western world. Even so, strong ideological and cultural factors inhibited the comprehension of this information. There was confusion and doubt over the origins of Nazi antisemitism, and its severity and impact on the Jews of Greater Germany before the outbreak of World War II. After September 1939 all the previous impediments to understanding intensified and new restrictive factors came into play. For Britain throughout the war and the United States after December 1941, the persecution and eventual extermination of the Jews took place behind enemy lines. Accounts of murder and wholesale destruction could therefore be dismissed as 'war propaganda'. Moreover, during the war the Allied nations and those under Nazi control inhabited different moral universes. Information about the crimes committed against the Jews in the latter was received with varying time lags in the former. The rate at which that information was assimilated greatly varied, for example, between Britain and the United States (although both exhibited important common tendencies). Both countries had their own chronologies connecting them to the Holocaust during the war.

The danger of accepting too readily the incomprehensibility of the Holocaust has already been examined. The question of 'why' may indeed be beyond human understanding both now and in the future. Nevertheless, some of the more mundane issues of 'how' have already become mythologized. Historians and others have thrown up their hands in despair at problems, which although highly complex, can still be teased out by using previously neglected approaches. One area in which such tendencies are already apparent as its historiography develops is that of the Allies and their knowledge of the Jewish fate in the war. This has become an important battle ground in the subject of the Allies and the Jews of Europe more generally. If nothing was known, or if the information available was misinterpreted, then the alleged lack of response to the Jewish catastrophe can be explained without need for further soul-searching. Alternatively, if the information was available and was more or less assimilated, other explanations have to be found for the 'abandonment of the Jews'.

Robert Ross asks: 'Who in America knew about the Final Solution?' His answer is clear: 'American Protestants knew. They gave money, offered prayers, wrote words of sympathy, and passed resolutions condemning Hitler, the Nazis, and anti-Semitism of the extreme form practised by the Nazis.' He concludes that 'Protestant Christians in America, based on reports published in the American Protestant press, could not have said then and cannot say now that they did not know'. Opinion poll material for the United States, which will be examined later, casts doubt on Ross's sweeping statements. It will become clear that the understanding and impact of the Holocaust on American society is more complicated than either of the extremes – total awareness, suggested by Ross, or the lack of impact, posited by Doneson.[6]

In the early historiography on the Allies and the Holocaust, a certain naiveté prevailed. Arthur Morse's study of American and British 'indifference' to the Jewish plight in the war assumed full knowledge of the changes in, and impact of, Nazi policies towards the Jews. A few years earlier, in 1964, Andrew Sharf published what we have already seen was the first major research into Allied knowledge of the Holocaust. Although suggesting that the British press 'knew well and printed accurately exactly what was happening', Sharf acknowledged that there was 'an inveterate British inability to grasp imaginatively what could happen on the continent of Europe'. He concluded that while antipathy towards the Jews at home played a role in this process and was more significant than any shortage of information, more important was 'the psychological commonplace that, with the best will in the world, it is hard to grasp the meaning of suffering wholly outside one's immediate experience and for which, moreover, there is very little historical precedent'.[7] Walter Laqueur, among others, further developed the approach started by Sharf, asking the essential question with regard to the Allies and the news of the Holocaust: 'what is the meaning of "to know" and "to believe"?' The dichotomy between the two is a crucial one. It has been taken on board in such a strident account as that of Robert Ross, who is forced to acknowledge that 'even in knowing, Protestant Christians in America did not seem to understand or grasp fully the enormity of the crime being committed against the Jews'.[8] Yet in the increasingly sophisticated literature on the Allies and their knowledge of the Holocaust, little or no work has been carried out on the reception of the information among the public in the liberal democracies. Walter Laqueur, particularly, has stressed that 'It is important to know how widely the information was distributed and whether it was read and accepted'. He has acknowledged that this is 'usually more difficult to document'. Nevertheless, Laqueur from partial evidence (mainly confined to state officials in the British and American governments) makes some important observations:

the fact that some information has been mentioned once or even a hundred times in secret reports or in mass circulation newspapers does not necessarily mean that it has been accepted and understood. Big figures become statistics, and statistics have no psychological impact. Some thought that the news about the Jewish tragedy was exaggerated, others did not doubt the information but had different priorities and preoccupations.

Laqueur followed Sharf not only in acknowledging that some could not accept the information because of their own antisemitic impulses, but also in suggesting that psychological factors were ultimately more important in the assimilation process. There is, therefore, a rather unsatisfying and mystifying tendency present when Laqueur concludes that 'when the veracity of the information becomes incontrovertible, continued resistance to it becomes almost inexplicable'.[9] In this study, greater attention will be paid to specific cultural factors and how they combined with more general psychological processes. By such a broader approach and through examining the responses and reactions of 'ordinary people', it is hoped to offer a more sophisticated (but less obscurantist) view of the manner in which the Holocaust was experienced in liberal democratic culture during World War II.

II

In late October 1939, the British government published a White Paper on German Atrocities. All the details of the White Paper referred to the pre-war period yet, in terms of material on the Jews and the reception to it, the document set a pattern in Britain and to some extent the United States for (with one major exception) the rest of the war. First, the British government, concerned about a possible counter-productive impact, wished to avoid, where possible, 'atrocity' propaganda. It was only goaded into the White Paper by Nazi accusations about *British* concentration camps during the Boer War. Second, the government was unhappy using stories involving Jews. This was partly because some British officials distrusted Jewish victims, 'who are not entirely reliable witnesses', but mainly a result of the British government's reluctance to identify in any direct way with the Jewish plight or to somehow connect the British war effort with the protection of the Jews.[10] In December 1939, in a private letter, the British Foreign Secretary, Lord Halifax, was willing to write to the Zionist leader Chaim Weizmann that

So far as this country is concerned, we are putting our whole energy into a life-and-death struggle with Nazi Germany, the persecutor of Jewry in Central Europe, and by ridding Europe of the present German regime we hope to render a supreme service to the Jewish people.[11]

This, however, was far from an explicit war aim of the British government; it would be a by-product of victory and not the first reason for fighting. Furthermore, only on one occasion, in December 1942, would British or American official and semi-official propaganda stress the sufferings of the Jews in particular under the Nazi regime. As will emerge, such policy was deliberate and was by no means an accidental oversight. But public reactions to the October 1939 White Paper indicate that state policy in this area cannot be treated in isolation. Indeed it is essential to take seriously the interrelationship between official Allied information concerning Nazi atrocities and popular opinion in the democracies.

The White Paper received considerable publicity on both sides of the Atlantic. In Britain the queues and orders for it might suggest it had a degree of success. Sales levels apart, however, the document was seen by the British government as another failed venture in terms of its official information and propaganda at the start of the war. A month earlier, the disastrous Ministry of Information poster campaign, 'Your Courage, Your Cheerfulness, Your Resolution, Will Bring Us Victory', had backfired and actually emphasized the distance between state and public at the beginning of the conflict.[12] Responses to the White Paper reveal that the British public again believed they were being manipulated by the government. Official explanations that the material had been suppressed until the start of the war were dismissed as

Absolute . . . and perfect rot.

I now feel that a stronger and less grandmotherly government would have had the honesty to publish the account in peace-time, while a more honourable government would have refrained from doing so in war.

All these details [concerning the German concentration camps] were known last September and yet we signed at Munich. This is the limit of hypocrisy unless it is more sinister and is the beginning of a hate campaign.

I hate the inconsistency of policy, that kept it all quiet while we were busy buying off the Nazis' Western threats at the expense of Austria, Czechoslovakia, the Ukraine, etc, & now brings out the story full-blast with exclamations of righteous horror.

With regard to the [White Paper] on seeing this I thought [to] myself 'How come the atrocity stories'. This opinion was shared by my sister who said she supposed people were not being sufficiently enthusiastic about the war, so the Government had to whip up some hate.[13]

Few, it should be emphasized, actually doubted the information contained in the White Paper (and those who did tended to be in the small minority actually sympathetic to the Nazi regime). Others referred back to the false atrocity stories of World War I which heightened public scepticism about any 'official' propaganda. Yet it was on such grounds that a university librarian from Leeds, while accepting the validity of the reports, still 'thought it was a thoroughly bad thing to publish it *as propaganda – as atrocity-stories*'.[14] The government later claimed that its first attempt at 'atrocity' propaganda had managed to produce the reverse of what had been intended. This was only partially true. On one level the White Paper did not lead to any sympathy towards Nazi Germany; indeed, quite the opposite was the case.[15] On another level, publication of the document did heighten concern among ordinary people that they were being taken advantage of and treated like children by the state. Also of great significance was the absence of any popular discussion about the atrocities being committed especially against the Jews. The state itself was largely responsible for this lacuna. It had decided to emphasize in

the first few documents [those] which are not so sensational as the Jewish ones but which show that perfectly good Aryans such as Niemoller and the German Catholics have also had to suffer.

Nevertheless, there was material in the White Paper on Jews in camps such as Buchenwald and also on the events of *Kristallnacht*. Yet it is significant that these elicited no specific comment from the public.[16]

Several clear tendencies did emerge from the White Paper, and these persisted for the rest of the war in Britain and the United States. First, all future Nazi crimes would be viewed through the prism of 'atrocities' and thus ran the risk in wartime of being dismissed as manipulative propaganda. Second, and crucially, Nazi atrocities would, in both British and American society, be connected to the German concentration camps of the late 1930s. There was some reluctance in both countries to accept the brutal reality of these camps before the war and the White Paper helped to dispel most lingering doubts.[17] Nevertheless, these concentration camps, located in Germany and Austria, were seen as the limit of Nazi inhumanity both in scope and geography. We have already seen how quickly the events of *Kristallnacht* passed from public memory in the liberal democracies. Rather than the mass-based, geographically dispersed and bloody pogrom of November 1938, it was the more obviously state controlled, centralized but less murderous brutality of the *1930s'* concentration camps that was to become a symbol of Nazi evil. In spring 1945, camps such as Buchenwald, Dachau and Belsen were liberated by the British and American troops. The disclosures from the camps in Germany/Austria were generally linked by the public in the two major democracies to what they believed was the situation in 1939. In the process, the possibility of different camps in other localities – of death factories in Poland such as Treblinka – thus bypassed most in Britain and the United States until well after the end of World War II.[18]

Third, the British and American governments were reluctant to emphasize any explicitly Jewish themes in their atrocity propaganda. Both believed that the Jews were problematic victims: reference to their persecution might not elicit popular sympathy in the democracies. The Permanent Under-Secretary at the Foreign Office, Sir Alexander Cadogan, thus defended the lack of prominence given to Jewish cases in the October 1939 White Paper on the grounds that he was 'not sure that sympathy with the Jews hasn't waned considerably during the last twelve months'. Similarly, in the summer of 1940, George Bernard Shaw was refused permission by the British government to broadcast on the Nazi persecution of the Jews for fear of upsetting public opinion, particularly that in the United States.[19] In 1941, the refusal to identify with the Jews as *specific* victims of the Nazis was made explicit by the British Ministry of Information in its infamous memorandum concerning 'horror stuff' which

must be used very sparingly and must deal always with treatment of indisputably innocent people. Not with violent opponents. And not with Jews.

A similar policy was followed in the United States after it entered the war. In 1943, a request from the American Jewish Congress to produce a film highlighting European Jewry's fate was met with the following response from the chief of the Bureau of Motion Pictures of the Office of War Information:

it might be unwise from the standpoint of the Jews themselves to have a picture dealing solely with Hitler's treatment of their people, but interest has been indicated in the possibility of a picture covering various groups that have been subject to the Nazi treatment. This of course would take in the Jews.[20]

The avoidance of the Jewish issue requires some explanation. The British government at the start of the war turned down a chance to expose the most brutal aspect of its enemy's policies. In 1943, when news of the horrific details involved in the implementation of the 'Final Solution' was well established, the American government similarly rejected such a propaganda opportunity. At the heart of both states' reluctance to stress Nazi antisemitism was the power of an exclusive nationalism. In the United States, the growth of pluralism in the 1930s was reversed after entry into the war and was replaced with a greater emphasis on Americanism. In Britain, there was no 'mainstream' model of diversity in operation before the war and the conflict reinforced the predominance of English nationalism. Ironically this occurred at a time when the country became, through various processes, blatantly mixed. A 1943 cartoon in a right-wing and xenophobic newspaper has 'the entirely imaginary meeting of two Englishmen'. It takes place in a London square packed with foreign soldiers and other war immigrants to Britain, whose origins were anything other than Anglo-Saxon.[21]

In the United States, 'Americanism' in the war led to the acceptance of most immigrants or former immigrants on condition that they conformed to a national norm. Britishness or Englishness was more exclusively defined and, potentially, had greater conservative tendencies. In both cases, however, such nationalism was tied to a powerful liberal discourse concerning the Jews. It has been shown for the 1930s how many in British and American society looked for a rational explanation of Nazi antisemitism based on an assumption that it was the result of Jewish difference. Antagonism was seen to be a natural reaction to the irritant of Jewish particularity. The *level* of Nazi antisemitism could not be explained by this classic liberal assimilationist theory, but few were willing to challenge their own adherence to it in the light of the Third Reich's persecution of the Jews. What is remarkable for the World War II period is how, in spite of all the anti-Jewish horrors exposed, the views of many in the democracies, both in the state hierarchy and the public, remained unchanged. Many government officials genuinely believed that to stress *Jewish* sufferings was against liberal, universalist principles. Their liberal perspective did not allow them to acknowledge that the Jewish case might indeed be unique. As Frank Roberts, a senior official in the Foreign Office stated as late as May 1944:

The Allies rather resent the suggestion that Jews *in particular* [my emphasis] have been more heroic or long-suffering than other nationals of occupied countries.

The writer and prominent commentator H. G. Wells had articulated the liberal opposition to Jewish particularity in the 1930s and in the war itself. His views on this matter were received positively by senior officials in the Foreign Office and Ministry of Information who stressed that the attitude of 'His Majesty's Government [is] that Jews must be treated as nationals of existing states'. To single out '"the Jew" as a separate category [would] perpetuate the very Nazi doctrine which we are determined to stamp out'.[22]

III

The net result of all these tendencies was that few on a popular level were aware that the war in its first months had already brought disaster to the Jews of Europe. In Britain, out of the several hundred people writing detailed war diaries for the social anthropology organization 'Mass-Observation', only three referred explicitly to the fate of the Jews in Poland. It is significant that for two of them, there was considerable reluctance to believe the news. A house-wife from Leeds heard an item on the BBC news that

the Poles were being very badly treated by the Germans, and the Polish Jews even worse. Up till now I have succeeded in believing that 80% of the stories of Nazi atrocities must be propaganda and exaggeration of the truth. But since reading in the U.S. 'Time' last week a report by an American photographer who had actually been in Poland during the war and taken photographs of some of the horror of the German destruction, I think differently.

A journalist from London registered the only other reaction to the fate of Polish Jewry based on information from the British media:

I read in the paper tonight that Jews being evacuated from 'German Poland' into 'Russian Poland' were thrown into the river if they couldn't pay the price demanded. It seems fantastic – the old epithet of barbarians seems the only one to use, if this is true.[23]

Otherwise the perception of German atrocities was confined to the concentration camps and would, even then, rarely refer to Jewish sufferings. In late 1939 and early 1940, both the British and American press reported the first major development of the Nazis 'resettlement' programme for the Jews, the Lublin plan. The movement of hundreds of thousands of Jews to an area which could not support them was, as *The Times* indicated, 'A Stony Road to Extermination'. Such reports, which incorporated the broadening geographical spread of Nazi antisemitism, made little impact on the general public. The coverage was not prominent, received little official backing and lacked a context.[24] Moreover, in the United States particularly, the massive and disastrous Jewish population transfer was still reported with reference to the Jews of Germany and Austria and to the earlier concentration camps. Press reports referred to the 'forced migration into a huge concentration camp in what was formerly Poland'. An American Jewish Committee publication forecasted that the likely outcome of the Nazi scheme to move up to two million Jews from Germany and German-dominated territories was 'a large concentration camp, where they would be doomed to degradation, misery, and death'. Indeed, a strategy seems to have developed among international Jewish leaders to explain the enormity of the Jewish plight across Europe by using this specific metaphor. In spring 1940, Nahum Goldmann, Chairman of the World Jewish Congress, stated how less than one million of the nine million Jews of Europe were leading 'normal lives'. Jews under Nazi rule were 'living in a big concentration camp'.[25]

For the first years of the war, it is far from clear whether the public in the democracies had understood either the intensification of Nazi antisemitism or its spread to Eastern Europe. Goldmann himself acknowledged that 'The full story of the tragedy of Poland has not yet been learned'. The fixation on Germany/Austria and on concentration camps was exposed in an article published in the *Buffalo Courier Express* in April 1940. Reacting to a report on the decline of German Jewry, it wondered how much was 'due to emigration and how much to death by slow torture in Nazi concentration camps'. A London journalist writing for Mass-Observation met one of her cousins, a Czech Jewish refugee whose mother and wife's relations were in Poland. Although a practising Christian, the Mass-Observer was aware of some of the problems facing her cousin's relatives and she added that 'his feelings can be imagined'. She concluded, however, that 'the state of Jews in Poland was nothing like that in the Reich, of course'.[26]

IV

The impact of this early news on the Jews of Britain and the United States was complex and varied. National Jewish papers in both countries reported all the information received from sources across Europe. The assimilation of this material, however, revealed the importance of the domestic agenda to both British and American Jews. A columnist in the *Zionist Review* commented at the start of 1940 that:

Speak to the average English Jew and he will agree that the Jews in what was once Poland are having an appalling time. It is questionable, however, whether one in a hundred here realise the full nature of the tragedy.[27]

At the start of the war, many Jews in the liberal democracies, particularly the refugees from the Third Reich, maintained an intimate connection to the events on the Continent. Lottie Gross, a young refugee in a hostel in Southport, wrote in her diary that

I could be perfectly happy if I had not to worry about my poor father, who is imprisoned since the outbreak of war. We do not even know where he is. I do hope with all my heart that the time is not too far when I can see my dear parents again . . .

In 1959 Werner Rosenstock of the Association of Jewish Refugees recalled how, 20 years earlier,

the letters we received in those late summer days from those we left behind were, apart from scanty and desperate Red Cross messages in the following two years, the last we heard from them.

The agony of the separation caused by the war was also shared by some Jews who had come from Eastern Europe at the turn of the century. In the collective autobiography of one such large family in the East End of London, a daughter recalls that 'The war brought terrible anxiety about our relatives in Europe – they were scattered in Belgium, France and, of course, Poland'. She adds that Red Cross messages soon stopped and that all other information about their relatives dried up. In her story of the war, and those of her ten brothers and sisters, experiences in the forces and other war work dominate. The fate of their relatives in Europe did not reappear as an issue until the end of the war.[28]

Two major factors appear to explain such developments. The first involved the pressures of living on the Home Front in Britain and, to a lesser extent, the United States. Shortages of goods, changes of occupation, concern over relatives in the forces and, in Britain, the very real danger of enemy attack on civilian targets proved difficult and often all-consuming. On top of these general difficulties, the Jews of both countries had to face the intensification of domestic antisemitism, which, in an atmosphere of global intolerance, further emphasized their marginality in society. The second factor was what Alex Grobman has called, with regard to American Jewry and the Jews of Europe, a 'feeling of impotence toward effecting any immediate change'. As early as summer 1940, the *Jewish Advocate* of Boston 'noted that as country after country came under Hitler's domination, American Jewry became incapable of further expression of pain'.[29] All these processes can be followed through the extensive diaries of Samuel Rich in Britain.

As we have already seen, Rich was a minor communal activist and teacher at the Jews Free School in London (he retired in 1938) who maintained links with prominent Jews across the world. He had expressed anguish throughout the 1930s at the plight of the Jews in Nazi Germany and was constantly aware of the marginality of Jews in the liberal democracies when campaigning on behalf of their persecuted co-religionists. In August 1939 he reported himself to be 'paralysed with fear of war'. He was relieved at the publication of the White Paper in October 1939 because 'at last they [the non-Jews] see that what happens *inside* Germany *is* the world's business'. In March 1940 his thoughts were still with the Jews of Europe. He believed that 'A negotiated peace w[oul]d seal the fate of the Jews, and of all other helpless groups in Europe'. By May, however, his thoughts had become obsessed by the fact that after the fall of the Low Countries, 'the invasion of England is possible'. In early June he recorded a conversation with a Jewish friend:

If Hitler comes to London? – we talked of euthanasia – gas-ovens etc. . . . *And*, if the French don't hold 'em now, it may happen soon.

Ten days later he added

France has surrendered! France! We are left *alone* to fight the beastly thing! . . . How long can *we* last? And the fate of English Jewry!

From this point, Rich became obsessed with the British war effort, the continuation of British Jewry and, most specifically, the survival of his own family. In July 1940 Stephen Wise, the American Jewish leader, called Rich. Wise related how he was going to Lisbon to become European boss of the World Jewish Congress. Rich added ruefully that 'They've [presumably American Jewry] no idea of the impossibility of European work *now*'. From that point on, the Jews of Europe rarely featured in Rich's prolific diary writing. This appears to have been a deliberate strategy as at times Rich actively sought to distance himself from the fate of persecuted Jewry which he seemed to think was beyond reach and doomed. His world view turned inwards and he became obsessed with the many real problems of life in wartime Britain. He was desperate to see the end of the war, and anxious that the late threat of the flying bomb raids on London would deprive him of the privilege. With the news of the German surrender he wrote in his diary 'So our family has survived [two] world wars – thank God!' Rich was by no means alone in such tendencies. In late 1942 the *Jewish Chronicle* commented on the discomfort that its readers reported on reading of the escalating persecution of European Jewry – of those who could not face the weekly stories of atrocities because it 'so harrowed their feelings'. Thereafter, for the sake of its audience, what was the leading Jewish newspaper in the democratic world gave less prominence to such stories.[30]

It is easy to criticize the Jews of the liberal democracies in the war, but the domestic pressures should not be minimized. This was particularly the case with British Jewry which, in addition to possessing neither the wealth nor the potential influence of its co-religionists in the United States, had also shouldered the impact of the war on the Home Front since September 1939. The commitment to maintain the refugees from Nazism had created an immense financial strain on the Jews of Britain. This was intensified due to the dislocation at the start of the war which left thousands of refugees unemployed and in need of support. Moreover, the evacuation of tens of thousands of Jewish children and adults caused great disruption to the maintenance of Jewish education and everyday life. On top of these problems, Jewish organizations (including alternative groups on the left), devoted scarce resources and time to combating antisemitism in Britain during the war. British Jewry during the conflict was a frightened community preoccupied with its own defence and the pressures to keep Jewish traditions alive in unfavourable circumstances.[31]

The distance from the events in Europe, but also the domination of a domestic agenda, was illustrated by a remarkable letter from the Chief Rabbi of the British Empire, Joseph Hertz, to the Archbishop of Canterbury in June 1942 (exactly at the point when the first news of the 'Final Solution' reached Britain and the United States). Hertz wrote with regard to religious dialogue, and the possibility of it leading to Jewish apostasy, that 'There are things that I fear more than pogroms'.[32] The persecution and possible total destruction of European Jewry led Hertz to take every care to maintain the future spiritual well-being of British Jewry. Attention had turned inwards to a situation in which Jewry seemed less powerless in its ability to influence events.

British Jewry had neither the moral energy, vision and self-confidence nor the financial resources to confront the horrors facing the Jews of Europe. Moreover, it was imbued with liberal values and did not want to emphasize the *specific* Jewish plight for fear of alienating itself from state and public. Highly visible protests on behalf of persecuted Jewry were rejected; these themselves might create antisemitism in Britain. There were important exceptions from groups on the religious and Zionist right and the political left who were not concerned about endangering the good name of British Jewry for the sake of deeply held principles. Nevertheless, the importance of those supporting alternative strategies should not be exaggerated. They were marginal within the organizational framework of British Jewry and generally remote from the power bases of society as a whole. In the United States, by 1942, although the American Jewish Committee shared a similar ideology to much of 'mainstream' British Jewry, alternative voices, especially those connected to the Revisionist Zionist movement, would, as we will see in the following chapters, play a more important role in pushing the American government into action on behalf of the persecuted Jews.[33]

V

In the first years of the war, therefore, the fate of the Jews of Europe, while not necessarily neglected, received little prominent attention in British and American societies outside the specific worlds of their Jewish minorities. Even here there was a distancing from and, at times, an avoidance of, the atrocities being committed in Europe. Neither the British nor the American governments gave any official lead to issues concerning the persecution of the Jews. In the media, reports of Jewish suffering continued but became less focused as other war news came to the fore. As Deborah Lipstadt suggests: 'Ironically, after September 1939 the importance the press accorded the story of the Jews' persecution diminished even further despite the fact that the treatment being meted out to them increased in severity'.[34] It is not surprising, therefore, that it became difficult for ordinary people in Britain and the United States to maintain an interest in, or an understanding of, European Jewry's situation in the early stages of the war.

In the autumn of 1940, Mass-Observation carried out an extensive survey on British attitudes towards 'nationalities', including the Jews. Its findings reveal the growing importance of domestic war issues in the interpretation of the fate of European Jewry as well as the continuing influence of a liberal ideology and its essential ambivalence towards the Jews. The ambivalence can be clearly located in the overall summary of the survey. Jews received by far the highest number of spontaneous comments in the category 'oppressed, wronged' but a much smaller percentage of mentions in terms of 'deserv[ing] sympathy, pity'. Moreover, they dominated the category 'a problem, embarrassment'. A more detailed investigation of the material used to generate these general conclusions reveals that there were still many who, while acknowledging that the Jews were a persecuted minority, believed that Jews were a malevolent force in society.[35]

A small number of the respondents were unambiguous in their sympathy for the Jews. Their treatment in Europe was 'most unfortunate. [They were] homeless and persecuted.' One, a young forestry commission worker in Norfolk, went further and stated that

The Jews are a great race and their sufferings under the [Third] Reich are quite sufficient indictment against the Hitlerian regime. Their deliverance is one of our chief war aims.

At the other extreme, a few commented that 'I still think they should be exterminated. This is one of the few things in which I agree with Hitler.' Most in the category of 'sharing Hitler's prejudices' added that they 'deplor[ed] his treatment of them, of course'. Those that 'intensely dislike[d] Hitler's methods of dealing with them' (in spite of Jews being 'a canker in the nation') revealed the dilemma in the liberal mind – how to explain the enormity of the anti-Jewish persecutions. Many in the survey continued to follow H. G. Wells and agreed with him that the Jews 'brought on their own problems by their failure to assimilate'. Another Mass-Observer was puzzled why there was antisemitism in Germany but added that the Jews in Britain were 'not very different'. Others struggled to reconcile their belief in Jewish power and influence in the world with the apparent ease with which the Nazis had carried out their persecution of the Jews in Germany. A miner in Yorkshire admitted to 'mixed feelings. [He] could never understand why world Jewry allowed Hitler to get away with it.' A teacher in Hertfordshire was 'puzzled why British and American Jews apparently take no steps to help the persecuted Jews'.[36]

The strains of the war were reflected in other responses. One woman in an evacuee reception area acknowledged that she had loathed antisemitism 'but recently felt antipathy' because of the behaviour of Jews coming in from the East End. Another added that she had 'become increasingly anti-Jewish, in spite of immense sympathy for them'. Perhaps most significant, however, were the responses which revealed that the persecution of the Jews had become just one out of many different foreign and domestic issues confronting those in British society. One observer commented how the Jews of Europe were no longer 'in the limelight now', a fact that another seemed to welcome: 'Must you? One had almost forgotten them, at any rate as a problem on their own.' Taking on board the misery of a persecuted people, both distant and unrelated, was a strain that few would welcome in addition to the difficulties already faced in wartime society. Avoidance of unpleasant stories was thus an understandable reaction. As a correspondent from Sheffield put it, with much honesty but more concern, that most of all

I would like not to believe the stories about the persecution of the Jews and the extermination of the Poles, but I think there is too much evidence not to believe.[37]

As early as April 1940, the liberal *Time and Tide* suggested that with all the military disasters, 'the fate of the German Jews has been forgotten'. Even this journal, which was generally sensitive to the Jewish cause, forgot the problems of East European Jewry.[38] At the end of 1940 and throughout 1941, the amount of evidence available in the democracies concerning the fate of the Jews in absolute terms (and even more so in relation to the escalation of murder), continued to decline. In the 'fateful months' of summer/autumn 1941, Nazi policy moved towards the implementation of the 'Final Solution'. The activities of the *Einsatzgruppen* in murdering hundreds of thousands of Jews in the area formerly controlled by the Soviet Union received very little prominent coverage in the West. In the United States, Deborah Lipstadt reports that 'Although by the fall of 1941 news of the slaying of Jews had begun to appear, the press generally focused far more attention on Jewish life in Germany and German-occupied Western Europe'. A similar pattern developed in Britain. In both countries, discussion of Jewish issues had moved from the international to the domestic, with complaints in Britain that the Jews were not pulling their weight in the war effort. It was not until the summer of 1942 that an accurate picture of the scale of the destruction since the invasion of the Soviet Union was recognized. It took even longer for it to be accepted that the killings were part of a plan for total destruction of the Jewish people.[39]

In January 1942, limited coverage was given in the democracies to a note from the Soviet Union on German atrocities. Following the pattern of the British White Paper, little attention was paid in the note to the Jews and, in Britain at least, these limited references made almost no impact on public perceptions. The British and American people were by now out of touch with the enormity and the geographical spread of the Nazi crime against the Jews.[40] Slowly, however, the limitations of knowledge and understanding would be challenged in 1942. More information became available about the mass killings perpetrated by the *Einsatzgruppen* in Eastern Europe. It reached a new level of authority in June 1942 when the *Daily Telegraph* published a report of the Jewish Labour *Bund* in Warsaw. The report referred to the mass shootings and liquidation of the ghettos but also to the development of gassing at Chelmno. The *Bund* account indicated that already 700,000 Polish Jews had been killed and stressed that the Nazis were intent on killing all the Jews in Europe. This information, along with other details from Poland, received widespread coverage in the British and American press in late June/early July 1942. At a press conference to publicize the report, the MP Sidney Silverman (who was chairman of the British Section of the World Jewish Congress) said that his organization 'felt that there had been something like a conspiracy of silence in the Press about this tragic situation of the Jews in Europe'. The *Bund* report was, however, published in a wide range of national and local newspapers across Britain and received some press attention in the United States. At this point, clear differences between the two Allied nations first emerged in assimilating the information from Europe. In Britain, Deborah Lipstadt suggests, the *Bund* report was covered in a prominent 'direct and forceful style' whereas the American press 'did not highlight this news and often omitted from its reports key pieces of information or burdened them with various disclaimers'.[41] Nevertheless, the news started the slow process of mobilizing Jews and their supporters on both sides of the Atlantic. Otherwise the new information about the intensification of persecution appears to have made only a limited impact on the public. Some of the press reported the *Bund* account in terms of a pogrom rather than a systematic programme of mass killing. Indeed, the ever-increasing news in the second half of 1942 of the scale of killing actually confirmed the view that atrocities in the form of *ad hoc* massacres were taking place rather than a deliberate *planned* extermination. Summer/autumn 1942 was the only period in the Allied camp when the destruction of *Polish* Jewry was emphasized. Just as the concept of atrocities committed against German Jews in the concentration camps was limited to past perceptions, so the murder of Polish Jewry was connected to the bloody, but essentially limited, pogroms of Eastern Europe at the turn of the century. There was, however, one essential difference. The memory of the destruction of Polish Jewry would be very brief in the liberal democracies whereas there was a general awareness that German Jewry was one of the chief targets of the Nazi regime. This process continued after the war and has only recently been challenged. As Zygmunt Bauman has stated: 'Both in the East and in the West, Eastern European Jews have been left, for decades, without spokesmen of their own'.[42]

VI

In August 1942, Gerhard Riegner, representative of the World Jewish Congress in Geneva, sent a telegram to Washington and London outlining the 'alarming report' he had received concerning a plan in which all the Jews in countries occupied or controlled by the Nazis would 'be exterminated at one blow to resolve once for all the Jewish Question in Europe'. David Allen in the Foreign Office was aware of all the deportations that had taken place and also the destruction in the Warsaw ghetto, yet he could not see that 'this rather wild story' confirmed that there was a policy to

'exterminate at one blow'. The German policy seems to be rather to eliminate 'useless mouths' but to use able bodied Jews as slave labour.[43]

More and more evidence came to the West in 1942, yet officials such as Allen were reluctant to accept that the anti-Jewish massacres were 'the result of a plan drawn up on a given date at Hitler's headquarters'. As we will see in the following chapter, in the autumn of 1942 pressure grew from the Polish government in exile and Jewish and pro-Jewish lobbyists for an Allied Declaration on the Nazi crimes committed against the Jews. The Foreign Office was opposed to such a move, not wishing to emphasize the particularity of the Jewish fate. If there was to be a Declaration, Allen believed that it should 'avoid specific reference to the *plan* of extermination'. Similarly, Eleanor Rathbone found that, in early December 1942, the Political Warfare Executive, responsible for British propaganda abroad, 'don't feel sufficiently satisfied that Hitler actually signed a decree for mass extermination'.[44]

Similar sentiments were expressed on a popular level in Britain. The widespread reports in the press on the atrocities committed in Poland, followed by the Allied Declaration in the middle of December 1942, created much anguish but there was disbelief that there could actually be a plan of extermination. As a clerk from Bury St Edmonds wrote: 'I quite believe many are getting massacred, but I can't understand *any* Government deliberately ordering it'. A minority thought the reports were part of a deliberate hate campaign or were the result of Jewish or Soviet invention – a theme with some resonance in pacifist and right-wing Catholic circles. The influence in such matters of the popular writer Douglas Reed (whose theories of what would now be called Holocaust denial became ever more paranoid in the war) also grew.[45] Yet, even if few in Britain realized the full horror of what was happening in Europe, there was still great awareness that the Jewish plight was dire. The British government's Home Intelligence reported at the end of December 1942 that the public's response towards the Jews could be summarized as 'Abroad – greatest sympathy; in England – general feeling that they badly want controlling'. Jews were blamed for the existence of antisemitism in Britain, yet this very rarely implied any support for Nazi techniques or an opposition to helping the Jews of Europe to escape. One Observer who admitted to 'a certain repugnance to Jews as a whole' added that

For the Jews abroad I have nothing but sympathy and see no reason why we should not welcome them and offer them asylum as long as they need it or wish for it.[46]

Individuals in Europe attempting to communicate the information about the fate of the Jews to those who seemed reluctant to believe it stressed that the latter needed to 'use [their] imagination'. In Britain the limitations of the liberal imagination made it hard for most to accept the reality of irrational facts such as the planned extermination of the Jews. Nevertheless, there was still widespread sympathy in Britain for the Jews of Europe at the beginning of 1943. Those in the United States in contrast seemed less concerned. The greater distance from the European continent, and the predominance of a domestic agenda in which Jews were seen to be a major problem at home, allied to less intensive press reporting (and discrediting of the information by mainstream publications such as the *Christian Century*), made the fate of the Jews less a matter of public concern at this point in time. In January 1943 less than half the Americans polled believed in the accuracy of reports that up to 2 million Jews had been killed. Over one-quarter believed the story was just a 'rumour'.[47] Doubts about the scale of the Jewish disaster were much deeper and longer-lasting in American than in British society. Nevertheless, news of the Holocaust peaked in Britain during December 1942 and January 1943. Thereafter, although there was much detail available, neither the government nor the media, as we will see, was anxious to give it much attention. The assimilation of the sudden rush of information at the end of 1942 has therefore a particular significance. How much impact did it have on the British public?

Aside from the significant but numerically small number who for ideological reasons totally denied the reality of the persecutions, others could be found in Britain who avoided 'the word "Jew" in the paper[s because] the news about [them] is pas[t] bearing'. The reluctance to confront the information, and the evasion of the process of 'knowing and believing', is revealed in the reactions of a left-wing electrician from Blackburn. Throughout early December 1942 he recorded headline after headline, mainly from the *Manchester Guardian* (which continued to provide by far the most comprehensive coverage of the persecutions in the democratic world outside the Jewish press), relating to the 'Plight of the Jews, [and] mass annihilation'. Yet it was not until 10 December that he reported any personal reaction:

It wasn't until I read in such details in the *Guardian* today that I realised the enormity of the crime against the Jews. It seems that the evidence is irrefutable.[48]

It thus took constant repetition of the Jewish plight, prominent reporting and the reinforcement of an official announcement to make any lasting impression. This occurred only once in the war, on either side of the Atlantic – at the end of 1942. As we will see, the Allied Declaration was seen as a mistake by both the British and American governments and attempts were made throughout 1943 to dampen down the issue and thus to remove its *presentness* from both war societies. There were those, such as Rathbone, who desperately tried to keep the fate of the Jews at the forefront of the public mind in 1943. Yet, even in Britain, without state support such campaigners on behalf of European Jewry found by the summer of 1943 that the public had become 'hardened to atrocities'. In November 1943 the MP and journalist Harold Nicolson believed that 'the Press was bored with atrocity stories'. Just a year after the Allied Declaration, there was evidence that accounts of destruction were being rejected in Britain as well as the United States as war propaganda. In the spring and summer of 1944, the quite blatant and open deportation and extermination of Hungarian Jewry to the death camps of Poland elicited little public or press interest in either country.[49]

On 23 July 1944, Majdanek camp, where several hundred thousand inmates died, including roughly 125,000 Jews, was exposed to the world by the Soviet Union. The disclosures received widespread attention in the Soviet press; it was not until 12 August that *The Times* reported the information, and even then little prominence was given. The BBC refused to give the camp any publicity. A report from the first British journalist to visit the camp, Alexander Werth, was rejected because 'they thought it was a Russian propaganda stunt'. The *Illustrated London News* did give the camp full photographic treatment, including pictures and details of the use of gas chambers. Nevertheless, continuing a pre-war tendency and one that would continue well after the end of the conflict, its extensive feature on 'The Most Terrible Example of Organised Cruelty in the History of Civilisation' did not mention the word 'Jew' once.[50] In January 1945, Soviet troops liberated Auschwitz but again the event received very little publicity in the West and it would take a long time before the full significance of this camp for Nazi crimes in general, and the destruction of European Jewry in particular, was realized. Neither liberation made a significant impact on American or British society at that time. One of the few Mass-Observers to comment on the Majdanek disclosures was, significantly, a foreign correspondent of a newspaper. She wrote later that 'last August when the reports of Lublin [the location of Majdanek] were issued there was no public stir'. She added that partly because the Soviets had liberated the camp 'people did not believe that Lublin was true, they thought it was propaganda'. Remarkably, in spite of all the new information available, public knowledge and awareness of the destruction of European Jewry actually declined in Britain between 1943 and the end of the war.[51]

VII

The key to this development was the determined and continued refusal of the British government to connect the plight of the Jews to the British war effort. Without that bond, it is not surprising that a boredom threshold was soon reached. The stories concerning the Jews lacked a context: there was no attempt to identify with the victims on a human level, and therefore the only appeal of the information was as 'atrocities'. Arthur Koestler, a leading writer who had arrived in Britain as a refugee in 1940, was one of the few people who met Jan Karski at the end of 1942. Karski, a non-Jewish Pole, went to Britain and the United States to give his eye-witness account of the 'Final Solution'. Koestler reproduced this information in a literary account, 'The Mixed Transport', which outlined the journey of a cattle wagon taking Jews to their death. He pointed out how three million Jews had already died, including deaths by the use of gas. Koestler published the story in a progressive literary magazine at the end of 1943 and was furious that it was rejected by some of its readers as 'atrocity propaganda'. He replied 'There is no excuse for you – for it is your duty to know and to be haunted by your knowledge.'[52]

Koestler was asking much of the public, yet there were some who were prepared in the liberal democracies to acknowledge the appalling reality of the Jewish plight and to let it become part of their moral universe. It was not an easy task, since it involved the employment of a progressive liberal framework which rejected exclusive nationalism and, instead, supported a pluralistic vision of society. They also accepted the existence and need to confront mass evil in the world. The diaries of a married couple, the Ws, provide us with insights into the minds of those rare individuals who were at least prepared to confront the reality of the events in Europe. Their moving testimony indicates the difficulty of acknowledging the horror and, ultimately, the powerlessness that acknowledgment produced given the reluctance of the liberal democratic states to involve themselves with the fate of the Jews.

When the news of the Warsaw ghetto rising was being reported in Britain, Mr W, a radio operator, reflected on the 'intellectual effort [needed] to produce a concrete picture' of what statements such as 'umpteen million Jews are believed to have died in Poland since 1939' meant in terms of the individuals involved. He added that the 'ghetto . . . does not somehow seem real, we know so little and none of the people in it have anything to make them actual to us'. He and his wife, a railway clerk, were willing to make that effort. In October 1944 she wrote in her diary that

I cannot write what I feel about all this evil. My soul cries out in distress. I am a Jew, a Pole, a Greek, I am all women who are tortured, all children who are hurt, all men who die in agony.

A month earlier, Mr W had given his reaction to the news concerning the Nazi death camps:

we hear that they are going to slaughter all the Poles in the concentration camps of Oswiecim & Warsaw. . . . When I first heard about such things, many years before the war, they threw me into a state of sick horror from which it took me as much as a day to recover. . . . Part of my intellect, which regards human life as supremely valuable & the only ultimate good, continually argues with me that I ought now to live perpetually in such a state . . . But of course it is impossible to live perpetually in contemplation of such things & remain sane. In practice I find I think of them comparatively little. For five minutes or so when I read an account in the newspapers, or my thoughts drift off to something else. Very occasionally, when I laugh, something inside me asks what right have you to laugh in a world where such things are? But it is only for a moment. No doubt it is inevitable and necessary. I tell myself however little I think of these things they have entered too deeply in my heart's core for me to be in any danger of really forgetting them. I hope I am not mistaken. For they appear to make very little impression on most people. One still meets some who try to make out that these stories are not true, that they are lies, or propaganda, or rumours. . . . Perhaps this is one of the greatest of problems for civilised life; how is one to combine a sense of universal responsibility with ordinary day-to-day sanity.[53]

Their concern was not merely theoretical. The W's family had been involved in the rescue of a refugee child before the war and they campaigned on behalf of persecuted Jewry during the conflict. In December 1942, rumours (not without strong foundation) circulated that the British government was refusing to allow the entry of a small number of Jewish refugee children because of concern that it would generate domestic hostility. Mr W commented 'Can it really be true that anti-Semitism in this country is too strong to allow of it?'[54] Those actively campaigning on behalf of the persecuted Jews had to face a government that lacked faith in the British public and which refused to accept a genuinely pluralistic vision of society. It is perhaps not surprising that many of the campaigners were outsiders in society. Mrs W stressed her Welshness in being able to confront the problems of other, marginal people. Harold Laski, Louis Golding and Victor Gollancz were on the fringes of the British Jewish community. Christians such as Blanche Dugdale, James Parkes, Bishop Bell, Harold Nicolson, Eleanor Rathbone and Storm Jameson were, as has been illustrated for the 1930s, in their own ways also unconventional figures. All accepted a vision of society that was essentially diverse and plural and were willing to challenge the nationalistic and monocultural liberalism of their government. To these exceptional individuals, the Holocaust was very present in their war experiences.[55]

At the other extreme there were those such as H. G. Wells, who, when meeting Jan Karski in December 1942, questioned without any expression of emotion 'why antisemitism emerges in every country the Jew resides in'. Few in the democracies would be so callous. Writing in February 1944, George Orwell suggested that the stories of the atrocities committed against the Jews 'bounce off consciences like peas off a steel helmet'. A year later, a senior figure in Foreign Office propaganda suggested that both the British and American people were 'still not as a whole willing to believe that German atrocities abroad and the Gestapo reign of terror at home, has been anything like what it is'.[56] Nevertheless, at points in the war the fate of the Jews *did* become of concern for those in the liberal democracies. That the Jewish plight was not placed more prominently in the minds of British and American societies during the war reflected the force of a combination of factors. It was partly a result of a process of avoidance. Facing the Jewish tragedy meant confronting mass human misery. A member of the Women's Land Army wrote in 1943 that 'The plight of Jews in Europe does not bear thinking about', and added that she believed there was no longer as much sympathy as there had been in 1938/9 because of general war weariness.[57] Primarily, however, the absence of consideration given to the persecuted Jews can be explained by the absence of any state initiatives on this matter. This in turn reflected the domination of a nationalistic and monolithic liberal framework in which there was no place for the particular fate of the Jews as a despised minority group. Only the efforts of a remarkable group of activists in both Britain and the United States kept the issue alive at all. Their isolation and marginality was intensified by the resistance of both the American and British governments to the publicity and campaigning efforts of the pro-Jewish groups.

Even with the growing scepticism over Nazi atrocities as the war came to its conclusion, there was a general awareness in both Britain and the United States that the Jews had suffered in the conflict. The problem for campaigners was that there was rarely a clear picture in people's minds about the changing nature and scope of the anti-Jewish persecutions. Sir Herbert Emerson was a rare British government official who realized, in December 1942, that

There can be no doubt that it is the policy of Germany literally to exterminate all Jews in Germany and Austria and the occupied countries in Europe, not only German and Austrian Jews but Jews of all nationality.

In contrast, at the same point in time John McNair, General Secretary of the Independent Labour Party, wrote in sympathy to the World Jewish Congress about the atrocities committed against the Jews. Revealing his ignorance of what was really happening, he added that 'Unfortunately this is no news to us as for the last four years we have realised that programs [sic] were continuing in savage brutality'. It is thus not surprising that in December 1944 a survey carried out in the United States found over three-quarters of a poll sample believed that the Germans had 'murdered many people in concentration camps' but put the figure killed at 100,000 or less.[58] The vagueness of such assumptions can be at least partly explained by the lack of specific and up-to-date information (outside detailed and unprominent press reports).

VIII

In Britain, only one film during the war dealt with the persecution of the Jews – *Mr Emmanuel*, which was based on the novel by the Anglo-Jewish writer, Louis Golding. Its publicity included the slogan that it was 'a daring picture on a daring subject' yet, as Ilan Avisar points out, the film only dealt with the plight of the Jews in Germany in 1938.[59] The film did not minimize Nazi cruelty, but it was released in 1944 when the scope of Nazi antisemitism had moved beyond the borders of Germany. Moreover, the film was at pains to stress the kindness of the liberal British nation and people in comparison to the Germans/Nazis: 'We in England don't look at Jews in this way'. The film also features a young Jewish refugee boy saved by escaping to England. Mr Emmanuel, a foreign-born but loyal British Jew, attempts to rescue the boy's mother (a non-Jew) from Germany. When Mr Emmanuel returns, the young boy 'gradually acquires English manners and customs . . . [with] scarcely a trace of a foreign accent'.[60]

More films dealing with Nazi persecutions were made during the war in the United States but they also reveal some of the tendencies present in *Mr Emmanuel*, particularly their underlying domestic agenda. Hollywood had a desire to show the evilness of the Nazi regime, but in important films such as *The Mortal Storm* (1940) and *So Ends Our Night* (1941) there were only muted references to Jewishness *per se* by portraying victims as 'non-Aryans'.[61] There was a desire, as we have seen, to avoid any concentration on the specific antisemitism of the Nazi regime. The other important parallel between American films and *Mr Emmanuel* was their focus on Germany/Austria and particularly on the Nazi concentration camps. Yet again, it was pre-war Nazi atrocities which continued to dominate such imagery, even after the 'Final Solution' had been put into operation and had been reported in the West. In this sense, as he later realized, Chaplin's *The Great Dictator* (1940) did a disservice not only by mocking the fascist leadership but also in presenting the German concentration camp as a ridiculous set-up, rather than a frightening indictment of man's capacity for evil. Only one film, *None Shall Escape* (1943), which was not a prestige film, managed to portray elements of mass murder in its presentation of Nazi horror.[62]

The dilemmas facing film makers and their government watchdogs in Britain and the United States cannot be dismissed as minor factors. If Golding wished to show Jews and refugees as loyally British, it can partly be explained by reference to other contemporary representations. Refugees in many popular British novels, films and plays of the time were shown as dangerous subversives, dirty and untrustworthy. In both Britain and the United States, plays and films were written during the war which presented the Jews as military heroes and as patriots attempting to counter the widespread image of Jews as war shirkers. That time and money was spent on such apologetica reveals the power and fear of domestic antisemitism. There was not enough confidence, therefore, to produce the feature film exposing the horror of the 'Final Solution' demanded by the American Jewish Congress in 1943. Such unease was not totally misplaced – there were antisemitic disturbances in the cinemas of London when *Mr Emmanuel* was shown and similarly in New York and Boston with *None Shall Escape*. Moreover, audiences on both sides of the Atlantic became impatient with Chaplin's moralizing speech on the need for religious and racial tolerance at the end of *The Great Dictator*.[63]

It must be stressed that pictorial and filmic images of persecution made a far greater impact on the public than stories of anti-Jewish atrocities hidden in the inside pages of newspapers and journals. In this respect, the powerful cartoons of David Low and 'Vicky' in the British press during the war are remarkable both for their accuracy (including the images of Jews herded on cattle trains, queues, use of gas) and their isolation. It is significant that Low, as a New Zealander, and 'Vicky', a Hungarian Jewish refugee, were outsiders in British society. The influence of drama in the war was far less substantial. The one major exception was the pageant *We Will Never Die* (1943), which was scripted by the revisionist Zionist Ben Hecht and seen by over 100,000 Americans. *We Will Never Die* was intended as a memorial to the murdered Jews of Europe and outlined their extinction at the hands of the enemy as well as the more typical, defensive portrayal of Jewish contributions to civilization and the Allied war effort.[64]

In the theatre, performances of the ever-popular *Merchant of Venice* changed little to accommodate Hitler's persecution of the Jews. John Gross in his study of Shylock across the ages points out that

Ideally, it is true, one might have hoped for a shift of emphasis in productions of *The Merchant of Venice*, an oblique recognition that contemporary events had given the play frightening new overtones. But while such a thing was always possible, it was never very likely; and in the event, it was not to be.

In 1943, the British theatre critic James Redfern attacked 'Those humanitarian critics who have found in Shakespeare's *Merchant of Venice* an enlightened tract, particularly suitable for these times of antisemitism abroad'. To Redfern, they had 'let their feelings overrule their judgement'. Shylock was a villain, a bad Jew who should be portrayed as such. Redfern resented what he saw as the contemporary impossibility of decent men referring to bad Jews just because of 'The idiotic, base and wholesale persecution of Jews in our time'. He thus praised Frederick Valk's performance in London during 1943 because his uncompromising Shylock could never be viewed with sympathy. It was not irrelevant, one should add, that Valk was a refugee from Nazism who, like many fellow exiled actors, was forced to play unpleasant roles in film and theatre.[65]

In the general absence of cinematic and other popular representations of the changes in intensity and location of Nazi antisemitism, it is, therefore, not surprising that the full nature of the scale of the Jewish disaster in the war escaped most ordinary people in the democracies. When specific and recent information was presented, such as that by Arthur Koestler, doubts were expressed concerning authenticity. Harold Nicolson was one who was privy to much of the information concerning the destruction of East European Jewry reaching the West in 1942. He published some of this information in a leading British weekly magazine but was told by an irate reader that

As a propagandist, Mr Nicolson . . . stretches the bounds of human credulity in making the statement of 433,000 Warsaw Jews congregated in a ghetto behind a high wall. The figures are twice the number of the whole of the population of Warsaw, and I should like to see the wall enclosing nearly half a million people.

In actual fact, by the time Nicolson had published his account, much of the ghetto had already been liquidated. His readership, however, had difficulty relating their image of pre-war Poland to the reality of the situation just two years later. Christopher Browning has shown with brilliant clarity that

In mid-March of 1942, some 75 to 80 percent of all victims of the Holocaust were still alive, while some 20 to 25 percent had already perished. A mere eleven months later, in mid-February 1943, the situation was exactly the reverse. Some 75 to 80 percent of all Holocaust victims were already dead, and a mere 20 to 25 percent still clung to a precarious existence. At the core of the Holocaust was an intense eleven-month wave of mass murder. The center of gravity of this mass murder was Poland, where in March 1942, despite two and a half years of terrible hardship, deprivation and persecution, every major Jewish community was still intact; eleven months later, only remnants of Polish Jewry survived in a few rump ghettos and labor camps.[66]

Throughout this period, the Western world had difficulty in coming to terms with first the news of the *Einsatzgruppen* murders and then the destruction of Polish Jewry. A major discordance of chronology and location took place between comprehension in the liberal democracies and the Jewish reality in Eastern Europe. It was for this reason that both the British and American public had less difficulty in accepting the reality of the images coming out of the liberated *western* camps in 1945. In location, and sometimes even in name, these concentration camps could be seen as part of a continuum, however horrific they had become, with the Nazi atrocities of the 1930s *and* their cultural representation in the war. The heart of the Holocaust, the crucial period between summer 1941 and summer 1944, in spite of the often detailed information available, had yet to be assimilated.

It has been necessary to highlight the complex ideological and cultural processes through which the destruction of European Jewry was channelled in the Western democratic world. Such lack of comprehension can be partly explained by the enormity of the crime committed and the lack of a precedent. Nevertheless, other issues were involved in the confusion and lack of understanding about the Jewish plight. First, the importance within liberal ideology of playing down Jewish particularity and the concomitant tendency to view antisemitism as a response to Jewish separatism should not be minimized. Second, the limitations imposed by the power of exclusive American and British national frameworks in contemporary perceptions of the war were also crucial. These factors combined but did not stop some individuals in both democracies identifying and campaigning on behalf of European Jewry throughout the conflict. More often, however, although the antisemitism of some (particularly in the United States) hindered any such bonding, *ambivalent* views predominated in the liberal world. Many in Britain at least, while hazy about the full scope of the Jewish disaster and antipathetic to some if not all Jews at home, were still sympathetic to the persecuted Jews of Europe. A complex matrix developed, made up of partial understanding and chronological/geographical confusion; of sympathy, antisemitism and ambivalence towards the Jews; of state and public in interaction; and of the limitations imposed by national exclusivity and liberal universalism. It was out of such diverse and often contradictory tendencies that practical issues concerning the destruction of the Jews would be confronted in Britain and the United States.

5

From 'The Enemy Within' to 'This Bestial Policy of Cold-Blooded Extermination': Britain, the United States and the Jews, September 1939 to December 1942

At the heart of the Allied responses towards the Jews of Europe during World War II was a battle between Britain and the United States over self-image. In essence, the governments of both countries resented the Nazi persecution of the Jews for genuine humanitarian reasons but also because it presented awkward questions regarding state policy. The two impulses possessed immense contradictory potential. It became crucial, however, for the British and American governments that they followed policies with regard to the Jews of Europe which at least *appeared* to be liberal in origin and execution. From September 1939 until December 1941, Britain wished to impress the American people of the moral rightness of its cause in the fight against Nazism. After the United States entered the war, the two countries were in competition with one another to prove which had the best liberal credentials. Yet, for almost the first half of the war the difficulty for those campaigning on behalf of persecuted Jewry was to push the issue onto a foreign policy rather than a domestic agenda.

Neither country possessed a clear channel through which pressure could be exerted on the government. The refugee organizations created in the 1930s were one obvious channel through which concern could be articulated, but these were divided both in terms of ideology and religion. There was also great diversity within the organized Jewish community in both British and American Jewry which militated against a coordinated approach. In the summer of 1938 an attempt was made to coordinate the rescue/relief activities of the

American Jewish Committee, the B'nai B'rith, the American Jewish Congress and the Jewish Labor Committee. While a general Jewish Council was formed, the ideological and bureaucratic barriers against a unified approach were too great. The American Jewish Congress left the Council in 1941 but the loose grouping had never functioned in any meaningful way before then.[1] With the outbreak of war in September 1939 there was simply no administrative structure in place in either country to launch a national campaign. Hundreds, if not thousands, of individuals had been involved in the rescue of refugees during the 1930s and perhaps millions of ordinary people in the liberal democracies were sympathetic to the Jewish plight in Europe. Yet the diffuse nature and organizational weakness of those favouring help and refuge was exposed during the summer of 1939 when the Wagner-Rogers Bill was defeated in the United States. There were positive responses to the Bill at the official hearings from church groups, organized labour and other secular bodies. A desperate attempt was made to bolster this support by the formation of the Non-Sectarian Committee for German Refugee Children. Government reluctance to challenge the restrictionist lobby was the crucial factor in the Bill's demise. Nevertheless, the prior lack of coordination of those supporting the entry of 20,000 refugee children made the defeat of the Wagner-Rogers Bill much easier and less embarrassing to the government.[2]

In Britain the centralization of the liberal refugee bodies, Christian and Jewish, at Bloomsbury House at least allowed greater standardization of responses, but the restraints imposed by its ideology and close links with the state limited the scope of any criticism it would level at the British government. Nevertheless, it was, if only indirectly, through contacts made at Bloomsbury House that one of the first organizations was formed in the war with the specific aim of helping the persecuted Jews of Europe. This grouping, which was eventually to become the Council of Christians and Jews, was not assembled until November 1941. It was therefore as late as two years after the start of the war before such a body consisting of Jews and non-Jews came into existence on either side of the Atlantic. It is a detail which will require some explanation.[3]

I

George Orwell, pondering the persistence and intensification of antisemitism in the modern world, wrote in 1944 that it was

very doubtful whether modern Europe cares enough for doctrinal questions to want to persecute people merely because they are not Christians.

Orwell was not alone in this analysis. Indeed, as late as 1988, the leading historian of Nazi Germany, Ian Kershaw, could point out that 'Given the self-evident importance of the subject, it is somewhat surprising how little sustained analysis has been undertaken of the stance taken by the Christian Churches toward the Jews, both inside and outside Germany, during the Nazi era'. Reviewing the first major collection of essays on the subject, published a year earlier, Kershaw stressed the lack of attention given to Eastern Europe and Poland in particular. Dealing with the one contribution devoted in the volume to the churches in the 'free world' (in this case England), Kershaw highlights how it was concerned 'with a completely different scenario and one in which the stance of the Churches was the for the most part a commendable (if more or less helpless one)'.[4] It will be necessary to query Kershaw on both counts. The attitude of the Churches in Britain (and also the United States) was far less straightforward. Moreover, their influence and overall importance in the determination of liberal democratic responses and reactions to the plight of European Jewry should not be minimized.

In spite of the increasing secularization of both British and American society as the twentieth century progressed, and the loss of faith after the horrors of World War I, Christianity was an essential ingredient of national identity in both countries. In Britain, with its established Church, Jewish groups were too marginal, small and financially weak to have much influence in government circles. The situation in the United States was similar, at least until the last stages of World War II, in that the Jews were too insecure and divided to use their greater numerical, monetary and political influence to much effect.[5]

In the late 1930s and early 1940s, pressure to help the Jews of Europe within the two liberal democracies of Britain and the United States required a partnership with the non-Jewish world. Christian, or Gentile, responses were thus of vital significance. It is no coincidence that the pressure to rescue refugee children in both Britain and the United States was led by church groups, although it is important to recognize that it was a movement inspired by the grass roots rather than being imposed from the top down. The centrality of the churches' role was shown in the hearings for the Wagner-Rogers Bill in which only one Jewish witness, Stephen Wise, was called on to speak in favour. The Non-Sectarian Committee, anxious to minimize the Jewishness of the debate and therefore marginalize antisemitic sentiment, used a series of Christians as witnesses. In terms of the secular response, it was the supporters of the Bill who persuaded organized labour to take part. As we have seen, the sincerity of the leaders of the AFL and CIO with regard to this child refugee scheme is not in question. Nevertheless, as was the case in Britain, there was little chance of the labour world providing an actual lead over the European Jewish crisis in general.[6]

Before *Kristallnacht*, the official responses of the churches in either country had been meagre. In July 1938 James Parkes wrote to Bishop Bell of Chichester complaining that British Christian action on behalf of the persecuted Jews had so far been 'superficial. . . . In addition, in so far as merely signing letters of protest, etc, is concerned, it enters the field somewhat late.' It had been reported in 1933 that the Archbishop of Canterbury, Cosmo Lang, had been unwilling to address a protest meeting concerning Nazi Germany and the Jews because 'the Government's foreign policy might be embarrassed'.[7] Other Christians wrote to Bell in 1938 suggesting that a group could be formed through

which Christians could show their sympathy and discover ways of cooperation with Jews in face of the tragic extension of antisemitism in Europe.

They added that in terms of issues such as antisemitism and 'blood and race' in general 'It is plain . . . that Christians in this country have underestimated both the present and the future perils of . . . Nazism'. Similarly it has been suggested that, for American Protestants at least, 'the plight of the Jews was never a dominant concern of the mainline denominations . . . the attention given to this matter before November 1938 was at best sporadic'.[8]

The pogrom undoubtedly increased Christian awareness and involvement in both countries concerning the plight of the Jews. Nevertheless, there was still an absence of a coherent framework through which such sentiment could be expressed. In spite of efforts made by the Dean of St Paul's and the Board of Deputies of British Jews in the late 1930s, James Parkes wrote in February 1940 that Jewish–Christian cooperation so far had 'rarely been effective, largely because it has neither been continuous nor coordinated'. To Parkes, 'Jewish–Christian relations [were] among the most vital responsibilities of the Church', but his views on such matters were isolated. The Secretary of the Board of Deputies of British Jews, A. Brotman, confirmed this situation at the start of 1940. He had contacted a group of leading churchmen, suggesting the formation of a new organization to be concerned with the menace of antisemitism. Brotman reported back that he was 'afraid there seemed to be little enthusiasm for it'.[9]

II

The possibilities of fresh initiatives at the start of the war on behalf of European Jewry were thus remote. The likelihood was made even more improbable as domestic opposition to the refugees already present in British and American society intensified. With the outbreak of war, the refugees' previous marginality increased as they became the potential 'enemy from within'. The fluidity of the status of the refugees in the liberal democracies during the 1930s has already been highlighted. In particular, the widespread categorization of the refugees as 'aliens', although legally correct (and emphasizing the fact that both Britain and the United States continued *immigration* policies in the 1930s), damaged both the image and self-worth of the exiles from Nazism. The danger of this label was recognized by the *Daily Herald* in a controversial editorial published before the war:

'Aliens.' Not a very nice word, but when you want to stir passion and fan race prejudice, then a fine word.

'Aliens.' They are coming to Britain 'in hordes'. They are taking the 'bread from our mouths'. They do not understand 'our British ways'. Let them see they can't 'sneak in here'. Out they go!

The *Daily Herald* realized that this was 'the way to stamp out pity and love and graciousness' and in response it tried to answer the question '"Aliens." What are they?':

They are human beings, to begin with. They are men and women, who have girls and boys, as we do. They are men and women who are made unhappy by the very things that make us unhappy, who find their happiness in the simple things that give us happiness.

Revealing the pressure operating in the liberal democracies to explain that persecution was not the refugees' fault, the editorial stressed that

They have done nothing that in this free country we would regard as either a legal offence or a moral crime. They are law-abiding people, courteous, patriotic, hard-working.

It concluded by emphasizing that 'above all that, they are men and women and children in distress, in the very kind of distress that British people themselves would find intolerably agonising'.[10]

The emotions and connotations behind the word were not lost on the refugees. In 1931 a Dutch academic in Britain had commented how people like himself

must consent to be called an 'alien' – *alienus*, an outsider, one who is different – instead of a 'foreigner' – one who comes from outside the country, a word which kindly ignores those notions of difference, of being other than English, which to the English means less-than-English, an inferior. 'Alien' dwells on quality, 'foreigner' only on locality.

The continuity in such attitudes, even against those who were victims of foreign oppression, was revealed in the comments of Alfred Perles who was in the Richborough refugee camp in Kent at the start of the war:

I do not like that word, *alien*; the word has a derogatory, almost cruel ring. I should have much preferred being called a stranger. But stranger was, perhaps, too vague a term; anybody from Yorkshire, or Dorset, would be a stranger in Kent, without being an alien. Why, then, couldn't we just be foreigners? It would have sounded less humiliating than alien.[11]

In both Britain and the United States opposition to the refugees focused on economic issues, but underneath such concerns was the more fundamental fear of the threat posed by the refugees to national identity. There were, however, subtle differences between the two countries. The exclusive framework of Englishness was such that all 'aliens' could be seen as essentially 'other'. In the United States, the animus was directed against aliens who were likely to engage in 'un-American' activities, essentially any form of radical politics. Although there was a reaction to the threat of Bolshevism in Britain after 1917, the 'Red Scare' was far more intensive and long-lasting in American society. The alien/Bolshevik connection was behind deportations of foreign Jews in Britain during the 1920s, but by the Nazi era was far less pronounced in society as a whole outside the more paranoid world of the security forces. MI5 had warned about the possibility of Nazi spies masquerading as Jewish refugees as early as 1938, but such worries made little impact on British state policy towards the Jews of Europe before the war. In contrast the charge of communism was levelled at prospective Jewish refugees repeatedly by American restrictionists in the late 1930s.[12]

At the start of the war, however, Britain effectively closed its doors to Jewish refugees by cancelling any visas previously granted to enemy nationals. It was assumed that anyone emigrating from German-controlled lands would have needed Nazi permission to leave and therefore was automatically suspect. In February 1940 Eleanor Rathbone wrote to the Home Secretary, John Anderson, asking the government to consider allowing in those with pre-war visas, especially individuals threatened with deportation to Lublin. Rathbone offered the assurances of the Czech Refugee Trust that the individuals concerned would not be a danger to the state. Anderson replied that it was his

duty as Home Secretary to regard this problem from a more objective point of view, and considerations of sympathy with the unfortunate persons . . . cannot be allowed to override considerations of what is best for the security of the country and for the public interest.

It is significant, however, that Anderson's decision was not simply taken in the interest of 'national security'. Anderson added that he did not think that it would be in the interests of the refugees themselves who are at present in this country to allow a further influx of refugees from territory under enemy jurisdiction. There [was] already considerable uneasiness about the number of aliens in this country, and fresh admissions would add to the public uneasiness and might do much to prejudice the position of refugees already here.

Such concerns were to be a common feature of British governmental responses to the Holocaust and ensured that Britain would not be a major place of refuge. Indeed, throughout the war Britain had no explicit refugee policy to help Jews to escape. Several thousand Jews may have entered Britain from the Continent during the conflict, but they came as a result of other movements, such as that of troops and civilians from Holland and France in the crisis months of spring 1940, rather than because of a deliberate rescue policy.[13] Yet, in the phoney war period, with the country effectively closed to new arrivals, the British government was at pains to prove that its treatment of 'enemy aliens', as the refugees from Nazism had then become known, was inspired by humanitarian sentiment. It was particularly anxious to impress the United States in such matters.

The role of the refugee organizations in the implementation of policy towards aliens was still crucial at the outbreak of war. Indeed one reason for the cancellation of visas after 3 September 1939 was because of, in the words of a senior Home Office official, 'the practical difficulties of making contact between the refugee in enemy territory and the refugee organizations in the United Kingdom which are likely to be almost insuperable'. The Home Office had become totally reliant on Bloomsbury House vetting the suitability of refugees abroad. There would have been no desire on behalf of the refugee organizations connected to Bloomsbury House to challenge the new ruling. The problems of maintaining the refugees already in Britain were great enough. At the start of the war these bodies were effectively bankrupt and relied on the British state to re-finance them through grants and loans. It prompted Sir Alexander Maxwell, Permanent Under-Secretary at the Home Office, to comment that the new financial arrangements would 'reverse the historic practice by which governments have borrowed money from the Jews and will introduce a new procedure by which the Government will lend some money to the Jews!'[14]

In spite of government annoyance at the cost involved to the British tax payer, power still rested with the refugee bodies at the start of the war as attempts were made to categorize the 'enemy aliens'. Tribunals were set up to classify the Germans and Austrians into various degrees of loyalty and trustworthiness. The information provided by Bloomsbury House about individual refugees was of great importance. A Home Office memorandum for the guidance of tribunals emphasized that

While care must be taken to check the information supplied by these representatives, full use should be made of such information as they can give and they should be given facilities to assist the tribunal.[15]

The contrast between the perception of the refugees in United States and Britain was exposed in these tribunals. Rather than alien radicalism, the key issue in the tribunals was a less clearly defined fear that Englishness was being undermined by the refugees. The contrast between tribunals for refugees under the liberal Bloomsbury House aegis and those sponsored by the Chief Rabbi's Emergency Council was plainly exposed in the autumn of 1939.

Richborough camp was the proudest exhibit of the Bloomsbury House approach. Its charges had been urged from the start to 'LEARN TO THINK ENGLISH' and had assimilated this approach. At the outbreak of war, a Richborough camp member wrote that

Great Britain's cause is our cause! Our fate is inextricably bound to the issue of England's fight. We must help the country which gave us a new home and helped us to start a new life.

He added, although it was probably unnecessary, that 'England's task is to preserve Justice and Freedom'. The setting up of tribunals, however, unnerved many at the camp. But the training provided by the refugee organizations had not been in vain. The English gentleman in charge of the tribunal was suitably impressed, exclaiming to one refugee that 'You are a friend!' Those in the Richborough camp, 'when trusting in Great Britain's hospitality and reasonableness . . . were right'.[16]

This was certainly the image that Britain wanted to put across to the Americans. An official in the Foreign Office stressed that the fact that the vast majority of refugees remained at liberty showed that 'internment *en masse* has not been our policy and we can state principles which will fully correspond with American ideas'. Sir Alexander Maxwell went further and even suggested that the BBC cover a tribunal at work

with a view to giving the public, and particularly the American public, some information as to the methods we are following in dealing with the enemy aliens in this country.[17]

It became essential to stress the difference in approach between Britain and the Nazi dictatorship and to justify British treatment of enemy aliens. For some refugees the tribunals became a chance to witness 'The fairness of the English' as well as an 'opportunity to prove themselves as loyal friends of Great Britain'. For others, the tribunals became an ordeal as they tried to prove their right to freedom. Their battle was as much concerned with culture as it was with security.[18]

In Stamford Hill a group of young Talmudic scholars had been placed in a hostel through the efforts of Solomon Schonfeld, Secretary of the Chief Rabbi's Emergency Council. Facing the Presiding Officer of Tribunal No. 8, it soon emerged that the refugees had not 'the slightest idea of anything English at all. They [were] living in a ghetto.' Had it not been for the assurances from an English Jew present at the tribunal as a liaison officer (who assured the tribunal chairman that 'they would be in future looked after and guided by the Jewish community'), all the refugees would have been interned. Attempts were made to mobilize the assimilationist wing of Anglo-Jewry to take action against the hostel and its refugee leader. In response, Neville Laski, the anti-Zionist President of the Board of Deputies of British Jews, wrote to the Chief Rabbi to complain about the hostel. Hertz was not impressed about the complaint and wrote back that he

[did not] regret and certainly need not apologise for, my having rescued these Yeshivah students from Nazi concentration camps. Nor was it my first duty to teach them either British geography or English games, but to enable them to *live*. And I have yet to learn that ignorance of British geography or of English games on the part of a poor hounded human being is sufficient reason for him being interned.

The liaison officer responded that Hertz was mistaken and that any aliens tribunal would be concerned

that the people whom it exempts from internment are not only beyond suspicion, but are likely to prove loyal citizens. Rabbinic studies alone in a German-ghetto atmosphere can achieve absolutely nothing to this end.

How can this loyalty be demanded of any body of young men who are taught nothing about English ways, English history, or the English outlook? If they are not to be trained in this loyalty from the very first week of their arrival, what chance have they of merely comprehending, let alone feeling, that love of England which is the veritable fountainhead of these traditions of Anglo-Jewry of which we English Jews are so proud and which is itself the strongest bulwark against the antisemitism in our midst?[19]

A chance was being offered to the refugees to show that they were making an effort to become British. Some of the tribunal magistrates were impressed by the 'normalized' refugees. The conditional acceptance of the liberal approach was exposed by a judge in charge of a tribunal in Kent. He referred to young Jewish men and women in a training farm and classified them as 'an outstanding element'. In spite of their traumatic background

they were full of hope, learning English and Hebrew and looking forward to settling on the land in Palestine. They were pictures of youthful health.

He added, however, the second half of his bifurcated image:

There could be no greater contrast than that between them and the sleek and voluble Jews too often seen and heard in law courts as litigants and witnesses.[20]

Some tribunals differentiated less between types of 'enemy aliens' and placed all their cases in 'B' category – of uncertain loyalty. Individual prejudices led to regional variation, but the significantly lower percentage of refugee domestic servants placed in 'C' category (loyalty unquestioned) – 64 per cent as against 90 per cent for the 'enemy aliens' as a whole – reveals that more general class/ethnic/gender prejudices were also at work. In fact by the second week of the war some 8,000 Jewish domestics had been sacked. Their removal was partly a result of the dislocation caused by the war but was mainly due to 'the unwillingness of British employers to continue to employ Germans'. The sackings and tribunal classifications emphasize again how the plight of these Jewish women had never been fully comprehended by large sections of the British public.[21]

III

Most refugees, 64,200 out of 71,600, were left both at liberty and without restrictions in the early part of the war. Their status as friendly 'enemy aliens' was bizarre, and in stark contrast to those in France: at this stage, some 15,000 German and Austrian refugees in France were rounded up and held in primitive *camps de concentration*.[22] For a minority of the refugees in Britain, however, the opportunity never arose to prove their loyalty to the tribunals. Several hundred individuals were immediately interned at the start of the war as a result of decisions taken by the security forces. Possibly half of those placed in detention were refugees and there is some evidence that this was a result of MI5 prejudice against foreign (especially Jewish) radicals/communists.[23] The potential for future, more widespread, prejudiced action was revealed in the first few months of the war but the refugees were as a whole left alone and not perceived as a security threat. Their major problem continued to be one of maintaining a livelihood in Britain. The war opened up new opportunities and the government began to ease some of the restrictions on refugee employment. Apart from a desire to meet the needs of the war economy, there was another element of self-interest in the government's desire to let the refugees work: unemployed, the refugees were a burden to the refugee organizations and, in wartime, to the state. Nevertheless, the government was aware that there was trade union and popular resistance in this area, especially as unemployment, although on the decline, persisted in the first months of the war. Therefore, Peake, the Parliamentary Under-Secretary at the Home Office wrote to Assheton, his equivalent in the Ministry of Labour, asking him to 'consider as sympathetically as possible how to reconcile the interests of the refugee organizations with the need for protecting British labour interests'. Government sensitivity more generally with regard to popular perceptions of British war aims was revealed by the response of the Ministry of Labour. Further relaxation of refugee employment was not advisable as

the greatest care must be exercised to prevent any impression getting about that, whilst our young men are going out to fight, their employment is being taken by young aliens who are neglecting to take the opportunity of volunteering.[24]

Economic fears, with their underlying ethnocentricism, dominated all other concerns about the refugees in the phoney war period in Britain. As late as the end of April 1940, only one in a hundred interviewed on the aliens question 'spontaneously suggested that refugees should be interned *en masse*'. From May to at least early July 1940, the situation reversed as Britain became engulfed in a 'Fifth Column' panic. The net result was that over 20,000, or roughly one-third of the refugees from Nazism, were interned in Britain. Several thousand more were deported to Australia and Canada.[25] The speedy reversal of a 'liberal policy' which had set out, in the words of the Home Secretary, Sir John Anderson, 'to avoid treating as enemies those who are friendly to the country which has offered them asylum', has bewildered many. By stressing that internment was a 'minor blot . . . a result of momentary panic', continuities and important impulses in British aliens policy have been neglected. There were, however, some exceptional individuals within British Jewry who suggested as early as July 1940 that

The only possible explanation of the action recently taken against the refugees . . . must be that the Government has yielded to the agitation of certain circles whose attitude to the victims of Nazi persecution has never been sympathetic.[26]

The government later defended its action on the grounds that internment was designed to protect the refugees from public animosity in the tense months of spring 1940 when Western Europe collapsed under the Nazi invasion. Opinion poll and other contemporary material would suggest that mass internment of 'enemy aliens', at least until July 1940, had widespread public support. Nevertheless, there is little evidence of violence or even potential violence aimed at the refugees in this period. Ironically the government's measures and pro-paganda merely legitimized and intensified public antipathy, rather than the reverse. The limited documentation available strongly suggests that mass internment was carried out through pressure from above and not below. A particular victim was the refugee domestic, described by one government figure as 'a menace to the safety of the country'; refugee servants represented the ultimate threat. They were foreign, female and inhabited that dangerous world below stairs.[27]

The policy of mass internment was implemented by the Swinton Committee, whose activities were not subject to public scrutiny. Its membership included individuals who were deeply hostile to the refugees. Other influential and publicly unaccountable bodies, such as MI5 and the Joint Intelligence Committee, also distrusted the Jewish exiles and played key roles in alien internment.[28] Power had been simply removed from the liberal-inspired Home Office and its close allies in Bloomsbury House.

IV

The British internment of aliens is an important episode with regard to the broader Allied confrontation with the plight of European Jewry. Although only a temporary development for most refugees from Nazism, internment, and the tribunal procedure before it, had exposed how the issue had become internalized as a *domestic* matter. The tribunals, largely representing the triumph of the liberal phase, were concerned to prove that at least some of the refugees, even if only as temporary guests, could become a worthwhile addition to the British war effort. Mass internment revealed that sections of the state were unhappy at the presence of refugees in Britain – even in the short term. The policy of deportation to the colonies was carried out with no public discussion, and would have continued had the practice not gone so hideously wrong. It has been remarked that the deportations, which would have rid Britain of many of its refugees, 'might have worked had every ship [sailing to the Dominions] not been plagued by scandal'. Hundreds drowned when one ship, *The Arandora Star*, was torpedoed. The refugees and their fellow Italian internees were subject to abuse and robbery by British troops in all the other voyages. The British captain of perhaps the worst example of this unpleasantness, *The Dunera*, described the Austrian and German Jews on board as 'subversive liars, demanding and arrogant'. The failure to comprehend just who these aliens were was brutally exposed with internment and deportation. Although camp life soon settled to a reasonable standard of decency in Britain and its colonies, the refugees were taken aback by the slur cast on their loyalty.[29]

Mass internment also revealed the limitations of those previously supporting the refugees. The Bloomsbury House organizations refused to challenge the overall government policy and in some ways welcomed the action as it both took away the expense of maintaining refugees at liberty and removed their charges from the public eye.[30] Refugee invisibility had been the aim of Bloomsbury House, even though it had not been envisaged that this objective would be fulfilled by the alien internment camps of the Isle of Man.

The ambivalence of the labour world towards the refugees was further exposed by internment in spring/summer 1940. The TUC's own newspaper, the *Daily Herald*, which had previously so eloquently warned about the dangers of viewing the refugees as 'aliens' rather than as human beings, now applauded the government's measures and proclaimed 'Country Saved From Fifth Column Stab'. Orwell suggested that behind such support was

the working-class line . . . 'What did they want to come here for?' Underlying this, a hangover from an earlier period, was a resentment against these foreigners who were supposedly taking Englishmen's jobs.[31]

Later, after the panic had died down, it should be added that the *Daily Herald* criticized the hardships caused by the government's indiscriminate measures. But the return of the TUC's individualist policy with regard to the exiles from Nazism (as well as its limited vision) was shown in July 1940 when the Secretary of its International Committee was willing only 'where he thought it useful and justifiable . . . [to] endeavour to obtain the release of some of [the refugees]'.[32]

Although slow and haphazard (and with an initial bias against the 4,000 women internees), the release procedure enabled many refugees to embark on work in the British war economy or enlist in the Pioneer forces. The internment process, which had involved prejudice against the German and Austrian Jewish domestics, effectively ended this most common form of refugee occupation. In May 1943, a survey of 134 female refugees in the Manchester area found only 14 in domestic service. Most had moved on to work in factories or offices which, although limited in terms of pay, at least allowed greater overall freedom. After July 1940 anti-alienism based on security fears became increasingly unimportant in Britain. This decline in concern coincided with the receding threat of invasion. With the establishment of full employment, even economic opposition to the refugees declined. By 1941 it was reported with regard to the TUC that 'All except two societies had agreed to take refugees into membership'. At the start of 1942, Orwell reported to the United States that 'Of late feelings have grown more friendly [towards refugees], partly because there is no longer a scramble for jobs, but partly, also . . . owing to personal contacts'.[33]

Almost as soon as mass internment had been completed, the British government embarked on a damage limitation exercise, emphasizing that the process had actually been carried out with the greatest of care and attention to liberal sensibilities. Internees, it suggested, were released at all possible speed and the favourable conditions in the camps were highlighted. Even those critical of government policy were encouraged to stress that 'no other country would have behaved with such consideration and sense of fairness and desire to do the proper thing as our own country'.[34] Yet again, there was an anxiety to avoid any criticism from the United States which would tarnish Britain's liberal image and thereby damage American support for the war effort. In 1941 hostile press comment in the United States about the British internment camps prompted the following concern from the Home Office:

In view of the vital importance of securing the sympathies of the United States . . . and the well-known susceptibility of the American public to propaganda of a sentimentalist nature, I should imagine that this policy would fall within the sphere of National Policy.[35]

V

Ironically, however, from the summer of 1940, fifth column panic had also taken control within both the American government and public. An opinion poll carried out in July 1940 suggested that over 70 per cent of Americans believed that the Germans had started to organize a fifth column in their country. The historian William Leuchtenberg suggests that, 'unable to agree on what to do about the enemy without, the nation hunted fifth-columnists within'.[36] What is striking about this panic was its indiscriminate nature. It is true that in Britain the *Sunday Dispatch*, at the heart of the invasion scare, warned that alien refugees, part of 'Hitler's fifth column', were 'in league with Berlin and Moscow'. But such hysterical conspiracy theories were relatively rare, certainly in comparison with the United States. With ever-growing intensity, such beliefs took root in American society in 1940. One of the leading adherents in government circles was Breckinridge Long, head of the Special War Problems Division of the State Department. In this position, as Richard Breitman and Alan Kraut suggest, 'Long sat at the vortex of the controversy over how much America ought to moderate its refugee policy in a humanitarian gesture toward European Jewry'.[37]

In June 1940 he wrote in his diary:

Discussed further restriction of immigration, including those who have visas. It is very apparent that the Germans are using visitor's visas to send agents and documents through the United States and are using their Consulates in the United States as headquarters for their nationals who enter on transit permits and who are carrying confidential documents.

Breitman and Kraut add that 'Between 1940 and America's entry into the war in 1941, Long opposed a liberalization of America's restrictive policies because he believed that with the newcomers would come spies and saboteurs'. As late as August 1942 Long was convinced that

The refugee problem is a thorny one – and there is plenty of criticism either way the decision lies. One side is dissatisfied in any case. But I weather that – and try to play it safe against any possible Fifth Column.[38]

Serious debate has subsequently taken place concerning whether Long's resistance to a refugee influx was motivated by antisemitism. It must be suggested that much of the discussion has been marred by a failure to define terms with sufficient clarity. David Wyman has suggested that Long was not 'overtly negative toward Jews simply because they were Jews', but this generalized statement needs to be made more specific. It is clear that Long was not a pathological antisemite who hated all Jews. Yet it does not follow from this that 'Long's stubborn embrace of law and regulation in the light of the Holocaust's reality was typical of a public servant wearing the blinders of bureaucratic responsibility' and had nothing to do with the *Jewishness* of the refugees concerned.[39] There is no doubting from Long's meetings with Jewish representatives, such as Stephen Wise, and his diary comments that Long was capable of real sympathy for persecuted Jews. In September 1942, on hearing of the deportation of French Jews, he wrote that 'The appeal for asylum is irresistible to any human instinct and the act of barbarity is appalling'. But he was also at pains to stress that 'We can not receive into our own midst *all* – or even a large fraction of the oppressed'. Two years earlier Long stressed that 'We have been generous – but there are limitations'.[40]

In fact Long revealed classic liberal tendencies with regard to the Jews of Europe and more generally. He was disgusted by Nazi atrocities against them but believed that to emphasize the persecution of the Jews, as was demanded by large sections of American Jewry in 1943, would 'produce a reaction against their interest'. He added that

One danger in it all is that their activities may lend color to the charges of Hitler that we are fighting this war on account of and at the instigation and direction of our Jewish citizens.

Long's liberalism was reflected in his commitment to individualism. He told the American Federation of Labor in 1944 that one of the most important reasons to liberate countries under Nazi occupation came out of 'our deep and abiding interest in the restoration of individual liberty'. On such grounds Long was thus genuinely anti-Nazi and also hostile to the idea of Jewish group solidarity. Nevertheless, his opposition to Jewish particularism did not preclude giving help to individual or carefully selected small groups of Jewish refugees, and this was offered with regard to religious and labour leaders under threat in Eastern Europe. Long's greatest animus was directed towards foreign radicals and subversives. East European Jews were just one of many groups whom he suspected of such tendencies. He agreed with a colleague that Russian and Polish Jews were 'lawless, scheming, defiant – and in many ways unassimilable' but believed that the same charges could be levelled at 'the lower level of all that Slav population of Eastern Europe and Western Asia'. Long's restrictionism was thus not specifically aimed at one group, but in considering his impact on American refugee policy from 1940 until 1943 his essential *ambivalence* with regard to the Jews needs to be taken into account.[41]

Unlike Britain, where the fear of alien subversion was all but dead by the end of 1940, the alleged menace of the fifth column intensified in American society throughout 1941. Its existence was hardly doubted. The AFL had warned in 1940 of the possible dangers to American civil liberties inherent in measures taken against aliens. A year later, its rival, the CIO, continued to campaign against

legislation in any form which seeks to set alien residents aside for special persecution. It does so in part because of our devotion in principle and in practice to the widest operation of democratic methods.

At the same point, however, the AFL warned of

new problems . . . [concerning] the admission into our borders of war refugees, as well as of infiltration of spies, propagandists, fifth columnists, and other persons engaged in activity inimical to the American form of government.[42]

It is not surprising that, in this atmosphere of suspicion, immigration figures to the United States from areas of persecution in Europe declined rapidly in 1941. As in Britain, attention had turned inwards and concentrated more on monitoring and controlling refugees at home than on rescuing them from abroad. There were few, before 1942, who were willing to question the overall policy of restrictionism, even in American Jewry.[43] In 1940, Friedrich Stamper, representing the German Trade Union delegation, spoke at the AFL annual convention of the help given to him and other activists in escaping from Southern France:

Through the brotherly help of your President William Green and the continuous assistance of the Jewish Labor Committee a group of . . . endangered labor people were able to come here. We were successful in leaving all that horrible misery behind us and in reaching the free shores of America.

I want to state here publicly that only by that marvelous and energetic continued action of our American brothers here, the lives of my friends, my family, and my own person were saved.

In its equivalent convention in 1940, the CIO also drew attention to the plight of 'thousands of our brother trade unionists [who] are trapped in concentration camps in France and are unable to return to their native lands because to do so would mean long imprisonment or death for them'.[44]

The limitations of this concern are clear. There was still a stress on individuals in concentration camps and attention was focused on the rescue of prominent labour leaders (Jewish and non-Jewish). David Dubinsky, the leader of the International Ladies Garment Workers Union and a prominent member of the Jewish Labor Committee, recalled a meeting with the Secretary of State, Cordell Hull, to discuss visas for persecuted people in 1940. Realizing that the list provided by the Jewish Labor Committee was 'all bigshots – political leaders, writers, artists', he screamed at the Committee's executive secretary 'Where are the plain people? Where are the tailors and the textile workers? Where is Hershel and Yonkel and Mordechai?' Dubinsky appears to have forgotten himself the existence of Sarahs and Rebeccas, but he had a point. Eventually through the efforts of the Jewish Labor Committee, orthodox Jewish bodies and the World Jewish Congress a list of some 1,200 names was presented by William Green to the State Department. Not all these people could be located but 800 visas were issued, which, with family, led to the rescue of 1,500 individuals.[45]

It was not until the horrifying news of the destruction of Polish Jewry reached the West in the summer of 1942 that the Jewish Labor Committee offered a serious challenge to the AFL's restrictionism. Its freedom to do so before then is questionable. At the 1940 convention, in which the AFL received praise for its rescue of labour leaders imprisoned in concentration camps, the Federation's Executive Council had supported restrictive alien naturalization measures 'Aimed at Communists, Bundists and others of that ilk'. President William Green stressed that his was 'an American institution'.[46] In the face of such insular and intolerant nationalism, there was little scope for the Jewish Labor Committee (which depended for its success on its close relationship with the AFL) to challenge the American labour movement's restrictionism and extend its agenda beyond the rescue of prominent Jewish labour leaders. The emphasis on internal matters with regard to 'aliens' was even present in the CIO. Its opposition to anti-alien legislation of 1940 and 1941 has been mentioned. It should be added, however, that it feared one possible result of these measures was that they would create a special class of workers which, because of the reprisals made possible through this legislation, cannot be expected to participate in the various organizations and activities of the labor movement. Indeed such legislation would tend to force alien workers into an anti-labor role as strikebreakers, and possibly, informers.

In such an atmosphere it is not surprising that no coordinated initiatives came out of the United States with regard to the Jews of Europe in 1941 and the start of 1942.[47] Indeed, it will be argued that, throughout 1942, perhaps the most murderous year of the Holocaust, it was Britain that was to become the focus of pressure to take action on behalf of the persecuted Jews.

VI

After the invasion panic in Britain, Hans Eysenck, a refugee from Germany, became a member of the Air Raid Precaution Service in London. There was some suspicion of him as an enemy alien. Eysenck had learnt to play cricket and his skill at this most English of games

posed a severe problem for them. 'This man has a slight foreign accent and is a spy; such people can't play cricket. However, he obviously *can* play cricket.' They finally arrived at the solution. They decided I must be Welsh! The Welsh have a funny accent, but they do play cricket. From then on, whenever we played some other post at cricket, they introduced me as their Welshman.

No better example could be found of George Mikes' theory that aliens, no matter how hard they tried, could become British 'but [they] can never become English' (Eysenck, it should be added, found himself abused as a Welsh-man!).[48] The poet and writer Stephen Spender was dismayed to find that one of his fellow dinner guests in the war, Sir Joseph Addison, formerly British Minister in Prague, was boasting at the table

that he had succeeded that day in preventing his Club (the Travellers) from electing as a member 'a dirty little Czech Jew' by threatening to resign.

Spender walked out but found himself ostracized. He later heard that Brendan Bracken, the Minister of Information, had said that Spender 'didn't have the right to walk out of a dinner party just because he didn't approve of the conversation'. Refugees were certainly not members of the 'club'.[49] They were also highly marginalized within the organized world of British Jewry. In spring 1940, an attempt was made to form an independent Refugee Liaison Group and thereby establish 'a permanent relation with the Anglo-Jewish community'. It fell apart with the chaos caused by internment but was revived a year later with the formation of the Association of Jewish Refugees (AJR). Inevitably much of its energy was taken up with securing

the removal of restrictions which prevent full utilisation of the services of those refugees in the common cause against Nazism, and for recognition that loyalty to this cause should be the guiding principle of release from internment.

By 1942 the AJR had 1,000 members and had links with various Jewish and international bodies, within which it raised questions concerning the status of European Jewry after the war. Compared even to the Selfhelp refugee organ-ization in the United States (which helped send relief to over 5,000 people in France during 1941), the AJR had only a limited influence. Nevertheless, the status of refugees from Nazism in British society more generally from the end of 1940 had recovered from its abyss in the spring and summer. Their efforts to help the war effort were more or less welcome and, although pockets of resistance still existed, few cared much either way about their presence as the conflict progressed, beyond allegations that they were profiteering as black marketeers.[50]

By the summer of 1941, most refugees had been released from internment but the panic had taken its toll on pro-Jewish activists. Leading campaigners, such as Eleanor Rathbone and Solomon Schonfeld, expended enormous energy throughout the second half of 1940 and early 1941 to obtain the release of refugees from the internment camps. The focus of attention in liberal circles, as George Orwell recognized in the spring of 1941, had moved from the issue of Nazi atrocities to the British measures taken against the refugees.[51] Only by the summer of 1941 could attention return to the Jews still in Europe. The issue was raised by W. W. Simpson to James Parkes in July 1941:

when one thinks of Hitler's anti-Jewish acts . . . the sum total of all that everybody has tried to do in this country seems very small indeed.

Efforts from this point on were made to re-activate the earlier attempts at a Christian–Jewish organization focusing on the Jewish catastrophe in Europe.[52] Even though, as we have seen, news of the Jewish fate was not prominent at this point in Britain, there was an awareness among a minority of Christians and Jews in Britain that the situation had deteriorated rapidly. A member of the International Hebrew–Christian Alliance thus wrote to the Bishop of Chi-chester in November 1941 warning that, unless Jewish–Christian cooperation was achieved soon, 'the real question is, will there be any Jews left in Europe to concern oneself about?'. Through the efforts made by Parkes and Simpson, and building on the 'close, friendly and fruitful cooperation that had developed in the Bloomsbury House experience', a conference of prominent British Jews and Christians was finally arranged in November 1941.[53]

At the conference, Joseph Hertz, the Chief Rabbi, emphasized with regard to combating antisemitism 'that Jews alone could do nothing'. Hertz added that he 'thought the press was callous in the matter of Jewish victims of the Nazis' and pointed to an article in *The Times* that day which underestimated the total number of killings. Nevertheless, although it was the intensification of antisemitism that forced the conference into existence, it was domestic issues that dominated its proceedings. The Dean of St Paul's stated that he was 'chiefly concerned with the situation in this country and perhaps did not take so wide a view of the problem [as] had been presented to the present meeting by . . . the Chief Rabbi'.[54] After several more months of delicate negotiations the Council of Christians and Jews (CCJ) was eventually formed in March 1942. The issue of antisemitism in Britain, and its Christian and Jewish roots, dominated the activities of this organization until well after the end of the war. The Nazi persecution of the Jews had prompted the formation of this organization against both Christian and Jewish unease about cooperation, but the concern about the global dangers of antisemitism perversely pushed its activities to concentrate on domestic matters. Nevertheless, in spite of its internal limitations, the CCJ was to become an important forum through which pressure on behalf of European Jewry could be voiced in Britain.[55]

One internal limitation within the CCJ was its reluctance to move away from a liberal ideology and emphasize the particularity of the Nazi antisemitism. It had a desire to emphasize universal principles common to Christianity and Judaism, which was seen to be important for the internal cohesion of the organization. Thus the preamble to the aims of the Council stressed that

the Nazi attack on Jewry has revealed that antisemitism is part of a general and comprehensive attack on Christianity and Judaism and on the ethical principles common to both religions which form the basis of the free national life of Great Britain.

In April 1942, at the second executive meeting of the CCJ, a model resolution was drawn up for church groups so that they could

place on record [their] increasing concern at the Nazi treatment of the Christian Church and of the Jewish community in Germany and German-occupied territories.[56]

Given the lack of response elsewhere this was an important initiative to mobilize popular opinion in Britain. The fate of European Jewry was still not prominent in British society during the first months of 1942 and such a resolution, although broadened to include Christians as well, at least put the issue back onto a domestic agenda. Within the Christian world in Britain, there was still resistance to accepting that the Jews had not somehow earned their persecution. A survey carried out just before the war had found those who believed that 'The Jews crucified Christ. They are now suffering for their actions.' Such views continued in the war. An article published in May 1941 on 'The Nazi Creed' in the *Christian News-Letter*, repeated the prevalent view of the 1930s. It was the 'irresponsible and conspicuous behaviour' of 'A small clique of profiteers, many of them Jews, [who] managed to settle down on the top platform of society' that had enabled Hitler to come to power. The editor of this liberal Christian journal welcomed the article as a 'masterly interpretation of the German situation'. He later reported that it was 'met with great appreciation from our members'.[57] Late in 1941, W. W. Simpson broadcasted on the BBC, warning his listeners about the evils of antisemitism at home and abroad. He received many letters of protest from Christians reminding him of the Jewish responsibility for the death of Jesus. There was thus a major battle waged within the CCJ and in the Christian community more generally concerning whether antisemitism was, or was not, the fault of Jews. Acceptance of James Parkes' belief that Christianity itself was responsible for the genesis and development of antisemitism, even in the modern world, would have to wait for another generation.[58]

It is perhaps not surprising, therefore, that the persecution of the Jews was not a prominent issue in the CCJ agenda in the summer of 1942, even though the devastating news of the destruction of Polish Jewry was growing daily. Yet, by December 1942, the level of information was such that the CCJ was stung into action. In spite of some misgivings, it decided to send a deputation to the Foreign Office. Part of the CCJ's anxiety came from a reluctance to accept the scale of the Jewish disaster. It was thus proposed to ask the Foreign Office to establish 'the authenticity of the reports which had been received from various sources as to the treatment meted out to Jews in Eastern Europe'. A CCJ delegate told the Foreign Office that 'there was a tendency even amongst the clergy to discount general statements about these atrocities'. Indeed, at this point, Selig Brodetsky, since 1940 the Zionist President of the Board of Deputies of British Jews, wrote that with the notable exception of the Archbishop of Canterbury he found a general spirit of disbelief within the CCJ itself.[59] The role of William Temple, Archbishop of Canterbury since 1942, was indeed unique. Although in poor health, it was through his tact and diplomatic skills that the CCJ was still in existence. Temple was deeply moved by the persecution of the Jews and had taken part in joint Jewish–Christian deputations on European Jewry as early as October 1942. At a meeting with the Home Secretary, Herbert Morrison, Temple and other Christians were horrified to hear that the risk of domestic antisemitism was stopping the possible rescue of a small number of French Jewish children. News of

Morrison's views further stimulated Christians in Britain to campaign against the negative response of their government.[60]

Although there were doubts and hesitations in the Christian response in late 1942, prominent leaders such as the Archbishops of Canterbury and Westminster played a central role in pushing the plight of European Jewry onto the national agenda. In late November 1942, Eleanor Rathbone asked her fellow Christian campaigner and leading Zionist Blanche Dugdale 'why the Jews [in Britain] did not do something demonstratively' in protest against the persecution of their brethren on the Continent. The point was raised at the executive committee of the Jewish Agency for Palestine. It was decided, however, that the best strategy was for Christians to raise the subject so that it would not be dismissed by the government as a matter only of Jewish self-interest. Thus, rather than the Jewish Lord Samuel, it was decided to ask Christian leaders to raise the subject in the House of Lords. It was for the same reason that the Jewish Agency approved of the Christian delegation going to the Foreign Office in December 1942.[61]

These tactics expose the defensive world view of British Jewry, including its mainstream Zionist wing, at this crucial point in time. Nevertheless, the Jewish assumptions on which such strategies were based were not totally without foundation. The British government *was* more susceptible to public pressure articulated through non-Jewish channels. In late December 1942, after the Allied Declaration, a senior Foreign Office official minuted, with regard to 'illegal' Jewish immigrants from Romania stranded in Turkey but making for Palestine, that

This is not the moment to raise objections of any kind to facilitate the escape of refugees, unless we are prepared to risk further archiepiscopal reproaches.

A few months later, at the time of the Bermuda conference on refugees, Richard Law, Parliamentary Under-Secretary at the Foreign Office, revealed the government's continued concern about pressure coming 'from an alliance of Jewish organizations and Archbishops' to help the Jews of Europe.[62]

Beyond the end of 1942, the role of national British Christian bodies in the publicizing of the Jewish plight declined. Even in the CCJ there were complaints as early as March 1943 that the organization was spending too long on the persecution of the Jews. Thereafter it spent little time or energy on the topic and concentrated on domestic antisemitism matters (including whether or not the allegations of Jewish black-marketeering were justified).[63] As was also the case in the United States, Christians were prominent among those who doubted the stories of Nazi persecution of the Jews. Nevertheless, those such as Archbishop Hinsley, Archbishop of Westminster, who, in public, parliament and in meetings in Whitehall, drew attention to 'the brutal persecution of the Jews', were crucial in the process of the issue becoming one of national significance in Britain at the end of 1942.[64] Although often responding to Jewish pressure, the sympathy of Christian leaders for the persecuted Jews, and their unhappiness at British government inaction, was absolutely genuine. But Christian action alone was not enough in this matter and the impetus in Britain during the second half of 1942 with regard to the Jews of Europe required an additional impulse.

VII

The Polish Bund report in June 1942 had been disseminated to the media by the British section of the World Jewish Congress. For the rest of 1942, with erratic support from the Polish government in exile, the British section was of central importance in both publicizing the fate of the Jews and in seeking the help of the Allied governments. At the British section press conference in June 1942, Sidney Silverman emphasized that the world was

witnessing an attack by the Axis, not upon the freedom of the people, not upon the country of a people – but an attack on the people themselves, designed expressly to exterminate them physically from the face of the earth. . . . The facts proved that the casualties already suffered by the Jewish people in Axis-controlled lands, far exceeded the casualties of any other people in any other war.[65]

For the next six months the British section concentrated its efforts almost solely on giving publicity to the information coming out of Eastern Europe. In autumn 1942 it attempted to do so by using its contacts within the British press, especially though liberal elements such as the *Manchester Guardian*. Convinced of the authority of the information, the British section released reports such as the 'Mass Slaughter of Jews in Europe', 'Nazis Carrying Out Policy of Extermination' and 'Seven Million Jews Threatened With Extinction', and highlighted how 'The Jews of Europe are now being systematically massacred by the hundreds of thousands, from one end of Europe to the other'.[66]

In early October 1942, the desperate urgency of the Jewish situation was reinforced by a further telegram from Gerhard Riegner in Geneva to Silverman and Easterman in the British section:

I yesterday had a new call of the same person who gave me the information on the general plan of extermination which I communicated to you by my special message some months ago. I was told anew that the whole plan is already in execution on a large scale and that action must be taken *immediately* if we want to save anything.

This and more detailed information that Hitler had 'ordered, planned and put into execution by organised mass murder the total extermination of the Jews in the European territories in his occupation' was passed on to the British government.[67] For a period of weeks no response to these reports was forthcoming from Whitehall or Westminster. In November 1942, pro-Jewish activists, such as James Parkes, despaired that it was

practically impossible to get proper attention for the consideration of a single issue like the Jewish question.

The continued silence of the Government in relation to the massacres is evidence of the strength in places of power of the reactionary forces – from whom we have nothing to hope.[68]

In early December, the British section intensified its activities and launched a campaign to get a United Nations' Declaration on the Jews. The Declaration, it hoped, would emphasize that those involved in the killing of Jews would be held personally responsible; it would call for an end to mass murder and the seeking out of refuge for those who could escape:

The Congress believes that such a Declaration, supported by similar expressions of opinion on the part of the Churches, Trade Unions and Co-Operative bodies, will be able to influence wide circles of the population in the occupied countries and especially in countries like Hungary, Roumania, Italy and Bulgaria, and save hundreds of thousands of Jewish lives.

The aim of the British section in seeking a Declaration was not to guarantee post-war punishment for the perpetrators: it was a matter 'not only for the conscience of the world but for the *consciousness* of all the civilised peoples – to arouse not only their sympathy – not even their protest – but to awaken them to action'. British parliament was to be asked to do its utmost to prevent further massacres and to help the surviving remnants to find a place of rescue and safety.[69]

In January 1943 the British section reported that the Allied Declaration of 17 December 1942 was 'the result of the most intense activity by the World Jewish Congress in London and Washington'.[70] There is no doubt that the British section in particular played a vital role in building up momentum in the first two weeks of December. Nevertheless, in spite of their efforts and the pressure from non-Jewish bodies in Britain, the British government still showed great reluctance to embark upon the Declaration. Ultimately it was the decisive action of the Polish government in exile that finally forced the Allied Declaration.

Relations between the Polish government in exile, its Jewish representatives and British Jewry had been strained since the arrival of the Poles in Britain from France during 1940. Accusations of Polish army antisemitism on the British mainland had led to tension on both sides. The Poles were embarrassed at the publicity the issue achieved in British society and the Jews believed that the evidence of discrimination and harassment of Jews in the army revealed that pre-war Polish antisemitism was alive and well.[71] Further disagreements occurred over accusations that Polish Jews were not receiving their fair share of relief distributions and over the treatment of Jews in the evacuation of Polish troops in the Soviet Union. In spite of all these problems, as David Engel has suggested, the Polish government in exile was reluctant to sever all relations with the Jews. It believed, perhaps alone outside Nazi circles, 'that world Jewry could exercise significant influence [in Polish–Allied–Soviet relations] if not for good, then certainly for ill'.[72] In World War I, individuals such as Chaim Weizmann had been able to use the myth of Jewish power to further the cause of Zionism. By World War II, Britain and other Allied nations realized that international Jewry had little real power and was unlikely to hinder the prosecution of the war effort against the Nazi regime. There was thus little scope to exploit Jewish bargaining in diplomacy. In a situation of general impotence, it is perhaps unsurprising that Jewish leaders in Britain and elsewhere were slow to realize the potential of the misguided beliefs of the Polish government in exile. Nevertheless, Polish obsession about Jewish influence was used advantageously in December 1942. The government in exile was unhappy about the limited attention given in Allied media and propaganda concerning atrocities committed against the Polish people by the Nazis. In the summer and autumn of 1942, it had itself given uneven publicity to the explicit fate of the Jews. Rather than sheer antisemitism, tactical considerations appear to have been at play in this matter. To the government in exile, the Jewish card had a special significance. As Engel concludes, it was 'Most likely they believed that Jewish suffering stood to arouse more sympathy in the West than the suffering of the Poles'.[73]

In November 1942, the Polish government in exile received the devastating information from Jan Karski outlining the implementation of the 'Final Solution'. Apart from considerations of diplomacy and an undoubted element of genuine distress and humanitarian impulse, pressure was placed on the exiled government by Jewish organizations to support rescue measures for the Jews. As a result, on 10 December, a note was sent to Anthony Eden, the Foreign Secretary, detailing the Nazis' extermination of the Jews and calling for a way 'of offering hope that Germany might be effectively restrained from continuing to apply her methods of mass execution'. The significance of this note was great. It was, as Engel suggests, 'the first time that any Allied government had undertaken to act as a spokesman for the Jews under Nazi rule'. He also adds that 'It led directly to the . . . joint declaration' of 17 December.[74] It must be suggested, however, that the decision to embark on the Declaration can only be understood as the culmination of pressure from *various* sources. A combination of Jewish, Christian and, finally, Polish campaigning eventually forced the British government to accept the Declaration (even though it stood against all its previous policies on this issue). For the first and only time in the war, the specific fate of the Jews in Nazi Europe was highlighted. As Alex Easterman of the British section wrote shortly after:

I do not know yet what practical results will emerge from the Declaration, but we are now heavily engaged in trying to evolve at least the schemes whereby Jewish lives can be saved. We are satisfied, however . . . that we have succeeded at long last in rousing the public conscience to the facts of the terrible situation of the Jewish people in Europe. That is something for which we must all be grateful. That also was not an easy job and there were times when we felt very disheartened at the lack of response to our efforts to get the facts into the public mind of Jews as well as non-Jews.

Another member of the British section believed that there was now a 'glimmer of hope that the awakening of opinion [would] result in practical measures of relief if only to a few'.[75]

In fact the Allied Declaration had been drawn up explicitly to avoid any promise of rescue. Anthony Eden in the House of Commons, responding to a question from Sidney Silverman, confirmed that

the German authorities, not content with denying to persons of Jewish race in all the territories over which their barbarous rule has been extended the most elementary human rights, are now carrying into effect Hitler's oft repeated intention to exterminate the Jewish people in Europe.

Having briefly described the transportation of Jews to Eastern Europe and the destruction of the ghettos, Eden suggested that 'The number of victims of these bloody cruelties is reckoned in many hundreds of thousands of entirely innocent men, women and children'. The Declaration concluded by stressing that the Allied governments

condemn in the strongest possible terms this bestial policy of cold-blooded extermination. They declare that such events can only strengthen the resolve of all freedom loving peoples to overthrow the barbarous Hitlerite tyranny. They re-affirm their solemn resolution to ensure that those responsible for these crimes shall not escape retribution, and to press on with the necessary practical measures to this end.

Later, Eden was asked if the Declaration could 'be followed up and consideration given to the possibility of rescuing such of the Jewish people as may
escape from these massacres'. Eden replied that he had 'doubts . . . whether
it would be useful' and the request from Eleanor Rathbone for a debate on
the Declaration was ignored.[76]

Rathbone had in fact prepared for such a debate on the fate of the Jews.
Her notes, however, survive with her own annotation that it was 'one of many
[speeches] not given on this question'. She had wanted to stress that 'it is not
enough to warn the enemy Governments. The warning may fall on deaf ears.'
She added that

Until a few weeks ago, there was a Conspiracy of Silence about this dreadful tragedy
– silence in the Press, silence in Parliament. *That must end.*[77]

Rathbone's frustration with the Allied governments intensified as she believed
that they were committed only to post-war retribution instead of immediate
rescue. But, unbeknown to Rathbone, the British government was starting to
recognize that the Allied Declaration, in spite of its lack of reference to practical
measures, had nevertheless placed it in a difficult situation. In September 1942,
there was discussion in the Foreign Office over the possibility of adverse
publicity if Britain refused to rescue Jewish children in Vichy France. It led
a senior official in the Foreign Office, A. W. G. Randall, to send a brief to
the Ministry of Information outlining what Britain had already done for the
refugees. Randall commented that

The dramatic publicity given to the plight of several thousand abandoned Jewish children
in France will make a completely negative policy on our part very difficult in the face
of public opinion here and the United States.[78]

Concern over the British government's liberal reputation at home and abroad
was even greater after the Declaration of December 1942 and the public outcry
that had greeted it. As another Foreign Office official minuted, this 'new
situation [could] only be met by a new policy, or modification of the present
one'. In response, a secret Cabinet 'Committee on the Reception and Accommodation of Jewish Refugees' was set up and held its first meeting on the last
day of 1942.[79] Until this point there was little disagreement between the British
and American government with regard to the Jews of Europe. But, had Britain
now changed the rules of the game?

6
The Rules of the Game: Britain, the United States and the Holocaust, 1943 to 1945

By the time of the Allied Declaration, most of Polish Jewry had been destroyed and the mass deportation of West European Jews had been in operation for six months. In the last few months of 1942, there was a growing awareness in the West that Polish Jews were being killed in the hundreds of thousands but, because 'the German attack on the Polish ghettos was not a gradual or incremental program stretched over a long period of time, but a veritable blitzkrieg', it is hardly surprising that few were aware of the immensity and thoroughness of the destruction that had already taken place. One contemporary who had very clearly understood the situation of European Jewry was Eleanor Rathbone. With the help of the publicist Victor Gollancz, Rathbone succeeded in altering the rules of the game through which first Britain and then the United States would confront the Jewish disaster in the last years of the war.[1]

Rathbone had wished to start her campaign in the House of Commons on the day of the Allied Declaration. The debate on the Declaration failed to materialize and her prepared speech remained unused. Her speech notes, however, reveal both her deep understanding of the Jewish plight at the end of 1942 and her proposed programme of rescue. Both aspects of the aborted speech are remarkable for their penetration and prophecy. Rathbone acknowledged that much of European Jewry had already been wiped out: 'The best we can do now will be too little and too late'. In fact roughly three-quarters of the eventual total of victims were dead at this stage. It was still essential, believed Rathbone, to see 'that even that little is not left undone'. In spite of all the confusion of information about the persecution of the Jews and the domination of other war news, Rathbone realized that it was the Balkan states which were to become crucial if any sizeable numbers of Jews were to be saved:

It should not be assumed that even Hitler's unwilling Allies – Hungary, Roumania, Bulgaria – cannot be influenced. In their treatment of their own Jews, these States have indeed a *Black Record*, especially Roumania. But by this time they must know in their hearts that the United Nations are going to win the War. They must be haunted by the fear of retribution. If the Voice of Christianity, of compassion for tortured humanity, appeals to them in vain – and there are men and women in every country to whom it will appeal – they may listen to a Voice which tell[s] them that before it is too late, they had better buy off some of the vengeance that will otherwise overtake them, by showing a *reluctance to participate* in this last and worst of Nazi crimes – the extermination of a whole people.

Rathbone, however, was determined to place the issue on the domestic agenda of the Allied nations. It was essential that those in Europe 'must be convinced that this is a matter about which we and our Allies *really care* – care passionately, care to the extent of being willing to make great efforts and sacrifices ourselves. *What have we done to convince them of that?*'[2]

Of critical importance to Rathbone was that the Allied response 'must not be only a War of Words. There must be Action.' Rathbone and her fellow campaigners were already bitter about the stance taken by the British government (and especially the Home Secretary, Herbert Morrison) with regard to the entry of Jewish refugees to Britain from the Continent in the autumn of 1942. She believed that a lead had to be given to other countries and wanted to 'implore the Home Secretary and the whole War cabinet to give immediate attention to this subject of practical proposals for rescue'. Having met official recalcitrance, Rathbone was now willing to play the only card left to the pro-Jewish campaigners – a popular campaign to embarrass the government and force action. Rathbone was aware that the government knew that the fate of, and possible help for, the Jews depended on 'arousing increasing concern in the public mind'.

At the end of 1942 and the start of 1943, Rathbone had faith in the British public:

It would be an insult indeed to suggest that there is anything to fear from anti-Semitic influences here. Anti-Semitism is an ugly infect[ious] disease, like scabies or leprosy, born of dirt. But ou[r] people, even the anti-Semites among them, are not so callous that they would rather let Jewish men and women and children be tortured to death than see them admitted here. Until recently they have been kept in ignorance of the terrible facts. They are not to blame if they seemed indifferent.

To Rathbone, the battles to win the war and to save the Jews were inseparable:

I suggested the other day, when the ringing of Church bells at Christmas was under discussion, that if the Church bells were considered . . . joy bells, it would be a mockery to ring them when the nation which gave us the Bible was in [the] course of extermination. Of course I do not really grudge the people their bells. They may bring joy to the children and the young. [B]ut for older people, if they have hearts and consciences, how can there b[e] joy?[3]

In this Rathbone and the British government were clearly far apart, hence Rathbone would have to wait five months in Parliament before she was able to put such views across. Yet both shared a common belief with regard to the Jews of Europe in fearing that the country's liberal reputation was at stake. Throughout the remainder of the war the government was at pains to show the generosity of Britain's record in offering help to the persecuted. Rathbone believed as early as December 1942 that the image was already tarnished, perhaps beyond repair:

If peace came to-morrow, we could not forget the millions for whom it would come too late, nor wash our hands from the stain of their blood.

For indeed, the responsibility does rest on us, though to a very different degree from that of the malefactor Nations. If before the War, we and the other nations had shown greater foresight and courage there would have been no War, and if our policy towards refugees had been less miserably cautious, selfish and unimaginative, thousands of those already dead or in danger of death, might be now free and happy, contributing from their rich store of talent and industry to the welfare of mankind.

There are those who believe that at least before the War, our policy towards refugees was generous. I do not share that belief.

Her bitterness towards government inertia notwithstanding, Rathbone acknowledged that 'the past is past' and concentrated her energies on those for whom rescue was still a possibility. She asked, 'What can we do ourselves as a Nation and in union with other nations? There should be *a concerted plan.*' On the same day as the Declaration, Rathbone published a more specific proposal, suggesting that a minister be appointed whose 'undivided attention' would be devoted to the refugee question. Only then would the enormity of the crisis of European Jewry be dealt with adequately by the Cabinet.[4]

The chasm between Rathbone's expectations of the Declaration and those of the government was immense. The British government hoped that the promise of post-war retribution was self-contained and could be separated from the problematic issue of rescue. Its reluctance to even consider schemes of rescue rested on two foundations which remained unchanged for the remainder of the war. First, it was assumed that there was no real possibility of wide-scale rescue and that expectations of action would be built up which could not, in practice, be matched. Second, the British government feared that if such a scheme *was* successful it could lead to an influx of Jews either at home and elsewhere in the British empire or in Palestine. Such a movement would have disastrous consequences in terms of generating antisemitism and putting back diplomatic efforts. In each scenario the outcome would be at least embarrassing and at worst positively dangerous to the government. Rather than being consciously hypocritical, the British government's policies had an inner consistency which emerged from a distrust of the Nazi government, potential refugee Jews and the British public. It was determined to maintain both Britain's liberal image *and* its adherence to liberal principles when dealing with Jewish matters. Both the government's determination to keep to a policy which effectively ruled out the possibility of mass rescue and the sincerity with which it believed that it was doing all that it was realistically able to do to help made the lives of individuals such as Rathbone extremely difficult. Yet, for a few months, a public campaign in Britain after the Allied Declaration threatened to destroy the government's equilibrium.

I

In a frenzied day of writing, one week after the Declaration, Victor Gollancz produced one of the most astonishing pieces of polemical literature published in war-time Britain. Gollancz had come from a leading British Jewish family with strong orthodox rabbinical links. Nevertheless, Gollancz remained ambivalent towards his Jewish roots and was caught between a spiritual interest in both Judaism and Christianity. At times he veered away from Jewish particularity, such as the occasion in April 1938 when he refused a request from Lord Bearsted to contribute to a fund for Austrian Jewry:

No one grieves more deeply than I do for the fate of our people: but I also grieve no less deeply for the fate of those non-Jew[s] who are the victims of this same persecution. I cannot see the problem in isolation. . . . In my view the salvation of Jewry depends on the whole political fight against Fascism in general.[5]

At the end of the war, Gollancz would balance his Jewish particularism and general universalism by producing two pamphlets simultaneously on the fate of the Jewish survivors and the unnecessary misery imposed on the German people. In December 1942, and for several months after, however, Gollancz devoted all his attention to the fate of European Jewry. He was prompted to do so after a meeting with Jan Karski. As with others such as Arthur Koestler, the images of the 'Final Solution' so graphically described by Karski would haunt Gollancz for the rest of the war. A week after the Allied Declaration, on Christmas day (appropriately for one so intrigued by the Christological tradition), Gollancz wrote *Let My People Go*. Like Rathbone, Gollancz saw the Declaration as only a first step. He did not doubt 'the genuineness and warmth of Mr. Eden's sympathy', but added that the policy outlined in the Declaration, 'it must be plainly said, [would] not save a single Jewish life'. Indeed, the pamphlet was subtitled 'Some Practical Proposals for dealing with Hitler's MASSACRE OF THE JEWS and an appeal to THE BRITISH PUBLIC'.[6]

In the pamphlet, Gollancz, staggered by the uniqueness of the European Jewish situation, moved away from his earlier universalist position. Most importantly, he rejected the persistent government line that the only way to help the Jews was to win the war: 'There are practical things that might be done *now*', he stressed. Following Rathbone, he also put his trust in the British public and dismissed government claims of its antisemitic tendencies. Gollancz asked the public to show support for the Jews and to demand an active policy of rescue: 'In this way you will put to shame any doubts, if doubts there can really be, about your humanity'. Gollancz called for the British government to allow increased Jewish immigration to Palestine and to provide the necessary visas for refugees reaching neutral countries. Encouragement should also be given to neutral countries to allow more refugees to pass through their territories. To coordinate such activities, Gollancz called for the formation of a special United Nations body with sole concern for refugees.

The impact of the pamphlet was immense. Within days, the first print run of 100,000 copies had sold out and by the end of January 1943 a further 50,000 had been distributed. As a result of Gollancz's appeal for public support, hundreds of petitions and letters offering money, accommodation and food were sent to MPs and the Foreign Office.[7] The British government had been concerned that the Allied Declaration would lead to demands for rescue. In the first weeks of 1943 its fears were being realized. The Foreign Office had deflected several pro-Jewish deputations in January and was also faced with parliamentary demands for action through a newly formed Committee for Rescue of Victims of Nazi Massacres (Committee for Rescue). Delaying tactics were used against both, but the Foreign Office realized by February that the government had at least to *appear* to be doing something. In a rather desperate Foreign Office *aide-mémoire* to the American Chargé d'Affaires, attention was drawn to

the intense public interest shown in the United Kingdom over refugees from German oppression and in particular over the fate of the Jews . . . intensive representations [had been made] to His Majesty's Government that every effort should be made to meet the extermination policy by rescuing such Jews as are able to escape into neutral countries, and facilitate the reception of more.

The Foreign Office called for a meeting with the United States to discuss a coordinated policy so that public opinion would be satisfied.[8]

On 7 January 1943, a meeting at Burlington House, London, of sympathetic MPs and Jewish representatives took place to demand action from the British government. At this gathering, the President of the Board of Deputies of British Jews, Selig Brodetsky, pointed out that in spite of all the delegations to the government, 'little had yet been done, and that consequently continued influence had to be brought to bear in order that something should be done'. At the same point, Solomon Schonfeld, the Secretary and leading force in the Chief Rabbi's Emergency Council (CREC), addressed MPs and Peers, also stressing that 'Official negotiations and deputations have not produced the desired result in the question of victims of Nazi Massacre'. With the support of roughly 80 MPs and prominent members of the House of Lords, Schonfeld produced a motion calling on the British government

following the United Nations declaration . . . to declare its readiness to find temporary refuge in its own territories or in territories under its control for endangered persons who are able to leave those countries, to appeal to the Governments of countries bordering on enemy and enemy-occupied countries to allow temporary asylum and transit facilities for such persons; to offer to these Governments, so far as practicable, such help as may be needed to facilitate their co-operation; and to invite the other Allied Governments to consider similar action.[9]

In a two-week period Gollancz, Schonfeld and the Burlington House group had demanded action from the British government. Although there was a limited overlapping of individuals, these forces had emerged independently and with a large amount of mutual ignorance of each other's existence. Some conflict emerged between the groupings based on personality clashes as well as principles of ideology (including the recurring problem of Zionism) and tactics.[10] Nevertheless, in the short term, the ability of all three to appeal to different constituencies in British society added to the pressures building up on the government. Even organized British labour had changed its attitude. The TUC, 'In view of the continued persecution of the Jews by the Nazis and their campaign for the extermination carried out by orders of Hitler and Himmler . . . vigorously condemned this brutal and inhuman policy'. Moreover, the National Council of Labour called for action by the British government to provide asylum for any Jews who could escape from Nazi oppression. Church groups and others registered their horror at Nazi measures and their disappointment with the lack of response from the British government. In short, an important transformation had occurred between the end of December 1942 and the start of February 1943.[11] Before and during December the battle had been to force the British and other Allied governments to recognize the particularity of the Jewish fate under Nazism, and to move concern away from the refugees at home to the persecuted abroad. By February 1943 the pressure from lobbyists had pushed the Foreign Office to recognize that the *rescue* of refugees was now 'the main problem, which is so much agitating the public conscience'.[12]

II

In early March 1943, the group meeting at Burlington House formally constituted itself into the National Committee for Rescue from Nazi Terror (National Committee). At its first meeting, Eleanor Rathbone, who was to provide its energy and main focus, indicated that in spite of all the public pressure, there had still been no major change in government policy since the Allied Declaration. The Committee therefore called

for continued demonstrations of public opinion in this country in favour of immediate and adequate action by His Majesty's Government and other Governments of the United Nations to provide rescue for as many lives as possible.

A few weeks later Victor Gollancz anxiously reported that the

original intention in forming the Committee had been to organise public opinion on this question and to maintain it at high pressure throughout the country. There were signs that public interest was now diminishing.[13]

The main reason that the momentum was lost in the spring of 1943 was because of the delaying strategies employed by the British government. It placed the pro-Jewish groupings in a difficult position although their attempts at accommodation with the government limited rather than promoted their cause. Schonfeld for the Committee for Rescue had, 'In reference to [Eden's] and [his] colleagues' wishes', modified its initial parliamentary motion to remove 'all controversial points'. Thus, in the revised version, in Schonfeld's words, 'No mention [was] made either of admission of refugees to this country, or to Palestine, leaving it open to His Majesty's Government which are the best methods of rescue'. The revised motion also moved towards the government's universalist line, calling for immediate measures of rescue 'on the largest and most generous scale' but these had to be 'compatible with the requirements of military operations and security'.[14] Throughout February and March 1943 this motion, now supported by 280 MPs, was tabled in the House of Commons without success. On 1 April 1943, a Parliamentary question was asked about the refusal to debate the motion. The Prime Minister, in response, asked for the motion to be delayed further until discussions with the United States over such matters had been concluded. The following day Schonfeld wrote in frustration to *The Times*, referring to the Prime Minister's recent comments about Britain's 'treasures of the past . . . decent government and fair play'. Schonfeld highlighted the dilemma of the pro-Jewish activists in their relationship to the British government:

[Churchill had] touched the core of a problem upon which there seems to be serious divergence between the Government and public opinion. While the former wishes to concentrate purely on winning the War, the people are clamouring for victory plus fair play, that should enable us, in the words of the Primate, to stand 'at the bar of history and of God'. England's sportsman's-heart revolts at the idea of standing by inactive in the presence of the colossal murder.

Schonfeld concluded that the support for the Parliamentary motion was 'uttering a definite call: His Majesty's Government, do the right thing now!'.[15]

From the perspective of the British government, matters were more complicated. It recognized that there was a growing constituency demanding action which was sympathetic to the plight of the Jews. Within the boundaries of its own strategy, the British government believed it *had* shown flexibility, most notably in granting visas for a limited number of individuals still in enemy-occupied countries. By mid-March, in response to requests from Schonfeld, 20 visas had been given and another 100 were under consideration. Even this limited gesture had to be kept confidential.[16] The government was well aware that nothing had been done that would satisfy the demands which had been built up among the British public for action. The government, however, believed it could not act in isolation, yet was faced by American vacillation on the subject. The joint conference which Britain had demanded was thus delayed until late April 1943. As Henry Feingold has suggested, the State Department was concerned that Britain would gain a moral lead in the refugee stakes through the conference. A rushed conference which took into consideration British public sympathy might have a policy outcome beyond that desired by the American government. Nevertheless, resistance to a more generous policy could lead to the reputation of the United States being embarrassed. Procrastination by State Department officials, such as Breckinridge Long, thus enabled greater American control of the eventual conference.[17]

One reason for the ability of American bureaucrats to delay the conference was the slower mobilization of public opinion in the United States. In March 1943 Gollancz had called for fresh campaigning in Britain but also the activation of popular pressure across the Atlantic. In fact the American Jewish Congress had planned public protest meetings for January and February 1943 but both were postponed. The Zionist Revisionist 'Committee for a Jewish Army', led by a small group of Palestinian Jews who had settled in the United States (the 'Bergson Boys'), began a press campaign in February 1943 to emphasize the desperate plight of the Jews and the need for action. But it was not until the following month that events such as that organized by labour and church groups in Madison Square Gardens, New York, which attracted tens of thousands of people, took place. At the same point the American Joint Emergency Committee for European Jewish Affairs was created. It called for meetings to be sponsored by local Jewish, labour and Christian groups to be organized across the United States. Such gatherings, planned to take place in April 1943, would outline 'the full horror of what is happening to the Jews of Europe today'. The intention was 'to marshall the public opinion of your community behind the proposals that are being submitted to the United States Government and to the United Nations'.[18]

From April 1943, Britain lagged far behind the United States in efforts to mobilize public opinion concerning the Jews of Europe. Nevertheless, the importance of activists' efforts, such as those of Rathbone, Gollancz and Schonfeld, in spite of their immediate lack of success, should not be minimized. In May 1943, a memorandum sent to Breckinridge Long on the image of the United States with respect to aiding refugees highlighted the importance of the British campaigners in such questions. The official pointed out that 'the slogan of "action – not pity" [had] become the watchword of the pressure groups who are interested only in a particular class of refugee'. It had been, he added, developed in

England, where certain emotionalists and impractical dreamers adopted it and shipped it on to Rabbi Wise and Goldman in New York. There it was made the keynote of a mass meeting in Madison Square Garden.

One could go further than the analysis of this cynical State Department official. The practical proposals suggested by Gollancz in *Let My People Go* were similar to those produced by the Joint Emergency Committee in March 1943.[19] Frustrated as they were with the lack of progress made on the domestic front, the 'emotionalists and impractical dreamers' of Britain had succeeded in opening up the debate and placing it on the agenda of the United Nations. Much, however, would depend on the delayed conference at Bermuda.

III

The Anglo-American Bermuda conference revealed much about the limitations of the liberal approach when confronted with the Jewish catastrophe. Universalism and sympathy for the Jews combined with national exclusivity and antipathy towards Jewish particularity. The conference discussed the plight of the Jews but public declarations were to refer only to *refugees*. To these Allied governments, emphasizing the Jewishness of the victims was to play the Nazis' game. Such universalism meant that no specific Jewish representation was allowed at Bermuda as 'the refugee problem [was] not confined to persons of any particular race or faith'. Yet Bermuda itself was not a neutral location, for it precluded the possibility of Jewish lobbying from Britain and the United States. Moreover, two years earlier, Chaim Weizmann had objected to a meeting at Bermuda because he believed that there was antisemitic feeling on the island.[20] At Bermuda the British government re-established the importance of linking the refugee question to the danger of aggravating antisemitism at home. The Cabinet even arranged for this view to be prominently expressed in the parliamentary discussion on Bermuda in May 1943. Neither side embarrassed one another about their most obvious weak points – their respective immigration quotas in Palestine and the United States. Flexibility about visas for individuals might increase, but wide-scale rescue was not on the Bermuda agenda. On the negative side, the Americans had asked for the Inter-Governmental Committee on Refugees (IGC) to be revived but, although suspicious of this development, the British government was given no indication that it would play an active role. Its reappearance at least enabled public declarations to be made that something positive had emerged from the conference. The British cabinet thus believed that Bermuda was 'a marked success'.[21]

Not surprisingly, the pro-Jewish groupings in Britain and the United States, having waited powerlessly for several months for its outcome, did not see the Bermuda conference in such positive terms. There was immense disappointment and anger. As Eleanor Rathbone put it: 'A mountain has been in labour; it has thrown up a mouse'. The long-awaited debate in the House of Commons gave her a chance to express her views and to stress again the need for a 'Ministry for Refugees'. She acknowledged the frustrations that had emerged from brief meetings with ministers, when pro-refugee deputations came out 'thinking not only that we care more, which is natural, but that in a sense we know more about it'. With a new ministry it would be possible for the government to share the lobbyists' expertise and sense of concern. Instead she was given the impression that the government was 'trying . . . to buy off public agitation as cheaply as possible'. Acknowledging that only victory would bring an end to all the killing, Rathbone stressed with regard to the Jews that

meantime let no one say: 'We are not responsible'. We are responsible if a single man, woman or child perishes whom we could and should have saved. Too many lives, too much time has been lost already. Do not lose any more.[22]

Through the assistance of several backbench MPs, the government managed to lose the impetus provided by Rathbone. The discussion in the House of

Commons focused on problems of domestic antisemitism relating to refugees and the possibility of hostility increasing with any fresh influx. Eden, the Foreign Secretary, then defended the results of the Bermuda conference and reconfirmed the government line that he 'did not believe it [was] possible to rescue more than a few until final victory is won'.[23]

At this stage Rathbone and her fellow campaigners were unaware of the Cabinet Committee on Refugees. Its existence since late December 1942 might have depressed the lobbyists even further. The successful stimulation of British public opinion appeared to have been in vain. Much was expected from the Bermuda conference and the long-delayed parliamentary debate but both had hardly altered the situation. Meanwhile the murder of the Jews was six months more advanced. At the end of June 1943, Rathbone told the Executive Committee of the National Committee that 'the position seems extremely unsatisfactory. We seem to have reached a stalemate or a dead-end'. She indicated that in meetings with ministers 'We are treated kindly and courteously, but kept at arm's length as much as possible'. Rathbone, whose earlier animus had been directed at the Home Secretary, now concluded that the Foreign Secretary

has no time for us. . . . The implication of it all seems that the Government has very little sense of urgency over the whole matter, very little hope of doing anything for rescue except on a small scale and a strong desire to avoid pressure.

She was also aware, however, that

if we refrain from publicity and from organised pressure, there is a real danger that the Government will assume that public interest has weakened and their present tendency to dismiss a painful subject from their own minds will be encouraged.

Revealing the fatalism and sense of despair that the government's attitude had by the summer of 1943 installed in her and the National Committee, Rathbone concluded 'What, if anything, can we do about it?'.[24]

At this point the National Committee published a pamphlet, *Rescue the Perishing*, which included a 12-point programme for immediate rescue measures, evidence of public concern and an indication of the lack of action by the government since the Declaration. The programme reflected, with some refinements and updating, the proposals made in Gollancz's *Let My People Go*. On one issue, however, there was a change of policy. Gollancz had called for a United Nations body to be set up with sole concern for refugees. At the meeting in January 1943 which laid the foundations for the National Committee, there was debate concerning whether there was a need for an international or a British organization to deal with the problem. Rathbone was in favour of a British body and in *Rescue the Perishing* called for the formation of a new instrument within the British Government, such as will ensure that the whole problem of measures of rescue will receive the undivided attention of at least one or more persons of high calibre with full authority.

Rathbone was aware 'that while Ministers are excusably preoccupied with the immediate responsibilities concerning the war, they show no inclination to use the services of outside experts on the subject'. The National Committee was sceptical about the revival of the IGC (especially considering its limited role after the Evian conference) but was willing initially, in the absence of other likely alternatives, to give it some support.[25]

Although the revived IGC was accepted by the British government with some reluctance, by the autumn of 1943 it was being seen by the Foreign Office as a blessing in disguise. Its reconstruction, as the leading British representative at Bermuda, Richard Law, put it, 'answers [Miss Rathbone's] chief complaint about there being no-one with sole interests in refugees'. It would also deflect attention away from the Foreign Office. As for pressure 'to get enthusiasts like Miss Rathbone appointed to the [IGC]', the Foreign Secretary was adamant:

I'm convinced we can't use Miss Rathbone or any of her kidney as assessors. Assessors are concerned with facts: Miss R is interested in policies, [and] would sit there trying to force her particular views down the throats of the committee. Anyway, the Americans won't have her.[26]

By the autumn of 1943 the British government had recovered from its earlier loss of balance when public opinion threatened to push it away from its set strategy on refugee matters. This was certainly not one of total inaction, as Richard Law explained in a Foreign Office memorandum on the 'The Refugee Situation' in September 1943:

Fundamentally the refugee problem remains within the same limitations, and the persistent propaganda of large-scale 'rescue' remains as unreal as ever, short of victory. Nevertheless since the Bermuda Conference distinct progress within practical limits has been made.[27]

Indeed, the Foreign Office now welcomed the IGC as a way to avoid what it saw as the total and unjustified inertia of the American State Department with regard to refugee matters. In reality this meant slightly greater flexibility in granting visas for refugees heading for Palestine, and a move away from the rigid interpretation of the 1939 White Paper. Earlier policies had resulted in the brutal turning away of those who had escaped from Europe, culminating in the tragic loss of life on *The Struma* in February 1942. In the first three weeks of November 1943, for example, Martin Gilbert has indicated that 83

Jewish refugees from Hungary (who had escaped through Romania, Bulgaria and Turkey) and 19 from Bulgaria were allowed into Palestine by the British authorities. Solomon Schonfeld had also been granted visas to cover 100 rabbis and their families from Nazi-occupied territories where it was hoped that they would be allowed to enter neutral countries. British Passport Control officers in Madrid, Lisbon and Ankara had been instructed by the Foreign Office to give the necessary transit or entrance visas. But these were essentially tokenist measures. In broader questions of mass rescue from both Romania and Bulgaria, where the Jewish populations were in a highly precarious position, officials such as Law stressed that there was 'little hope of any large movement'. Simultaneously, however, the fear that Hitler might encourage 'a quite unmanageable flood' of Jews from the Balkan countries still haunted government circles.[28]

In the United States, during the autumn of 1943, the government appeared to be even less accommodating towards the Jewish and pro-Jewish lobbyists. Activists continued to organize mass meetings and blatant propaganda against the government through the Emergency Committee to Save the Jewish People of Europe. A broad coalition consisting of Jewish, church and labour groups combined to demand rescue but Breckinridge Long and the State Department stood resolutely against any change of policy.[29] Ironically, at the same point, British campaigners who had instituted such tactics in the first place dropped their open campaigning. The departure of Victor Gollancz (who had suffered a nervous breakdown partly through the pressure of addressing so many audiences on this traumatic subject) weakened the public profile of the National Committee. More generally, however, constant government warnings about the danger of stimulating antisemitism in Britain appears to have diminished the faith of the activists. Earlier in 1943, Rathbone had boldly argued that it was 'an insult to the British people to suppose that even those who "don't like Jews" would rather leave them to be massacred than find asylum for a few thousand of them'.[30] A good example of such tendencies occurred when support for the Parliamentary motion was being elicited. Colonel Medlicott MP wrote to Schonfeld pointing out that there were already hundreds of thousands of refugees in Britain, most of them Jewish. He added, with a clear emancipation contract in mind, that he was

unhappy over the attitude of the Jewish people themselves towards this problem [of European Jewry], which is so essentially their own. I feel that the Jews lose a very great deal of sympathy which otherwise would be gladly given to them if only they themselves would take more active steps to further the Allied cause.

Apart from the refugees who have come here as a direct result of the Hitler persecution, there are hundreds of thousands of Jews who have enjoyed the protection and hospitality of this country for years, indeed generations. One would so much have liked to see them, as a community, take some active steps, and indeed undergo some definite sacrifice, as a thank offering for all that this country has done for them. How gladly the British people for example would have welcomed a great Jewish fund in aid of British prisoners of war in Germany.

Yet in spite of all these clear reservations, Medlicott was anxious to stress

in conclusion that the . . . points which I have made in no way qualify my agreement with you that every effort must be made to rescue as many Jews as we possibly can from the terrible fate which Germany with her ingrained and nation wide brutality is preparing for them.[31]

By the autumn of 1943, Rathbone and others in the National Committee seem to have followed the government in mistaking such ambivalent views for outright and unequivocal antisemitism. It started a campaign to combat anti-semitism 'which is inseparable from our work and which considerably hinders our success'. In 1944 the National Committee spent energy and some of its limited resources producing anti-defamation literature, material with a highly apologetic tone. The British government, if only indirectly, had forced the campaigners onto the defensive. Debate was again focused on friction at home rather than the rescue of Jews abroad. It was only after another frustrating meeting with senior Foreign Office officials late in 1943 that British activists became convinced that the government was still not sufficiently interested in the subject. At the start of 1944 the National Committee announced

in Great Britain, those mainly responsible for guiding public opinion on refugee questions have deliberately discouraged public agitation during recent months, believing it fair to give the government time to develop the plans made at the Conference at Bermuda, without indiscreet publicity. However, the results of the government policy do not justify continued silence, and the National Committee for Rescue from Nazi Terror has decided once again to enlist the active support of public opinion for their humanitarian policy.[32]

But by this time the public mood in Britain had changed. With a lack of lead given by the state and the press no longer providing the extensive coverage of late 1942 and early 1943, public lack of interest and scepticism about the reports of extermination had grown. The situation was well summarized a year after the Allied Declaration by Ignacy Schwartzbart, Jewish representative in the Polish government in exile. Schwartzbart believed that public mistrust of news concerning European Jewry came largely out of the fact that the infor-mation reported was 'fragmentary and incoherent'. It was therefore hard for ordinary people in Britain to keep up with all the changes and shiftings of Jewish populations across Europe (such as Jews being moved into areas where others had been killed). On top of this, the normal imagination could not cope with the scale of the annihilation process. Schwartzbart concluded that the stories were now being 'dismissed as propaganda'. The barriers to comprehension were now immense and the attempts of the National Committee to revive the interest of the public throughout 1944, in pamphlets such as *Continuing Terror*, were generally unsuccessful.[33]

The problems of Rathbone and the National Committee at the end of 1943 were immense. Public sympathy had diminished and there appeared to be little hope of the British government changing its policies. The situation in the United States seemed even bleaker. In September 1943, Congressman Will Rogers Jr of the Emergency Committee to Save the Jewish People of Europe came to Britain to coordinate lobbying efforts on both sides of the Atlantic. Although pleased at the greater activity of American campaigners, the National Committee was sceptical about such activists' influence on the government of the United States. The National Committee decided in November 1943 that

The [Emergency] Committee which had been established as a result of the Conference [in New York during July 1943] was not sufficiently representative to act as an analogous body, and we therefore declined to exchange liaison officers.

The British government also shared the National Committee's doubts about progress being made in the United States. Indeed, it was still concerned in the autumn of 1943 that the Americans wished to do too little and not too much on the refugee question.[34] The formation of the War Refugee Board (WRB) in the United States was again, however, to change the rules of the game.

IV

On one level it appears curious that it was to be the United States, rather than Britain, that was to take the major lead with regard to the Jews of Europe in the last stages of the war. If domestic antisemitism is taken as one comparative indicator, then it is clear that not only was hostility much stronger in the United States, but that it actually reached new heights at the time of the formation of the War Refugee Board in 1944. Surveys carried out on the American public in 1942 found that 47 per cent of the population believed that antisemitism was on the increase, whereas the figure for 1944 was 56 per cent. Similarly, over the same period, fear of Jewish power in the United States rose from 51 per cent to 56 per cent. In Britain, Mass-Observation surveys on the Jews were carried out in 1941, 1943 and 1944. Those expressing strong disfavour towards the Jews declined in 1943 to 13 per cent (just half the level recorded two years earlier). The percentage fell even further the year after. The present author's analysis of Mass-Observation material for 1943 suggests that less than one-fifth of the British population was concerned over the level of Jewish influence in the world. Moreover, British antisemitism was, if anything, on the decline in the latter part of the war. The government's Home Intelligence unit had been monitoring attitudes towards the Jews since early in the war. Its final report on the subject was produced in July 1944 and concluded that 'during the past eight weeks [antisemitic] comment has . . . continued at a low level'. Thereafter, the subject merited no further comment from the government investigators. In the last year of the war, there was little in the way of hostile press or public discussion of the Jews in Britain whereas in the United States mini-riots against the Jews occurred in New York and Boston.[35]

Other factors could be added to reinforce the strangely divergent paths taken by Britain and the United States in 1944. Although there were a few minor exceptions, Britain had no equivalent restrictionist or even antisemitic lobby in Parliament as existed in the House of Representatives. Indeed, the widespread support for Schonfeld's rescue motion had shown the goodwill that existed in Britain, especially in the House of Commons. Moreover, the State Department had been even more stubborn than the Foreign Office with regard to the dissemination of news concerning the 'Final Solution' and its attitude towards rescue.[36] There were, however, crucial differences between the United States and Britain that enabled the formation and relative success of the WRB – in spite of all the domestic problems. In essence they relate to the possibility of ethnic pluralism in American politics which contrasts to the monocultural nature of the British system in World War II. In turn, changes in American policy depended on the power and influence of American Jewry.

In late 1943, lobbying by the Emergency Committee to Save the Jewish People forced the issue of European Jewry into the heart of American politics. The 'enemy within' was no longer the alien subversive but consisted of untrustworthy officials in the State Department. Embarrassing Congressional hearings on the rescue of the Jews in November, and especially the inadequate responses of Breckinridge Long which were publicized in December, focused public anger on government inaction, particularly from American Jewry. This on its own, however, may not have been enough to change government policy. It was the action taken by Treasury Secretary Henry Morgenthau and the support of his progressive non-Jewish colleagues in the Treasury Department that proved decisive. In a document, initially entitled 'Report . . . on the Acquiescence of this Government in the Murder of Jews', presented to Roosevelt, allegations of deliberate attempts by the State Department to stop the circulation of news about the destruction of the Jews were made. In addition, the report suggested that the public had been misled about the action taken by the American government. Morgenthau, in effect, was willing to use his influence to blackmail the President in an election year. As he put it in negotiations before seeing Roosevelt:

I personally hate to say this thing, but our strongest out is the imminence of Congress doing something. This is our strongest out. Really, when you get down to the point, this is a boiling pot on the Hill. You can't hold it; it is going to pop, and you have either got to move very fast, or the Congress of the United States will do it for you.

The report, presented to Roosevelt on 16 January 1944, spelt out the situation very clearly:

[T]here is a growing number of responsible people and organizations today who have ceased to view our failure as the product of simple incompetence on the part of those officials in the State Department charged with handling this problem. They see plain Anti-Semitism motivating the actions of these State Department officials, and, rightly or wrongly, it will require little more in the way of proof for this suspicion to explode into a nasty scandal.[37]

A few days later, the WRB was formed by a Presidential Executive order. In spite of its non-particularist title, the main concern of the WRB was to rescue Jews who were potential victims of the Nazis' extermination programme. Moreover, the establishment of the WRB broke the tacit agreement between Britain and the United States that the only way of helping the Jews was to win the war. There have been subsequent criticisms of the WRB that it was too little and too late. Yet it has also been suggested that over 100,000 Jews were saved by its activities, as well as the lives of thousands of non-Jews.[38]

The role of the American government was crucial in the success of the WRB. This was less in terms of money (less than $500,000 of government money was eventually spent by the WRB) and more in the form of help given in facilitating the movement of payments and people. Most of its funding, some $20 million, was provided by American Jewry, mainly through the American Jewish Joint Distribution Committee. Whatever its internal weaknesses, and generally it functioned effectively, and in spite of its late arrival, the WRB, as Yehuda Bauer concludes, 'was an expression of moral and political support by the [American] administration to save Jews with Jewish means'. The contrast with Britain could not be more stark.[39]

The National Committee, the only central non-sectarian body in Britain dealing with the fate of the Jews in Europe, depended on an insecure budget of several hundred pounds. Some of this tiny sum was provided by the Board of Deputies of British Jews. In June 1944, a grant of £150 was given to it by the Chief Rabbi's Emergency Council for the 'excellent work on behalf of our suffering Brethren on the Continent'. Hertz, the Chief Rabbi, added that the National Committee was in need of funds, but Jewish leading personalities and religious bodies showed little interest and understanding. He felt that as the lay leaders failed to encourage this work, he had to do it.[40]

In February 1944, the leading British Zionist and MP Maurice Rosette wrote to the editor of the *Jewish Chronicle*, Ivan Greenberg, on a similar question. Rosette had remarked at a private meeting that British Jews had not done enough to help their European brethren and his comments had been picked up by the non-Jewish press. Rosette was apologetic about the adverse publicity this had generated but added that

In the matter, however, of saying that [Jewry in] this country has not done enough, I am unrepentant. If you compare the record of Palestine, for example, which has unceasingly agitated for work and organisation since the news of the massacres became known, with the comparative calm acceptance in this country, you will see what I mean. Even Eleanor Rathbone has privately from time to time expressed amazement at the way in which we are dealing with the situation here.

I am not at all in agreement with you that no appeal for money could have been made. You probably know . . . that there is work going on of which we cannot speak publicly, and whilst no one can pretend that it is saving large number of Jews, it is at least saving some, and it is done at the cost of enormous sums of money and prodigious human effort. Where is this money coming from? Either from the Yishuv, at tremendous sacrifice, or even from the Joint in America. What have we done in this country to help? It seems to me that even if it means a saving of a single human being no amount should be considered too great. I know that there has been no public appeal, and, therefore, perhaps the man in the street cannot be blamed, but we, who are responsible, and I include myself without hesitation, should have done more . . . .

As for public agitation, can we honestly say that we have done anything approaching even that which is being done in America, and I would not exonerate them entirely. The American Government has, however, moved and allowing for the fact that in some respects this is a political move, nevertheless it appears to mean business, and American Jewish public opinion has played some part.[41]

Criticisms were also made of the financial contributions of British Jewry by the Jews of Palestine. In the defence of Britain's Jewish minority, it should be emphasized that the huge commitments made in the 1930s, and at the start of the war, to maintain the refugees from Nazism had created an immense burden on the community. Yet, it is clear that the growing distance from the reality of the fate of European Jewry in the last stages of the war also made a crucial impact on the level of money offered by British Jews for rescue/relief work. Of perhaps greater importance was the lack of political power that British Jewry was willing to exercise. Its mainstream leadership was still insecure in its position in society. British Jewry was certainly unwilling to embarrass the government in the manner finally executed in the United States in late 1943/early 1944. In deputations to the Foreign Office and to leading politicians, the Board of Deputies of British Jews was always hindered by attempts to show gratitude with the net result that their 'reasonable' and 'moderate' demands were easily deflected.[42]

Yet, in Britain the Jews represented less than 1 per cent of the total population. It is significant that there was little financial or moral support for the efforts of British campaigners from the churches or organized labour in the latter half of the war. Thus the Council of Christians and Jews withdrew its small grant to the National Committee in late 1943. Again the contrast with the United States, where national church bodies as well as the AFL and CIO played leading roles in the rescue campaign, is plain. Although it acknowledged that there were some sympathetic individuals in the non-Jewish world, such as Eleanor Rathbone and James Parkes, British Jewry saw itself isolated in a society in which there was little room to emphasize ethnic difference.[43] How then did Britain react to the *particularistic* policies of the WRB?

V

There is irony in the great similarity between Roosevelt's Executive order of 22 January 1944, establishing the WRB, and the programme of the National Committee. It could be argued that, indirectly, the British organization's outline of positive action, formulated in early 1943, acted as a model for the WRB. Yet, throughout 1944 the British government both resisted attempts to set up an equivalent body and deeply resented the activities of the American Board. The problem in Whitehall in 1944 was to resist American demands for what it saw as the extravagant and dangerous measures of rescue, while continuing to help the Jews in a more 'realistic' and limited way. Ultimately, however, in this process, the 'liberal' image of Britain had to be preserved. It was a tightrope the government succeeded in walking because, unlike the United States, public opinion could be ignored. Nevertheless, in making no fundamental changes in policy, the British government's balancing act was precarious. In 1944 the Nazis attempted to destroy the remnants of European Jewry but, as their grip on the Continent lessened, so the opportunities for mass rescue increased. On the one hand, the Nazis' determination to finish the 'Final Solution' limited such possibilities. On the other, the success of the WRB showed some of the potential for rescue.

Two weeks after the formation of the WRB, the British Cabinet Committee on Refugees met to discuss its response to the new development. There was some belief in British government circles that the WRB was created as a sop to the Jewish electorate of New York State, but it was perceived as having little substance in reality. Anthony Eden therefore believed that 'we should welcome the President's move', and this was the message sent to the United States. The Foreign Secretary, however, was concerned to find out more about the WRB 'and, in particular, whether "rescue" indicates any new diplomatic, military or economic measures with which the United States Government would wish to associate HMG'. A month later Eden reported to the Cabinet Committee that he had

received information from Washington which suggests the possibility of serious differences of opinion between HMG and the United States Government over details of refugee policy.[44]

The conflicts that would continue to cloud relations between Britain and the United States concerned the fate of Balkan and, especially, Hungarian Jewry in 1944. Randolph Braham has suggested that, while the Holocaust has no historical equivalent, 'the tragedy that befell the Jews of Hungary in turn involved unique factors that differentiated it from that of other national Jewish communities of Europe'. Braham indicates the speed and ruthlessness with which these half million victims were killed in 1944. He also points to the precise level of information available to the 'free world' of the mechanics of the 'Final Solution' at this stage in the war.[45]

The initial concern of the British government was the WRB's licensing of $100,000 to be spent in Hungary and Romania on goods for the relief of Jews. Eden saw this as an important 'departure from the principles of economic warfare [the blockade] agreed upon between our two governments'. For the second time in the war, the British government faced the possibility of having to change its refugee strategy. A year earlier it had avoided this due to State Department delay. Now, ironically, the pressure to move was coming from the American government itself. Eden, pondering on what the British response should be to the purchases, put the dilemma to the Cabinet Committee:

If we object we risk being held up by the War Refugee Board, which is engaged in a publicity campaign, as obstacles to a humanitarian measure which would probably save many Jewish lives. If we merely acquiesce, we allow the U.S. Government to get credit for a piece of rescue work which critics will say should have been attempted long ago, while [if] we, too, agree to remit money to the Intergovernmental Refugee Committee [for the purchases] we may be committed to a relaxation of our financial blockade which may prove of real advantage to the enemy.

Eden concluded, however, by stating that the WRB

has been officially welcomed by us. We have also stated our wish to co-operate with the United States Government in every way possible, and to leave no means of saving refugees untried which was consistent with the efficient prosecution of the war.[46]

The solution to this difficulty was to come up with new proposals – ones which met the restraints seen by the British government as vital in the formulation of policy. First, large-scale rescue was impossible but also dangerous. Second, practical, limited measures would both help the Jews as far as it was realistic to do so and would also show the genuine concern of the British government. Rather than licences, which broke the economic blockade, the British government proposed the use of a credit system. This was in fact already in operation through the Joint Distribution Committee and its agent Saly Mayer in Switzerland. Through this system, no hard currency was exchanged in enemy territory, only pledges which would be redeemed in dollars after the war. Moreover, the British government, encouraged by the Treasury, would put in a fixed amount – £1,500,000 – whereas the American licence system threatened to cost much more.[47]

The WRB bitterly opposed the credit scheme. First, they believed it undermined the licence system (individuals inevitably preferring cash to the promises of payment). Second, they saw it as a too limited rescue measure. The issue created tremendous tension across the Atlantic, and throughout the rest of 1944 the Cabinet Committee and the Board indulged in criticism of one another. The British resented what Eden referred to as the tendency of the 'War Refugee Board . . . to give the impression that only the United States Government takes the refugee problem seriously'. It therefore produced a series of reports of 'Recent Activities of His Majesty's Government on Behalf of Refugees' to 'help to put the matter in correct perspective'. In the first such report of June 1944 it indicated the encouragement that had been given to countries such as Sweden, Switzerland and Turkey to help the Jews. More specifically, the rescue of Jewish Yugoslav refugees from Italy to Egypt and the arrival of over 1,200 Jews in Palestine from Constantza, Romania, via Istanbul between 15 March and 15 May 1944, was stressed. The Cabinet Committee also believed that the WRB had 'extravagant hopes' which had been unable 'to produce appreciable results'. The WRB, however, was convinced that the British were slow to move, leaving all the burden on the American side. This clash in approach came to a head in the summer of 1944 over the crisis of Hungarian Jewry.[48]

In its second meeting in 1944, the Cabinet Committee considered the proposals brought to the Allies by Joel Brandt – the notorious 'blood for guns' offer of Adolf Eichmann. The Cabinet Committee wanted nothing to do with what it saw as Gestapo blackmail which had no likely chance of success. Again, however, the other major consideration – that the scheme might actually come off – was considered. Both the Home Secretary and the Secretary of State for the Colonies were anxious lest it lead to an influx of Jews into the United Kingdom or Palestine, thereby provoking serious anti-semitism. At the same time the Committee was aware

that the scheme might secure sympathy beyond its merits in Washington, where the President's War Refugee Board, backed by Mr. Morgenthau, had, partly for electoral reasons, committed itself to the 'rescue' of Jews.

A telegram was thus sent from the Foreign Office to Washington stating that

while . . . refusing to deal with this scheme and the channels through which it has come, we realise [the] importance of not [offering] a mere negative to any genuine proposals involving the rescue of any Jewish and other victims which merit serious consideration of the Allied Government. [The] whole record of United States and His Majesty's Government is a proof of their active sympathy with victims of Nazi terror.

Much to British surprise, the Americans agreed not to pursue the Brandt proposals.[49]

But shortly after this episode, the Cabinet Committee was faced with another offer, that of Admiral Horthy, the Hungarian Regent, to let the Jews leave his country. It was one that Eden this time regarded as genuine. Both Britain and the United States believed that the offer should be accepted, but yet again differences between the two countries created problems. In particular, and as with the Brandt proposal, the British government believed that the American 'statement that it is unlikely refugees will leave Hungary in such numbers that the Allies cannot cope with the situation as it develops is not borne out by the facts'. There was fear that the Germans were actually inspiring the offer so as to embarrass the British by flooding the Middle East with Jews. Thus, although there was agreement to accept the Horthy offer, the British stated to the Americans that there would be limitations to their commitment to rescuing the Jews for 'strong military reasons'. In addition, the Foreign Office wanted the IGC consulted over this matter. It was a demand which the British government did not believe would jeopardize lives through delay. Rather than accepting the Americans' pleas for urgency at face value (and thereby avoiding consultation with the IGC), Eden concluded that the United States was 'inspired by a fear that the Intergovernmental Committee might steal the thunder of the War Refugee Board'. The net result was that the pleas of the National Committee and others 'to accept with the least possible delay the Hungarian offer to release Jews' was not acted on until the second half of August, over three weeks after it had initially been tendered. Eleanor Rathbone suggested to Eden that Horthy's weakening on the Jewish question in August 1944 had not been helped by the slowness of the Allied response to his offer. Indeed, a few days before the British and American governments publicly declared their willingness to help Jewish refugees from Hungary, the Hungarian government had agreed with the Germans to resume the deportations.[50]

After the Hungarian episode, the possibilities of significant rescue disappeared. Later in 1944, Paul Mason, the head of the Foreign Office Refugee Department, reflected on this fact and what he saw as the belated recognition by the WRB 'that large scale evacuation of refugees from Hitler's Europe was almost impossible, and that there was no scope for spectacular work'. Mason incorrectly believed that the Board had been dissolved and that it was surprising that this supposed decision had not been taken earlier. It was a body which always had 'an eye on public opinion and a disregard of what was or was not practicable which made it hard for the [IGC] to keep step'. George Hall, Parliamentary Under-Secretary at the Foreign Office, agreed with Mason and suggested that the 'demise' of the WRB 'justifie[d] the work of [the] Intergovernmental Committee'.[51] Was this analysis correct and how did the British government succeed in turning down requests for a British War Refugee Board?

VI

A note from the United States Embassy at the start of February 1944, informing the Foreign Office of the establishment of the WRB, also requested that the British government issue 'a declaration of policy similar to that made by the President'. This communication, as well as pressure from the refugee lobby to create a similar body in Britain, forced a detailed response from the Foreign Office. The official response was given by the Foreign Secretary in the House of Commons after a question by the Jewish independent Conservative, Daniel Lipson. Eden welcomed the formation of the Board and stressed the government's desire to cooperate with it, although he stressed the 'unavoidable limitations' which had to be faced over the question of rescue. There was no need, however, for a new body in Britain, due to the Cabinet Committee on Refugees, whose existence the government now publicly acknowledged. Furthermore, it was possible for the government to work with the United States through the IGC. Both Lipson and Rathbone queried whether the Cabinet Committee was equivalent to the WRB, which had access to the President and an executive director. Eden replied that the Cabinet Committee had 'a responsibility to the Foreign Office. We think, that, on the whole, that is the best way.'[52]

A month later, in March 1944, a fuller discussion of this question took place in a debate on supply when the Commons was considering the payment of £50,000 to the IGC. Here Richard Law stressed 'that the fact that the War

Refugee Board has been set up in the United States is not in any sense a criticism of the Intergovernmental Committee'. The reality of the situation was somewhat different. Morgenthau's documentation sent to Roosevelt in January 1944 from which the WRB emerged had actually stressed the failure of the IGC. In the debate in the Commons, Rathbone criticized the size and organization of the IGC: with its small London office and staff of four

It is just a little as though, seeing a number of people escaping from a hungry tiger, you sent after them a stage coach, drawn by four white horses, when what you needed was a Rolls-Royce. It seems rather a leisurely machine, and a small machine.[53]

Law defended the IGC and stressed again that it was the appropriate body through which the government should work. Rathbone responded that because the IGC was inter-governmental this strengthened the case for a British body (similar to the WRB) to supplement it. This forced Law back to a defence of the Cabinet Committee which he claimed was 'exactly what she wants . . . . I do not think there really is the practical difference that some Hon. Members imagine there to be.' In spite of these rebuttals, the campaign for a British Board continued in 1944 through the work of the National Committee. It pointed out that 'the success achieved by [the WRB's] work, so far, is an added argument for the establishment of a similar body, and similar machinery, in the United Kingdom'. In a letter to *The Times* the National Committee suggested that the size of the WRB and its access to the President made it, contrary to what Law had claimed, a much more powerful body than the Cabinet sub-committee. They concluded by asking whether 'a question so difficult and involving the fate of such innumerable victims deserve[s] a more amply equipped machinery here?'.[54]

In private the British government did acknowledge that the WRB was a different animal. It was for this reason that opposition to the WRB was so profound. As Sir Herbert Emerson, Director of the IGC put it: 'refugee questions in which the Board is interested are apt to assume an importance out of relation to bigger questions'. The Director of the WRB, John Pehle, according to a perceptive British Treasury Department official, 'feels that his first loyalty is not to Anglo–American co-operation nor to the British conception of a financial blockade but to the Jews in Europe'. No British body, and certainly not the Cabinet Committee, shared that philosophy. It was one, as Rathbone and her Committee realized, that was vital if the challenge of rescuing Jews was to be matched. The staff of the WRB, which included Jews and non-Jews, was, in Emerson's words 'young, able and keen. They feel that they have a job of work to do and they have to do it quickly.' In Britain, those like Rathbone were carefully, if politely, kept out of any decision-making process. Access to the government was a privilege, not a right, forcing the National Committee to a cautious approach and to gratitude when meetings with officials were arranged. In the summer of 1944, the National Committee's delegations and memoranda sent to the Foreign Office and IGC made little impact other than to irritate the government and to reinforce the sense of impotence in the pro-refugee lobby.[55]

On 26 July 1944, the last big delegation of the National Committee, headed by the Archbishop of Canterbury, told the Foreign Secretary 'that [British] public opinion was highly alarmed over the treatment of the Jews in Hungary' and that there was a willingness to make great sacrifices and admit 'considerable numbers of Jewish refugees to this country'. There was indeed some evidence of this. The government's Home Intelligence unit reported 'Horror at their treatment and sympathy with the victims'. But, unlike the outcry 18 months earlier, it was less intense and certainly less vocal. The Foreign Office had little difficulty in dismissing the demands of the Archbishop. Since Bermuda, both the Foreign and Home Office were agreed that refugee Jews must be kept out of Britain. In terms of Palestine, a trickle of Jewish survivors arrived from the Continent throughout 1944, most of them Romanians who had escaped through Turkey. Colonial Office officials were capable of generosity when it concerned individuals or small groups of survivors attempting to reach Palestine. Mass rescue to Palestine, however, was still ruled out.[56]

There was, in fact, a general consensus between British government departments on refugee issues. There is some evidence that individuals in the Treasury Department were, by early 1944, facilitating a more positive strategy of rescue, and, as with the credit system, they had some success in helping to negotiate the saving of Jewish lives in enemy territory. Nevertheless, this was neither on the scale of the US Treasury revolt in late 1943, nor were these individuals dominant in the British Department. Ultimately then, the government avoided the demands for a British War Refugee Board throughout the last stages of the war. The British government managed to continue its 'rescue' policy within narrow constraints – ones that certainly differentiate it from the approach of the United States from the start of 1944.[57] What can be concluded from these differences?

VII

The dominant explanation for both the British and American government's failure to respond to the crisis of European Jewry has been that of 'bureaucratic indifference'. Some have gone further with regard to Britain in the latter stages of the war and suggested that 'the anti-Jewish prejudices of officials in all the offices . . . hindered, obstructed, and finally paralysed every initiative that could have saved Jewish lives in 1944'. It is important to stress again that the terms 'indifference' and 'antisemitism' have been used too loosely and require more precise definitions.[58]

The possibility of these terms being employed at the time by critics worried both the British and American governments. Nevertheless, they were also highly critical of each other's response to the crisis of European Jewry in the second half of the war. In 1944 the British government was particularly worried about being accused of apathy on the issue. Documentation was thus regularly sent to the Americans to show that 'we are far from being indifferent to the sufferings of the Jews'. It is easy to criticize such statements and similar ones from American officials in the light of actual policy. It does not follow, however, that either government was being self-consciously hypocritical on this issue. If they had been genuinely indifferent, government officials would have been unconcerned about the fate of the Jews, and it would have made no difference to them if the Nazis massacred the Jews or not. The evidence suggests that both in public and private, civil servants and ministers were appalled by the Nazi atrocities.[59] Yet the question remains, why was the British response to these crimes so limited compared to the United States after the formation of the WRB?

The question of antisemitism and the Allied response has been one of the most controversial in the continuing debate. But again it is not clear what is meant by the term. First of all, Allied *support* for the genocidal policies of the Nazis must be dismissed. This was first suggested by Goebbels at the time of the Allied Declaration and revived in a more sophisticated form in 1966 by Reuben Ainsztein in one of the first articles on the British response. Ainsztein argued that although the British ruling establishment figures were rarely Judeophobes, they nevertheless realized 'that the Germans were solving the Jewish problem for them'. There is, however, no evidence that the destruction was actually welcome (even in the cynical and hostile atmosphere of the Colonial Office where Jews were often greatly distrusted). But the absence of Nazi-style prejudice in British government circles does not mean that the question of antisemitism should be discarded. If antisemitism was a factor in the British case, then it is hardly surprising that it did not take a Nazi form.[60]

We have seen how the British commitment to liberal values, and especially individual freedom, led to a revulsion against Nazi methods. Nevertheless, the commitment to individualism also required of the Jews that they cease to be a collective body. Persistent antisemitism in a liberal nation was explained by the tendency of the Jews towards particularism. With remarkable consistency and in partial contrast to the United States the British government held closely to these liberal values *throughout* the war. The view of the government was that the 'Jews must be treated as nationals of existing states'; they were 'a purely religious community, on the same national footing as their fellow citizens'. When the Chief Rabbi asked that the Jews of Hungary be given a status of being protected by the British in the summer of 1944, the response was clear:

it is not the policy of HMG to regard Jews as belonging to a separate category. It is felt that discrimination of this kind savours too strongly of the Nazi attitude towards Jews.[61]

Out of this philosophy came a reluctance to accept publicly the Jewish dimension to the Nazi atrocities. The Cabinet Committee on the Reception and Accommodation of Jewish Refugees soon removed the word 'Jewish' from its title. A similar policy, as has been noted, was in operation at Bermuda and the British government was hostile to any Jewish or pro-refugee representation in the reconstituted IGC. Its choice of Chairman, Lord Winterton, added further to the discomfort of campaigners such as Rathbone. Winterton's anti-Zionism and social antipathy towards Jews was well known – he was rejected as Lord Moyne's replacement in Cairo in 1944 because, in the words of Churchill's advisor, he was 'chairman of the Antisemitic League'. It was out of opposition to stressing the Jewish aspects of the impact of the Nazis' crimes, and the implications this had for rescue, that the British government objected to the WRB.[62] The Board, in spite of its neutral title, had been formed in Whitehall's eyes as a way of satisfying the particularistic demands of New York's Jewish voters. Moreover, it was believed that because of the presence of Jewish members, the WRB was following policies that put saving the Jews before the universalistic goal of winning the war. To the British government, such ethnic or racial particularism was abhorrent. Indeed, in the major House of Commons debate on the WRB, Richard Law stressed that if an equivalent organization was set up in Britain it would involve major constitutional changes: it would 'institute an independent body which would control Ministers and heads of other Departments outside it'.[63]

But the liberal critique of Jewishness also affected refugee policy. Whenever a major possibility of rescue presented itself, the fear of a flood of Jews either to the Middle East or to Britain dominated the minds of British government officials. The assumption was that the introduction of large numbers (that is, more than a few thousand) of foreign, unassimilated, Jews would create hostility towards them. The government's concern at the time of the Horthy offer, for example, was not due to indifference, or to a blatant Nazi-inspired anti-semitism. It came out of an ambivalence towards the Jews; a sympathy towards their plight but an equal concern that they would create antisemitism if released out of the Nazi hell. Liberal values were thus harnessed to an exclusive nationalism, in which Englishness and Jewishness were seen to be incompatible. Yet, vital to understanding British policies from 1943 to the end of the war was the government's fear that it might be seen as illiberal. This meant that in 1943 (due to public pressure) and in 1944 (because of the WRB) it had to face modifying its two, genuinely held, prime beliefs – that wide-scale rescue was impossible, and that it was also potentially dangerous. In both cases, however, it managed to preserve its own strategy. It was an indication of its strong desire not to bend from its universalist principles – of winning the war first, and refusing to discriminate in favour of the persecuted Jews.

In the United States, until the formation of the WRB in January 1944, similar policies operated – in fact it could be argued that it was the British government throughout 1943 that was willing to exercise greater flexibility. But the formation of the WRB owed much to the money and influence of American Jewry which enabled the successful public campaigning (which involved thousands of non-Jews and many non-Jewish organizations) after spring 1943. The success of the Board also depended on the continuing finance provided by Jewish sources. Nevertheless, the successful Treasury revolt led by Henry Morgenthau showed the potential of pluralistic politics in the United States, an option not available to campaigners in Britain. Even so, differences between the two countries in the last years of the war should not be exaggerated. The United States, like Britain, was wary of letting in any sizeable number of Jewish refugees for fear of stimulating domestic antisemitism. The camp established in Oswego, New York State, in 1944 for 1,000 Jews from Europe was quite clearly a 'token refuge'. Moreover, official pronouncements about the activities of the WRB shied away from stressing any specific Jewish connection. Yet it remains that experts whose sole concern and energy could be directed to saving Jews were employed by the United States government in 1944 and 1945. In Britain their equivalents in the National Committee were left powerless and frustrated. Government officials were more concerned with the post-war removal of those refugees in Britain than with efforts to help the victims of Nazism in Europe.[64]

In January 1945, Eleanor Rathbone visited Ignacy Schwartzbart of the Polish government in exile. In total despair at the destruction of his own people, Schwartzbart commented that

This pigeon-hearted woman is one of the most gentle phenomenon among the M.P.s. Unfortunately her influence is only a moral one, which in [British] political life is tantamount to no influence.

Rathbone was to die shortly after the war, ill and exhausted by her activities. Indeed, the high death rate among the National Committee as a whole is very evident.[65] Their efforts in mobilizing the sympathy of the British public in the first half of 1943 eventually had little impact on government policy. Ironically, their impact, although indirect, was felt in the United States, where antisemitism was more powerful and sympathy towards the Jews less pronounced. It was the domination of universalist values, welded to an exclusive nationalism, that explains the stubbornness and homogeneity of the British government's response to the Jewish catastrophe. Its relative failure, especially when compared to that of the United States from 1944 until the end of the war, was not, therefore, due to the politics of 'indifference' or even that of 'antisemitism' – it was the politics of liberal ambivalence.

Part III

The Post-War World

7
Liberal Culture and the Post-War Confrontation with the Holocaust

It is now widely assumed that the liberation of the concentration camps in Western Europe during April/May 1945 ended the Holocaust and brought home its grim reality across the world. Both assumptions are extremely problematic. Tens of thousands of Jews, weakened and ill as a direct result of Nazi brutality, would die soon after liberation. The mental and physical scars of the persecution for many more would last throughout their lifetimes. For a sizeable minority, the moment of liberation was not in itself a notable event, reflecting the physical exhaustion and low morale of the victims. Hadassah Rosensaft who arrived in Belsen from Auschwitz in November 1944 recalls how for her the point at which she was liberated by British soldiers 'seemed a dream which soon turned into reality'. Nevertheless, she adds

How tragic it was that the great majority did not even realize that we were free, because they were unconscious or too sick to understand what was happening. . . . For the greatest part of the liberated Jews at Belsen, there was no ecstasy, no joy at our liberation. We had lost our families, our homes. We had no place to go to, nobody to hug. Nobody was waiting for us anywhere. We had been liberated from death, and the fear of death, but not from the fear of life.

In similar vein, Primo Levi in *The Drowned and the Saved* commented that 'In the majority of cases, the hour of liberation was neither joyful nor light-hearted. . . . Not "pleasure the son of misery": misery the son of misery.'[1] Furthermore, it is true that in the last quarter of the twentieth century the filmic and photographic images of the survivors of camps such as Belsen and Buchenwald have come to symbolize the horrors of the Holocaust. The scenes which were witnessed by the British and American photographers and cameramen have been used to represent the full extent of human degradation which emerged from the Nazis' programme of destruction and humiliation. It is also the case that the American and British troops, by liberating camps in Germany and Austria, confronted tens of thousands of Jews who had somehow lived through the mass murder in the camps of the east. More Jewish survivors were liberated from Belsen than any other concentration camp. But it would take some time for the gruesome sights of the liberated camps to be connected to a specifically *Jewish* tragedy or, indeed, be associated with the war itself in any direct way.

James Parkes, a leading campaigner on behalf of European Jewry, wrote a study in the war on *The Emergence of the Jewish Problem*. As the book was to be published by the state-sponsored Royal Institute of International Affairs (Royal Institute) and had implications for future peace conferences, Parkes had to seek British government approval for its content. He later related that when

the section on the Nazis was being written, news was filtering in of the reality of the 'final solution'. In the first draft I had written that there had been 50,000 Jews murdered in cold blood. The Foreign Office crossed off a nought. More news came in. In the second draft it was half a million – and the Foreign Office crossed off a nought. When they did the same to five million, I gave up and no figure is mentioned in the book.[2]

If there was a problem in understanding the scale of the disaster, there was an equal dilemma in finding a context for the Holocaust. Those involved in contemporary constructions of the war had great difficulty in assimilating information about the destruction of the Jews in their overall chronologies. On the surface the extermination programme appeared separate from the military struggle. Throughout the conflict the Royal Institute produced three-monthly chronologies of 'principal events' that had taken place at home and abroad. Information concerning the persecution of the Jews was limited to two passing references, both in 1942 (reinforcing the point that knowledge of the Holocaust peaked in that year in Britain). The first concerned the World Jewish Congress press conference in June and the second related to the Allied Declaration in December 1942. There was no material on the persecution of the Jews in the contemporary chronologies for 1943. Moreover, for 1944 and 1945, there was only information on one concentration camp liberation – that of Dachau in April 1945. Two years after the end of the war, however, a supplemented version of these chronologies was published by the Royal Institute. References to the extermination of the Jews were still limited but included a brief mention of persecution in Holland, Hungary and the Warsaw ghetto rebellion. Nevertheless, information on the camp liberations (although still unconnected to the Jewish disaster) was now more prominent. There was material on the liberation of Majdanek, Auschwitz, Belsen and Buchenwald, as well as Dachau.[3]

It was thus to take some time before the concentration camps would even feature in attempts to provide a cohesive war narrative. The realization, however, that the western camps were not at the heart of the extermination process has even now, half a century later, yet to be achieved on a popular level. The Holocaust, it must be stressed, is now more present in the cultures of liberal societies such as Britain and the United States than ever before. This is also true of some countries occupied by the Nazis in the war. Henry Rousso has written of France since the late 1970s and its confrontation with the Vichy years (including its antisemitism). He comments on 'the *immediacy* of the period, its astonishing presentness, which at times [has risen] to the level of obsession'.[4] Yet this greater awareness has not stopped the influence of ideological and nationally specific frameworks from shaping and often distorting contemporary conceptions of the Holocaust. For British and American societies especially, the spring 1945 liberations have been particularly important in the process of creating a memory of European Jewry's destruction. The particularistic frameworks of Englishness and Americanness have been employed to confront the horrors of Nazism. As Ilan Avisar has written, more generally, 'as the war-torn countries were licking their wounds, reflection on the war experience gradually developed and concentrated on the specific national problems of each society'.[5] For many years (and continuing trends that were present throughout the Nazi era), neither British nor American society was able to come to terms with the specifically antisemitic aspect of the Nazis' extermination programme. Liberal universalism continued to be welded to forms of nationalism which precluded the consideration of the Jewish fate. Only in recent decades has a different pattern emerged so that the Holocaust is recognized widely as a special entity. It is now seen as being linked to other forms of genocide and racism, and to the Nazis' destructive capacity, but it is also perceived as possessing its own unique features (including the specific devastating impact on a particular people and their culture). Although there has been great change in recent years, this process of understanding is, in Britain, far from complete and there is a contrast to the situation in the United States. This chapter will explore how and why different patterns have emerged in these two liberal democracies in their post-war confrontation with the Holocaust.

I

Although their responses would vary later, at the time of the liberation of the western concentration camps there was great similarity between Britain and the United States as they tried to make sense of the human misery and death they had exposed. The Soviet forces, as we have seen, liberated eastern camps such as Majdanek (in July 1944) and Auschwitz (in January 1945). They found the evidence of mass murder with some victims (dead and alive) still in the camps. But the Nazis had been able to abandon these camps and leave them in a relatively sanitized form. Horrific as they were, there was less immediate and open evidence of mass human misery in the liberated eastern camps compared with what was to face the British and American soldiers in the final stages of the war in Europe. Camps such as Buchenwald, Dachau and Belsen were not centres of direct extermination or death factories. Belsen, for example, as its historian, Eberhard Kolb, comments, 'occupied a relatively special place within the National Socialist concentration camp system'.[6] It began functioning in 1943 and was not initially designed exclusively for Jews (although it did operate as an exchange camp for a few privileged Jewish prisoners). Only in the last few months of the war (with the arrival of the survivors of the death marches) was a clear link made to the extermination programme in the east. But it was the sight and smell of the western camps that would confront the liberators. The link between camps such as Auschwitz and Belsen would emerge much later. In spring 1945, it is not surprising that those witnessing the horrors within the liberated camps would assume that they had come across the very worst of Nazi atrocities, 'the lowest point of degradation to which humanity has yet descended' as the British White Paper on Buchenwald put it. Such tendencies were reflected in a popular *Victory Book* produced in Britain during the summer of 1945. In a section on liberation, 'Victims of the Nazis', there was a vague and fleeting reference to a 'Silesian death camp' (that is, Auschwitz) but the report suggested

It was, however, within the frontiers of Germany itself that the most horrific sights were discovered. The great Nazi concentration camps of Buchenwald, Dachau, Belsen and the like were overrun by the Allies and discovered to be crammed with thousands of half-starved, disease-ridden wrecks of men progressed beyond human aid.[7]

In early 1945, British officials had received information from the Soviet Union about the liberation of Auschwitz. Doubts were expressed by senior civil servants about the scale of the destruction that had taken place in the camp. By May 1945, however, Ian Henderson of the Foreign Office wrote that it was 'generally agreed that Oswiecim was the worst of all the camps'. But this was a perception far removed from popular notions in Britain and the United States. Another Foreign Office official noted in February 1945 that information on the camps liberated by the Russians had received only 'the scantiest indications in the Press'.[8] The lack of understanding was exposed even in the Houses of Parliament. There was discussion on the liberation of the western camps and particularly Buchenwald, which was to be subject to a visit from a parliamentary delegation. By contrast, Auschwitz lacked any real meaning in terms of its geography, scale and purpose. It was referred to as 'Aeushwald' and 'Aeuschwitz' in what was the briefest of mentions in the House of Commons. Significantly, this was in response to a question of whether any *British* subjects 'were confined in Aeschwitz Camp in Germany [sic]'. Such national exclusivity was to condition other responses to the camp exposures.[9]

A journalist in London, reflecting why the reports of Belsen were being generally accepted as genuine – whereas those concerning Majdanek less than a year earlier were rejected as propaganda – concluded that it was probably 'because it is our forces which are up against these present horrors'. Of central importance with regard to understanding popular responses to the liberation exposures in spring 1945 is the connection that was made to knowledge of the concentration camps of the 1930s. In Britain particularly, the White Paper of October 1939 was a point of reference, marking the time at which the government gave official credence to the information that had already been widely reported on Nazi atrocities.[10]

There were few, as we have seen, who disbelieved the information contained in the White Paper. The small group of individuals who doubted such material were at that point mainly connected to pro-Nazi organizations (with elements from the pacifist movement also suspecting the British government of atrocity-mongering to whip up support for the war effort). As the war progressed, however, those refusing to accept that the Jews were being exterminated as part of an organized programme of destruction broadened to include many outside the world of antisemitic extremism. Indeed towards the end of the conflict in Britain, and also in the United States, there was a greater tendency to believe that stories of the destruction of the Jews were 'atrocity propaganda'. Yet the films, newsreels, photographic displays, newspaper and radio reports of the liberated western camps were to change fundamentally the public perceptions of Nazi atrocities in Britain and the United States. In both societies the information was generally accepted and believed. An opinion poll carried out in the United States during May 1945 found that 84 per cent of the sample believed the reports that 'the Germans have killed many people in concentration camps or let them starve to death'. A further 9 per cent thought the stories were 'true, but exaggerated', and only 3 per cent doubted them seriously. Just 1 per cent stated that the reports were 'doubtful, hard to believe'. The proportion of those believing that the Germans had killed 'many' in the concentration camps had increased slightly since the end of 1944 (by 8 per cent) but the major difference in public perceptions concerned the actual number murdered. The most common figure given in December 1944 of people killed in the camps was 100,000 or less. By May 1945 the figure had risen to a median average of one million.[11] This was still only a fraction of the total murdered in the Nazi concentration camp system but indicated that there was now some awareness that killing on an enormous scale had taken place. Yet the very wording of these Gallup polls highlights the continued focus on Nazi *concentration camps*. Other locations of mass murder and the possibility of death camps remained largely unrecognized in the liberal democratic world. Moreover, the surveys made no specific mention of Jewish victims of extermination.

The work carried out by Mass-Observation during the spring of 1945 revealed a similar situation in Britain. There were some who were suspicious of the revelations but they were in a small minority. In an investigation carried out when the first liberation reports/pictures were released in April, over 80 per cent were convinced that they were genuine whereas 'Four months ago a quarter of the people who were interviewed had no opinion about the validity of the atrocity stories' and only 37 per cent regarded them as true. Just 3 per cent of the April 1945 sample believed that the atrocity stories were false whereas the figure for December 1944 was over one in ten. It is important, however, to move beyond the surface tendencies exposed in such statistics. A detailed analysis of the material gathered by Mass-Observation reveals other important aspects of the British debate when the news of the liberated western camps was circulating.[12]

The clearest feature which emerges was the profound impact that the reports had on ordinary people. Discussion in diaries during the second half of April and early May 1945 was dominated by discussion of the disclosures:

The horrors of the German prison camps have got people properly now. One hears nothing else talked about. (18 April 1945); Everyone in the hospital was talking of the awful Hun Concentration Camps. I've rarely seen the British People so moved. (23 April 1945); [in response to a letter describing Belsen] I just can't forget it. It doesn't seem possible that such things would happen in a civilised world. (24 April 1945); Everybody everywhere in the tram, in the office, [is] talking about the German atrocities now being uncovered and really, our wildest imaginings couldn't have pictured things as bad as they are (18 April 1945).[13]

The second aspect of the contemporary debate concerned the veracity of the stories. As will be discussed shortly, the consideration of the disclosures along the limited lines of 'true' or 'false' was partly in response to the British government's presentation of the concentration camp material. The emphasis in the semi-official newsreels was summarized by the commentary in Pathe's treatment of the camps: 'The responsibility for these terrible crimes falls squarely on the German people'. As Nicholas Pronay suggests, the purpose of these newsreels was not so much to shed 'light on what the Germans had been up to . . . but rather in the spirit expressed in the title which Paramount News gave its version of the Belsen footage: *Proof Positive*'. In a pattern very similar to the one that emerged with the October 1939 White Paper, the British public were generally convinced of the evidence of Nazi atrocities. Neverthe-less, it is important to add that there were a significant number who were suspicious of the British government's motives in releasing the material.[14]

Lingering doubts about the nature of Nazi crimes against humanity were largely removed by the camp disclosures, especially by the photographic and filmic images. As one contemporary put it: 'The film is mightier than the pen. I'm always hearing bits of conversation in shops and buses: "it must be true, because I've seen the pictures".' It was reported 'how the concentration camp revelations have impressed and changed the outlook of many men and women. They realise that these are hard facts and not just atrocity propaganda.'[15] Another Observer noted the talk in his office after newspaper pictures were circulated: 'Even the confirmed sceptics are shaken by these pictures of Belsen camp and agree that the Germans are a bad lot.' A film strip producer in London commented that 'Details of some of the horror camps seem unbelievable, yet one is forced to believe that they are true'.[16] It should be stressed, however, that belief about the stories was in spite of, rather than because of, their semi-official exposure to the public. A middle-aged man emerging from a cinema showing one of the camp newsreels in late April 1945 highlighted the importance of this factor:

There's one or two even now [who] won't believe it. Just stubbornness. Think it's clever to believe nothing you hear. That's the trouble about too much propaganda – you get people thinking everything's propaganda. Well, I don't think that myself, but after all, there's plenty been written about these camps, all these years since Hitler came to power. Anybody that wasn't deaf and blind and daft knew all about it. The suspicious thing to my mind is why they start making all this din about them now. I suppose it's a question of seeing is believing.

A clerk in Essex was even more troubled by the 'official' nature of the revelations yet ultimately was forced to accept the truth of the reports:

I find it hard to keep an open mind on this matter. I have not forgotten the recent controversy over the last war atrocity stories, and to me they have always smacked of propaganda – the Germans are our enemies. [Cruelty is one of Nazism's trade marks but] it is hard to believe, however, that this mass cruelty has been perpetrated on so many thousands of victims. Yet what else can we believe? Here is the evidence, in the soberest newspapers, as well as the *Daily Mirror*.[17]

The *Daily Express* designed an exhibition in Trafalgar Square of 22 photo-graphs from Belsen, Buchenwald and Nordhausen. The motto 'SEEING IS BELIEVING' accompanied the images. In the extensive surveying carried out by Mass-Observation, there was evidence of only one exception to this rule – a 15-year-old was reported as saying that he/she thought 'it must have been all a stunt . . . because the pictures weren't all that bad'. But this teenager's response was totally isolated. Observers at the cinema and in the photographic exhibitions reported the audiences' and visitors' stunned silence. An Oxfordshire housewife related how she 'felt too rotten for words so did nothing all day'. Others were so sickened that their health and sleep were affected. The visual images were simply too powerful to be dismissed.[18] Indeed the British government itself decided to exploit the strategy of 'seeing is believing' in the choosing of its official delegation to visit Buchenwald camp.

On the morning of 19 April 1945, General Eisenhower, Commander of SHAEF (Supreme Headquarters Allied Expeditionary Forces), invited Churchill to assemble a party to visit a camp at Weimar (Buchenwald) as the 'new discoveries . . . far surpass anything previously exposed'. Churchill told the Commons later that day that Eisenhower wanted a British parliamentary body to go 'in order that they may themselves have ocular and first-hand proof of these atrocities'. In the preamble to the White Paper published in late April 1945, the selection of the ten parliamentary delegates was explained as follows: the choosing of two peers and eight MPs was designed to have representatives from both houses. The larger number of MPs allowed a cross-section of the Commons to be present (three from the Conservatives, three from the Labour party and one each from the Liberals and Liberal Nationalists). The White Paper also noted that the delegation included a woman, two doctors, a solicitor and 'a member of the Jewish race'.[19]

In announcing the formation of the delegation, Churchill asked the party whips to come up with representatives in what appeared on the surface to be a free process. Behind the scenes, however, pressure was being applied on the whips. James Chuter Ede, soon to become the Home Secretary, reported in his diary how in the Labour party there had been 'some comment on the selection of Ness Edwards and Sloan as the Labour representatives'. It was explained to Chuter Ede by the Labour whip that Churchill 'wanted the unbelievers to go'. Churchill had hinted at such machinations in the House of Commons when, in response to a plea that it not 'be represented by the usual official delegates', he drily commented that he could 'see some to whom it might do a lot of good'. In fact, the eventual choosing of Sidney Silverman, the British Chair of the World Jewish Congress, was due to the illness of Sloan, rather than a recognition of Jewish suffering in the camps. Immediately after the war the British government was reluctant to allow specifically *Jewish* relief organizations to visit the liberated camps. The initial totally non-Jewish make-up of the parliamentary delegation reflected the government's continued refusal to accept any hint of Jewish particularism. Only the illness of a Labour 'doubter' gave room for a Jewish member of the team to participate. Churchill's strategy certainly worked for the individuals involved. The final sentence of the White Paper concluded that 'The memory of what we saw and heard at

Buchenwald will haunt us ineffaceably for many years'. Tragically, one member of the delegation, Mavis Tate, was to commit suicide not long after the visit to Buchenwald. The delegation's objective had been 'to find out the truth'. The parliamentary team reported the stench, disease, overcrowding and evidence of cruelty found at the camp and their evidence was accepted as being beyond doubt. But their scope, as their report stressed, was self-consciously limited. Their aim was

to test the accuracy of the reports already published. We therefore determined to exclude from our report statements of which no material evidence was still visible.

This point brings into focus the exact nature of what was and was not discussed in official and semi-official reporting from the liberated western camps and how this in turn was assimilated by the public.[20]

II

Historians and others have an enormous desire to believe that the liberation of the camps in spring 1945 exposed to the world the horrors of the Holocaust. In so doing they impose later perceptions on contemporary interpretations and provide a deceptively simple chronology on what was, in reality, a prolonged and complex process of understanding which is yet to be completed. The assumption that an immediate connection was made at the time of the liberation of the concentration camps to what is now known as the horrors of the Holocaust has rarely been checked by reference to detailed evidence. Surprise is therefore expressed when the reality turns out to be somewhat different from the expected pattern. Thus, in the first monograph devoted to the liberation of the camps (significantly entitled *The End of the Holocaust*), Jon Bridgman appears to have been thrown off guard when he found that 'In all the contemporary accounts of the Bergen-Belsen liberation there are remarkably few references to Jews'. Yet Bridgman does not analyse why this was the case and later suggests a popular identification with *Jewish* victims of Nazi persecution immediately after the war which precluded 'even supposedly innocent [antisemitic] remarks'. He thereby ignores the logic of his own findings. The liberal imagination demands that the concept of progress be restored as quickly as possible. As Primo Levi put it, there is a false optimism which desires to believe that 'After the disease, health returns; to deliver us from imprisonment "our boys" arrive just in time, the liberators with waving flags'.[21] Bridgman, however, was not mistaken in pointing to the absence of Jews in the Belsen reports. This was the case with the newsreels and the official British government film on the liberations, as well as radio and newspaper accounts of Belsen. But the process was not confined to Britain and Belsen. The same tendency was clear in the equivalent American media liberation reports. The absence was hardly an accidental oversight as, for example, at the time of its liberation, 40,000 Jews were present in Belsen (representing up to two-thirds of its final population).[22]

There are three interrelated reasons for the absence of Jews in the contemporary reports. First, those facing the horrors had difficulty in making any sense of the situation. Curtis Mitchell, an American military photographer, was taken to see Belsen very shortly after its liberation and later related how

you got over feeling that these were people any more. They were so thin and so dried out that they might have been monkeys or plaster of Paris and you had to keep saying to yourself, these are human beings, and even when you said it your mind was not believing it because nothing like this had ever happened before and it just couldn't happen.

Similarly, John Dixey, a medical student who took part in the relief team, commented that

If it had been several hundred bodies one might have been really desperately upset and affected by it, mentally or psychologically at any rate. But no, it was on such a huge scale, it was rather like trying to count the stars. There were thousands and thousands of dead bodies and you couldn't really consider them to be your mother or your brother or your father because there were just too many and they were being bulldozed into graves.

Joy Trindles, a nurse who had served on the western front, added that 'We thought we had seen it all. Until Belsen'.[23] Richard Dimbleby in Britain and Ed Murrow in the United States, the two leading broadcasters in their respective countries, attempted to describe the scenes that confronted them in Belsen and Buchenwald. Both refused to compromise and produced perhaps their greatest work from the liberated camps. Dimbleby told a BBC colleague that 'I must tell the exact truth, every detail of it, even if people don't believe me, even if they feel these things should not be told'. Murrow told his American listeners 'If I have offended you by this rather mild account of Buchenwald, I am not the least sorry'. Both struggled to communicate the enormity of the situation. Murrow added that 'I pray you believe what I have said about Buchenwald. I have reported what I saw and heard, but only part of it; for most of it I have no words.' Dimbleby was furious when at first the BBC refused to broadcast his account until it had been verified by newspaper reports. (The BBC also used Murrow rather than its own reporter to describe Buchenwald. By using an American with great standing in Britain they hoped to impress upon their listeners the authenticity of the revelations.) Dimbleby's report dealt with some of the crazed, starving individual inmates he had encountered. But it was his descriptions of the mass dead that dominated his broadcast:

In the shade of some trees lay a great collection of bodies. I walked around them, trying to count – there were perhaps 150, flung down on each other. All naked, all so thin that their yellow skins glistened like stretched rubber on their bones. Some of the poor, starved creatures whose bodies were there looked so utterly unreal and inhuman that I could have imagined they had never lived.[24]

In these powerful accounts, which had an immense impact on the British and American public, the victims emerged as devastated people without a past or a future. The scale and immediacy of the horror limited the possibility of understanding the specific background of the camp inmates. It was also the very awfulness of Buchenwald, Belsen and Dachau which initially acted as a barrier to an understanding that these were not the worst of the Nazi camps. This is the second factor that has to be taken into account when explaining the silence on the Jews in contemporary liberation accounts.

In the White Paper on Buchenwald, the parliamentary delegation reported that

One of the statements made to us most frequently by prisoners was that conditions in other camps, particularly those in Eastern Europe, were far worse than at Buchenwald. The worst camp of all was said by many to be at Auschwitz.[25]

It would take some time, however, before it was realized that the eastern camps were fundamentally different to those in the west. The official Soviet report on Auschwitz published in the summer of 1945 did little to change the situation as it received very little publicity in Britain and the United States. In short, although many of the survivors in the camps such as Belsen had been through the death camps of the east, those reporting the liberations did not make the connection to a wider Nazi extermination programme. The western camps were perceived as self-contained and as representing, on their own, an indict-ment of the Nazi system/German people. It is crucial, however, to go beyond such pragmatic and localized explanations of why the Jews did not feature in the early reports. Yet again, the answer lies within the nature and strength of liberal ideology.

As early as February 1945 the British Ministry of Information considered the production of a film highlighting the 'terror methods of Germany'. After the liberations of Buchenwald and Belsen, there was financial approval for the film and it was to 'be given top priority'. Sidney Bernstein was entrusted with assembling the film using footage from British, American and Soviet cameramen. Alfred Hitchcock was also employed to ensure that there could be no accusations that the material had been faked. The aim, as Bernstein later recalled, was to place the blame for the atrocities with the German people and not just with the Nazi elite. But the strong ideological roots of the film's purpose did not stop at such narrow nationalism. A universalism was also at work. It was one that continued the tendencies which had been so important in the war, especially the exclusion of any specific consideration of Jewish suffering. A top-level British government memorandum linked to the film and post-war atrocity material stressed with regard to German documentation that

preference [was to be given] to those which specify the nationality and/or religion of the victims and documents should be selected involving as great a variety of nationalities and religions as possible. It is especially desirable to document the extent to which non-Jewish German nationals were the victims of the German concentration camp system.[26]

In the Bernstein film (which, because of a softening attitude towards Germany in the autumn of 1945, was never shown), no mention was made of Jewish victims in Auschwitz or Buchenwald. The strength of liberal opposition to any form of Jewish separatism, even when the reality of the Nazi extermination programme became clear, was thus still maintained. In the British case it might be suggested that the fear of giving any credence to the Zionist case prohibited any particular mention of the Jews. Yet there was no difference between the British and American media when dealing with the concentration camps. The word 'Jew' is conspicuous by its absence. Indeed, in one or two cases of reporting, there was positive resistance to the very suggestion that the victims may have been predominantly Jewish. A leading liberal British journalist, James Hodson, wrote in the liberal *Time and Tide* that although he had been told by a Rabbi (quite accurately) that 70 per cent of Belsen's victims were Jewish, he insisted that the figure did not exceed 20 per cent. On the Trotskyite left, *Socialist Appeal*, which had earlier claimed that the atrocities against the Jews had been exaggerated, now stated that the only real victims of the Nazi camps had been the German working classes.[27]

Given the media's presentation of liberated camps, it is not surprising that little public debate focused on the Jews as specific victims of Belsen and Buchenwald. Nevertheless, the information as presented by official and semi-official accounts was not simply accepted uncritically by ordinary people. The American cultural critic, Susan Sontag, has written how she came by chance across photographs of Bergen-Belsen and Dachau in a bookstore in Santa Monica during the summer of 1945:

Nothing I have seen – in photographs or in real life – ever cut me as sharply, deeply, instantaneously. Indeed, it seems plausible to me to divide my life into two parts, before

I saw those photographs (I was twelve) and after, though it was several years before I understood fully what they were about.[28]

As a very young person, Sontag had no framework in which to place such images. Yet for many adults in Britain and the United States, there was such a context to place the appalling images – that of the Nazi concentration camps of the 1930s. Mass-Observation found that over half of their sample believed that the camp exposures could be related to Nazi atrocities before the war. Their comments show how little was really understood about what had taken place *since* the 1930s: 'I'd read a great deal about it before, so it wasn't new to me'; 'I'd read about it and guessed what it was like ever since 1936'; 'I'd heard about it long ago back in 1935–1936.' Those who had been critical of the Conservative appeasers were particularly prone to anger along such lines at this point. The novelist Naomi Mitchison commented in late April 1945 that 'I keep on saying that when some of us talked about concentration camps three years before the war the people who talk about them now wouldn't listen'.[29] This led many to be suspicious of the British government's motives in releasing the concentration camp material as the war came to an end. It rarely led to doubting the atrocity evidence but it pushed many to construct their own interpretation of the place of Belsen and Buchenwald in history. As one observer put it:

It made me feel pretty sick; but somehow I feel too much is being made of it. So much commentary I mean, it makes you wonder what they're up to. You can't trust them. They never said anything about it before the war, why all this hullabaloo now?'[30]

By connecting the 1945 exposures to the camps of the 1930s (which in the case of Buchenwald and Dachau at least allowed for continuity in name), the sheer size of the Nazi extermination programme escaped most people in the liberal democracies. Nevertheless, there was still surprise at the images of the liberated camps. One man in his twenties commented that 'I'd heard about it years ago. No doubt I didn't realise they were quite so bad.' Similarly a middle-aged woman commented that although she was aware of German atrocities since 1935, she 'didn't think [she] realised altogether the extent'.[31] The immensity of the images of Belsen and Buchenwald thus confused many. The journalist in London who was intrigued why, in contrast, the Majdanek disclosures a year earlier had made so little impact reminded her colleagues about the reality of the *extermination* camps but they responded by suggesting that

they thought [Majdanek] was less horrible. If people are gassed they don't suffer. Some of the people at Buchenwald have been there 12 years. And they are Germans too, their own folk.

Nevertheless, the attempt to interpret the evidence independently of the government line allowed at least a small minority to make the connection to the Jewish disaster:

Well, in a way I did know, I knew they had been torturing the Jews for years, but to see all these terrible pictures – poor starved people dying worse than animals – seeing it as if you'd stood there yourself – it made something you could never forget.[32]

In addition, hundreds if not thousands of non-Jews in Britain had developed intimate ties with Jewish refugees or Jews stranded in Europe. They thus understood earlier than most what had actually occurred to the Jews of the Continent. A housewife in Sheffield related meeting a Czech Jew in August 1945 who had just arrived from Prague:

After 39 months in a concentration camp [he] saw his mother and brother gassed. Bears lashes on his back still. He, a 12 stone man, weighed 90 lbs when liberated . . . says nine million died at his camp alone. Knows that [he] isn't believed here, but says after first census is taken in Europe, we will know he speaks the truth. . . . How he can still smile and be courteous, he does and is, is amazing.

Another housewife, in Winchester, mentioned in her diary in September how her husband

had just received a letter from a Polish Jew with whom he was at college. The Pole had spent five years in a concentration camp and he and his sister were the only survivors in his family. [Her husband] said: 'We grumble here, but we've none of us been through anything like the things that that man has endured'.[33]

Yet, before the evidence presented at the early war crimes trials in the autumn of 1945, such connections to the Jewish fate (and an awareness that it had been fundamentally different to the experience of others) were comparatively rare. The objective of the British and American governments in revealing the nature of the crimes of their enemy had not been to focus on the victims of the Nazis (and especially not the Jews), but to emphasize the rightness of the war effort through the demonization of the German people. Ironically the impact of this strategy was to be felt most strongly by the refugees from Nazism in the liberal democracies.

Many on the left in Britain were suspicious of the thinly disguised anti-German hate campaign. One woman commented that

They say it's the fault of all German people . . . [but] I'm afraid it doesn't make me feel anti-German; it makes me feel anti-humanity, that man could do such a thing to man.

Would the same have happened here, I wonder, if we'd had the same government? I've heard some violent anti-semitic talk which makes me think it would. I feel it's the fault of humanity at large, not the Germans in particular.[34]

In the summer of 1945, Victor Gollancz in particular was anxious to show in pamphlet form *What Buchenwald **Really** Means*. He stressed that his latest work was not concerned with the extermination camps in Poland where millions of Jews had been slaughtered, but with the western camps and the high percentage of German opponents that had suffered in them. Gollancz's attempt to oppose the accusation of German collective guilt was accompanied by a powerful David Low cartoon of the concentration camp victims. In response to a bowler-hatted Englishman's indignant comment that 'The Whole German People Should Be Wiped Out For This!', the survivors reply: 'Don't Forget Some of *Us* Are Germans, Friend'.[35]

Although some could not face the concentration camp films and exhibitions, the majority of the British public felt it was important to endure the images. Huge queues formed outside the *Daily Express* exhibition in London. A visitor commented: 'Awful pictures, enough to make one feel ill, but everyone, like me, wanted to see them'. Such visits reinforced the rightness of the war effort and, often, a parochial realization of what Britain itself might have experienced. It is therefore not difficult to understand why, for many, the government's emphasis on collective German guilt, in spite of the efforts of Gollancz and Low, was highly successful. In the spring and early summer of 1945 a genocidal attitude towards Germany was common in British society: 'I don't think we could ever be hard enough on the Germans; their behaviour is more like animals.'[36] For the refugees from Nazism this was an especially difficult time. Out of the chaos of liberated Europe many were piecing together news of family and friends killed in the extermination programme. For the majority of exiles, there was little to celebrate at the end of the war, yet they found little space to grieve in British society. The Association of Jewish Refugees in Great Britain wrote to Eleanor Rathbone at the end of April 1945 despairing that

The publication of the atrocities committed in the concentration camps have influenced part of the public to mix up Jewish Refugees with German nationals . . . we therefore beg to put before you some material about the suffering undergone by Jews in concentration camps between 1933 and the outbreak of war.

This Association has always made it clear that no bonds are left between Jewish Refugees and Germany, but it seems necessary to show once again that the Jews were Hitler's first victims in the concentration camps as they were anywhere else. A great part of the refugees who could escape to this country and to other places of refuge had to go through the hell of the concentration camps.[37]

Yet again the limiting prism of the concentration camp hindered comprehension of the Jewish plight. In a bitter ironic twist, however, the camp exposures of spring 1945 actually led to increased hostility towards the Jewish refugees. As the National Committee for Rescue from Nazi Terror reported, 'A certain feeling of hate against "all Germans, even those living here", has doubtlessly arisen amongst parts of the population through a misconception of the implications of the Buchenwald revelations'. At the start of May 1945 in the House of Lords, Lord Ailwyn and others attacked 'the infiltration of Germans into various activities of our national life' and there were equally unpleasant asides in the House of Commons.[38] Refugees in Britain were frightened that their already marginal status as aliens was under further attack. Few had become naturalized and the fear of being forced to return to the Continent haunted many Jewish refugees in 1945. One German Jew who had spent six months in Sachsenhausen concentration camp wrote to Victor Gollancz in July 1945. He explained that while he was trying

to build up what is still left of my life . . . [he could not] get rid of the idea or rather the fact that once again our very existence is in the balance, as I do not know what will become of us. How can anybody expect us to go back to a cemetery!

He added that

one hour ago I received a confirmation that my dear father died in one of those extermination camps. I did not cry because I never expected anything else. And I cannot cry any more.[39]

In the autumn of that year the British national and local press gave a new dimension to the anti-German/anti-alien campaign. The suggestion was made 'that the housing shortage could be greatly eased if foreigners were made to leave this country'. By October 1945 such sentiment had moved onto a street level in the area of greatest refugee concentration – the borough of Hampstead in north-west London. Over 2,000 signatures were obtained for a petition to remove the 'alien presence' from the area. The petition movement consisted of a mixture of local Conservative party members and figures with strong connections to quasi-fascist organizations. It was, however, the links with the extremists which limited the success of the anti-aliens. Indeed, the strengths and weaknesses of the Hampstead Petition movement in the autumn of 1945 set the pattern in Britain for the post-war period. At a local level there appeared to be little understanding of the traumas and difficulties facing the several thousand Jewish refugees in Hampstead. It was thus possible to label them as 'aliens' or 'foreigners' and to exploit their Germanness and even Jewishness to stimulate local animosities. Yet the connections with organizations which could be linked to the former enemy ultimately destroyed the movement's credibility. Liberals and those on the left particularly stressed the dangers of Nazism (including the use of race hatred) inherent in this anti-German movement. Eleanor Rathbone, as always, went further. In what was one of her last public speeches before her untimely death she addressed a protest meeting in Hampstead. She pointed out that, for the refugees, the war had hardly ended. Rathbone added that if she too had to confront the 'fate [of] their dearest, [I] think I'd go mad'. Stressing a particularity that both the anti-alienists *and* the anti-petitionists had generally avoided, Rathbone asked:

Who are these aliens? Jews. Hitler adopted *your* policy – throw them out (later exterminated them). Do you want to follow *his* policy?[40]

The revelations from the western camps thus provided a problematic matrix which, rather than aiding comprehension of a specific Jewish tragedy during the war, actually hindered, distorted and ultimately delayed understanding of the grim reality. The British and, to a lesser extent, the American government had succeeded in whipping up hatred of the German people. In the process the nature and background of the victims had been by-passed. For some the images of the concentration camps made only a passing impact. Often their presentation did not help – for example, in Britain and the United States the liberation newsreels were sometimes sandwiched between mundane and parochial news items and the flippancy of a Donald Duck cartoon. Yet for a majority the images were so powerful that they would remain indelibly ingrained in memory. It has been said that 'Many still remember exactly where and when they first saw these awful images'.[41] Yet the historicizing, re-processing and re-interpretation of these images would take individuals many decades. Some would never attempt the process. It is vital to stress that in 1945 only those with specific interest in the Jews themselves would connect the horrendous scenes to what would become known as the Holocaust. As Neil Ascherson has written of Bernstein's liberation film:

The film-makers had not, in fact, had time to grasp the horror within the horror. The scale of the 'Final Solution of the Jewish Problem' had scarcely dawned on them, and it was to be many years before the word 'Auschwitz' (implying the gassing of millions), replaced 'Belsen' in Britain as the ultimate metaphor of evil.[42]

Three groups can, however, be identified which did make the connection between the camp revelations and the Jews at an early stage. The first and numerically the most significant were the Jewish minorities of the democracies. However, with some notable exceptions (individual and organizational), American and especially British Jewry were, as we have seen, increasingly removed from the reality of the situation in Europe as the war progressed. Even with the camp revelations in spring 1945, many Jews in Britain and the United States had difficulty in understanding what had occurred. A Jewish British army chaplain who was present in the early days of the Belsen liberation recalls the incredulity of Jewish audiences back home when he related his experiences. A survivor entering the United States remembers that when she first arrived 'the most ignorant people in the whole country about the Holocaust were the Jews'.[43] The specific details of the Jewish experience on the Continent during the war still escaped many established Jews in the democracies. Nevertheless, the information received throughout 1945, including that coming through family communication, brought home to Jews of both Eastern and Western European origin that something totally unprecedented had occurred. Not only had individuals' families and friends been killed, but a whole culture – the very roots of those who had come to live in the 'free world' – had also been wiped out. The suddenness of this realization in 1945 (although it would take much longer for the information to be properly assimilated) was perhaps the most important factor shaping, directly and indirectly, Jewish post-war identity in countries such as Britain and the United States. An American Jewish journal, *Opinion*, in the spring of 1945 described how

The most shocking [disclosure] of the war, indeed of all history, is the extermination of close to five million European Jews! Almost equally shocking is the indifference of the civilized world.

Similarly in Britain the Anglo-Jewish Association a few years after the war reported that

We have to deal with the emotion of insecurity – it arises from the recollection that not so long ago in Europe a highly advanced State turned upon its long established Jewish Community and eventually destroyed nearly the whole of European Jewry before a world which, though professing to be horror struck, was not prepared really to put itself out in order to save those who were threatened. Insecurity arises from the fear that the same thing might be repeated. . . . Such anti-Semitic incidents as occur in this country are doubtless magnified and produce a reaction in Jews which increases rather than diminishes tensions.

Nevertheless, the sense of marginality in these two Jewish communities led to the adoption of different strategies and responses to the surviving Jews of Europe. The *Opinion* article moved on to the suggestion that

More painful than the world silence [was] the failure of American Jewry and of American Jewish leadership to do anything themselves or to compel government action on behalf of the victims. . . . If American Jews had really been deeply aroused, our public officials would have been compelled to initiate real rescue work.[44]

Jews in the United States after 1945 were prepared to use their financial and political muscle at high government level. Moreover, as Yehuda Bauer has illustrated, they gave massively to relief measures on behalf of the Jews still in Europe: 'A bad conscience, a desire to make amends and help wherever possible, and an improving fund-raising organization all helped to produce what was then considered amazing results'. A sum of close to $200 million was received by the American Jewish Joint Distribution Committee between 1945 and 1948. In contrast British Jews responded to the news from Europe less in the form of guilt and more in terms of concern about their own status in society. British Jews lacked the wealth, numbers and potential influence of their American counterparts. In addition, the immediate post-war years were marked by the 'agony of Anglo-Jewry' over the British–Jewish conflict in Palestine and the intensification of domestic antisemitism. This reached a climax in the autumn of 1947 with riots against the Jews in major British towns, violence that lasted several nights. Those appealing for funds and clothing on behalf of new organizations such as the Committee for the Care of Children from the Camps were disappointed by the response from British Jewry. It reflected both the relative poverty and the narrow concerns of a Jewish minority that was now the largest in Western Europe. The Holocaust made a deep impact on British Jewry but this would be largely reflected in an increasingly inward-looking and insecure world-view. Few Jews in Britain and the United States would be involved immediately in measures of relief and rescue for the survivors, but practically all would be scarred by the realization of what had occurred, responding with a mixture of fear, insecurity and guilt.[45]

The two other and numerically much smaller groups interested in the Jews were to be found at polar extremes. The first were those who had been involved in helping Jews before and during the war and who continued to be involved in helping the survivors. In Britain, Victor Gollancz struggled not only to convince the public that not all Germans were guilty but also to show that the concentration camps contained hundreds of thousands of survivors. Concerned about contemporary obsession with only the horror of discovering mass death in the camps, Gollancz suggested with regard to the Jews of Belsen, Auschwitz, Dachau and Buchenwald that 'I am not concerned with those who have gone: let the dead bury the dead. I am concerned with the living.' Gollancz received much public response to his pamphlet *"Nowhere to Lay Their Heads": The Jewish Tragedy in Europe and Its Solution* but, as will emerge, many were more concerned with domestic matters than with helping the surviving Jews of Europe. A minority who had been stirred to action by Gollancz's *Let My People Go* were similarly 'very moved by [*"Nowhere to Lay Their Heads"*] and deeply thankful to [him] for having written it'. One of his readers suspected, however, that the 1945 pamphlet was simply preaching to the converted. There was not in Britain during 1945 the huge public demand for action which had so typified the situation after the publication of *Let My People Go* at the end of 1942. A woman from Carlisle wrote to Gollancz in the summer of 1945 explaining that 'Just before the war I spent a holiday in Germany and it was only then that I realized what anti-Semitism meant'. She was subsequently drawn into the fate of the Jews and 'now Belsen, Buchenwald and all the other horror camps have become a very personal sorrow to me'. It was, however, the rarity of this response in 1945 rather than its typicality which gives it significance.[46]

At the other extreme were those to whom the 'Jew' was the enemy and the source of all problems in the modern world. The destruction of European Jewry provided a dilemma for such extremists. First, they faced the problem of explaining how this all-powerful international force had managed to let itself be destroyed. Second, many extremist antisemites were attracted to forms of Nazism which lost any semblance of respectability with the revelations of the concentration camps. Denial of Nazi antisemitism, as we have seen, was not new and had its roots in the 1930s before developing further during the war itself. After the war, however, those who publicly denied that the Jews had been persecuted by the Nazis tended to be animated by fascist-style antisemitism alone. Mass murder of the Jews, they alleged, was due to Jewish invention (thus confirming the power rather than the ultimate weakness of world Jewry). The photographic and filmic imagery of the camps in 1945 proved a specific target for such extremists as they realized the strength of its impact. As early as May 1945, Frederick Bowman's *The Talking Picture News* commented with regard to the 'atrocity pictures' that there 'never was a worse fallacy than the idea that the camera can't lie'. In November 1947 the British fascist Oswald Mosley came out of retirement to announce to the press that 'Buchenwald and Belsen are completely unproved. . . . Pictorial evidence proves nothing at all.' Bowman and Mosley had both been detained by the British government during the war and their influence after 1945 was not great outside the small coterie of organized antisemitism. The same cannot be said of the journal *Truth* or Douglas Reed, whose paranoid rantings about Jewish conspiracies continued to be published by the widely respected Jonathan Cape until the 1950s. Reed told his readers that 'no proof can be given that six million Jews "perished"' and surveys in 1945 and 1946 suggest he was still not without influence. A shorthand typist's diary in September 1945 indicates how such views could still percolate through to non-extremists:

Notice that a lot of fuss and rumpus is being made about the Jews again. I wonder if it is all true, or merely what Douglas Reed says 'Because of the organised state of Jewry, we always know if 20 Jews suffer, but not if thousands of non-Jews do'. If only one *knew* what was true. I am a little suspicious.

Another Mass-Observer was less doubtful. At first he was incredulous about Reed's claims 'but after thinking about them came to believe that they must be in large measure true'. The Nazi persecution of the Jews was 'a hoax being magnified by the propaganda of International Jewry to obtain special privileges'.[47] It must be stressed that such views were isolated in Britain. Nevertheless, they were part of a very limited pattern in which a similarly small group of sympathizers at the other extreme (as well as the Jewish minority itself) made up those connecting the 1945 camp revelations to the fate of European Jewry.

It has been necessary to assess the initial reactions to the liberations (and Belsen and Buchenwald especially) in great detail for these proved to be a durable template with regard to popular understanding of Nazi atrocities. Indeed the battle to establish the singularity and specificity of the Jewish tragedy in the war would have to waged *against* the perceptions of spring 1945; ones that both by-passed the fate of the Jews and the possibility of the murder of millions.

III

In his *"Nowhere to Lay Their Heads"*, the universalist Victor Gollancz agonizingly explained his need in 1945 to justify morally a case for Jewish particularism: 'For my part, when human suffering is concerned I don't care a fig whether a man is a Jew or a gentile, an Englishman or a German'. He had to add, however, 'The plain fact is that, relatively to their total number, the Jews have suffered in this war more, terribly more, than any other people in the world'. Gollancz was more than sensitive to the possibility that such claims would upset British parochialism. It was still essential for him to refer to the fact that over four million Jews had been killed, at least a quarter of the total number of Jews in the world, and ask

Of what other people can that, or anything like it, be said? I would not say a word which might seem to make light of British suffering, and in particular of British suffering during the period when, in the phrase which must never be allowed to lose its glory however often repeated, 'we stood alone'. But if, to rebut a cynical libel, a comparison has to be made, remember that the number of British dead and missing, soldiers and civilians, was . . . 339,891; and this out of a total population of 48 millions.

Gollancz was taking a massive risk in daring to challenge the powerful myths that had developed of the British war effort and the sacrifices made, and particularly so given that he desired to win the sympathy of his British audience.

Some of his correspondents were indeed affronted by this attack on English nationalism by a 'wealthy' Jewish publicist:

Is there one of your people who has done more than his equal of ours? Yes, Jews have suffered more, but if the British had been distributed amongst almost every country in Europe, wouldn't they have suffered in like manner?[48]

Such narrow British parochialism with regard to the war and the Jews was to receive its first challenge in the Belsen Trial in autumn 1945. At the trial the camp's intimate connection to Auschwitz and therefore to mass murder in the east was established. Even here the particularity of the Jewish case did not receive a great deal of attention either in the trial or in subsequent media accounts. The *Zionist Review* reported with some frustration that 'the word "Jew" was not mentioned once in the preliminary formal proceedings'. More important in terms of knowledge of the Jewish catastrophe were the mammoth Nuremberg Trials which started shortly after. Michael Marrus has suggested that the crimes committed against the Jews 'never assumed a prominent place' at Nuremberg. Nevertheless, it was here that the figure of six million came into popular usage as well as the exposure of the methods of mass murder (including the use of gas chambers in the eastern camps). But in Britain and the United States the public soon tired of the meticulous attention to detail in the trials and there was relief when they finally finished nearly a year later in 1946.[49] Even after the Nuremberg Trials, Auschwitz and the other death camps had still to capture the popular imagination whereas Belsen became a term used in popular culture and everyday life. By the time of the Eichmann trial in 1961 the question was asked that 'The name Belsen is remembered, but are the facts which made it notorious so well remembered?'. In this respect it is important to note that the Auschwitz trial in 1947 received little attention or interest from the Western media.[50] What then was known on a popular level about the destruction of the Jews a year after the end of the war?

In July 1946, Mass-Observation carried out another detailed report on the Jews. Although there were no explicit references to the numbers of victims killed in the lengthy responses received, it is clear from this material that there was widespread awareness that the Jews of Europe had been subject to an attempted extermination (and that, through the use of gas chambers, Hitler and the Nazis had been largely successful). The survey was, however, carried out at a time of tension between Britain and the Jewish world over Palestine. Rather than the evidence of the Holocaust being used in a sympathetic way to support the Jewish cause, the reverse was often true:

I have always been of the opinion that Hitler's treatment of the Jewish problem was the right one. I mean I should be glad if the entire Jewish nation was utterly exterminated.

I should not approve of torturing them. . . . The only thing I disapproved of with regard to Hitler's Gas Chamber was that there were not enough, and what there were, were not very efficiently run.

I am inclined to agree with Hitler that the best solution of the Jewish problem, for the Gentiles that is, would be to gas the lot.

[With regard to the explosion at the King David Hotel] I could not have loved a Jew before, now I think Hitler was more right than wrong in his idea of extermination.[51]

Yet, apart from such temporary genocidal leanings, what emerges most strongly from this survey was the persistence of the assimilation solution as the answer to the 'Jewish problem'. With a tenacious adherence to liberal principles, Jews were still blamed for the existence of antisemitism, even *after* the evidence of the Nazis' extermination programme:

The Jewish problem is created by the Jews themselves. Nobody would interfere with Jews, not even Nazis, if they had not made themselves so conspicuous and hateful. The best solution would be for the Jews to pipe down and . . . to assume the nationality of the countries in which they live.

If such a miracle were possible, in a few generations, if they dropped their practice about marriage with non-Jews, there would be no Jewish problem. Hitler had another method and I wonder if . . . ?

Others were slightly uneasy about blaming the Jews after the immensity of what had occurred; a crime which to them could not be condoned:

On the other hand nations don't get persecuted for a long period by a lot of people for nothing.

Of course the cruelties of the Nazis are intolerable whatever the Jews were like – but I sometimes wonder if there was a *little* fire – even if only a spark – to account for so great a conflagration of smoke!

It is accepted that Hitler's disgusting bestiality to them could never be excused by whatever sins they had, or were said to have committed . . . [Yet all nations occupied by Germany] took advantage of the situation with suspicious alacrity, and proceeded to the 'solving of their own Jewish problem'.[52]

In May 1945 a journalist in London reported an office conversation in which the possible solutions to the 'Jewish problem' were discussed. One clerk was appalled at what the Germans had done to 'God's Chosen Race'. He suggested that 'The Germans could have passed laws, curtailing Jewish business. They shouldn't have tortured and killed the Jews.' This 'moderate' view was not accepted and 'Opposition was strong: "You can't pass laws against people in

power. The Jews have the banks and the industries".' In a desperate attempt
to explain away the seeming irrationality of the Nazis' antisemitism, some
were anxious to contrast the behaviour of the Jews of Europe with that of
British Jews who were 'less a thorn in the flesh'. Another added that

The Jews on the Continent were far more of a problem to their States than they are in
England; [that is] there are, or were, far more 'bad' Jews on the Continent than in the
United Kingdom.

These views were not confined to Britain. A poll of American GIs found that
'a very high proportion' believed that 'Hitler was *partly right* in his treatment
of Jews'.[53]

The determination to hold on to such attitudes was shown when they were
focused even on the survivors of the concentration camps. A Cambridge
University student was convinced that conditions in Belsen 'were due to the
filthy habits of the Jews themselves'. After viewing newsreels on the liberation
of Belsen one woman remarked: 'It must have been their fault. There's no
smoke without fire, you know.' Nor were such views kept to the private
realm. At the Belsen Trial in 1945 the British officer defending Josef Kramer,
the camp commandant, called the Jewish inmates the 'undesirable elements
from the dregs of the ghettoes of Central Europe'. *Truth*, a journal still with
strong links to the Conservative party, fully accepted this analysis of why the
Nazis had treated the Jews as they did in the camps. A similar attitude was
expressed by General George Patton, who was in control of much of the
American army administration of the displaced persons camps in Germany.
Patton disliked all the displaced persons but 'particularly . . . the Jews who
are lower than animals'. He believed that the 'Jewish type of DP is, in the
majority of cases, a sub-human species without any of the cultural or social
refinement of our time'. Unsurprisingly, Patton followed policies which were
often biased against the Jewish survivors. Yet, initially, on an official level,
both the British and American governments refused to 'discriminate' between
Jewish and non-Jewish displaced persons, as this would challenge liberal
universalism. Jews were thus mixed in camps with many who had fought for
the Nazi regime.[54] A disastrous cocktail of animosity against Jewishness (especially against the *ostjuden*) and opposition to Jewish particularity continued
to dominate British and American thinking about the Jews of Europe for the
first few months after the end of the war. The Jewish survivors still faced the
problem, as they attempted to leave the Continent, that their specific tragedy
had yet to be widely recognized. It would become, in fact, easier for those
previously sympathetic to the Nazi regime to enter some countries than the
Jews themselves.

IV

Although in the late stages of the war British and American responses to the European Jewish crisis took very different paths, both countries had effectively closed their doors to Jewish survivors. After the end of the conflict, however, there was to be a marked contrast in their respective immigration policies with regards to the Jews. In the six years of the post-war Labour governments, Britain allowed in, at most, several thousand Jewish survivors (at the same time as recruiting several hundred thousand displaced persons for labour purposes). In roughly the equivalent period the United States gave entry to well over 100,000 Jews from Europe, or one-quarter of the total permits it gave to displaced persons.[55] There was, therefore, a huge discrepancy between the number and proportion of Jews allowed entry into Britain and the United States which has to be accounted for. Rather than reflecting its undesirability as a country of immigration, the fact that so few Jewish survivors were accepted by Britain reflected the power of a mono-cultural liberal assimilationist ideology at work. The same tendencies were present in the United States and briefly became dominant in the passing of the 1948 Displaced Persons Act (which both directly and indirectly discriminated against the Jews in the European camps). Nevertheless, the pressure that built up after the war for a liberalization of immigration laws and the eventual liberal interpretation of the 1948 Act revealed (as with the formation of the War Refugee Board in 1944) that United States government policy was then based on the concept of ethnic plurality, in which the Jews were to be given proper consideration. This was the first of many areas in which British and American responses to the Holocaust were to take radically different directions in the post-war period.

The first hint of the changes ahead came with the Harrison Report on displaced persons in Europe. Criticisms had been levelled at the American military's handling of Jewish displaced persons in 1945 and Earl Harrison was dispatched to Europe by a not unsympathetic President Truman to recommend changes. In total contrast to General Patton, Harrison stressed that the Jews had 'suffered most and longest' and should therefore 'be given first and not last attention'. Breaking the assimilationist taboo, Harrison argued that 'The first and plainest need of these people is a recognition of their actual status and by this I mean their status as Jews'. Treating them simply as nationals of their country of origin meant ignoring the reality of their catastrophic war experiences. In what was to be a blunt attack on British policies, especially with regard to Palestine, Harrison pointed out that

Refusal to recognize the Jews as such has the effect, in this situation, of closing one's eyes to their former and more barbaric persecution, which has already made them a separate group with greater needs.

Treatment of Jewish displaced persons in the American-run camps did not become perfect after the circulation of Harrison's report, but it made enough difference for a British official to comment in 1946 that the 'Americans take very great trouble with all Jewish refugees, and woe betide any U.S. officer who leaves himself open to a complaint'. No such sensitivity was apparent in the British camps. In addition, by the end of 1945 a contrast had also already built up between Britain and the United States with regard to the entry of Holocaust survivors.[56]

In December 1945, under pressure from Jewish and non-Jewish lobbyists, President Truman announced a scheme of preferential treatment for displaced persons within the United States' immigration quota. At this point Britain and the United States were in increasing conflict over the former's refusal to allow any significant number of Jews into Palestine. In response, British officials were then critical of American immigration policy towards European Jewry, accusing the United States of hypocrisy in not wishing to burden itself with unwanted Jews. The truce that had operated on a public level between the two countries on these sources of mutual contention was, by the end of 1945, well and truly broken. The Foreign Office therefore dismissed Truman's proposals with regard to preferential treatment of displaced persons. British officials suggested 'that the number of displaced persons that can be dealt with under the scheme will be quite small, and . . . amounts to little more than a gesture'. In fact some 28,000 Jews entered the United States under its provisions until it was replaced by the Displaced Persons Act of 1948. The number was indeed relatively small compared to the number of Jews trying to leave Europe, but it still amounted to more than a token gesture. This becomes particularly apparent when comparisons are made with the equivalent British Distressed Relatives scheme.[57]

In the case of the United States, restrictionism/antisemitism inside and outside of Washington did not diminish towards the end of the war or immediately after it. Nevertheless, the consensus that had built up throughout 1943 in labour and church groupings in support of helping the Jews also persisted. Such popular pressure in harness with Jewish lobbying had led to the formation of the War Refugee Board. In late 1945 it pushed Truman to announce his preferential treatment scheme. A year later, a non-denominational Citizens Committee on Displaced Persons was formed which aimed to bring 100,000 Jews to the United States. To broaden the appeal of the Committee, its goals were widened to include the taking in of non-Jewish displaced persons (who represented three-quarters of those in the camps in Europe).[58] The Citizens Committee realized that its success was dependent on receiving the support of organized labour. This was achieved in 1946 when William Green of the AFL gave the movement his backing. In fact, at both its 1946 and 1947 Congresses, the AFL unanimously supported resolutions from Jewish unions to help displaced persons reach the United States. Rather than a break with its refusal to modify existing immigration laws, the success of these resolutions showed the continuity of AFL strategies pursued in the latter part of the war. AFL anti-Nazism and sympathy towards the victims of totalitarian oppression were made compatible with adherence to firm immigration control by using unfilled annual quotas from the war years. In 1947 the AFL supported the proposal from representatives of the International Ladies' Garment Workers' Union to allow the entry of 400,000 displaced persons during a four-year period. It was stressed that this was 'less than half the number of persons who could have legally entered our ports, but did not do so because of the war'. The AFL's desire to show that the United States would 'remain a place of refuge for those fleeing totalitarian oppression', was now translated into support for generous interpretations of the immigration laws (albeit belated and at a time of economic prosperity).[59]

This consensus of opinion (involving Jews, Christians and secular groups) in favour of relaxed immigration procedures for displaced persons was in stark contrast to the situation in Britain. After their brief interest in late 1942 and early 1943, the churches and labour movement were effectively silent on the question of European Jewry. Little changed after the end of the war. In the religious world, even the Council of Christians and Jews studiously avoided discussion of the Jewish tragedy and continued to concentrate its energy on fighting domestic antisemitism. James Parkes was almost alone in the Christian community in realizing not only the scale of the killing that had taken place but also that, particularly with regard to Polish Jewry, the centre of pre-war Jewish life had 'been exterminated as a living force'. Moreover, most of the churches in Britain remained hostile to the idea of a Jewish state in the Holy Land and were thus unsympathetic to Jewish immigration to Palestine.[60] The close ties between the TUC and the Labour government also precluded the continuation of the British labour movement's pre-war sympathy towards Zionism. The relative weakness of the Jewish trade union movement, certainly compared to the United States, was also exposed in the post-war period with regard to bringing Jews to Britain. In 1947, Jewish representatives of the National Union of Tailors and Garment Workers (whose membership was 15 per cent Jewish) forwarded a resolution to the National Council of Labour, calling upon the government to open its doors to the Jewish displaced persons still 'languishing in the most dire conditions'. It concluded by suggesting that, apart from the humanitarian motive, 'H.M. Government will be enabled to fill these vacant places in the ranks of British Industry, to assist in the economic recovery of Britain'. The TUC response was negative, especially to the last point. It argued that to claim that the Jewish survivors could help the British economy was 'wide of the mark'. Unemployment did not disappear in Britain during the immediate post-war period and was still a major concern of the trade union movement. Nevertheless, as the Tailors and Garment Workers suggested, one the most important economic problems facing the British government after 1945 was a *shortage* of labour – hence the granting of work permits to over 600,000 aliens between 1945 and 1950. But the trade union movement still regarded Jewish immigrants as especially problematic. Their analysis was shared by the government. It was a factor which largely explains why British schemes of immigration for Jewish survivors after the war were so feeble, especially when compared to the vast numbers of other aliens allowed in.[61]

In October 1945 the Home Secretary, Chuter Ede, reported that he was 'being pressed to admit to this country survivors of German concentration camps who have relatives here able and willing to look after them'. An official reported that 'The Home Office is being inundated with applications for the admission of distressed foreigners to this country'. Detailed discussions over this matter took place between the Ministry of Labour, the Home Office and the Foreign Office, eventually leading to the Distressed Relatives scheme. Although neutral in title, it was effectively designed for Jewish survivors in Europe. The scheme, administered by the Home Office, set restrictions so tightly that in practice it turned out to be nearly unworkable. Two Jewish sisters from Breslau, who had survived Auschwitz, reveal the huge bureaucratic obstacles placed in the way of those attempting to enter Britain. They

had always wanted to go to England, because our older sister was there, as well as a number of other relatives. The question of *how* was more difficult. At that time there was still no category under which we could go to England, despite representations made by my family to the Home Office.

After three months in Brussels waiting for a response from the British Passport Control Office, the two sisters applied under the new Distressed Relatives scheme. They then found they were ineligible because they had an uncle in the United States and 'to qualify for Britain we were supposed only to have relatives there'. The only way they could then qualify was 'to malign our poor uncle dreadfully and say that he'd never take us in'. Eventually after some minor deception the two sisters were allowed into Britain.[62]

The government was aware that under the Distressed Relatives scheme 'The majority of the foreigners concerned would be Jews of German nationality'. They thus designed procedures whose confines would be so narrow that the number qualifying 'would be in 100s rather than 1000s'. It was, as a Ministry of Labour official put it,

really a problem of balancing our own needs against humanitarian considerations. The Home Office feel that any large scale immigration is out of the question but that there are some cases where we ought, for humanitarian reasons, to admit the foreigners and accept the burden involved, such as it is.

Even the tiny numbers involved created some problems for the officials and ministers involved. The interdepartmental debates over what amounted to several hundred Jewish survivors revealed how problematic 'the Jew' had become in the mind of the British government. The key to all this concern rested with the question of the Jewish ability to assimilate. In effect, the Jews were being excluded on classic liberal grounds.[63]

The politician who revealed these tendencies most clearly was the Foreign Secretary, Ernest Bevin. Bevin's role in the struggle over Palestine from the end of the war to the formation of the Jewish state has led him to be seen by many as a great enemy of the Jewish people. What has been little understood, however, is the tenacity with which Bevin clung to liberal principles with regards to the Jews. To Bevin, the Jews had to be treated as full members of their country of origin. Any form of Jewish particularism beyond their religious attachment was anathema to Bevin. He was thus determined that the surviving Jews of Europe should return to their birthland. Pogroms in Poland and the antipathy of other countries on the Continent did not convince the British Foreign Secretary that the Jews might have a sincere reason for not wishing to return 'home'. Bevin's unshakeable convictions led him to send back to Germany Jewish survivors who had arrived on the shores of Palestine in the infamous 'Exodus' affair in 1947. Bevin had rejected the possibility of Jews from the 'Exodus' boats coming to Britain as he believed it would lead to serious antisemitism. His opposition, however, to any sizeable foreign Jewish presence in Britain preceded the climax of the Palestinian episode.[64]

In November 1945 the Home Secretary reported a meeting with Bevin:

he mentioned the recent decision to permit the entry into this country of refugees from Europe. He is anxious to avoid the concentration of large numbers of refugees, especially Jewish refugees, in the towns and he suggested that it might be possible to work out a scheme whereby young Jewish male refugees were admitted on condition that any work they undertook should be in agriculture and that young Jewish females might similarly be steered into some profession like nursing.

Bevin was in fact continuing policies he had supported as Secretary of the Transport and General Workers Union to help Jewish refugees train as agricultural workers. Coming from a poor agricultural background himself, Bevin believed that this was the only way to 'normalize' the Jews. In Bevin's eyes, the Jewish 'problem' emerged from the parasitical role they played in the cities. Indeed his oft-quoted insensitive jibe against Jewish displaced persons 'getting to the head of the queue' in the autumn of 1945 reflected his belief that cosmopolitan Jews had engaged in unfair profiteering in the war. By the spring of 1946 it had emerged that few of the Jews coming to Britain under the Distressed Relatives scheme had taken up the manual or rural pursuits desired by Bevin. The Foreign Secretary found this disappointing. Bevin told George Isaacs, Minister for Labour, that he hoped that the people coming under the scheme 'might be steered into agriculture or any other sphere where they would be most useful, thus avoiding undesirable concentration of them in towns'.[65]

A similar Home Office criteria of 'usefulness' even existed for the emotive issue of child survivors of the concentration camps. An article in the *Sunday Express* on these orphans led to much sympathy from the British public. Although not on the scale of that following the Baldwin appeal in 1938, the sense of outrage led to the offering of thousands of British homes for the children. A member of the British army, T. H. Tilling, wrote in anger to the Home Office that these survivors had been 'apparently forgotten by us'. Tilling pointed out that 'For six months in Germany I had my HQ at Belsen', somewhat sarcastically adding, for the bureaucrats in Whitehall, 'perhaps you've heard of it!'. There were, he believed, 'still about one or two thousand of the wretched people whom we liberated from the Camp who, for one reason or another, *cannot* get to Palestine'. Tilling concluded that Britain '*ought* to help them and *now*'.[66]

The Home Office regarded the matter in a different light. The estimate of 'one or two thousand' was underlined by an official and a minute added that 'There can for the present be no question of extending the eligible categories of the scheme of the admission of distressed relatives'. Another Home Office official added that 'it would be quite impossible for this country to meet all the claims which are being made on its hospitality'. With more than a little distortion of the reality (especially given the dismissive attitude towards the policies outlined by Truman in December 1945), it was suggested that 'a very considerable number of persons come within the scope' of the Distressed Relatives scheme. A tiny project was, however, implemented by the Home Office to help child survivors of the concentration camps. One thousand children were to be given temporary refuge to enable them to recuperate in Britain. Again the limitations of the proposals were so great that less than three-quarters of the proposed number could be found who were eligible. Just over 700 children were eventually brought to Britain under a scheme administered and paid for by the Jewish community through the Central British Fund. Twenty-eight hostels were opened for these children across the country.[67]

Evidence of sympathy shown by ordinary people to these children and to the plight of other survivors of the concentration camps was dismissed by many in the British government. Alleged utilitarian criteria were at work in the choosing of post-war immigrants. Jews had no place in such considerations as they were seen as unsuitable workers and harbingers of antisemitism. In some exasperation, a Ministry of Labour official wrote with regard to Bevin's concerns that

We cannot escape from the fundamental fact that these aliens are being admitted on humanitarian grounds and will be given shelter by the relatives or friends who have invited them to come. . . . We . . . need to bear it always in mind that this scheme was meant to provide some immediate relief to aliens in the difficult conditions this winter in Europe.

Even this more sympathetic official added that 'permanent residence is not intended'. Nevertheless, C. J. Dennys of the Ministry of Labour was appalled at the 'rather oppressive' procedures and restrictions that the Home Office had instituted through the Distressed Relatives scheme. Dennys added that its 'very narrow categories' were making it near-impossible for survivors to come to Britain:

My own feeling is that if we were to try and exclude near relatives whilst admitting other foreigners, the general public could not be expected to appreciate the reasons for such a policy or to accept it as fair.

Dennys proposed that these near-relatives be allowed into Britain under a revived scheme to bring alien domestics to the country. The Home Office was opposed to any liberalization of policy but Ministry of Labour pressure, in the light of revived demands from middle-class women for servants, led to limited flexibility. Thus a few Holocaust survivors, such as Elizabeth Weisz, sister of the cartoonist Vicky (who had to campaign long and hard and use his influence in government circles), were allowed into Britain. As Vicky's biographers comment: 'She entered – such were Britain's requirements of a concentration camp victim – on a Domestic Service Permit which allowed her to be somebody's maid'.[68]

It is thus hardly surprising that when British officials began recruiting displaced persons on a massive scale from the camps in Europe the Jews were either at the bottom of desirability lists or excluded altogether. The key to the selection of suitable groups was their ability to assimilate into British society and to provide the necessary labour. Jews, in the minds of many British officials in the Home and Foreign Office, failed on both counts. Underlying such policies was the fear of domestic antisemitism. Concern about this issue increased in the war and reached new levels of paranoia after 1945. It was believed that any sizeable Jewish influx (in effect anything over several hundred) would lead to serious trouble. Few if any Jews would thus be among the hundreds of thousands of displaced persons who came to Britain to solve its post-war labour shortage. Ever narrowing definitions of Englishness had combined with a liberal commitment to assimilation to exclude anything other than a token entry of Jews.[69]

The essentially problematic view of Jewish displaced persons which operated in British government circles was shared with other liberal democracies. On the grounds of ability to assimilate, both Australia and Canada discriminated against the Jews while also recruiting massively in the displaced persons camps of Europe. Indeed, antisemitic pressure in the American Congress ensured that the Displaced Persons Act of 1948 was also clearly biased against the Jews. Clauses relating to the date of arrival in the camps and in favour of 'agriculturalists' were inserted which were blatantly designed to limit severely the number of Jews eligible. Anti-radicalism, which had acted against Jews trying to escape to the United States in the 1930s and during the war, re-emerged in 1947/8 as a force against the entry of Eastern European Jews. It was only the sympathetic administration of the 1948 Act that stopped it being used to exclude Jewish survivors, and this was also the case in other English-speaking countries. In the following years, therefore, Jews entered the United States in the same proportion as their numbers in the displaced persons camps.[70]

One of the further ironies of such policies was that while Jewish survivors were seen as problematic (especially as the bringers of their own misfortune) and therefore excluded, those who had played a role in the implementation of the 'Final Solution' were allowed into the democracies with few obstacles placed in their way. In a tiny minority of cases, some known Nazis and sympathizers were actively recruited for their specific intelligence, technical and scientific knowledge as the battle against fascism quickly gave way to the new realities of the Cold War. More generally, the need for what was seen as the right kind of labour was the only consideration motivating British, American, Canadian and Australian officials recruiting in the displaced persons camps. In spite of the Allied declarations in the war promising post-war retribution, screening of these individuals for possible war crimes was not a priority. As Christopher Mayhew (who was involved in such screening processes in Britain) later recalled: 'if "some monsters" came in this was a small price that had to be paid'. The re-emergence of the war crimes issue in the democracies will be examined later. Here, however, it is important to highlight the paradox which the Association of Jewish Refugees had pointed to as early as 1946. Hundreds of thousands of non-Jewish displaced persons, some with fascist sympathies, were being recruited to the democracies without a word of objection. Jewish concerns regarding the possible entry of perpetrators of mass murder remained unconsidered or were totally overruled. At the same time, schemes for helping distressed Jews in Europe were marked mainly by their meanness.[71] There was, therefore, in liberal state policy during the immediate post-war period, little consciousness of or sensitivity towards the Jewish trauma in the war. On a practical level, was this also true of ordinary people in the democracies? Were the survivors of the Holocaust who managed to reach countries such as Britain and the United States treated with sympathy and understanding?

V

In the autumn of 1945, when considering the possible entry of distressed relatives, a Ministry of Labour official was concerned that

There will be, I feel, a public outcry if persons of German nationality, however deserving their case, are brought back while there are still British subjects awaiting transport, and I think that in any statement the Home Secretary should say that British subjects will have priority.[72]

Yet the British public was given little chance by its state to consider the Jewish catastrophe in general or the plight of the survivors in particular. It is not surprising, therefore, that many of the Jews reaching Britain from Europe after the war were to be treated with little understanding. More than anything else, the exclusive national framework which had developed with regard to the British war effort hindered any possibility of considering the horror of the European Jewish experience. Indeed there was even an antipathy towards the survivors because their stories threatened to disturb the complacency and immense self-satisfaction of 'Britain alone'. Kitty Hart, who survived Auschwitz, was one of the first to come to England after the war. Moving to Birmingham, she was 'soon to discover', in both the Jewish and non-Jewish worlds,

that everybody in England would be talking about personal war experiences for months, even years, after hostilities had ceased. But we, who had been pursued over Europe by a mutual enemy, and come close to extermination at the hands of that enemy, were not supposed to embarrass people by saying a word.

To her, the years of isolation after liberation were especially difficult: 'People didn't understand. In some ways the suffering I endured in the early post-war years was worse than it had been in the KZ [concentration camp]. Personally, I certainly found that time more traumatic.' A survivor of Westerbork and Belsen, settling in north-west London, had similar post-war experiences to Kitty Hart:

I found it better not to talk about the concentration camps, and not to do or say anything that would make me appear different from anyone else. People simply didn't understand what we'd been through, and they didn't make allowances for anything. I just thought it was safer to say nothing. I felt so threatened. I am very angry about what happened to me. From the time I left the camp I was shunted about, and there was nothing solid, nothing firm in my life; and I am angry when I look back and consider how we were treated when we came to England.[73]

Rather than acting as a bridge between the two, British suffering in the war acted as an insurmountable obstacle in the way of understanding the Holocaust. Gena Turgel, who had survived Auschwitz and Belsen, recalls how when she first

came to England, people seemed very preoccupied with themselves. Some said: 'We also had a hard time. We were bombed and had to live in shelters. We had to sleep in the Underground.'

I said: 'Yes, I'm sure it must have been bad, but at least you weren't living in constant fear that someone would hit you or shoot you at any moment, or that you might starve.' These people lived in a different world. They had blackouts, but they had amusements, dances. . . . They were able to go out and enjoy themselves.[74]

Some exceptional individuals, including non-Jews such as Charity Blackstock, immersed themselves in the fate of the survivors. Blackstock was involved in the placing of some 150 Jewish orphans in 1948. She recalls with much honesty the difficulty of attempting to comprehend a different world:

How in the name of sanity could a kindly, well-intentioned woman who had lived her life in the suburbs begin to understand the state of mind of a boy, who had, six years back, been dragged out of the gas-chamber by his hair, and flung into a mountain of corpses where he lay for a day and a half until it was safe for him to crawl away.

Through reading and, more than anything else, talking to the children, Blackstock began to realize the 'full horror' of what her charges had been through. It has often been suggested that after the war most Jewish survivors wished to put their past experiences behind them and move on to building a new life. In some cases this was undoubtedly true, and in the United States a minority of the Jews arriving after the war purposefully avoided moving to areas where fellow survivors or other Jewish communities had settled. Many were, however, anxious to talk about their lives during the war. Charity Blackstock recalls how her Jewish children often volunteered their stories to her. 'But,' she adds, 'they seldom discussed these things with anyone outside.' With the frustration that could come from lack of comprehension or sheer disbelief, Blackstock believed that this was the right strategy for her children to adopt. Mutual support between survivors, at first at an informal level, thus became important from the start of their lives in Britain. It was not made easy by the small numbers involved and their dispersion across the country. Nevertheless, by

1963 those who had come on the Children from the Concentration Camp scheme had formed themselves into the '45 Aid Society. It offered practical self-assistance in the form of material and psychological support.[75]

In Britain in the years after the war the Jewish survivors were thus pushed to submerge their war experiences. It was a strategy which helped their short-term acceptance into society but did little for their future personal adjustment. A tiny proportion of the population realized, or came to realize, what these individuals had experienced, but few made that effort. Even some of those offering hospitality to the camp children were unable to cope. They were, as Blackstock relates, 'confronted by strangers so alien that they might have come from outer space'. The British media did not help in the process of understanding. Stories such as that of Gena Turgel, who married her British Jewish liberator, were exploited by the press for their freakishness and sensationalism rather than for the very humanity illustrated by her experiences. Gena Turgel, as the 'bride of Belsen', became another label from a world which was treated as if coming out of science fiction and unrelated to the human experience. Although portrayed positively, Turgel, as an individual, was almost as unreal as the demonized 'Beast of Belsen' (Josef Kramer) and the 'Bitch of Belsen' (Irma Grese). Turgel came to Britain late in 1945 and, echoing the comments made by Blackstock, added that with all the media attention she 'felt as if I had come from outer space'.[76] Was the situation any different in the United States?

Testimony from survivors reveals a similar pattern in which the failure to communicate the scale of the Jewish disaster during the war became a huge frustration. In some cases attempts were made by Americans to equate their war experiences with those of the survivors. Dorothy Rabinowitz reports how the survivors

soon learned that they might be asked, by friends and relatives, what it was like to starve, and after being told that starvation was very bad, the friends and relatives might respond that yes, they knew, because there had also been shortages of many things in America during the war, such as sugar.

She adds that many other Americans were 'intent on hearing nothing'. Ignorance and disbelief were also common: stories of selections and the gas chambers were met with responses such as 'You have a terrific imagination'. The dean of a law school wondered why a camp survivor was 'wearing [her] laundry numbers on her arm'. The tendency when dealing with survivors to see them as freaks was also apparent. Abraham Foxman who came to New York in 1950 as a ten-year-old recalls how the survivors'

isolation, or whatever else they felt, was reinforced by our neighbors. They expected us to look like we had come right out of a camp – emaciated, wounded. They hinted that they wanted to know what we had gone through, only they didn't really. My parents tried to explain at first. But they stopped. It simply wasn't worth it.[77]

There were, however, subtle differences between the United States and Britain. On the one hand, the greater distance from the events in the war made it even easier to dismiss descriptions of the 'Final Solution' as war propaganda. On the other hand, the much larger number of survivors present in the United States and the greater influence of American Jewry helped create more awareness of the Jewish tragedy. Ernest Michel survived a series of camps and was one of the first to enter the United States under Truman's scheme in 1946. He got a job in a small town, Port Huron, Michigan, where he related his war experiences to a local college society. This led to a series of talks in the town and then across the United States sponsored by the United Jewish Appeal. It is hard to imagine such a tour taking place in Britain in the years following the war. Although its significance should not be overestimated, some of the first post-war literature in English dealing with the destruction of European Jewry, such as John Hersey's *The Wall* (1950), came out of the United States. In October 1947, the mayor of New York unveiled a plaque to the 'Heroes of the Warsaw Ghetto Battle' in what has been described as 'a massive public ceremony'. Nevertheless, it is important to add that the proposed memorial to accompany this plaque in Riverside Park was never built. Overall, by the time Hersey's book (also on the Warsaw Ghetto) was published there was no real interest or understanding of the immensity or specificity of the Jewish plight in the war. It was left to the survivors themselves and a tiny minority of others to ensure that the European Jewish experience during the war would be constructed into a coherent story and embodied in popular memory. The task for survivors in both Britain and the United States was to be long, frustrating and, for the main part, lonely.[78]

VI

In October 1945, Ignacy Schwartzbart, who had come to Britain from Poland during the war and played a prominent role in the Polish government in exile, was in a state of despair. He surveyed the brightly lit area of Oxford Circus but wrote in his diary 'for us Jews even on lit streets there is darkness. No spark of hope. No spark of joy.' His sense of isolation was made worse because of his problems in relating to British Jewry. After a meeting with Zionists in London he reported how 'I felt again so estranged among English Jews'. An earlier confrontation with a leading force in the Bloomsbury House organization revealed the huge gulf that existed between British Jewry and those of the Continent:

The conversation was rather unpleasant. The Jewish assimilationist did his best to show up his British-alleged superiority to me, the Polish Jew. . . . The gentleman boasted over his mother's British origins some 300 years back, and of his father's British origins some 175 years back. To this I replied that I stem from a Jewish family who lived in Poland 600 years.

The chasm in outlook between Schwartzbart and British Jewry was revealed in April 1945. In spite of, or even possibly because of, his pleas, the English Zionist Federation's *Zionist Review* printed not one line about the second anniversary of the Warsaw ghetto rebellion. In the autumn of 1945, at the first post-war Zionist Congress, a plan was put forward to establish a permanent memorial in the future Jewish state to the Jews who had perished under the Nazi regime. It was ironic that this Congress, which adopted the plan, would take place in England, the liberal democracy in the post-war world which was perhaps the slowest to commemorate the Holocaust.[79]

In both Britain and the United States, the Warsaw ghetto rebellion was to become the first major focus of Holocaust memorial. To the Jewish world, and especially to the left and the Zionists, the rebellion was an illustration of Jewish solidarity and a useful antidote to the widespread belief in Jewish passivity. To non-Jews trying to make sense of the Jewish catastrophe, the ghetto revolt could at least be placed in the context of armed resistance during the war. As we have seen, the event was one of the very few to be inserted into the Royal Institute of International Affairs revised war chronology. At the start of 1948 a 'Warsaw Ghetto Memorial Committee for Great Britain' was established. It was created in response to the decision of the Central Committee of Jews in Poland to establish a memorial on the site of the ghetto to mark the fifth anniversary of the uprising. A British body consisting of representatives of the Federation of Polish Jews, the Polish Jewish ex-Combatants Association, other Polish-Jewish groupings and the Board of Deputies of British Jews was assembled with the assistance of the World Jewish Congress. In fact the Board played only a limited role in the small fund-raising effort undertaken by the Memorial Committee. Selig Brodetsky, as President of the Board of Deputies, was keen to emphasize 'the deep sorrow felt by all classes of the Anglo-Jewish Community at the tragic fate' of Polish Jewry. With a few notable exceptions, however (and mainly those connected to the World Jewish Congress), Jews of British origin would play only a minor role in Holocaust commemoration in the post-war years. Refugees from Nazism and the post-war survivors were to commemorate anniversaries of the destruction process. These only slowly gained support from first the Jewish community in general and then, more gradually still, society at large.[80] Across the Atlantic a similar process occurred. William Helmreich perceptively points out that, although it is assumed commemoration of the Holocaust began after the Eichmann trial, 'it is . . . clear that the survivors themselves were memorializing the Holocaust almost from the time they arrived in the United States'. He adds that all of the major cities 'with substantial survivor populations had "Newcomer" organizations'. In addition, organizations such as the Wiener Library in London and what was to become Yad Vashem in Jerusalem began the process of collecting testimony of survivors at the end of the war.[81]

One of the problems for survivors and refugees in Britain and, to a lesser extent, in the United States was their marginality within the power structure of their adopted Jewish communities. This was clearly exposed in 1956 when the question of reparation payments from Germany was raised. The Central British Fund, Anglo-Jewish Association and Board of Deputies of British Jews did not push the issue in governmental/international negotiations and the Council of Jews from Germany was effectively excluded from the policy-making process. It reported how it was 'forced into the miserable role of people who had to beg for a morsel of their own property'. The Association of Jewish Refugees was appalled at the collective decisions of the British Jewish establishment and concluded that the leadership

apparently did not realize that the Refugees from Germany constituted about one eighth of the Jewish population in Great Britain and had a right to expect the spokesmen of Anglo-Jewry to stand up for the interests of their group. We record with deep regret and disappointment this sad result.[82]

In the early 1950s, knowledge levels and comprehension of what had occurred during the war to the Jews was, at best, sketchy. In 1953 it was suggested that Gerald Reitlinger's *The Final Solution* was 'needed as a record of what has already become blurred in many minds'. A year later, the publishers of Lord Liverpool's *Scourge of the Swastika*, which dealt with Nazi crimes in general, defended publication of the book 'because we . . . feel that the horrors of Buchenwald and Auschwitz, which were so close to us ten years ago, have been too easily forgotten'.[83] What had occurred after the camp revelations in 1945 was in fact a continuation of tendencies from the war itself and even before. The images from Belsen and Buchenwald in particular were undoubtedly powerful, but they were placed only in the context of Nazi atrocities. In his *"Nowhere to Lay Their Heads"*, Victor Gollancz was concerned that the revelations of the concentration camps would go the same way as those after the Allied Declaration in December 1942 relating to the extermination of the Jews: 'interest very rapidly declined, and was soon more or less to vanish'. A correspondent to Gollancz shared his concern. The individual had a close friend who had been involved in the liberation of Belsen and wanted to increase public knowledge and interest in the concentration camps (and particularly the plight of survivors). He/she shared Gollancz's concerns and with much foresight warned as early as July 1945

How right you are – the public memory is all too short – and Belsen and Dachau and the people who still live will be forgotten by many (although in justice to the public I add – as an ordinary citizen – that the simple business of living absorbs most of one's time and energy).

Another correspondent, a member of the RAF, confirmed such an analysis. He told Gollancz that although he was

one of the general public who 'seemed not unmoved' I confess that my horror of the conditions at Belsen evaporated in a short time, under the stress of living my own life.

Charity Blackstock found by the second year of her project with the child survivors that

people were beginning to say, 'There are no more concentration camps, the war is forgotten, these children have been well looked after and should by now be able to look after themselves.' . . . That was in 1950.[84]

The frustrations such attitudes caused were not limited to the survivors. The liberators too had been traumatized by their experiences but found few who would listen to their experiences. The impact of this repression of memories was in some cases severe and led to later nervous breakdowns. A former member of the Royal Army Medical Corps unit which had been involved in the liberation process wrote in 1956 to the *Daily Telegraph* about the neglect of the memorial at the Belsen camp. He added that the indignation of the British public when he tried to describe the horrific scenes involving the bulldozing of the dead bodies 'shows only too clearly that we, as well as the Germans, are only too anxious to forget the whole ghastly episode'. He added that 'old soldiers may never die, but the causes for which they fight are very soon put quietly to death'. Similarly, a survivor in New Orleans came into contact with a truck driver who advised him

don't try to tell people here what happened over in Europe. I was in the American army, I walked into those camps and I saw all those things the Germans did, and people here don't believe it when you tell them.

He told the survivor that he had given up describing the state of the liberated camps to Americans (with the exception of former inmates or fellow liberators).[85]

The battle to forge a place for the Jewish catastrophe was hard fought in the 1950s. The atrocity material of 1945 made an impression but it was not connected to the plight of the victims, let alone the Jews. Moreover, the images were such that many wished to put them out of mind as quickly as possible. The early attempts to historicize the subject by Reitlinger and Poliakov, while laying the foundations for future research, made little popular impact at the time. On a cultural level, the horrors of the war made a deep impression on writers such as William Golding, who realized, in a rather patronizing way, that the atrocities committed had not been carried out by 'some primitive tribe in the Amazon. They were done, skilfully, coldly, by educated men, doctors, lawyers, by men with a tradition of civilisation behind them.' The writer Martin Amis relates discussing the Holocaust intensively with his father, Kingsley Amis. Yet Kingsley Amis, William Golding and other leading British writers who emerged in the 1950s did not write directly about the Holocaust.[86] This was also true of British Jewish novelists who emerged at the same time. If the Holocaust had made an impact on them, it was only in an indirect way by increasing Jewish insecurity. The result was that these new Jewish writers would focus on domestic issues. They thus wrote not about European Jewry but their own roots, especially in the East End of London. British Jewry as a whole shared the same attitude in the post-war world. In 1946 a Mass-Observer wrote with regard to the Jews of Britain 'what right have they to make a fuss as long as their skins are safe and they're not in a gas chamber?'. Such conditional acceptance was articulated from time to time to Jews, reminding them of their marginality in society. The cartoonist Mel Calman recalled how his outsider status was brought home to him by the comment of a workmate of three years: 'If we hadn't let you in you'd have been a lampshade'. In such an atmosphere it was hardly surprising that British Jewry wished during the 1950s to retreat to the domestic home, to achieve a comfortable material status and to put the plight of its brethren in Europe during the war to one side. The Holocaust lurked not very far from the consciousness of British Jewry but it was rarely confronted in a direct way.[87] It was only in refugee/survivor dominated cultural forums such as *AJR Information* (formed in 1946), *The Wiener Library Bulletin* (formed in 1949) and *The Jewish Quarterly* (formed in 1953) that history, testimony and literature relating to the Holocaust would be given prominence.

The situation was little different in the United States where little attention was devoted to the subject by both Jewish and non-Jewish writers. The cinema was another medium which stayed clear of this area. Anglo-American films on World War II tended to reconstruct it along more traditional military lines. In the immediate post-war period, Hollywood films such as *Crossfire* and *Gentleman's Agreement* (both 1947) had dealt with the menace of antisemitism but had placed the problem firmly in an American context. In contrast *The*

Desert Fox (1951) (an American film based on a British book) presented Rommel and the German war effort 'in an unambiguous, positive way'. The British film *Frieda* (1947) started the process of moving away from assumptions of German collective guilt. Nevertheless, ambiguity in the presentation of the major German character was present throughout the film and there were references to Nazi atrocities during the war. In contrast the British films of the 1950s dealing with the war 'retreated further from politics, until the . . . actualities of Nazism vanish, leaving [films such as *The Cruel Sea* (1952) and *The Dam Busters* (1954)] as pure adventure stories'. Moreover, they do so in an elitist and male-dominated manner. Within this narrow and nationalistic framework it is hardly surprising that there was no time for considering such issues as the fate of the Jews during the war.[88]

The Diary of Anne Frank was the only major exception to this general neglect of the Holocaust throughout the 1950s. It was first published in English in 1952 and went through many reprints throughout the decade and beyond. The diary was dramatized in 1955 and, from a similar script, made into a film released four years later. The play was originally shown on Broadway where it won national awards and was then shown across Europe the following year. *The Diary of Anne Frank* has since become the most important source of knowledge about the Holocaust for the Western world – hence the obsessive desire of neo-Nazis to question its authenticity.[89] What, however, was its original impact and how was it presented on stage and screen?

Judith Doneson relates how the play and film of the diary show 'the Americanization, and ultimate universalization, of the Holocaust through the *Diary*'. The universalization of the victims enabled Americans to identify with its subject matter but this, as Doneson adds, was inevitably 'at the cost of its Jewish particularity'. The filmic version went further and the president of the company producing it stressed 'this isn't a Jewish picture, this is a picture for the world'. Attempts to make the diary accessible were important and, to an extent, met the wishes of Otto Frank who wished to extend the message of his daughter's book as far as was possible. Nevertheless, on its own, and particularly in a highly selected format, the story of the diary told only a tiny part of the history of the Holocaust. The diary was accessible to people of all ages and of all backgrounds, but, placed out of context, it enabled the horrors of the destruction process to be avoided. In the 1950s, general knowledge of the overall picture of Jewish life and death during the war was limited in countries such as Britain and the United States. The strength of the text was in its ability to communicate the impact of Nazi persecution on the individual – an aspect so lacking in the de-humanized images of the liberated concentration camps. But, in isolation, the diary could not portray the immensity and geographical scope of the Jewish tragedy in the war. Moreover, in its universalized form as a play and film, the specificity of the Jewish fate was minimized.[90]

Doneson suggests that such universalization was essential for American society which, after the ruptures and paranoia of McCarthyism, was attempting to heal wounds and emphasize commonality. In Britain the continuing liberal opposition to Jewish particularity had the same result when the play was produced in 1956. The producer announced that he would

emphasise the universality of the theme as he had learnt from experience . . . that any attempt to stress the Jewishness of a character always ends in unreality.

The play struck a chord on the Continent but, in Britain, one critic sensed that the audience 'around me [did not feel] quite that profound disturbance of the soul which I had expected and which performances of the play in Germany seem to have accomplished'. He added, however, 'But then, this story has a very special significance for all decent Germans'. It must be suggested that in the Britain of the 1950s the play had little to say either about contemporary society or the memory of the war. A leading British liberal journalist, Jill Tweedie, recalls reading the diary in the 1950s. She found that after just three pages 'I was Ann[e]'. Yet Tweedie's background in being brought up in post-war Britain made it hard for her to understand the fate of Anne Frank: 'No-one and nothing prepared me for the shock of the end, I couldn't take it in, it broke all the rules.' Yet Tweedie herself states that

my most vivid childhood memory, apart from the bomb that blew in our house, is of being taken to see [aged nine] the filmed horrors of Belsen. Every detail is with me still, the half-dead with their somnambulist eyes, the dead looking more ancient than the corpses of ancient Egyptians.

Again it must be stressed that these images were rarely connected to the Jewish fate and were put to the back of the mind by most people. In reviewing the Anne Frank play in London during 1956, the critic Milton Shulman pointed out that

It takes such an effort of memory to recall the horrors of Belsen and Buchenwald. Time has inured us to the statistics of mass murder.[91]

Most of those in the secret annex would be killed in Auschwitz or Belsen, yet the play and film (which, true to their liberal ideology, would end on a note of hope) ignored this aspect of her life story. The death camps of the east, although well-documented in the testimony of survivors, were still not familiar symbols of Nazi evil during the 1950s. A Captain Delargy in Britain during 1958 reported with regard to Auschwitz that 'The real facts are not well known'. Delargy had described the camp at a public lecture. A former British Cabinet Minister 'exclaimed that before this talk he had thought that most of the deaths were caused by epidemics due to overcrowding and lack of sanitation'. Brief reference has been made to Lord Liverpool's *Scourge of the Swastika*, which sold 400,000 copies in 1956 alone. Although well-intentioned, this 'short history of Nazi war crimes' dealt in a sensational and at times voyeuristic manner with atrocities inside and outside the concentration camp system. One critic later commented that its exposures 'could still be regarded by many people as a shattering revelation'. These two popular texts together provided an unsatisfactory framework of reference for ordinary people confronting the Holocaust. Lord Liverpool's account still limited the subject of the Jewish fate in the war to the realm of atrocity stories, and a minor one at that. *The Diary of Anne Frank*, although itself a masterpiece, brilliantly written, moving and accessible, ultimately represented only a fragment of the whole story. Altogether the Holocaust had made little overall impact on British and American society and culture during the 1950s. Nevertheless, the differences between the two countries, which had started to emerge just after the war, began to widen further in this decade. With the play and film of the Anne Frank diary, the process of Americanizing the Holocaust had begun. In Britain there was no interest in attempting a similar process. Even the limited commemoration of events such as the fifteenth anniversary of the Warsaw ghetto rebellion achieved greater status in the United States than in Britain. The Eichmann trial in the early 1960s was to broaden the gap even further.[92]

VII

The Eichmann trial is often portrayed as the key turning point in popular perceptions of the Holocaust. There is no doubt that the lengthy proceedings and the extensive media coverage achieved by the interrogation of Eichmann in Jerusalem gave the Holocaust public exposure that had never occurred before, including in the earlier Nuremberg trials. Before the 1961 trial and Eichmann's execution in 1962, the persecution and extermination of the Jews had been one among many issues relating to the war and Nazism, and was not perceived in itself of having particular importance. In Jerusalem the whole trial concentrated on the Holocaust and brought home with graphic details the processes of destruction. Auschwitz would now become a term representing the evils of the modern world at least on a par with Belsen, Buchenwald and the other western camps. Yet, while adding new details and interpretations, the proceedings did not generally add anything of great significance that was not known before. It is thus highly significant that, in the late 1950s, Raul Hilberg had struggled to find a publisher for his monumental work *The Destruction of European Jewry*. It was eventually published in the same year as the trial and by the end of the decade was seen as a classic and definitive work on the Holocaust.[93] It was thus not so much the availability of new evidence as its accessibility and, more than anything, the new found willingness to make use of it that distinguishes the Eichmann trial. James Young writes with regard to Sylvia Plath and others:

Entered as it was onto the 'public record' during the Eichmann trial in Jerusalem, a time when images of the camps flooded the media and commanded world attention as they had not since the war, the Holocaust necessarily began to inform all writers' literary imagination as a prospective trope.

The trial also gave more space to the survivors who had been marginalized even in Israel. A correspondent in Jerusalem wrote to Victor Gollancz at the time of Eichmann's interrogation pointing out 'that the revelations at the trial came as a horrifying surprise also to us in Israel, where we meet each day people with their concentration camp numbers tattooed on the wrist'.[94] The greater prominence given to survivors after the end of the trial related less to their desire to communicate than to the willingness of others to listen to their testimony. Although concentrating on the perpetrators, the trial also revived the question of the Jewish councils and their role in the destruction process. After Hannah Arendt's polemic *Eichmann in Jerusalem* (1963), the debate broadened to consider Jewish resistance and from there to consider Jewish life in the Holocaust more generally. A context was at last slowly emerging for the growing but until then marginalized body of survivor testimony literature. Yet not all countries responded with equal concern to these developments. Indeed, the contrast between British and American responses to the Holocaust after the Eichmann trial illustrates how the new material and debate was not sufficient in itself to generate interest and involvement.[95]

The trial achieved a great deal of media attention in the United States. An opinion poll in May 1961 found that 87 per cent of Americans had heard of the event. The trial and subsequent controversies also generated debate in Britain but there was disappointment in some refugee/survivor quarters that 'the British press [did not] take this matter up with much more interest, and . . . let the people of this country know what had happened in those dark days'. One refugee wrote that he was

afraid that out here in [north London], so removed from the rest of the world, the sufferings of the Jewish people have never been really understood and to our shame the Eichmann case [has caused] hardly a ripple amongst the allegedly Christian population.

Indeed some sections of the Christian community in both Britain and the United States objected to the trial as they believed it showed Jewish vengeance as against Christian forgiveness. Revealing immense ignorance and insensitivity, some went even further and suggested that the similarities between the trials of Eichmann and Jesus were 'too great to be coincidental'.[96] Correspondence to Victor Gollancz at the time reveals a small section of the British population who did 'not beleive [sic] their six million story' and rejected the figure because 'in 1935 there were 665,000 Jews in Germany'. More significant, however, were those who had simply no desire to be reminded of the Jewish fate:

It simply adds to the evil to recount it. Those who know of the crime have no need to be reminded of it and those who know it not may take a ghoulish interest in it . . . so, in any case, the trial does no humane good to the cause of Jews or to those who do not wish them well.

The liberal tendency to argue that stressing the Jewish fate would actually increase antisemitism was thus still powerful in 1961. Although 35 per cent of the British population according to a Gallup poll in August 1961 reported themselves to be more sympathetic to the Jews as a result of the proceedings in Jerusalem, the Eichmann trial as a whole did not lead to any great interest in the Holocaust. Indeed, as we will see, there was still great resistance to referring to it at all throughout the 1960s.[97] Yet, during the same troubled decade, in the United States the subject began to take off in terms of cultural and intellectual interest. Films such as *Judgment at Nuremberg* (1961) and *The Pawnbroker* (1965) revealed that the processes which had begun during the 1950s had now developed much further. Thus, during the 1960s and after 'American films on the Holocaust reflect[ed] much in American society and contribute[d] to the Americanization of the Holocaust'. Questions of national and international justice, of racism and poverty at home, and, with Vietnam, wars abroad were all related to the Holocaust in a series of important films and books. The Holocaust was used as 'a metaphor for tragedy as well as a valuable lesson to prevent further tragedy'. At the same time the growing identity of American Jewry with the Holocaust, especially after the 1967 Israeli war and the parallel expression of ethnic pride by black Americans, meant that the particularity of the Holocaust was not ignored. The voice of survivors such as Elie Wiesel was now to be heard. Before the 1960s it has been suggested that Wiesel 'was just barely eking out a living. Nobody was interested then in what he had to say.' But tensions within American society (as well as its growing need, with the success of the civil rights movement, to emphasize plurality and to recognize the dangers of racism) enabled the Holocaust to become, even if at times abused, a part of everyday American consciousness.[98]

The dissimilarity to the British case can be illustrated at many different levels. One of the most blatant was in the continued marginality of survivors both inside and outside of the Jewish community. Earlier it has been shown how the concern over concentration camp children quickly dissipated and was transformed into a belief that they should just be left to their own devices. By the 1960s, Charity Blackstock believed that people could not 'even [be] trouble[d] to say it, they simply forget'. It was necessary to remind people that, 20 years after the camp liberations, although most survivors had settled into new lives, there were in Europe alone 'still *ten thousand* who exist – live is too kind a word – in bitterness and great misery'. Indeed no special facilities were made available for, or interest taken in, maintaining the mental health of the survivors/refugees in Britain until the late 1970s. Survivors and those few individuals intent on commemorating the Holocaust found themselves similarly marginalized.[99]

By 1960 a Warsaw Ghetto Memorial Committee had been formed by a group dominated by Jewish socialists. It was, however, sponsored by several Jewish and non-Jewish parliamentarians with the aim of establishing 'a permanent memorial to the heroes of the Warsaw Ghetto uprising; the 6 million Jewish and millions of other victims of Nazism'. The swastika epidemic that had spread across Europe during 1959 and 1960 created an awareness in Britain that a younger generation had grown up which was unaware of what had occurred during the war. In a series of newspaper articles presented in the form of letters to his daughter, a journalist pondered that 'No-one has ever told you about Warsaw, or Coventry, or Belsen, or Dachau. You would rather hear Elvis Presley (and who can blame you?).' With this in mind, the Warsaw Ghetto Memorial Committee's first imperative was

to remind those who have forgotten, to inform those who did not know, and to tell those who could not know, of the infamies of Nazism, and to learn the lessons therefrom.

In Britain, the pedagogical aspects of Holocaust remembrance were crucial in helping its importance to gain due recognition. Debate during the early 1960s revealed how far this was seen as being desirable in British society.[100]

Those in the Warsaw Ghetto Memorial Committee were not just alarmed at the 'ghost of the recent past' in the form of swastika graffiti. Reflecting concern about the evidence of attacks and general racism towards Britain's growing New Commonwealth migrants, the Memorial Committee aimed 'to promote activities to lessen racial tension, to condemn racial discrimination, and to work with others doing likewise'. Although other grass-roots bodies had emerged in Britain, especially after the racist riots in England during 1958, the response of the state was to solve the 'problem' by excluding black people. In an atmosphere in which the state itself blamed the victim for the existence of intolerance, it was to be difficult to promote Holocaust remembrance in the form of anti-racist initiatives.[101]

In 1961 two exhibitions took place in England dealing with the Holocaust. The first, at Coventry cathedral, revealed the problems of dealing with the non-British war experience. The second, in London, showed that the small number of enthusiasts who had campaigned for Holocaust remembrance were at last slowly starting to gain some recognition and support (particularly in the more favourable atmosphere linked to the interest generated by the Eichmann trial). In May 1961 an exhibition on Nazi concentration camps took place in Coventry cathedral. The original building had been bombed during the massive destruction of the town during the war and was preserved as a ruin alongside the new cathedral. The cathedral authorities saw their task as promoting international reconciliation and forgiveness. The concentration camp exhibition, designed by a Belgian, aimed to perpetuate the memory of past suffering and to stimulate among the younger generation a desire to avoid its repetition. Thus the cathedral authorities found themselves in the spring of 1961 with an exhibition with which they totally disapproved. The provost launched into a public attack on the exhibition and made clear that the cathedral authorities would 'continue to oppose it by every possible means in our power'. The objections to the exhibition were on fundamental grounds: the cathedral was 'automatically oppose[d] . . . to any sort of exhibition, no matter what its purpose, which is based on such a theme as the concentration camp'. It objected to the particularity of the exhibition and found the idea of it referring 'only to the concentration camps of the last war' puzzling. Given its supposed commitment to internationalism, it is ironic that the exhibition was lambasted because it was 'the work of one who can by no stretch of the imagination claim to be a Coventrian'. Rejecting claims that 'to remember these horrible events will ensure that they do not happen again', the *Coventry Cathedral Review* argued that this was 'the reverse of the truth'. For the sake of the future, it argued, the past should be forgotten. That such comments could be made at a national level by representatives of what was perhaps the most striking monument to the impact of the war in Britain illustrate the enormous problems for those trying to commemorate the Holocaust. On one level, commitment to liberal universalism and Christian forgiveness militated against remembering the fate of the Jews. On another, English parochialism insisted on the continued memory of the British war effort and the sacrifices made.[102]

The desire not to offend or upset was also present in the decision of the British Board of Film Censors in 1961 to ban the showing of footage from a film on the Warsaw ghetto. There were, however, dissenting voices and after protests from 100 MPs the film was eventually shown. The efforts of those on the Warsaw Ghetto Memorial Committee were also finally rewarded in 1961 when an exhibition on the rebellion was shown in a small venue in

London. The exhibition was run on a tiny budget (which the organizers still struggled to raise) and there was some difficulty in finding suitable display material as little existed in Britain. Nevertheless, it was still a landmark in Holocaust commemoration in British society. Messages at its opening from prominent individuals such as Lord Birkett, Lord Boothby and J. B. Priestley indicated that for some, at least, the scale and importance of the Jewish tragedy had been brought home. There was an awareness among a minority that there was a need to tell the story of Jewish sufferings under the Nazis 'because the facts have already been forgotten. It hardly seems credible that the extermination of six million Jews could be forgotten so quickly.' The Committee's plans for a permanent memorial in Britain were, however, far from being realized. This was starkly illustrated in 1965 as Britain commemorated the twentieth anniversary of VE Day.[103]

The international Association of Nazi Concentration Camp Survivors (ANCCS) was formed in 1960 as a response to 'the resurgence of neo-nazism' and the desire to keep alive the memory of what had occurred during the war. Its aim, similar to that of the Warsaw Ghetto Memorial Committee, was to think not only of the past 'but also of the present and the future, to help to prevent a repetition of what happened'. The paucity of Holocaust commemoration in Britain was illustrated when in 1965 the ANCCS raised a sum of less than £20 for a memorial plaque which was unveiled after a ceremony at St Martin-in-the-Fields, London. The ANCCS announced that

The plaque may not be very grand or on the same scale as similar memorials on the Continent, but we have at least the satisfaction to know that this particular plaque, which we initiated and produced, is the first and only one to the memory of Camp Victims in this country.[104]

Yet behind this ceremony was a story that emphasizes the total marginality of survivors in British society during the 1960s. The problem of connecting the British experience to those who suffered in Nazism was immense. It was recognized by Captain Hanauer, the chair of the ANCCS, when he wrote to Bill Simpson of the Council of Christians and Jews (CCJ) with regard to raising funds for a proposed memorial at Dachau:

we fully realise that this country was not as closely involved in the ghastliness of concentration camps as were those which were occupied by the Nazis during the war, all of which lost thousands of their best sons and daughters in these places. But we also know that between two and three hundred British service personnel, Secret Agents, RAF pilots were exterminated in Dachau, Buchenwald, Ravensbruck and other such infamous camps.

Rather than stressing the reality of the eastern camps, Hanauer was forced to make a slightly contrived and limited connection between British citizens and the western camps. In January 1965 the ANCCS approached the CCJ again, this time proposing a communal service in Trafalgar Square to commemorate the liberation of the camps. Simpson wrote back saying he doubted that the churches in Britain would cooperate. The date suggested by the ANCCS coincided with Christian Aid week which was 'positive and creative'. In contrast the liberation commemoration would be 'harking back to earlier bitterness, the reopening of old wounds, and an occasion to be avoided rather than shared'. The proposed event, at best, would be of 'secondary importance'. Hanauer was furious and responded bitterly:

Secondary importance of what and for whom? But for the victorious conclusion of the war against tyranny, 20 years ago in May, Christian Aid Week would certainly not be able to hold their admirable week at all. . . . Do you seriously suggest that the laying of wreaths at the Cenotaph and the holding of a '20th Anniversary commemoration service' by survivors, relatives and representatives of organisations which are actively employed in helping the many remaining and suffering foreign victims 'is a way of stimulating or perpetrating bitterness'? Again, I can ask you, in whom do we stimulate bitterness? That the suffering of the camp victims continues 20 years after their liberation is not our fault and I think it absolutely ridiculous to try to ignore it by sticking one's head into the ground for fear of offending people who have not got the strength of their own convictions. I, for one, most certainly think it my duty not only to remember those who died so that I could live, but also to pray for those who still suffer and for those splendid men and women who have taken it onto themselves to help them as much as they can. If this is thought to be stimulating or perpetrating of bitterness, then let it be so![105]

The CCJ opposed any attempt to hold a survivor event in the open air which might lead to antagonism and possible public disturbance (this being a time of disorder between neo-Nazis and anti-fascists in the capital). It was, however, the proposal of the ANCCS to connect their event to the Cenotaph which was the aspect that both Jewish and non-Jewish members of the CCJ found hardest to accept:

the Cenotaph is a national memorial to those who *gave their lives* for the freedom and security of the country and . . . [they opposed] the prospect of associating with the Cenotaph those who *came through* the war alive, whether out of Nazi camps, battle fields and naval operations.

Thus in the mass British commemoration of the twentieth anniversary of the end of the war, the survivors and the small group of people who recognized their history would be limited to a small private service. That it took place in a church reflected British Jewry's lack of involvement in the memory of the Holocaust. The episode had exposed the formidable barriers to comprehension in the liberal, Christian and exclusivist framework of Britain during the 1960s.

It had also shown the pervasive ignorance about the Jewish fate and the marginality of survivors in society.[106]

Even after the Eichmann trial very little material was published in Britain dealing with the Holocaust. The fantastical nature of Nazi antisemitism was avoided by major historians of Hitler and the Third Reich such as Alan Bullock and A. J. P. Taylor (who, instead, preferred to deal with matters of international diplomacy). One major exception to this trend was the work of the Jewish historian, Norman Cohn. His *Warrant for Genocide* (1967) revealed, through the history of *The Protocols of the Elders of Zion*, the importance of irrationality in history. Although she made the case too strongly, there was more than a little truth in Lucy Dawidowicz's comment that 'English historians of modern Germany . . . astonish us with the minimal attention they give to German anti-Semitism and to the destruction of the Jews'. In school textbooks in both Britain and the United States the Holocaust and Jewish history in general was generally avoided. The situation started to change in American textbooks in the 1970s but a survey in 1980 pointed out that in modern history books 'the story is completely glossed over'. This was the case 'especially in [Britain]'.[107]

This was also true of fiction for children. One exception was Kenneth Ambrose's *The Story of Peter Cronheim* (1962). At this point the Third Reich was rarely taught at schools either in Britain or the United States. Egon Larsen for the Association of Jewish Refugees believed that Ambrose's book was most welcome because the Nazi era was 'a period which teenagers know only from hearsay'. He added that

Twenty-odd years ago . . . [it] would have fulfilled the most important task of explaining to English children why so many young Central Europeans were turning up in their classrooms and at their playgrounds. It would have answered the recurring question, 'But *why* did you leave?', quite convincingly, and those teenage readers could then have passed on that explanation to their parents, who still did not know what this Hitler business was about. But I doubt whether such a children's book would have found a publisher at the time; in fact, there has altogether been very little juvenile fiction dealing with Nazi Germany, and hardly anything about the persecution of the Jews.

Other important works of children's fiction relating to the Holocaust, such as *I am David* by the Danish author, Anne Holm, were translated into English. It was not, however, until the 1970s that major works for children by British writers such as Judith Kerr (who was born in Germany) were published on the subject.[108]

Knowledge of the Holocaust, let alone informed debate and discussion on the subject, was thus still at a low level in Britain throughout the 1960s. It is with this in mind that the first major national attempt to deal with one aspect of it, the BBC's *Warsaw Ghetto* (1968), should be viewed. The film has been justly criticized by Lucy Dawidowicz and others for its uncritical utilization of Nazi propaganda footage of the ghetto. This material had been used earlier by the Nazis in the viciously antisemitic film *The Eternal Jew* (1940) to portray Jewish degeneration and disease. The BBC programme was unable to move beyond Nazi portrayals and thus failed to deal adequately with the reality of Jewish life and responses to Nazi barbarity in the ghetto. Yet the 1968 film was in no way intended to be malicious – it was, in fact, an attempt at a sympathetic portrayal of the Holocaust. Its limitations reflected the low level of British knowledge of the Holocaust as the 1960s came to a close.[109]

The differences between Britain and the United States in this matter during the 1960s and the early 1970s should not be overstated. Lack of consideration to the Holocaust in school education (and especially in the teaching of history, which in both countries remained essentially parochial) was one area of great similarity. Another related to the questions of memorials. Continued plans for a Warsaw ghetto memorial in New York were rejected in 1964. The Parks Commissioner explained that 'monuments in the parks should be limited to events of American history'. The awareness of pluralism but ultimate lack of commitment to ethnic particularism was also revealed in the comments of a member of New York's art commission: 'How would we answer other special groups who wanted to be similarly represented on public land[?]'. Jews as a 'special group' were still reluctant to put their full financial backing behind Holocaust remembrance – a committee for the 'Memorial to the Six Million Jewish Martyrs' which was formed in the late 1960s had raised only $17,000 of the required $1.5 million by 1973. Yet the awareness of the Holocaust as a universal symbol and the increasing involvement of American Jewry in the memory of the event during the 1960s ultimately differentiated the United States from Britain. By the late 1970s, and certainly by the early 1980s, the subject had become one of almost obsessive interest in American society. In contrast, George Steiner suggested that in Britain the Holocaust was 'Not our patch'. In recent years the gap between the two countries has diminished, and the Holocaust is perhaps more present than ever before in British society and culture.[110] Why, then, did Britain lag so far behind by the 1970s and how has it managed more recently to catch up at least some of the lost ground?

VIII

The increasing interest of American Jewry in the Holocaust during the 1970s was matched, if in a more limited way, by a new generation of British Jewish intellectuals. Writers such as Dannie Abse, Jon Silkin and D. M. Thomas engaged directly with the subject of the Holocaust and moved beyond the earlier Jewish apologist approach of Anglo-Jewish novelists such as Louis Golding and Naomi Jacob (who were motivated by a desire to outline in an almost pedagogic way to gentiles the story of the Jews during World War II). A growing self-confidence among sections of British Jewry meant that the new writers no longer needed to explain themselves to a non-Jewish audience when dealing with Jewish matters. On a more limited level the same was true in television, leading to important documentaries on the Holocaust by British-born Jews. These included Jeremy Isaacs' *Genocide* (1975) in the influential Thames Television *World at War* series and Rex Bloomstein's *The Gathering* (BBC, 1982) on the first major Holocaust survivor gathering which was held in Jerusalem. Bloomstein also produced the controversial *Auschwitz and the Allies* (BBC 1982). The latter, as has been noted in the introduction, was based on the work of Martin Gilbert who was starting to emerge as a major international Holocaust historian.[111]

It should be stressed, however, that these television documentaries of the 1970s and early 1980s were isolated events. Moreover, the fiction and poetry of the new Anglo-Jewish writers had only a limited circulation. More generally, the worlds of literature, art, music and film-making at a popular and high cultural level in British society rarely addressed the issue of the Holocaust. In addition, educational establishments from schools through to universities also managed to ignore the subject. There was, in short, still tremendous British ignorance of the Holocaust. A prominent journalist recalled watching the Isaac's *Genocide* in 1975:

It was the first time I had ever really seen those mountains of papery corpses, limbs and skulls that needed bulldozers to bury. Next day, among colleagues and friends, the sense of shock was palpable. And mystification, too. Why had we never been told before?[112]

Connected to such lack of knowledge was continued resistance to the commemoration of the Holocaust. It was shown in the tragi-comic struggle for a Holocaust memorial in Britain.

James Young has asked with regard to Germany: 'How does a state incorporate its crimes against others into its national memorial landscape?' Elsewhere he has written with regard to Holocaust memorials in the United States that, in contrast to those on the Continent, they 'inevitably call attention to the great distance between themselves and the destruction'. In Britain one could go further. The near-total absence of Holocaust memorials and resistance to the very idea of them has been used to distance the British experience from that of the 'diseased' Continent. The debate over Holocaust memorials in Britain has emphasized the Christian and exclusivist framework of society as a whole. In such discussions during the 1970s and early 1980s the dominant mono-cultural liberal creed had no place for the consideration of either the needs of its Jewish minority or a confrontation with the most illiberal occurrence in twentieth-century Europe.[113]

In 1973 and 1974, George Carter, an ordinary member of the United Reform Church in the Home Counties, suggested the construction of a centre in a British city which

would serve as a memorial to the many millions who perished in concentration camps during the Second World War. Those who fought and died to save our civilisation would also be remembered. The basic objectives of the proposal are firstly to provide recognition by the Christian community of the sufferings of the Jews and others, and secondly by using the holocaust as a foundation, erect a Centre to foster racial harmony and propagate good community relations.

Responses to Carter's proposals were not promising. Joan Lawrence, secretary of the Religious Weekly Press group, wrote to her fellow member of the CCJ, Bill Simpson:

where on *earth* does he think he's going to get enough cash? . . . The whole thing shows a total lack of any sense of realism. If you want to raise big money nowadays its got to be terrifically *emotive* (like starving children, or Israel).

Nobody here in this country (by and large) w[oul]d be moved by the Holocaust. Only we and James Parkes – and I doubt either of us are very viable financially!

Carter's proposals, which would become almost mainstream a decade later, were rejected as 'a kind of "lunatic fringe" effort, quite impractical to achieve and utterly high-flown'. The Archbishop of Canterbury wrote sympathetically to Carter but concluded that he wondered 'if Germany would not be a more suitable country to provide a memorial to those who died in Nazi concentration camps'. The Catholic Archbishop of Westminster was more terse: 'Britain [was] not the place, this [was] not the time'. If, for Carter, 'The size and details of the horror [were] really quite alarming and it's really only now that the "penny" has dropped', this was not true for many in British society.[114] There were others, it is true, such as those in the Warsaw Ghetto Memorial Committee, who were still campaigning for a permanent monument during the 1970s. Yet their argument that all previous 'calamities, disasters and epic struggles . . . pale into insignificance by comparison with the holocaust engineered by Nazism' was hardly accepted in the inward-looking atmosphere of British society. The Committee acknowledged that while it had managed to unite Anglo-Jewish communal organizations in the holding of 'large impressive Commemoration meetings on the anniversary of the Warsaw Ghetto

Uprising', its main aim, a permanent memorial, was still unfulfilled. It reflected sadly that 'Memorials are to be found in U.S.A., France, Poland, Israel and elsewhere. But, in England, nothing exists to mark this phase in history.' Both the memorials/centres proposed by Carter and the Warsaw Ghetto Committee aimed to stress both the particular tragedy of the Jews and the victims of Nazism more generally. The need, if success was to be forthcoming, to connect directly to the British and the Allied war effort in general was also recognized: 'The British people and all the nations who fought against Nazism in World War II have their martyrs, and victims in vast numbers, and their memory and sacrifice must be honoured too.'[115]

Carter, in particular, attempted to connect his idea to the burgeoning 'race relations' industry in Britain, but had little success with his project in the mid-1970s. Four years later, when a Holocaust memorial project was revived in Britain, he reflected on his past experiences. He had been repeatedly told that his scheme was 'too late and . . . the grim events had occurred on the continent and not in this country'. In refusing to accept the thinking behind either premise, Carter was isolated, especially within the Christian community in Britain. He believed, especially after the liberation of Belsen, in the principle of commemoration of the victims of Nazism and thought that reflections on the experience could be used to combat present and future intolerance. As a whole, the British churches believed the opposite.[116]

In 1979, during a claims conference for victims of Nazism at Geneva, the historian Yehuda Bauer stated with regard to Holocaust activities across the world that

In Britain, nothing at all has been done, and there exists an opposition on the part of the older generation in the Jewish community to introducing educational programmes specifically on the Holocaust.

Members of the Yad Vashem Committee of the Board of Deputies of British Jews were hurt by Bauer's remarks and drafted a response 'strongly rejecting the allegations made and pointing out the scope and intensity of the work being done by Anglo-Jewry in connection with the Holocaust'.[117] The gap in the two perspectives is made more understandable if alternative national and international frameworks are employed. From Bauer's global outlook, especially from an American or an Israeli viewpoint, the relative poverty of the British response was clear. By the late 1970s the subject had become highly popularized in American culture and society through television productions such as *Holocaust* (1978), often said in many ways to be a Jewish equivalent of the Afro-American *Roots* (1977). The Holocaust had also become part of the political identity of American Jewry. Judith Miller has described how in 1977 three Jewish officials in Jimmy Carter's administration promoted the idea of a national Holocaust museum in Washington. In the following years the idea took hold. Carter realized that support for such a venture might help heal the wounds between the Jewish electorate and the Democrats over the President's alleged sympathies for the Palestinian as opposed to the Israeli cause. In 1979 Carter announced his decision to appoint a Presidential Commission on a national Holocaust memorial. In subsequent debates, the question of who owned the Holocaust (and who was to be included and excluded in terms of victims of the Nazis and other groups who had suffered attempted genocides), generated much anger and heated debate in American society. Yet the Holocaust, as understood as a specific crime of the Nazi regime against the Jewish people, was, in spite of these discussions about uniqueness and ethnic particularity, firmly established in American consciousness by the time of the Presidential Commission and Bauer's comments on British neglect.[118] Although the process was uneven, and major distortions had occurred through the imposition of ideological and national considerations, the Holocaust had become established as a self-contained issue in a range of Western societies. On an international scale, therefore, Bauer was right to point out the relative weakness of British interest. For the small minority in Britain who had been actively involved in the process of Holocaust remembrance since the end of the war, however, it was hardly surprising that Bauer's remarks were deeply frustrating. It was especially galling given the relative progress they had made in the second half of the 1970s.

The failure and total isolation of George Carter's efforts from 1973 to 1975 indicated that if change was to occur it would need to be stimulated from abroad. This in fact happened in 1976 when, in an attempt to stimulate help from abroad, Yad Vashem in Jerusalem prompted the foundation of a support committee in Britain. Apart from largely unsuccessful fund-raising for Jerusalem, the new committee (which became part of the Board of Deputies of British Jews) aimed to stimulate teaching and commemoration of the Holocaust in Britain. The question of a Holocaust memorial soon returned to the agenda. Small memorials in synagogues, Jewish cemeteries and the like had been constructed by the late 1970s. These were, however, essentially private monuments and there were no such memorials in public places in Britain. The suggestion was made in 1979 for a Holocaust memorial to be erected 'in a central place in London as had been done on other European capitals'. There were some reservations expressed at the Yad Vashem Committee but generally the project had, for the first time, the support and backing of a major Jewish organization in Britain. The Committee, consisting mainly of British-born Jews with a minority of survivors and token Christian representation, showed a greater self-confidence (as well as a clear identification with the Holocaust) in its demands for such a national monument. But the national debate about the monument revealed that many in British society were yet to be convinced of its need or appropriateness. Indeed the project became within the CCJ 'the most controversial thing . . . in twenty years'.[119]

The debate and controversy was largely concerned with the question of the particularity of the Jewish fate and its relation to the British war effort. This partly arose out of the Minister of the Environment's promise of a site for a permanent memorial to the Holocaust in Whitehall, almost immediately opposite the Cenotaph. Greville Janner, MP, the President of the Board of Deputies, publicly announced the project in late 1979. The monument would not be confined to the Jews, but would include all the victims of Nazi extermination: 'The cataclysmic murder of some eleven million people, five million of whom were not Jewish'. Reporting of this statement distorted Janner's remarks and *The Guardian* indicated that 'The Board of Deputies of British Jews [was] to erect *its own* [my emphasis] cenotaph in Whitehall as a monument to victims of Nazi oppression'. It was to 'be the Jewish community's first public memorial in Britain to their war dead'. The CCJ, which had originally been one of the sponsors of the project, eventually withdrew its support. There was opposition to it from both the Jewish and Christian sides. The representative of its Manchester branch wrote that he could

see the case for memorials in the countries where the Holocaust was directly experienced, but not for such a Memorial in this country. If such a Memorial were erected I can well imagine its becoming the focal point of lunatic fringe activities against the Jews or the German peoples and I do not see why the CCJ should be involved in anything which might serve to harm relations between peoples.

A prominent Jewish member of the CCJ objected strongly to its location in Whitehall. He supported the idea of a Holocaust memorial, especially to all 11 million victims,

but there will be many people . . . who, like myself, would have objected very much to their being anything facing the Cenotaph, which is the memorial to the fallen of our country in World Wars I and II.

Another added that placing a Holocaust memorial next to the Cenotaph 'which, after all, commemorates all British subjects, regardless of Creed, who died in the war, was bound to cause some offence'.[120]

To the relief of many the site in Whitehall soon became unavailable. There was still, however, much opposition to the proposal of a monument *per se*. The British Council of Churches decided not to support the project as it believed it would act against 'the reconciliation of peoples of different race, faith and culture'. Its Executive Committee recognized that the atrocities had been committed in 'the midst of . . . European Christian civilisation', but ultimately its emphasis on Christian forgiveness allowed no space for Jewish commemoration. Immanuel Jakobovits, the Chief Rabbi, also had his own reasons for opposing the project, rejecting 'the sanctification of the Holocaust as a cardinal doctrine in contemporary Jewish thought and teaching'. While there had been greater support for the monument than five years earlier, there was general relief that the high profile project had not materialized. In the Christian community the belief was still widespread that such a memorial would act against reconciliation; there was also an objection to any form of Jewish particularism that might itself stir up antisemitism. It was to be four years after the Holocaust Memorial Foundation Committee originally proposed a public monument that a 'small and unobtrusive' memorial garden was placed in the Dell in London's Hyde Park. An annual commemoration ceremony, attended by several hundred people, has taken place since the mid-1980s.[121] Both this ceremony and the attempt to mark *Yom Hashoah* have had only limited success in Britain (although the number of synagogues commemorating *Yom Hashoah* through special services rose impressively in the early 1990s). Moreover, repeated attempts to create a museum of the Holocaust in Britain throughout the 1980s and subsequently have come nowhere near to success. Raising money for any Holocaust-related project in Britain both inside and outside the Jewish communities has proved a recurring problem. In contrast vast sums have been raised elsewhere, particularly in the United States for massive projects in Washington, New York and Los Angeles. The monument in the Holocaust Memorial Gardens in Hyde Park, apart from attracting its small number of visitors at the annual commemoration, has also been subject to vandalism by antisemites in the form of Holocaust denial graffiti. Yet in spite of all these limitations, it would be wrong to conclude that the Holocaust is still of limited interest in Britain. At various levels since the early 1980s the Holocaust has achieved great relevance in British society.[122]

The change in atmosphere was intimately connected with the move from a liberal assimilationist ideology to a more pluralistic vision of British society. Out of a growing commitment to multi-cultural and anti-racist strategies at a national and, particularly, local government level, the Holocaust became an important aspect of educational initiatives. This was marked by the reception to two exhibitions from abroad, *Auschwitz* (from Poland), which was first displayed in 1983 at the Whitechapel Art Gallery, and *Anne Frank in the World* (from Holland), which was shown two years later and has subsequently travelled across the United Kingdom and Ireland. They were not isolated events attended largely by Jewish audiences. These exhibitions attracted hundreds of thousands of visitors and were incorporated into school education. The new relevance of the Holocaust was shown by the involvement of the Inner London Education Authority (ILEA), which was at the forefront of anti-racist work, in the disseminating material such as 'Auschwitz: Yesterday's Racism'. The issue was still highly controversial, and the pack was never circulated due to political opposition. But there was still widespread evidence of general interest in the subject from a younger generation of non-Jewish educationalists (even if there was a tendency, with the desire to make the topic of contemporary relevance, to universalize the Holocaust and forget its specific place in Jewish history). Thus the title of the ILEA educational pack ignores the continuing legacy of the Holocaust for the survivors, their children and others. A further danger in such methodology was that it had a tendency to portray Jews as passive and limit their role in history to that of victims. More subtle approaches that show the richness and diversity of Jewish life destroyed by the Holocaust have been slower in developing.[123] But it was also in the 1980s that the Jewish community in Britain was beginning to campaign more openly and confidently with regard to Holocaust-related issues. For the first time, survivors achieved prominence both in society as a whole and within the British Jewish establishment. The experiences of survivors such as Kitty Hart, who made an important and harrowing television do-cumentary *Return to Auschwitz* (Yorkshire Television, 1979), Hugo Gryn, who has become prominent in the British media, Ben Helfgott, the founder and leading force of the '45 Aid Society and since 1986 Chair of the Yad Vashem Committee, and others have been listened to with increasing respect. It was British Jews, including survivors, who forced the issue of Holocaust education to be considered at the debate over the first national curriculum for England and Wales.[124]

The impact of the lack of Holocaust education in Britain was exposed in a 1989 opinion poll marking the fiftieth anniversary of the start of World War II. The survey aimed to establish popular knowledge levels concerning the war. The fact that one of the ten questions referred to the Holocaust (and that, in contrast, eight of the other nine were concerned with the *British* war effort) in itself revealed that the subject had received status as a self-contained and important part of the conflict, even in a parochially minded society. The specific question asked, 'What do you associate with the names Auschwitz and Dachau?', indicated, however, that the differences between the western and eastern camps had still to be widely recognized. Overall, only 23 per cent did not know or answered 'incorrectly'. The figure was much higher for the 18–24-year-old sample, with just 57 per cent answering 'correctly'. This age group reflected one born well after the end of the war, when there was little Holocaust education at British schools.[125] There was thus great dismay in the Jewish community when the first proposals relating to the National History Curriculum dealt only with the British experience in the 1930s. The Nazi regime generally and the Holocaust in particular were automatically ruled out. In what was a remarkable display of ethnic lobbying, the Jewish community, with the support of sympathetic non-Jewish MPs, campaigned through the Yad Vashem Committee, the related Holocaust Education Trust and an all-party group of parliamentarians for the subject to be reconsidered in the curriculum. The lobbyists argued that 'To ignore the phenomenon of how one of the world's most civilised nations could have condoned a State policy of mass murder and genocide is to leave unanswered one of the central questions of modern civilisation'. Following a by then well-established pattern, they also argued for the relevance of the subject with regard to questions of modern racism. They also patriotically linked the Holocaust to the British war effort in fighting the evils of Nazism. This campaign was highly effective and in the *Final Report* of the History Working Party on the National Curriculum, the international aspects of World War II were inserted, including the Holocaust.

Some problems remained. A crude universalistic tendency was present in the unsophisticated lumping together of Auschwitz, Hiroshima and Dresden as 'casualties of war'. More generally the History curriculum continued the long-standing problematic presentation of Jewish history in British textbooks: Jews only feature as a persecuted group and there is no attempt to deal with their religious and cultural development across the ages. Yet progress had been made. 'Genocide: The Holocaust' now featured as essential information that must be taught in the National Curriculum. In addition, surveys indicate that most teachers see the subject as an important one and some excellent source material has been produced on the Holocaust by British educators. As the twentieth century approaches its end, schools in Britain, Jewish and non-Jewish, are starting to produce high-quality Holocaust educational material. The contrast with the situation just over a decade earlier, when little material was available (and even many Jewish schools did not confront the subject), is clear. Britain no longer lags behind the United States in this area, and possibly now provides better Holocaust education at school level than the Americans.[126]

A similar pattern has emerged in higher education, where the resistance to the study of the Holocaust was perhaps even stronger. In the United States, in parallel to the growth of black and women's studies, the Jewish community lobbied for and contributed to Jewish studies programmes, including the Holocaust, at many American campuses. The situation in the United Kingdom until the late 1980s was, however, very different. There were simply no courses on offer on the Holocaust in any British polytechnic or university. In 1987 the Yad Vashem Committee carried out an investigation of Holocaust education at non-compulsory level. It found, in addition to the general neglect of the subject, a tendency to view the Holocaust as somehow being of interest only to Jewish students and educators. As the report concluded, this was a 'total misunderstanding of the complex and wide-ranging nature of the [Holocaust which] is so important historically that it does not and cannot "belong" to any particular group of humanity'. There was still resistance to considering the subject at all, a parochialism revealed in a collection of essays from leading British historians dealing with controversies emerging from the National Curriculum debate. Not one mention was made of the Holocaust. Yet, since the *Final Report* of the History National Curriculum was published in 1990, major changes have taken place. There are now important and sophisticated courses on the Holocaust in higher education institutions across Britain in disciplines such as History, Geography, Literature, Philosophy, German and Sociology. Jews and non-Jews, specialists and generalists have emerged who have recognized the central importance of the Holocaust in the modern world. Research of high quality has been produced and the general interest has been shown by the publication of the *British Journal of Holocaust Education*, which appeared for the first time in the summer of 1992.[127]

The change in atmosphere can also be charted in the case of the Imperial War Museum (IWM) and its representation of the Holocaust. The idea for a National War Museum first emerged in 1917 and was, due the interest of the Dominion governments, expanded to become the Imperial War Museum. It was established by Act of Parliament in 1920. By the 1950s, the IWM's role was defined as covering all military operations in which Britain and the Commonwealth had been involved since 1914. The IWM underwent a radical transformation in the 1980s, recognizing that many of its visitors had not experienced war directly. There was a desire to provide 'relevance to today's visitors and to make our displays more than a nostalgic journey into a near-forgotten reality'. If, however, in the minds of the IWM management, the broadening process of the 1980s made it 'perhaps the most comprehensive museum of the 20th century in existence', there were still only fleeting mentions of the Holocaust. In 1990 an exhibition was held at the House of Commons to mark the 45th anniversary of the Buchenwald report, which consisted of the material gathered by the parliamentary delegation. In the autumn of 1990 the exhibition transferred to the IWM. As a result it was reported that the museum director 'realised the lack of information they held on the Shoah, and has consequently agreed to hold more Holocaust material'. The IWM's response was 'to concentrate on material relating to Belsen Concentration Camp'. In 1991 a permanent exhibition at the IWM on 'Belsen 1945' came into existence. The exhibition and publications linked to it concentrate on the British relief effort (particularly on the work of medical teams) at Belsen after its liberation. The focus is thus on the British liberators rather than the liberated, but this was perhaps a necessary first step in the development of museum Holocaust representation. A similar, parochial process was apparent in early American proposals justifying Holocaust museums which would also concentrate on the connections made through the liberations of the western camps. The beginnings of a different approach were apparent during the spring of 1993 when the IWM commemorated the fiftieth anniversary of the Warsaw

Ghetto uprising. Although small in scale and funded by Jewish benefactors, it was the first IWM exhibition covering the Jewish experience of the Holocaust and one of only a very few presented by a national British cultural institution since 1945. It is thus a landmark in the story of Britain and the Holocaust, even if the further goal of a specific museum devoted to the Jewish catastrophe remains totally unrealized.[128]

The second area in which the Holocaust has made a controversial entry into British politics and society in general since the 1980s is that of war crimes. Again, comparisons with the United States are revealing. Both countries, and others such as Australia and Canada, allowed in through their displaced persons schemes significant numbers of individuals who had taken part in the destruction of European Jewry. Inadequate screening, and, in the United States, greater concern about communists than former Nazi sympathizers, meant that no action was taken against those coming to the liberal democracies. Half-hearted consideration was given by the British government in 1950 and 1951 to surveying those displaced persons who had arrived since the war, but no action was taken on the information received. The possibility that Britain and the United States had acted as a safe haven for those who had committed crimes against humanity was not an important issue in the Cold War era. Activists in both countries attempted to bring the issue out into the open in the 1950s and 1960s but it rarely became important. In Britain the popular media exploited such claims for their sensationalist value, but their news value was essentially temporary. The major change occurred in the United States in the late 1970s and related to American Jewry's new involvement and interest in the Holocaust. American Jewish lobbyists in 1977 demanded government action, which led to the formation of the Office of Special Investigations (OSI). The OSI took action against 80 persons suspected of war crimes, 30 of whom were deported or extradited. OSI activities and lobbying from the Simon Wiesenthal Center in Los Angeles resulted in similar investigations in Canada and Australia. By the mid-1980s, as David Cesarani has illustrated, 'Britain remained the only Anglo-Saxon country to absorb large numbers of East Europeans after the war that had not engaged in an exhaustive process of self-examination'.[129]

There were bodies, such as the anti-fascist journal *Searchlight*, which had campaigned for the prosecution of those guilty of war crimes living in Britain, but it took the impetus of fresh evidence from the Wiesenthal Center to force the British government, very belatedly, into considering action. The issue, as was the case with so many others in Britain with regard to the Holocaust, brought forth conflict over the issue of Jewish particularism and the memory of Britain and World War II. Nevertheless, the debate over war crimes also showed the changes that had taken place in British society since the 1970s.[130]

Jewish lobbying and the support of non-Jewish sympathizers, which had played a decisive role in the National Curriculum, had actually emerged earlier with the war crimes issue. An All-Party Parliamentary War Crimes Group was formed in 1986 as a result of the new information and the government launched the Hetherington-Thomas enquiry. The delay in bringing cases into consideration – a result of British neglect rather than ignorance – made the situation much harder. Even so, the evidence obtained shocked all who came into contact with it. The spirit of the House of Commons in its debates on war crimes legislation, with one or two notable exceptions, and in putting the issue on the statute books was remarkable in contrast to earlier post-war discussion of the Holocaust.[131] The discussion in the upper house, however, revealed that the tendencies which we have seen dominating all previous debates were still very much alive (if now more limited to an older generation). Whereas the House of Commons stressed the issue of moral justice, of Britain's reputation and of remembering what were still recent crimes against humanity, some in the House of Lords saw the question as being ones of an alien people demanding Old Testament revenge as against the British (Christian) sense of forgiveness. Other arguments emerged from the House of Lords which could easily have come from debates in World War II – Bishops and others claimed that raising the issue *now* would lead to increased antisemitism. These arguments against Jewish particularity also stressed the otherness of the Jewish minority in Christian Britain. The same points had also been used successfully against helping the persecuted Jews in the Nazi era. They were employed after the conflict in opposition to Holocaust memorials. The continued utilization of such thinking in the war crimes debate was, however, in vain in terms of halting fresh legislation if not its implementation. A minor constitutional crisis followed but the Commons finally got its way. The greater acceptance of pluralism and the active involvement of the Jewish community and many other sympathizers was ultimately successful. Britain had caught up with countries such as the United States in terms of its war crimes legislation. There were some, even in the House of Commons, whose opposition to the legislation appears to have been part of a general anti-'immigrant' perspective. Others, in the Lords and elsewhere, warned the Jews to keep their heads down over this and other issues. Although theirs was, ultimately, a minority position, their opposition has undoubtedly contributed to the continued delay in bringing prosecutions and has limited the potential scale of such trials: by July 1994, of 369 cases examined by the police since investigations began, 112 suspects had, in the intermediate period, already died. Nevertheless, British sensitivity towards the Holocaust, including Jewish feelings on the subject, had emerged in the war crimes debate in the late 1980s and early 1990s.[132]

The limitation of this new found sympathy in Britain (and in other countries, including the United States) concerns a third area – that of Holocaust denial.

The deep roots of this still persistent form of antisemitism have been charted throughout this book. It should be added that the British government considered taking action against Holocaust denial as early as 1943. In that year the extreme Scottish Protestant and pro-Nazi, Alexander Ratcliffe, produced a pamphlet claiming that 'there is not a single case on record of a single Jew having been massacred or unlawfully put to death under the Hitler regime'. One Home Office official believed that Ratcliffe's work would create 'animosity towards one section of His Majesty's subjects'. He was in support of new laws which would defend the Jews against attacks such as those from Ratcliffe. Herbert Morrison, the Home Secretary, refused to accept that a libel law was needed to protect the Jews and argued any such legislation would 'have an effect contrary to that intended'. It was not, in Morrison's view, the role of the state to protect its minorities and he maintained the right of the individual to freedom of expression.[133]

Holocaust denial became more and more organized in the post-war world and developed separately in many countries. From there it has expanded into an international network. For survivors, whose need to give testimony has often been an essential part of their post-war life, Holocaust denial has been particularly disturbing. Yet attempts in Britain to ban such material in the late 1980s and early 1990s have been rejected on the same grounds outlined by Morrison. The liberal British state has refused to protect one of its most vulnerable minorities – even though it now has the most powerful anti-racist legislation in Europe. Individual liberty has been put on a higher plane than the sensitivities of those who have suffered some of the worst abuses of the twentieth century. Apart from the hurt caused to survivors and others, the general influence of Holocaust denial is difficult to assess. There can be little doubt that its purveyors are motivated by antisemitism, often of a pro-Nazi variety. Nevertheless, its supporters have managed to operate in 'respectable' society both in Britain and the United States. Lady Mosley and David Irving have received much publicity in the British media for their views. The latter is not, as he says himself, 'your average loony'. He has functioned at many different levels in society – addressing neo-Nazis in Germany one minute, appearing on television and being quoted in 'quality' newspapers the next. Irving has shown that in spite of the greater sensitivity towards the Holocaust in British society, the subject can still be exploited for its sensationalism. Irving's denial of the Holocaust is absolute, yet he has been used as an 'expert' by several national newspapers over issues relating to the Nazi movement, including the Jews. He is still seen as one of Britain's 'leading historians' and has also been used along with Lady Birdwood (another Holocaust denier) by major television companies in what can only be described as insensitive freak shows in confrontation with Holocaust survivors. It cannot be argued that Britain is alone in giving such prominence to those holding such obscene views. Two major American politicians with national profiles, electoral success and presidential ambitions – Pat Buchanan and David Duke – both deny the Holocaust. In France the alarming rise to prominence of Jean Marie Le Pen is another example of someone who denies the Holocaust and yet has become a major force in national politics. In short, left to propagate their views by the state, those refusing to accept the reality of the Holocaust have still achieved success and respectability. It is not by any means clear, however, that such views have made a great impact in terms of popular belief. A poll carried out in 1993 by the American Jewish Committee found that only 7 per cent of British adults thought it possible that 'the Nazi extermination of the Jews never happened'. The figure was higher for the United States (22 per cent), perhaps reflecting the greater credence given to conspiracy theories in American culture and politics. Of much more significance was the finding from the same poll that only 2 per cent of American and 4 per cent of British adults believed that it was *not* important to know about and understand the Holocaust.

Holocaust denial undoubtedly causes distress to survivors and many others, but it is important to place its general influence in perspective. At the end of the war, as has been illustrated at the start of this chapter, the fate of the Jews was of interest only to a small minority of societies in countries such as Britain and the United States. This is far from the case today.[134]

IX

Judith Doneson has written with regard to contemporary American society that 'At every level – daily speech, politics, culture, Jewish life – the influence of the Holocaust is felt. It is part of the American vernacular.' It has increased even further with the massive success of the United States Holocaust Memorial Museum, which opened in Washington during 1993, and Steven Spielberg's *Schindler's List* (1994). In Britain the battle to achieve a presentness for the Holocaust has been harder. Until recently the limitations and strength of a mono-cultural liberal ideology provided a less favourable atmosphere for consideration of the Holocaust. Britain perhaps still has a long way to go. A documentary on British attitudes towards Germany included the following statement on Auschwitz: it 'means a lot of very unpleasant things to a lot of people'. A critic in response suggested that the individual was

so schooled in English understatement that he lacked a vocabulary which could embrace the subject. In this naive undefiled state, the British are almost unique in Europe.[135]

Yet, even in Britain, with its obsession with its own war experience, major change has taken place. Aside from developments already outlined in education and the war crimes debate, artistic works confronting the Holocaust are now constantly emerging. In 1991 two of the short-listed works of fiction in the prestigious Booker Prize dealt with the Holocaust and many major television documentaries and histories are being produced and written in Britain. The British Library, through its National Life Story Collection, is carrying out a major oral history of Holocaust survivors and their children. A younger generation of British people, Jewish and non-Jewish, are engaged with the Holocaust. Survivors and refugees from Nazism have acquired respect and such individuals are much in demand. One former child refugee reports that she is now giving 50 talks a year on her past experiences. Even Christian theologians in Britain are confronting this subject, when for so long Christian antipathy to Holocaust remembrance acted as an insurmountable barrier.[136] The growth and undoubted organization of Holocaust denial has to be put alongside such developments. We will soon enter an era in which the world does not have the benefit of the presence of survivors. But, much to the chagrin of the antisemites, there now exists a wealth of material on the Holocaust in terms of well-documented history, testimony of survivors and cultural representations. The last mentioned is, of course, of uneven quality and reflects ideological and national biases. Reflecting its cultural power generally, much representation of the Holocaust has already become Americanized. In Britain and elsewhere, Trotskyites and others on the extreme left have argued that Jews were responsible for their own destruction through Zionist 'collaboration'. Ironically, the extreme left's tendency to blame the victim recalls the persistent liberal opposition to Jewish particularity shown throughout this study. Such attacks on 'Zionism' have also appealed to the extreme right and there has been some limited crossover between the two extremes, both abusing the Holocaust for their own political purposes. Such tendencies need to be monitored carefully but their influence at present should not be distorted out of proportion. In more mainstream representations of the Holocaust, the problems, often ones of popularization, are much less severe. As James Young concludes, 'Better abused memory in this case, which might then be critically qualified, than no memory at all'. The subject of the Holocaust is now at least accessible to ordinary people, even in Britain. It has been a slow and ponderous process in the post-war world.[137]

Conclusion

Within the populace of the Allied nations, there were few who gave as much of their time and energy to the persecuted Jews of Europe as Eleanor Rathbone. Her acceptance of pluralism in a mono-culturally defined society and her ability to empathize with the people of a different faith and culture revealed an individual conscience of tremendous breadth and vision. In poor health already, Rathbone's willingness to identify and fight for the victims of Nazism showed courage and strength. From her privileged background, Rathbone could have accepted that the world was a just place and kept herself aloof from the plight of the needy and oppressed. Instead, she recognized the real condition of her age and saw its potential for evil and the perpetuation of human misery. At a time of frustration after the disappointments of the Bermuda conference in 1943, Rathbone pondered, with foresight, 'How many more are going to perish in the 20th century massacres of the innocents who might be saved[?]'.[1] As Rathbone feared, the Holocaust, in fact, only marked one stage of development in the history of genocide and was not in any way its epilogue.

As the twentieth century draws to a close, it has been estimated that genocide has brought death to over 50 million people. The number of cases of genocide, if anything, has increased since the end of World War II. In his last and most sombre book, *The Drowned and the Saved*, the late Primo Levi asked 'How securely do we live, we men of the century's and millennium's end and, more specifically, we Europeans?'. In pessimistic mood, Levi stressed that 'It happened, therefore it can happen again'. Although believing that it could 'happen everywhere', Levi thought that 'a mass slaughter is particularly unlikely in the Western world, Japan, and also the Soviet Union'. Levi hoped that in these places 'the Lagers of the Second World War are still part of the memory of many, on both the popular and governmental levels, and a sort of immunisational defence is at work'.[2] It now transpires that even this partial optimism was misplaced. Levi's untimely death in 1987 at least spared him from confronting the horrors of civil war in former Yugoslavia and the sight of concentration camps whose victims have been so reminiscent of those liberated in 1945. In the summer of 1992, descriptions of Muslim women and children in Bosnia incarcerated for five days in cattle-train wagons appeared in the Western media. Former refugees from Nazism, Holocaust survivors and other Jews could not help but draw parallels: it was 'too near the experience of our Jewish brethren under the Nazis for [them] to remain silent'.

Such evidence of genocide within Europe has to be placed alongside the continued rule of Saddam Hussein, an admirer of Hitler, who has attempted to carry out genocide against the Kurds and others in Iraq. Elsewhere the increasing influence of Pol Pot, responsible for the 'self-genocide' in Cambodia during the 1970s, and the massacres in Rwanda only emphasize further that this has been and continues to be a genocidal century.[3] Since 1945 there has been a series of international treaties outlawing genocide but these have had little influence, mainly because of the lack of international commitment to their implementation. Indeed, rather than acting as a deterrent, past examples of genocide appear to have encouraged later perpetrators. The authors of *The History and Sociology of Genocide* point out that not only has genocide occurred in all regions of the world, it has also been practised 'during all periods of history'.[4] This century, however, has a special place in the development of genocide. It is not simply the scale, frequency and geographical spread of twentieth century genocide that marks its uniqueness, frightening though these have been, it is the use of modern methods and the manipulation of bureaucracy, science and technology that make this century stand out. In this respect, the attempted destruction of European Jewry has particular significance. Hundreds of thousands, if not millions, of Jewish victims were killed by 'traditional' methods: first, by policies that brought starvation and disease in the ghettos and the western concentration camps during the last months of the war; second, through the massacres by shooting implemented by the *Einsatzgruppen* from the summer of 1941. But the production-line style of killing in the eastern camps and the determination to kill *all* Jews were developments that give the Holocaust, in this respect and many others, its unique horror. The use of mass communications, which was an essential part of the smooth functioning of the 'Final Solution', also highlights a feature of genocides in the modern world – the difficulty in keeping them secret, although there are contemporary examples of genocide for which no substantial records exist, such as two of the twentieth century's most devastating examples of genocide, namely those of the Armenians in the First World War and the Gypsies in the Second. The Nazis tried to disguise their crime against the

Jews, but as Levi again reminds us, even the *univers concentrationnaire* 'was not a closed universe'.[5]

In the first section of this book it has been stressed how the Nazi persecution of the Jews before the outbreak of World War II was practised openly. During the war, information about the Jews in Nazi-controlled Europe in the allied world was more problematic and sometimes involved a time-lag. Nevertheless, quite accurate and detailed information was available to both governments and ordinary people about the fate of the Jews. In short, the Holocaust became a global event with bystanders not just in the places of destruction but across the world.

Information was particularly accessible in the two leading liberal democracies of the Allied nations, Britain and the United States. Many similarities emerged between British and American reactions and responses to the Holocaust. But important differences, both in terms of the state and the population at large, have also become evident in this study. Can one therefore talk of a uniquely British (or American) confrontation with the Holocaust? Very little comparative work has been carried out in this area. There are few international studies of 'free world' diplomacy in the Nazi era with regard to the Jews of Europe, although some tentative league tables of generosity in providing asylum to refugees from Nazism have been attempted. But Helen Fein has been alone in attempting to build models of behaviour patterns in this area. Fein gives great attention to national traditions of antisemitism in explaining geographical variations in the success of implementing the 'Final Solution' in Nazi-occupied countries. She employed a similar technique when confronting Allied responses. Comparing Britain and the United States, Fein was forced, however, to recognize that antisemitism during the war was probably weaker in the former than in the latter. She was thus faced with the paradox that 'Unlike the American administration's response, which could be interpreted as an accurate reflection of public opinion, [the] British response did not reflect British public opinion'. By going into more detail in this area, Fein could have exposed the further inconsistency that American policy towards the Jews of Europe was at its most generous in 1944 and 1945 (with the formation of the War Refugee Board) at a time when antisemitism in the United States, as measured by opinion polls, was peaking.[6] This study has shown that the relationship between state policy and public sentiment was extremely complex and cannot be explained by simplistic notions of the existence or absence of antisemitism. In these democracies, the domination of liberalism determined that responses and attitudes would be fundamentally ambivalent. In its most basic and common form, there could be dislike of Jews at home and sympathy for the Jews abroad. It is important to add that in the United States during the second half of 1943 and early 1944, although antisemitism was reaching new heights, the efforts and success of those sympathetic to the plight of the Jews in the worlds of organized labour, the churches and American Jewry also peaked. The failings of Britain and the United States with regard to the Jewish crisis during the Nazi era may, therefore, be explained by the failure of state and society to solve the contradictions and ambiguities of liberalism. Only a tiny minority in these countries actually welcomed the persecution of the Jews. Nevertheless, the nature and origins of Nazi anti-semitism were rarely understood and the Jewish victims were frequently blamed for their own misfortune (which often affected treatment of refugees in Britain and the United States). Such tendencies reflected the tenacity of liberal ideology. The simultaneous existence of sympathy in these countries for the persecuted Jews should not be seen as evidence of blatant hypocrisy. Such ambiguity was shown clearly in the case of Harold Nicolson, one of those at the forefront of the campaign to rescue European Jewry. Although he did not like Jews, Nicolson genuinely 'loathed antisemitism'.[7]

In both countries, liberal ideologies were welded to exclusionary national frameworks, based on the notions of 'Englishness' and 'Americanness'. There were fears in Britain and the United States that certain alien groups would be unable to assimilate successfully and, if let in, would remain a constant danger to the well-being of society. Foreign Jews, especially those from Eastern Europe, were seen as particularly troublesome as it was believed that they would bring antisemitism with them. There were, however, crucial differences between the two countries in such nationalistic considerations. After 1918, Englishness was a near totally exclusive concept and was used to support the idea of a homogenous, non-immigrant, Christian nation. In contrast, although drastic restrictions had been introduced during the 1920s, some immigration was still possible through the quota system in the United States during the 1930s. Furthermore, by this decade Americanization at least allowed for some ethnic diversity within society. Against this, anti-radicalism was a much more powerful force in the United States and was marshalled successfully against potential Jewish immigrants who were discriminated against in the quota system. It was, however, the possibility of pluralism in society and ethnic representation in politics which ultimately differentiated the American re-sponse to the Holocaust from that in Britain. Through the War Refugee Board, the United States helped to save the lives of thousands of Jews. It was also the efforts of those in the United States, even more than those in Israel, which finally succeeded in giving the Holocaust a place both in history and present-day society. It has only been since the early 1980s, when multi-culturalism gained recognition and support, that the Holocaust has become the subject of serious discussion in post-war Britain. The paucity of the governmental response to the Jewish plight during World War II and the absence of debate for so long after 1945 might lead to the conclusion that British society was indifferent to the Holocaust. Indifference has become one of the most frequently used words to describe the responses of the allied nations (and also of popular opinion in Nazi Germany and occupied countries) to the fate of the Jews. In most of these cases the term has been employed inappropriately because it masks the mixture of sympathy and disdain that characterized most responses to persecuted Jewry. At varying levels, people became involved, even if, as was the case with the majority, their dominant response was silence and inaction. This was true also of ordinary people in the democracies.[8]

The distinguished historian of the Holocaust, Raul Hilberg, has commented that there were those 'in the United States and Great Britain for whom the reports of what was transpiring in Axis Europe meant very little, for whom persecution of any kind meant very little, until they underwent the shock of seeing something with their own eyes in 1945. They saw the camps.'[9] This is now a widespread view, but it is mistaken on two counts. First, Hilberg posits a total lack of knowledge and understanding on the part of the public in these countries during the war. Second, he suggests that the camp revelations revealed clearly the nature of the Holocaust to the world in the spring of 1945. Neither assumption, as has been shown in this book, is borne out by the evidence. But there has been a resistance to accepting alternative explanations. The strong liberal attachment to the concept of progress is threatened by the story of the Holocaust; myths have thus been constructed to make the subject more palatable. In contrast to the popular image that has grown up, the responses of the public in Britain and the United States to the plight of the Jews from 1933 to the end of the war were, in fact, highly complex. They were not, it must be emphasized, informed only by the state in a simplistic and one-directional manner. Information from above was frequently questioned or reinterpreted by those who received it. In fact, material presented by governments, the media and private sources was assimilated by ordinary people in an intricate way. The failure of many students of the Holocaust to recognize the complicated patterns of public opinion reveals a patronizing attitude to the populace of the liberal democracies. Henry Feingold stresses, with regard to the United States and other witnesses of the Holocaust, that it was ultimately the nation-state which determined action on behalf of persecuted Jewry. He adds that nation-states 'possess no souls, no conscience, and are not the containers of the spirit of civilization'. Yet, ordinary individuals and groups have been able to influence state policy, even when their numbers were not large. In the United States, the small but articulate restrictionist lobby had great success in keeping out Jewish children in 1939 during the debate over the Wagner Bill. The reverse process was at work with the agitation that led to the formation of the War Refugee Board. It is impossible to understand state policies towards the Jews of Europe in countries such as Britain and the United States without reference to public opinion. State and public informed one another, but did so in a complex and sophisticated relationship which can hardly be illustrated by a simple reliance on opinion poll data.[10]

The purpose of this book has thus been to chart the impact of the Holocaust on ordinary people in the democracies, rather than to outline in detail the implementation of state policy. It is consequently as much a contribution to Anglo-American social and cultural history as it is an account of the Holocaust. Primo Levi writes that the Lagers 'constituted an extensive and complex system which profoundly penetrated the daily life of the country'. But the Holocaust was also part of the everyday life of those far removed from its horrors.[11]

Helen Fein has suggested that

the implication of the Holocaust is that the life and liberties of minorities depend primarily upon whether the dominant group includes them within its universe of obligation; these are the bonds that hold or the bonds that break.

For ordinary people in Britain and the United States there were good reasons not to become involved with the fate of the Jews abroad. As the social psychologist, Ervin Staub, states 'To feel empathy results in empathic distress. To avoid that, people distance themselves from victims.'[12] Some did purposefully avoid confronting the fate of the Jews in the war, yet this was far from the only response in Britain and the United States. A small minority devoted themselves to helping in any way they could. To Harold Nicolson, in spite of all his social prejudices, there was no choice but to involve himself in the fate of the Jews after the Nazi rise to power. As a consequence, his everyday life was altered. In Britain, Storm Jameson and Eleanor Rathbone were examples of individuals who risked damaging their physical and mental health in the cause of European Jewry. Although the danger to their lives was in no way comparable, such individuals in the democracies acted as the counterparts of the rescuers of Jews on the Continent. They were, in Staub's terminology, 'good fanatics'.[13]

Nonetheless, focusing on ordinary people rather than on the responses of the state does not present human behaviour during the Holocaust in a more favourable light. The thousands involved in the altruistic rescue of Jews were numerically no greater than those who participated (without compulsion) in the murder of millions. The non-psychopathic ordinariness of the killers only serves to reinforce the frightening potential of mankind. Yet most people in the Holocaust occupied what Levi called the 'grey zone', the ambiguity inside and outside the camps in which 'Compassion and brutality can coexist in the same individual and in the same moment, despite all logic'.[14] This was also true of those in the democracies where the fundamental ambivalence of liberalism towards the Jews provided a coherent framework for the contradictory impulses of the individual. For a brief period in Britain at the end of 1942 and the start of 1943, pressure grew from below for government action on behalf of persecuted Jewry. Yet, in the process of mobilization and with the fate of the Jews receiving widespread attention, a greater awareness of those hostile to the Jews at home simultaneously came into existence. The British government decided to appease such potentially 'hostile' forces and to ignore the dominant sympathetic voice demanding action. The government mistook ambivalence for antipathy and attempted to satisfy only the lowest common denominator. In the process it made British identification with the Jews less attractive. If the government refused to take action; fighting on behalf of the persecuted could bring only frustration and despair. In the United States, popular pressure and high political lobbying was, at the start of 1944, successful. But the achievements of the War Refugee Board were not given publicity by the state and, as in Britain, the presentness of the Holocaust dwindled in the last 18 months of the conflict (even though, in this period, the amount of detailed information about the implementation of the 'Final Solution' increased dramatically). The 'fanatics' were left isolated – influential in the United States, but powerless and worn out in Britain.[15]

The recovery of the history of the Holocaust, as the last chapter explores, was long and difficult. In each country national and ideological factors combined to provide obstacles of varying size. Even the independent Jewish state had difficulty confronting the subject. The image of the Holocaust sat uneasily with the new country's attempt to prove its strength and self-reliance. It was in the United States where change occurred most dramatically. National self-questioning and the rise of ethnic politics coincided with the growing influence and confidence of American Jewry. The result was that there was the opportunity for survivors to receive a hearing and for the Holocaust to gain relevance for society as a whole. Elsewhere the battle for recognition took longer and in many cases remains to be completed. The domination of Stalinism in the Eastern Bloc precluded discussion of the ethnic particularism represented by the Jewish fate during the war. With the collapse of communism, some progress has been made in recovering forgotten history. This has even occurred in countries with such problematic histories of antisemitism as the Ukraine. In Poland the government, through the Auschwitz Memorial Museum, is attempting a presentation in which the centrality of the Holocaust is restored to its rightful place in the camp history. In the centre and west of Europe, problems still remain. German society has struggled, often valiantly, to come to terms with its past responsibilities. A reaction has now set in and matters have become further distorted owing to the problems caused by reunification. The myth of its own status as 'first victim' has acted as a barrier to Austrian reassessment of its role in the persecution of the Jews. In France, discussion of Vichy was taboo for a long time. With the breaking of that taboo in the

1970s, it became possible to discuss the role of Vichy in the fate of the Jews. However, the delay in prosecuting Paul Touvier (who acted as Klaus Barbie's assistant in the murdering of Jews and resistance workers) for crimes against humanity, and other recent cases, indicate that there is still some way to go before French society can acknowledge its past role. There is, nonetheless, increasing debate about Vichy and the Jews – discussion that would have been unimaginable 20 years ago – and the imprisonment of Touvier in 1994 illustrates these new tendencies.[16]

A similar transformation has occurred in Britain. The Holocaust has become, in a matter of a decade, a subject of major interest. For this to occur, barriers almost as problematic as those in Eastern Europe or formerly Nazi-occupied countries had to be overcome. First, the memory of World War II was so precious and untainted that anything that threatened to disturb this state of affairs was opposed. Second, the universalist liberal framework that dominated British society and culture was resistant to the particularity presented by the Holocaust. And, third, the domination of Englishness and Christianity meant that Jewish marginality was constantly emphasized. There was a remarkable durability in the belief that, somehow, Nazi antisemitism could be rationalized by blaming Jewish behaviour. Furthermore, Christians in the post-war world stressed the need for forgiveness and were consequently reluctant to consider the Holocaust in terms of guilt and the apportionment of blame. They continued to ignore Christian responsibility for past and modern antisemitism. All three factors combined powerfully after 1945. Both state and public ensured that the history of the Holocaust would remain marginalized and generally neglected. This was someone else's problem and was of no relevance to society. The comments of a leading churchman in the 1970s, that Britain was 'not the place, this [was] not the time', could be applied to the whole post-war period until that point. The recent changes, although by no means complete, are, therefore, all the more remarkable. They have been made possible by the introduction of pluralistic concepts and policies in British society. The belief and pleasure in diversity which were so essential to pioneers involved in the fate of the Jews, such as James Parkes, Storm Jameson and Eleanor Rathbone, have now become mainstream. The battle is not over – racism in Britain, as elsewhere, threatens to become an ever more powerful force in an increasingly exclusionist atmosphere. It has been encouraged by states which, like their predecessors from the Nazi era, are rewarding the prejudiced by closing their doors to the persecuted and excluding/expelling 'undesirable' aliens. The tolerant majority are, again, ignored.[17] More positively, in spite of the efforts of the revisionists, interest in the subject of the Holocaust continues to grow across the world. The subject is, again, accessible to ordinary people. In Britain, universalist principles made it hard to confront the Holocaust, both at the time and subsequently. In the post-war world, British society was one of the last to accept the importance of the Holocaust, even though its government and people had, at times, intimate connections with the Jewish fate during the conflict. It is a stark example of how the process of collective forgetting can be as important as that of collective memory. Ironically it is the *universal* aspects of the Holocaust which have made it accessible to the liberal imagination in a country as removed from its horrors as Britain. There is always the danger in universalizing the Holocaust that its particular significance to the Jews can be forgotten. But, ultimately, the message that 'The Holocaust belongs to all humanity'[18] remains essential as the millennium comes to a close and bloodshed and mass misery (including genocide) still threaten to engulf the world. Never has there been such a need for a global and inclusive 'universe of obligation' to establish those bonds of common humanity that were so lacking during the Holocaust.[19]

Notes

INTRODUCTION

1 William R. Perl, *The Holocaust Conspiracy: An International Policy of Genocide* (Shapolsky, New York, 1989), p. 75.
2 Cecil Genese, *The Holocaust: Who are the Guilty?* (The Book Guild, Lewes, Sussex, 1988), pp. 104, 114.
3 Public Record Office (PRO), FO 371/45383 E8450, memorandum, Nov. 1945.
4 Terminology for the attempted destruction of European Jewry has itself a complex history. See James E. Young, *Writing and Rewriting the Holocaust: Narrative and the Consequences of Interpretation* (Indiana University Press, Bloomington and Indianapolis, Ind., 1988), pp. 85–9 and Zev Garber and Bruce Zuckerman, 'Why Do We Call The Holocaust "The Holocaust"? An Inquiry into the Psychology of Labels', in Yehuda Bauer et al. (eds), *Remembering for the Future: The Impact of the Holocaust on the Contemporary World*, vol. 2 (Pergamon, Oxford, 1989), pp. 1879–92.
5 Shimon Huberband, in Jeffrey Gurock and Robert Hirt (eds), *Kidush Hashem: Jewish Religious and Cultural Life in Poland During the Holocaust* (Yeshiva University Press, New York, 1987), p. xi and Joseph Kermish (ed.), *To Live With Honor and Die With Honor: selected documents from the Warsaw Ghetto underground archives 'O.S.' (Oneg Shabbath)* (Yad Vashem, Jerusalem, 1986).
6 See the comments of Joseph Kermish, in Ilya Ehrenburg and Vasily Grossman (eds), *The Black Book* (Holocaust Library, New York, 1981), pp. xix–xxvi and Avraham Ben-Yoseph, 'Bibliography of Yiddish Publications in the USSR during 1941–1948', *Yad Vashem Studies*, 4 (1960), pp. 135–66.
7 Centre de Documentation Juive Contemporaine, *Ten Years' Existence of the Jewish Contemporary Documentation Center, 1943–1953* (CDJC, Paris, 1953); Sol Lipstein, *Yivo in America* (Yivo, New York, 1945). Lucy Dawidowitz, *From That Place and Time: A Memoir 1938–1947* (Norton, New York, 1989) highlights the transfer of Yivo to New York.

8   For the Wiener Library, see *Jewish Chronicle*, 13 Nov. 1987 and 1 Sept. 1989.

9   Jacob Robinson and Henry Sachs, *The Holocaust: The Nuremberg Evidence: Part 1: Documents, digest, index and chronological tables* (Yad Vashem, Jerusalem, 1976).

10 John Fox, *Teaching the Holocaust: The report of a survey in the United Kingdom (1987)* (National Yad Vashem Charitable Trust, Leicester, 1989), p. 14.

11 Antony Lerman, 'The art of Holocaust remembering', *The Jewish Quarterly*, 36 (Autumn 1989), p. 25; Michael Marrus, *The Holocaust in History* (University Press of New England, Hanover, NH, 1987 and Weidenfeld & Nicolson, London, 1988), p. xi.

12 Leon Poliakov, *Breviare de la haine* (Paris, 1951), published in English as *Harvest of Hate* (Elek Books, London, 1956), p. xiv; Gerald Reitlinger, *The Final Solution: The Attempt to Exterminate the Jews of Europe 1939–1945* (Vallentine, Mitchell, London, 1953), p. 531. In contrast, see K. Y. Ball-Kaduri, 'Evidence of Witnesses, its Value and Limitations', *Yad Vashem Studies*, 2 (1958), pp. 79–90. The Yad Vashem department for recording statements was set up in 1954. For its origins and earlier oral history projects, see Joseph Kermish's summary in Yehuda Bauer (ed.), *Yad Vashem: Guide to Unpublished Material of the Holocaust Period* (Yad Vashem, Jerusalem, 1975), pp. 25–7.

13 Poliakov, *Harvest of Hate*, p. xiii; Andrea Reiter, 'Literature and survival: the relationship between fact and fiction in concentration-camp memoirs', *European Studies*, 21 (1991), p. 259.

14 David Bankier, *The Germans and the Final Solution: Public Opinion under Nazism* (Blackwell, Oxford, 1992), p. 124 and p. 118.

15 There is, I would suggest, a tendency for male historians to avoid 'softer' aspects of the Holocaust such as the impact on Jews as individuals. It is significant that the pioneer work on the impact of the Holocaust on women and on children has been carried out by women. See, for example, Sybil Milton, 'Women and the Holocaust: The Case of German and German-Jewish Women', in Renate Bridenthal, Atins Grossman and Marion Kaplan (eds), *When Biology Became Destiny: Women in Weimar and Nazi Germany* (Monthly Review Press, New York, 1984), pp. 297–333; Vera Laska (ed.), *Women in the Resistance and in the Holocaust: The Voices of Eyewitnesses* (Greenwood Press, Westport, Conn., 1983); Deborah Dwork, *Children with a Star: Jewish Youth in Nazi Europe* (Yale University Press, New Haven, Conn., 1991); Joan Ringelheim, 'The Holocaust: Taking Women into Account', *The Jewish Quarterly*, 147 (Autumn 1992), pp. 19–23 (esp. p. 21).

16 Reitlinger, *The Final Solution*, p. 581.

17 Raul Hilberg, *The Destruction of the European Jews* (Quadrangle Books, Chicago, Ill., 1961), p. v; Ball-Kaduri, 'Evidence of Witnesses', p. 81.

18 The absence of the Jewish voice is a major weakness in the important collection by Ernst Klee, Willi Dressen and Volker Piess, *'Those were the Days': The Holocaust through the Eyes of the Perpetrators and Bystanders* (Hamish Hamilton, London, 1991) – originally published in German in 1988; Martin Gilbert, *The Holocaust: The Jewish Tragedy* (William Collins, Glasgow, 1986), p. 18.

19 Rhoda Lewin (ed.), *Witnesses to the Holocaust: An Oral History* (Twayne, Boston, Mass., 1990); Geoffrey Hartman, 'Preserving the Personal Story: The Role of Video Documentation', *Dimensions: A Journal of Holocaust Studies*, 1 (1985), pp. 14–18.

20 Lawrence Langer, *Holocaust Testimonies: The Ruins of Memory* (Yale University Press, New Haven, Conn., 1991), p. 66.

21 Allegations of Jewish passivity, particularly by Raul Hilberg and Hannah Arendt, led to a series of books on Jewish resistance. One of the first and, perhaps because of the need to counter earlier charges, the most emotive was Reuben Ainsztein's *Jewish Resistance in Nazi-Occupied Eastern Europe* (Elek, London, 1974). More recent and specific work includes S. Krakowski, *The War of the Doomed: Jewish Armed Resistance in Poland, 1942–1944* (Holmes and Meier, New York, 1984) and Dov Levin, *Fighting Back: Lithuanian Jewry's Armed Resistance to the Nazis, 1941–1945* (Holmes and Meier, New York, 1985).

22 Jacob Presser, *Ashes in the Wind: The Destruction of Dutch Jewry* (Survivor Press, London, 1968) – published in Holland in 1965. For an assessment of the book, see Henriette Boas, 'The Persecution and Destruction of Dutch Jewry 1940–1945', *Yad Vashem Studies*, 6 (1967), pp. 359–74. Dienke Hondius, *Terugkeer: antisemitisme in Nederland rond de bevrijding* (SDU, The Hague, 1990) deals with the hostility faced by Dutch Jewish survivors.

23 Janrense Boonstra and Marie-Jose Rijnders, *Anne Frank House: a museum with a story* (Anne Frank Stichting, Amsterdam, 1992), pp. 68, 78–9. See also Miep Gies, *Anne Frank Remembered* (Bantam, London, 1987).

24 Henry Rousso, *The Vichy Syndrome: History and Memory in France since 1944* (Harvard University Press, Cambridge, Mass. and London, 1991), p. 25. The book as a whole brilliantly charts the changes in post-war French society with regard to Vichy and the persecution of the Jews in particular. Robert Paxton and Michael Marrus, *Vichy France and the Jews* (Schocken Books, New York, 1983), p. xii.

25 Paxton and Marrus, *Vichy France and the Jews*, p. 366.

26 Jonathan Webber, *The Future of Auschwitz: Some Personal Reflections* (Oxford Centre for Postgraduate Hebrew Studies, Oxford, 1992), pp. 9–10.

27 For an indication of the scale of the former Soviet archives with regard to the Holocaust, see Lucjan Dobroszycki and Jeffrey Gurock (eds), *The Holocaust in the Soviet Union: Studies and Sources on the Destruction of the Jews in the Nazi-Occupied Territories of the USSR, 1941–1945*, (M.E. Sharp, New York, 1993) and Shmuel Krakowski, 'Documents on the Holocaust in archives of the former Soviet Union', in David Cesarani (ed.), *The Final Solution: Origins and Implementation* (Routledge, London, 1994) pp. 291–99; Dina Porat, 'The Holocaust in Lithuania: Some unique aspects', in Cesarani, loc. cit., pp. 159–74.

28 Martin Broszat, 'Hitler and the Genesis of the "Final Solution"', *Yad Vashem Studies*, 13 (1979), pp. 73–125.

29 Christopher Browning, *Fateful Months: Essays on the Emergence of the Final Solution*, 2nd edn (Holmes and Meier, New York, 1991), p. 79.

30 Ibid., p. 7.

31 Christopher Browning, 'German Memory, Judicial Interrogation, and Historical Reconstruction: Writing Perpetrator History from Postwar Testimony', in Saul Friedlander (ed.), *Probing the Limits of Representation: Nazism and the "Final Solution"* (Harvard University Press, Cambridge, Mass., 1992), p. 26.

32 See, for example, the approach of Lord Liverpool, *The Scourge of the Swastika* (Cassell & Russell, London, 1954), esp. chapter 6. I have been informed by individuals involved in the booktrade that such material was often to be found in the 'horror' section of second-hand bookshops in Britain.

33 Theodor Adorno et al., *The Authoritarian Personality* (Harper and Bros, New York, 1950).

34 Stanley Milgram, *Obedience to Authority: An Experimental View* (Tavistock,

London, 1974). For a favourable assessment of Milgram, see Zygmunt Bauman, *Modernity and the Holocaust* (Polity Press, Oxford, 1989), chapter 6.

35 Browning, 'German Memory', p. 27.

36 Christopher Browning, *Ordinary Men: Reserve Police Battalion 101 and the Final Solution in Poland* (Harper Collins, New York, 1992); Browning, *Fateful Months*, p. 7 and chapters 3 and 4 *passim*.

37 Klee, Dressen and Riess, '*Those were the Days*', pp. xvii, xix, 155–9.

38 See the comments of Yehuda Bauer, 'Against Mystification' in his own *The Holocaust in Historical Perspective* (Sheldon Press, London, 1978), esp. p. 44, on writers such as Katzetnik and Wiesel, and similarly Marrus, *The Holocaust in History*, pp. 2–3. The phrase *l'Univers concentrationnaire* was used by David Rousset, *The Other Kingdom* (Howard Ferley, New York, 1982), first published in 1947; Elmer Luchterhand, 'Knowing and Not Knowing: Involvement in Nazi Genocide', in Paul Thompson with Natasha Burchardt (eds), *Our Common History: The Transformation of Europe* (Humanities Press, Atlantic Highlands, NJ, 1982), p. 251.

39 Gordon Horwitz, *In the Shadow of Death: Living Outside the Gates of Mauthausen* (I.B. Tauris, London, 1991), pp. 2, 4. Luchterhand, 'Knowing and Not Knowing', pp. 251–72, an oral history of the local population and Hersbruck concentration camp, adds that this work was essential so that 'the everyday activities of perpetrators, victims and co-presents could be reconstructed with reasonable accuracy' (p. 251). The growing recognition of the importance of bystanders is acknowledged in Raul Hilberg, *Perpetrators, Victims, Bystanders: The Jewish Catastrophe, 1933–1945* (Harper Collins, New York, 1992), part 3.

40 Claude Lanzmann's film *Shoah* was released in 1985. The 'text' is unsatisfactorily reproduced in *Shoah: An Oral History of the Holocaust* (Pantheon, New York, 1985); Horwitz, *In the Shadow*, prologue. The information about the new sites was revealed by Schmuel Krakowski, an archivist at Yad Vashem, in a paper, 'Documents on the Holocaust in Soviet Archives', at the 'The Final Solution' conference, London, Jan. 1992.

41 See, for example, Reitlinger, *The Final Solution*, pp. 483–7; Poliakov, *Harvest of Hate*, pp. 8, 60, 82, 282–8. Perhaps a good indication of the limitations of historical research as late as the 1960s can be found through an English school history textbook which synthesized existing literature, B. J. Elliot's *Hitler and Germany* (Longman, London, 1966), which included a section with specific regard to the Holocaust entitled 'The Guilt of the German People'.

42 For new developments in German historiography see Ian Kershaw, 'Historians and the Problem of Explaining Nazism', in his own, *The Nazi Dictatorship*, 2nd edn (Edward Arnold, London, 1989), pp. 1–17, and Tim Mason, 'Intention and Explanation: A Current Controversy about the Interpretation of National Social- ism' reprinted in Michael Marrus (ed.), *The Nazi Holocaust*, vol. 3, part 1: *The "Final Solution"* (Meckler, Westport, Conn., 1989), pp. 3–20.

Early work on popular opinion in the Third Reich which stressed popular indifference to the fate of the Jews was carried out by Ian Kershaw, *Popular Opinion and Political Dissent in the Third Reich: Bavaria 1933–1945* (Clarendon Press, Oxford, 1983), esp. chapters 6 and 9, and Sarah Gordon, *Hitler, Germans and the 'Jewish Question'* (Princeton University Press, Princeton, NJ, 1984). A more negative assessment was produced by Otto Dov Kulka, '"Public Opinion" in Nazi Germany and the "Jewish Question"', *The Jerusalem Quarterly*, 23 (Fall 1982), pp. 121–44 and Michael Kater, 'Everyday Anti-Semitism in Prewar Nazi Germany: The Popular Bases', *Yad Vashem Studies*, 16 (1984), pp. 129–59.

43 Bankier, *The Germans and the Final Solution*, p. 155.
44 Ian Kershaw, 'The Persecution of the Jews and German Popular Opinion in the Third Reich', in Helen Fein (ed.), *The Persisting Question: Sociological Perspectives and Social Contexts of Modern Antisemitism* (de Gruyter, Berlin and New York, 1987), pp. 343–9; Lawrence Stokes, 'The German People and the Destruction of the European Jews', in *Central European History*, 6 (1973), pp. 167–91; M. Steinert, *Hitler's war and the Germans* (Ohio University Press, Athens, Ohio, 1977); Gordon, *Hitler, Germans and the 'Jewish Question'*, p. 267; Bankier, *The Germans and the Final Solution*, chapters 6 and 7.
45 See the profile of Reitz in *The Observer*, 4 May 1986. See also Anton Kaes, *From 'Hitler' to 'Heimat': the return of history as film* (Harvard University Press, Cambridge, Mass., 1989) and Eric Santner, *Stranded Objects: Mourning, Memory, and Film in Postwar German Society* (Cornell University Press, Ithica, New York, 1990), particularly chapter 3. Simon Hattenstone, 'The long way home', *Weekend Guardian*, 29–30 Aug. 1992, is a highly positive assessment of the film, which suggests that 'By showing how a genocidal ideology can creep up on and ultimately be embraced by ordinary decent people [Reitz] made it all the more horrific'. This ignores the fact that Nazism was played down in the film in order to show the continuities of the German experience and hence its normality. Reitz himself wrote that 'With Holocaust [he means the television series], the Americans have taken away our history'. See *New German Critique*, 36 (Fall 1985), p. 12. For the impact of the television series on German society, see Anson Rabinbach and Jack Zipes, *Germans and Jews since the Holocaust: The Changing Situation in West Germany* (Holmes and Meier, New York, 1986).
46 See Charles Maier, *The Unmasterable Past: History, Holocaust, and German National Identity* (Harvard University Press, Cambridge, Mass., 1988) and Richard Evans, *In Hitler's Shadow* (I.B. Taurus, London, 1989) for the *Historikerstreit*; Mary Nolan, 'The *Historikersteit* and Social History', in Peter Baldwin (ed.), *Reworking the Past: Hitler, The Holocaust and the Historians' Debate* (Beacon Press, Boston, Mass., 1990), p. 225.
47 A good, but still isolated, example is Frances Henry, *Victims and Neighbors: A Small Town in Nazi Germany Remembered* (Bergin & Garvey, South Hadley, Mass., 1986). A more recent and thoroughly researched study is Menahem Kaufman, 'The Daily Life of the Village and Country Jews in Hessen from Hitler's Ascent to Power to November 1938', *Yad Vashem Studies*, 22 (1992), pp. 147–98.
48 Anne and John Tusa, *The Nuremberg Trial* (Macmillan, London, 1983); Michael Biddiss, 'The Nuremberg Trial: Two Exercises in Judgment', *Journal of Contemporary History*, 16 (1981), pp. 597–615.
49 See, for example, R. Phillips (ed.), *Trial of Joseph Kramer and Forty-Four Others (The Belsen Trial)* (William Hodge & Co, London, 1949). The impact of the liberation on Britain and the United States will be examined in the final chapter.
50 Eleanor Rathbone, *Rescue the Perishing* (National Committee for Rescue from Nazi Terror, London, 1943); Victor Gollancz, *Let My People Go* (Gollancz, London, 1942); Morgenthau's diaries appeared in *Collier's Magazine*, Nov. 1947.
51 Anthony Powell on Reitlinger in *The Times*, 21 March 1978 and *Who Was Who 1971–1980* (Adam and Charles Black, London, 1991), p. 661.
52 Reitlinger, *The Final Solution*, pp. 463–9 for Belsen; pp. 406–7 for his treatment of the Allies' response. For the background and marketing of Reitlinger's book, see the records of Vallentine, Mitchell, 225/5/25 and 6/13, Southampton University archive (SUA). More promising, though almost as brief, was Poliakov's

Harvest of Hate, pp. 245, 260–1. Poliakov suggested (p. 245) that the struggles around the lives of European Jews 'and the repercussions these had even in the chancelleries of the Allies, have much to tell, though they constitute one of the least known aspects of the history of World War II'.

53 Reitlinger, *The Final Solution*, 2nd edn (Vallentine, Mitchell, London, 1968), p. 440.

54 Hannah Arendt, *Eichmann in Jerusalem: A Report on the Banality of Evil* (Viking Press, New York, 1963).

55 Gideon Hausner, *Justice in Jerusalem*, 4th edn (Holocaust Library, New York, 1978), pp. 243–4 for the treatment of Allied responses to the Holocaust at the Eichmann trial; *Davar* quoted by *AJR Information*, July 1961.

56 The Association of Jewish Refugees' *Information* started in 1946, *The Wiener Library Bulletin* in 1949 and *The Jewish Quarterly* in 1953. For early work on the United States, see David Brody, 'American Jewry, The Refugees and Immigration Restriction (1932–1942)', *Publications of the American Jewish Historical Society*, 45 (June 1956), pp. 219–47, and Henry Cohen , 'Crisis and Reaction', *American Jewish Archives*, 5 (June 1953), pp. 71–113.

57 The idea of a future memorial to those Jews who had perished in the war was first suggested at the Zionist Congress in London, Aug. 1945. It was formally established by the Knesset in Aug. 1953. See Reuven Dafni (ed.), *Yad Vashem*, 5th edn (Yad Vashem, Jerusalem, 1990), pp. 2–7; Andrew Sharf, *The British Press & Jews under Nazi Rule* (Institute of Race Relations, London, 1964), pp. v–vi. For a strong critique of the position adopted by the Institite of Race Relations at this point, see Chris Mullard, *Race, Power and Resistance* (Routledge & Kegan Paul, London, 1985).

58 Mason in *The British Press*, p. v.

59 Arthur Morse, *While Six Million Died* (Random House, New York, 1968); David Wyman, *Paper Walls: America and the Refugee Crisis 1938–1941* (University of Massachusetts Press, Amherst, Mass., 1968); Saul Friedman, *No Haven for the Oppressed: United States Policy Toward Jewish Refugees, 1938–1945* (Wayne State University Press, Detroit, Mich., 1973); and Henry Feingold, *The Politics of Rescue: The Roosevelt Administration and the Holocaust 1938–1945* (Rutgers University Press, New Brunswick, 1970). The critique is by Feingold, 'Guilt for the Holocaust', *American Jewish History*, 68 (March 1979), p. 262.

60 Leonard Dinnerstein, *Uneasy at Home: Antisemitism and the American Jewish Experience* (Columbia University Press, New York, 1987), p. 258.

61 For an acknowledgment of all these factors see the concluding remarks in Friedman, *No Haven for the Oppressed*, pp. 231–5.

62 From the cover of the British edition of Morse's book (Secker & Warburg, London, 1968).

63 Feingold, *The Politics of Rescue*, 2nd edn (Holocaust Library, New York, 1980), p. ix.

64 Marked by the publication of David Wyman's *The Abandonment of the Jews: America and the Holocaust 1941–1945* (Pantheon, New York, 1984) and a revisionist response by Richard Breitman and Alan Kraut, *American Refugee Policy and European Jewry, 1933–1945* (Indiana University Press, Bloomington and Indianapolis, Ind., 1987).

65 A. J. Sherman, *Island Refuge: Britain and refugees from the Third Reich, 1933–1939* (Elek, London, 1973); Bernard Wasserstein, *Britain and the Jews of Europe 1939–1945* (Oxford University Press, Oxford, 1979); and Martin Gilbert, *Auschwitz and the Allies* (Michael Joseph, London, 1981).

66 For the television version by Rex Bloomstein, see *The Listener*, 16 Sept. 1982. In addition to my own work, Louise London has undertaken important research on the whole of the Nazi era, although her thesis covers the period up to 1942. See her 'British Immigration Control Procedures and Jewish Refugees, 1933–1942' (unpublished PhD, University of London, 1992).

67 Irving Abella and Harold Troper, *None is too many: Canada and the Jews of Europe, 1933–1948* (Random House, New York, 1983); Michael Blakeney, *Australia and the Jewish Refugees 1933–1948* (Croom Helm, Sydney, 1985); Ann Beaglehole, *A Small Price to Pay: Refugees From Hitler in New Zealand, 1936–46* (Allen & Unwin, Wellington, NZ, 1988).

68 W. D. Rubinstein, 'Australia and the Refugee Jews of Europe, 1933–1954: A Dissenting View', *Journal of the Australian Jewish Historical Society*, 10 (1989), pp. 500–23.

69 Marrus, *The Holocaust in History*, p. 157.

70 Breitman and Kraut, *American Refugee Policy*, pp. 2–6, make some valid points about the loose use of the 'public opinion' in some of the existing literature. In the case of the United States, too much attention has been paid by historians to either manifestations of obvious public antisemitism in the form of organized fascism or the readily available but two-dimensional opinion poll material on Jews in the 1930s and 1940s. Such materials need to be supplemented by much wider ranging sources.

71 Wyman, *Paper Walls* and *The Abandonment of the Jews*; Friedman, *No Haven for the Oppressed*; Wasserstein, *Britain and the Jews of Europe*, chapter 3 is devoted to 'The Home Front' but remains disconnected to the rest of the book.

72 Mary Nolan, 'The *Historikerstreit* and Social History', p. 225.

73 G. M. Trevelyan, *English Social History* (Longmans, Green & Co, London, 1944), p. vii; Eric Hobsbawm, 'From Social History to the History of Society', *Daedalus*, 100 (Winter 1971), pp. 20–45.

74 E. P. Thompson, *The Poverty of Theory and Other Essays* (Merlin Press, London, 1978), p. 262.

75 Susan Mendus, *Toleration and the Limits of Liberalism* (Macmillan, London, 1989), p. 3. See also Susan Mendus and David Edwards (eds), *On Toleration* (Clarendon Press, Oxford, 1987).

76 See, for example, Mendus, *Toleration and the Limits of Liberalism*, chapter 1; Robert Wistrich, *Antisemitism: The Longest Hatred* (Thames Methuen, London, 1991), chapter 9: 'Britain: the Limits of Tolerance'.

77 Bill Williams, 'The Anti-Semitism of Tolerance: Middle-Class Manchester and the Jews, 1870–1900', in A. J. Kidd and K. W. Roberts (eds), *City, Class and Culture* (Manchester University Press, Manchester, 1985), pp. 74–102 (esp. p. 94). Paul Gilroy, *'There Ain't No Black in the Union Jack': The cultural politics of race and nation* (Hutchinson, London, 1987) is a brilliant exploration of similar themes for the Afro-Caribbean communities in Britain. More generally, see Geoff Dench, *Minorities in the Open Society: Prisoners of Ambivalence* (Routledge & Kegan Paul, London, 1986); Lionel Trilling, *The Liberal Imagination: Essays on Literature and Society* (Secker & Warburg, London, 1951), p. xiii; George Steiner, 'Book-keeping of torture', *Sunday Times*, 10 Apr. 1988.

78 See James Donald and Ali Rattansi (eds), *Race, Culture and Difference* (Sage, London, 1992); Robert Colls and Philip Dodd (eds), *Englishness* (Croom Helm, Beckenham, Kent, 1986); John Bodnar, *Remaking America: Public Memory, Commemoration, and Patriotism in the Twentieth Century* (Princeton University Press, Princeton, NJ, 1992).

79   Feingold, *The Politics of Rescue*, 2nd edn, p. xiii.
80   Perhaps the most obvious was the Oswego camp in New York state which took up to 1,000 Jewish refugees. See Sharon Lowenstein, *Token Refuge: The Story of the Jewish Refugee Shelter at Oswego, 1944–1946* (Indiana University Press, Bloomington, Ind., 1986).
81   Jonathan Steinberg, *All or Nothing: the Axis and the Holocaust, 1941–1943* (Routledge, London, 1990); Leni Yahil, *The rescue of Danish Jewry: test of a democracy* (Jewish Publication Society of America, Philadelphia, Penn., 1969).
82   Claude Lanzmann, 'Shoah as Counter-Myth', *The Jewish Quarterly*, 33 (Spring 1986), pp. 11–12.
83   Quoted in *The Observer*, 28 Dec. 1986; Gilbert, *Auschwitz and the Allies*; Gilbert, *The Holocaust*.
84   Leni Yahil, *The Holocaust: The Fate of European Jewry* (Oxford University Press, New York, 1991), pp. 10–11.
85   Yahil, *The Holocaust*, p. 11.
86   Hershel and Abraham Edelheit, *A World in Turmoil: An Integrated Chronology of the Holocaust and World War II* (Greenwood Press, Westport, Conn., 1991), p. x.
87   Edelheit and Edelheit, *A World in Turmoil*, p. 278; Blakeney, *Australia and the Jewish Refugees*, p. 285; Wasserstein, *Britain and the Jews*, p. 188 on what Wasserstein calls 'one of the savage ironies of history' by which Bermuda, the ghetto revolt and the first night of Passover all coincided.
88   Gilbert, *Auschwitz and the Allies*, chapter 14 is entitled 'Warsaw and Bermuda' and shows some of the dangers of directly confronting separate chronologies; Marrus, *The Holocaust in History*, p. 157 for moral judgments and bystanders to the Holocaust.
89   See chapters 6 and 7 of this study.
90   Lanzmann, 'Shoah as Counter-Myth', pp. 11–12.
91   Michael Marrus, *The Unwanted: European Refugees in the Twentieth Century* (Oxford University Press, New York, 1985), pp. 135–6.
92   For an indication of recent research on women and the Holocaust, see Joan Ringelheim, 'The Holocaust: taking women into account', *The Jewish Quarterly*, 39 (Autumn 1992), pp. 19–23.
      Jill Stephenson, *Women in Nazi Society* (Croom Helm, London, 1975), does not examine the role of German women in the persecution of the Jews but this is the focus of Claudia Koonz, *Mothers in the Fatherland: Women, the Family and Nazi Politics* (Cape, London, 1987). See also the latter sections of Marion Kaplan, *The Jewish Feminist Movement in Germany: The Campaigns of the Jüdischer Frauenbund 1904–1938* (Greenwood Press, Westport, Conn., 1979).
93   This troubled history is dealt with by Angela McRobbie, 'The many mothers who helped make Hitler's fatherland', *The Guardian*, 2 Aug. 1990, but the failure of some in feminist movements to acknowledge that racism often subsumed categories of gender is apparent from the heated debate in *Gender & History*, vol. 3, no. 2 (Summer 1991).
94   Dorothy Sheridan, *The Tom Harrisson Mass-Observation Archive: A Guide for Researchers* (University of Sussex, Brighton, 1991); Nick Stanley, 'The Extra Dimension: a study and assessment of the methods employed by Mass-Observation in its first period 1937–40' (unpublished PhD thesis, Birmingham Polytechnic, 1981).
95   Feingold, 'Who Shall Bear the Guilt', p. 261, has important observations on contemporary figures in the Allied camp.

96 Langer, *Holocaust Testimonies: The Ruins of Memory, passim*.
97 Work on the second generation is now receiving detailed attention. See Martin Bergman and Milton Jucovy (eds), *Generations of the Holocaust* (Basic Books, New York, 1982); Helen Epstein, *Children of the Holocaust: Conversations with Sons and Daughters of Survivors* (Putnam, New York, 1979); and Aaron Hass, *In the shadow of the Holocaust: the second generation* (I.B. Tauris, London, 1991).
98 Sander Gilman, 'German Reunification and the Jews', in Sander Gilman and Steven Katz (eds) *Anti-Semitism in Times of Crisis* (New York University Press, New York, 1991), p. 377.
99 James Young, *Writing and Rewriting*, p. 176.
100 Elie Wiesel, 'Art and the Holocaust: Trivializing Memory', *New York Times*, 11 June 1989.
101 Saul Friedlander, 'The Shoah between memory and history', *The Jewish Quarterly*, 37 (Spring 1990), p. 11.
102 Bauer, 'Against Mystification', p. 31.
103 Lanzmann, 'Shoah as Counter-Myth', p. 12.

1 LIBERAL CULTURE AND NAZI PERSECUTION, 1933–1939

1 William Parsons and William Ferkekes, 'Days of Remembrance: 1992 Lesson Plans' (United States Holocaust Memorial Museum, Washington, DC, 1992), p. 13.
2 Despite its title, an important exception is Michael Dobkowski (ed.), *The Politics of Indifference: A Documentary History of Holocaust Victims in America* (University Press of America, Washington, DC, 1982), chapter 8: 'Send These to Me: Pro-Refugee Sentiment in America'.
3 Richard Griffiths, *Fellow Travellers of the Right: British Enthusiasts for Nazi Germany 1933–39* (Oxford University Press, Oxford, 1983), chapter 6; Martin Gilbert, *The Roots of Appeasement* (Weidenfeld & Nicolson, London, 1966), p. 162.
4 Bob Moore, *Refugees from Nazi Germany in the Netherlands 1933–1940* (Martinus Nijhoff, Dordrecht, 1986), pp. 52, 91, 140, 170 and 173, on the Dutch Nazis (the *Nationaal Socialistische Beweging*). Moore is, though, reluctant to highlight antisemitism, focusing instead on 'the structure of the Dutch state and the inflexibility of the bureaucracy' (p. 108). On French organizations, see Michael Marrus and Robert Paxton, *Vichy France and the Jews* (Schocken Books, New York, 1983), chapter 2. And, more generally, see: Ralph Schor, *L'Antisemitisme en France pendant les annees trente* (Editions Complexe, Paris, 1992); David Wyman, *Paper Walls: America and the Refugee Crisis 1938–1941* (University of Massachusetts Press, Amherst, Mass., 1968), chapter 1; Michael Blakeney, *Australia and the Jewish Refugees 1933–1948* (Croom Helm, Sydney, 1985), chapter 1.
5 Vicki Caron, 'Prelude to Vichy: France and the Jewish Refugees in the Era of Appeasement', *Journal of Contemporary History*, 20 (1985), pp. 157–176 (esp. p. 168). See also Timothy Maga, 'Closing the Door: The French Government and Refugee Policy, 1933–1939', *French Historical Studies*, 12 (Spring 1982), pp. 424–42, and Gary S. Cross, *Immigrant Workers in Industrial France: The Making of a New Laboring Class* (Temple University Press, Philadelphia, 1983). Cross's work on the 1920s indicates how the selective policies of those years paved the way for later restrictionism.

6 For the general background to the 1919 Aliens Act, see Colin Holmes, *John Bull's Island: Immigration & British Society, 1871–1971* (Macmillan, Basingstoke, Hants, 1988), pp. 93–114. A. J. Sherman, *Island Refuge: Britain and refugees from the Third Reich, 1933–1939* (Elek, London, 1973), chapter 9, 'A Balance Sheet', does attempt a league table in which he suggests that British policy was 'comparatively compassionate, even generous' (p. 267). Greater sophistication has recently been achieved in researching the bureaucratic history of liberal democratic civil servants and the persecution of the Jews. See particularly Richard Breitman and Alan Kraut, *American Refugee Policy and European Jewry, 1933–1945* (Indiana University Press, Bloomington and Indianapolis, Ind., 1987) and Louise London, 'British Immigration Control Procedures and Jewish Refugees, 1933–1942' (unpublished PhD thesis, University of London, 1992). The focus on Britain and the United States does not imply that the liberal tradition in other countries, such as France, was any less significant during the 1930s but, because this study covers the period from the 1930s through World War II to the present day, the continuity of liberal democratic government in these two countries gives them a special significance.

7 Robert Murray, *Red scare: a study in national hysteria, 1919–1920* (University of Minnesota Press, Minneapolis, Minn., 1955); William Preston, *Aliens and dissenters: Federal suppression of radicals, 1903–1933* (Harvard University Press, Cambridge, Mass., 1963). For the vicious parliamentary debate about the Alien Restriction Bill, see *Hansard* (HC), vol. 114, cols 2745–818, 15 Apr. 1919. See Vaughan Bevan, *The Development of British Immigration Law* (Croom Helm, London, 1986) and, more generally, David Cesarani, 'An Alien Concept? The Continuity of Anti-Alienism in British Society before 1940', in David Cesarani and Tony Kushner (eds), *Alien Internment in Twentieth Century Britain* (Frank Cass, London, 1993), pp. 25–52; Neil Evans, 'Regulating the Reserve Army: Arabs, Blacks and the Local State in Cardiff, 1919–45', *Immigrants and Minorities*, 4 (July 1985), pp. 68–106; and Paul Rich, *Race and Empire in British Politics* (Cambridge University Press, Cambridge, 1986), chapter 7.

8 For the threat and reality of alien deportation in the 1920s, see the Home Office file PRO HO 45/24765/432156. Questions of naturalization are dealt with in David Cesarani, 'Joynson-Hicks and the Radical Right in England after World War One', in Tony Kushner and Kenneth Lunn (eds), *Traditions of Intolerance: Historical Perspectives on Fascism and Race Discourse in British Society* (Manchester University Press, Manchester, 1989), pp. 118–39, and *idem*, 'Anti-Alienism in England after the First World War', *Immigrants and Minorities*, 6 (Mar. 1987), pp. 5–29.

9 Labour Party Research Department papers, vol. 1 'Aliens 1925–42', Labour Party Archives, National Labour Museum, Manchester; Paul Foot, *Immigration and Race in British Politics* (Penguin, Harmondsworth, 1965), p. 105; Gilmour in *Hansard* (HC), vol. 275, cols 1351–2, 9 Mar. 1933; Angell quoted in Samuel Rich diaries, 18 Apr. 1933, AJ 217, Southampton University Archive (SUA); Jewish Association for the Protection of Women and Children, Gentlemen's Sub-Committee, 24 June 1919, 173/2/2/6, SUA; Joynson-Hicks in *Hansard*, vol. 180, cols 313–4, 11 Feb. 1925.

10 Breitman and Kraut, *American Refugee Policy*, introduction and chapter 1; Irving Abella and Harold Troper, *None is Too Many: Canada and the Jews of Europe 1933–1948* (Random House, New York, 1983); W. D. Rubinstein, 'Australia and the Refugee Jews of Europe, 1933–1954: A Dissenting View', *Journal of the Australian Jewish Historical Society*, 10 (1989), p. 515, referring to 'Australia's

consensual Anglo-Celtic immigration policy'; Ann Beaglehole, *A Small Price to Pay: refugees from Hitler to New Zealand, 1936–46* (Allen & Unwin, Wellington, NZ, 1988); for Holland, see Moore, *Refugees from Nazi Germany*, pp. 2–3; Gideon Shimoni, *Jews and Zionism: The South African Experience 1910–1967* (Oxford University Press, 1980), chapter 5; Maga, 'Closing the Door', pp. 424–7, and Cross, *Immigrant Workers in Industrial France* for France.

11 See the essays by Cesarani, Cheyette, Kushner and Rich in Kushner and Lunn, *Traditions of Intolerance*, for further elaboration of the discussion of liberalism, 'race' and national identity.

12 Andrew Sharf, *The British Press & Jews under Nazi Rule* (Oxford University Press, London, 1964), p. 193.

13 A. J. P. Taylor, *English History 1914–1945* (Oxford University Press, Oxford, 1965), pp. 419–20.

14 Stephen Glassock, 'Early Interpretations of Nazism: The British Press and Hitler, 1922–1928' (BA dissertation, Department of History, University of Southampton, 1985); Brigitte Granzow, *A Mirror of Nazism: British Opinion and the Emergence of Hitler 1929–1933* (Gollancz, London, 1964), esp. p. 125; Sharf, *The British Press*, chapter 1.

15 *Baptist Times*, 6 Apr. 1933; for a contemporary critique of the British press with regard to the Jews, see Samuel Rich diaries, 2 May 1933, AJ 217, SUA.

16 Rathbone in *Manchester Guardian*, 2 May 1933. For the background to this letter, see Eleanor Rathbone papers, X14/2.6, University of Liverpool archives (ULA).

17 Mr Flenley to Eleanor Rathbone, 10 May 1933, X14/2.6, ULA; John Fox, 'Great Britain and the German Jews 1933', *Wiener Library Bulletin*, 26, nos 1–2 (1972), p. 42.

18 See chapter 5 of this study for the December 1942 Declaration.

19 Granzow, *A Mirror of Nazism*, p. 160.

20 On such questions, see Bryan Cheyette, 'Jewish stereotyping and English literature 1875–1920: Towards a political analysis', in Kushner and Lunn, *Traditions of Intolerance*, pp. 12–32, and his *Constructions of 'the Jew' in English literature and society: Racial representations 1875–1945* (Cambridge University Press, Cambridge, 1993).

21 'The Nazi Pogrom', *Daily Telegraph*, 18 Mar. 1933.

22 Winston Churchill, *The Second World War*, vol. 1 *The Gathering Storm* (Cassell, London, 1948), p. 65. For his earlier views, see *Illustrated Sunday Herald*, 8 Feb. 1920, and, more generally, Michael Cohen, *Churchill and the Jews* (Frank Cass, London, 1985), chapter 1.

23 *Observer*, 20 Mar. 1932 (from its own Berlin correspondent).

24 *Saturday Review*, 20 Jan. 1934, quoted by Sharf, *The British Press*, p. 36. See also loc. cit., pp. 34–8 for similar examples; *Columbus Dispatch*, 16 Apr. 1933, quoted by Deborah Lipstadt, *Beyond Belief: The American Press & the Coming of the Holocaust 1933–1945* (The Free Press, New York, 1986), p. 47, and the section 'Why Antisemitism? Seeking a Rational Explanation', pp. 41–8; and, similarly, Robert Ross, *So It Was True: The American Protestant Press and the Nazi Persecution of the Jews* (University of Minnesota Press, Minneapolis, Minn., 1980), pp. 31–6.

25 Hadley Cantril (ed.), *Public Opinion 1935–1946* (Princeton University Press, Princeton, NJ, 1951), p. 381. A similar conclusion was reached by Mass-Observation in Britain. See Mass-Observation archive (M-O A), University of Sussex, FR A12, Feb. 1939.

26 Martin Gilbert, *Sir Horace Rumbold: Portrait of a Diplomat 1869–1941* (Heinemann, London, 1973), p. xiii.
27 Ibid., pp. 319, 418.
28 The despatches of 28 Mar. and 13 Apr. 1933 are reproduced in E. Woodward and R. Butler (eds), *Documents on British Foreign Policy 1919–1939*, vol. 5 (HMSO, London, 1956), pp. 3–6, 38–44.
29 Quoted by Gilbert, *Sir Horace Rumbold*, p. 379.
30 13 Apr. 1933 despatch in Woodward and Butler, *Documents*, pp. 40, 44.
31 Ernest Tennant, *True Account* (Max Parrish, London, 1957). For the Fellowship, see Griffiths, *Fellow Travellers*, pp. 182–6. See J. Douglas-Hamilton, 'Ribbentrop and War', *Journal of Contemporary History*, 5, no. 4 (1970), p. 62, for Tennant in 1939; Tennant journals, 29 Jan. 1932 and May 1933, W. W. Ashley papers, BR 81, SUA.
32 Journal entry, 5 Sept. 1934, Ashley papers, BR 81, SUA.
33 Tennant to Mount-Temple, 24 Sept. 1935, Ashley papers, BR 81, SUA.
34 F. Watson, *Dawson of Penn* (Chatto & Windus, London, 1950), p. 292.
35 'Einstein in England', *Manchester Guardian*, 4 Oct. 1933.
36 *The Persecution of the Jews in Germany* (Joint Foreign Committee of the Board of Deputies and the Anglo-Jewish Association, London, 1933), which appeared in three editions during the 1930s and, similarly, *Germany and the Jews* (Board of Deputies of British Jews, 1937 and 1939). The time and energy wasted on such statistics is indicated in the correspondence between the Board of Deputies, James Parkes and Ernest Tennant over the 'Jewish role' in Germany. See Parkes papers, 16/706, SUA. An alternative strategy was adopted by Israel Cohen in *The Jews in Germany* (Murray, London, 1933), which stressed how much the Jewish minority were part of German society.
37 Griffiths, *Fellow Travellers*, *passim*; Lipstadt, *Beyond Belief*, p. 39; Ross, *So It Was True*, p. 30.
38 Trevor Wilson, 'Lord Bryce's Investigation into Alleged German Atrocities in Belgium, 1914–15', *Journal of Contemporary History*, 14 (July 1979), pp. 369–83; G. E. O. Knight, *In Defence of Germany* (Golden Vista Press, London, 1933), pp. 9–13.
39 Tennant, journal entry, 5 Sept. 1934, in Ashley papers, BR 81, SUA.
40 Beverley Nichols, *News of England* (Jonathan Cape, London, 1938), pp. 300–3. He also had a series of articles on Germany in the *Sunday Chronicle*, Sept. 1936. See Sharf, *British Press*, p. 79, and Griffiths, *Fellow Travellers*, p. 227; Geoffrey Ward Price, *I Know These Dictators* (Right Book Club, London, 1937), pp. 118–20; and, similarly, Lord Londonderry, *Ourselves and Germany* (Robert Hale, London, 1938), pp. 169–71.
41 Douglas Reed, *Insanity Fair* (Jonathan Cape, London, 1938), pp. 152–5, and Cape's own journal, *Now and Then* (Spring 1939), for an indication of its success.
42 For Reed's remarkable career, see Tony Kushner, *The Persistence of Prejudice: Antisemitism in British society during the Second World War* (Manchester University Press, Manchester, 1989), pp. 99–100, and Richard Thurlow, 'Anti-Nazi Antisemite: The Case of Douglas Reed', *Patterns of Prejudice*, 18, no. 1 (1984), pp. 23–34. The impact of Reed's Holocaust denial views will be dealt with in later chapters. The assessment of Ward Price is in F. Gannon, *The British Press and Germany 1936–1939* (Clarendon Press, Oxford, 1971), p. 34.
43 Rathbone papers, X14/2.6, ULA.
44 See the notes of her talk, 'Jewish Refugee Problem', given to the Union of Jewish Women, 19 Feb. 1934, in Rathbone papers XIV/3.15, ULA. For her career as a

whole, see Mary Stocks, *Eleanor Rathbone: A Biography* (Gollancz, London, 1949). Rathbone's position was all the more remarkable given her earlier racialized world view. For a recent evaluation of Rathbone's career and her move away from eugenics-influenced race thinking, see Susan Pedersen, 'Eleanor Rathbone (1872–1946): The Victorian family under the daughter's eye', in Susan Pedersen and Peter Mandler (eds), *After the Victorians: Private Conscience and Public Duty in Modern Britain* (Routledge, London, 1994), pp. 105–28.

45 Sharf, *The British Press*, chapter 2; Colonel Meinertzhagen, *Middle East Diary 1917 to 1956* (Cresset Press, London, 1959,) p. 158, written shortly *before* the Nuremberg Laws were announced. See Mark Cocker, *Richard Meinertzhagen: Soldier, Scientist and Spy* (Mandarin, Gilmour, London, 1990).

46 Mr Fenn to Rathbone, 27 Oct. 1935, and Rathbone to Fenn, 29 Oct. 1935, in Rathbone papers, XIV/2.6, ULA.

47 Rathbone to Michael Franklin of Wayfarers Travel Agency, 5 Feb. 1936, in Rathbone papers, XIV/2.6, ULA.

48 Haim Genizi, 'American Non-Sectarian Refugee Relief Organizations (1933–1945)', *Yad Vashem Studies*, 11 (1976), p. 219.

49 Beatrice Wellington to K. Courtney, Apr. 1939, in Rathbone papers, XIV/2.15 [16], ULA; Nigel Nicolson (ed.), *Harold Nicolson: Diaries and Letters*, vol. 1 *1930–39* (Weidenfeld & Nicolson, London, 1966), pp. 347–8, letter from Harold Nicolson to Vita Sackville-West, 17 June 1938; Storm Jameson, *Journey From the North: Autobiography*, vol. 1 (Collins & Harvill Press, London, 1969), p. 344.

50 Louis Adamic, *America and the Refugees* (Public Affairs Committee, New York, 1939), pp. 26–7; Genizi, 'American Non-Sectarian', pp. 164–220 (esp. p. 219); A. Wilkinson, *Dissent or Conform? War, Peace and the English Churches 1900–1945* (SCM, London, 1986), pp. 124–6 and *passim*.

51 Headlam in 1933, quoted by Wilkinson, *Dissent or Conform?*, p. 148. See also Griffiths, *Fellow Travellers*, pp. 176–7 for Headlam's career.

52 R. Jasper, *George Bell* (Oxford University Press, London, 1967); H. Henson, *Retrospect of an Uninmportant Life*, vol. 1 *1920–1939* (Oxford University Press, Oxford, 1943), pp. 376, 413–4; James Parkes, *Voyage of Discoveries* (Gollancz, London, 1969), p. 117. The issue of Christians in the liberal democracies and the Jews will be covered more thoroughly in chapter 5.

53 Developments in the boycott campaign can be followed in the annual congress reports of the American Federation of Labor and the Trades Union Congress, 1933–1939.

54 For the British agreement, see PRO CAB 24/239 CP 96/33 and general comment in Louise London, 'Jewish Refugees, Anglo-Jewry and British Government Policy, 1930–1940', in David Cesarani (ed.), *The Making of Modern Anglo-Jewry* (Blackwell, Oxford, 1990) pp. 168–70; for Holland and the agreement reached in 1933 between the government and the central Jewish refugee body, the CBJB, see Moore, *Refugees from Nazi Germany* pp. 29–30.

55 In Britain, Sir Samuel Hoare, the Home Secretary in 1938, was 'urged by British Jewry – as strongly as any other group – that mass immigration would lead to an unacceptable growth in domestic antisemitism'. See J. Cross, *Sir Samuel Hoare: A Political Biography* (Jonathan Cape, London, 1977), p. 284; Hoare's own *Nine Troubled Years* (Collins, London, 1954), p. 240; and Leonard Dinnerstein, *Uneasy at Home: Antisemitism and the American Jewish Experience* (Columbia University Press, New York, 1987), *passim*.

56 For the diversity of approaches adopted in the 1930s, see Sharon Gewirtz,

'Anglo-Jewish Responses to Nazi Germany 1933–39: The Anti-nazi Boycott and the Board of Deputies of British Jews', *Journal of Contemporary History*, 26 (1991), pp. 255–76, and Saul Friedman, *No Haven for the Oppressed: United States Policy Toward Jewish Refugees, 1938–1945* (Wayne State University Press, Detroit, Mich., 1973), pp. 45–50.

57   Morris Beckman, unpublished memoirs, pp. 75, 77, London Museum of Jewish Life, 79–1990. See also, in the same collection, Aubrey Rose, 'A Memoir of the Old East End', p. 5.

58   The role of the refugee bodies and the specific involvement of Jewish women within them through organizations such as the National Council of Jewish Women is documented in Dobkowski, *The Politics of Indifference*, pp. 426–62. For Britain, see Elaine Blond with Barry Turner, *Marks of Distinction: The Memoirs of Elaine Blond* (Vallentine, Mitchell, London, 1988), chapter 4. See also the memoirs of a Manchester refugee organizer, Jean Gafan, 'Welfare of the Refugee' in Manchester Central Reference Library, Misc 879/4. The chaos in the British refugee organizations and the problems of its voluntary workers are referred to by Barry Turner, ... *And the Policeman Smiled: 10,000 Children Escape from Nazi Europe* (Bloomsbury, London, 1990), pp. 48–9. London, 'Jewish Refugees', pp. 163–90, highlights the crucial role of such bodies in the implementation of policy.

59   Martin Gilbert and Richard Gott, *The Appeasers*, 2nd edn (Weidenfeld & Nicolson, London, 1967), p. 6; Jeffrey Richards, 'The British Board of Film Censors and Content Control in the 1930s: Images of Britain', *Historical Journal of Film, Radio and Television*, 1, no. 2 (1981), pp. 40, 42; Robert Donington, 'Words and Music', in Ian Kemp (ed.), *Michael Tippett: A Symposium on his 60th Birthday* (Faber, London, 1965), pp. 91–2; David Matthews, *Michael Tippett: An Introductory Study* (Faber, London, 1980), p. 31; Meirion Bowen, *Michael Tippett* (Robson, London, 1982), pp. 22–3. The opera was not performed until 1944.

60   American films of the 1930s included *The House of Rothschild* (1934). See K. R. M. Short, 'Hollywood Fights Anti-Semitism, 1940–1945', in K. R. M. Short (ed.), *Film and Radio Propaganda in World War II* (Croom Helm, London, 1983), pp. 146–52, and Judith Doneson, *The Holocaust in American Film* (Jewish Publication Society, Philadelphia, Penn., 1987), chapter 1.

61   Samuel Rich diaries, 12 and 15 Nov. 1938, AJ 217, SUA.

62   Fox, 'Great Britain', p. 40.

63   Lionel Kochan, *Pogrom: 10 November 1938* (Deutsch, London, 1957), p. 11.

64   For moral indignation over the pogrom, see Sharf, *The British Press*, p. 58; Gannon, *The British Press and Germany*, p. 226; and Lipstadt, *Beyond Belief*, pp. 104–9. For photographic imagery, see particularly 'Back to the Middle Ages', *Picture Post*, 26 Nov. 1938; Kochan, *Pogrom*, pp. 126–7.

65   From 'Kristallnacht' exhibition, Wiener Library, London, Nov. 1988.

66   Headlam diary, 13 Nov. 1938. I am grateful to Mr Nicholas Crowson, a postgraduate at the University of Southampton, researching Conservative party responses to Nazi Germany at a constituency level, for this reference. Cantril, *Public Opinion*, p. 382.

67   Naomi Shephard, *Wilfred Israel: German Jewry's Secret Ambassador* (Weidenfeld & Nicolson, London, 1984), pp. 141–3; Kochan, *Pogrom*, pp. 141–5. Von Dirksen, the German Ambassador in Britain, assumed that the pogrom would create a barrier between the two countries. See E. Woodward and R. Butler (eds), *Documents on British Foreign Policy 1919–1939*, vol. IV (HMSO, London, 1950), pp. 333–4, 360.

68   Lionel Kochan, 'Inquest on Appeasement', *AJR Information* (July 1963), called

for a detailed study of appeasement policy and the persecution of the Jews which has still not been carried out; Roosevelt quoted by Sander Diamond, 'The *Kristallnacht* and the Reaction in America', *YIVO Annual of Jewish Social Sciences*, 14 (1969), p. 205; Kochan, *Pogrom*, pp. 141–5.

69 For overviews of the Evian conference, see S. Adler-Rudel, 'The Evian Conference on the Refugee Question', *Leo Baeck Institute Year Book*, 13 (1968), pp. 235–73 (esp. pp.237–8) on Palestine, and Shlomo Katz, 'Public Opinion in Western Europe and the Evian Conference', *Yad Vashem Studies*, 9 (1973), pp. 105–32; for Anglo-American diplomacy, see Sherman, *Island Refuge*, chapter 5, and Henry Feingold, *The Politics of Rescue* (Holocaust Publications, New York, 1980), chapter 2. The romantic interpretation of Roosevelt's decision to promote the international conference is that he was responding sympathetically to the powerful article on refugees by the journalist and campaigner Dorothy Thompson in *Foreign Affairs*, Apr. 1938. For a more realistic assessment of Roosevelt's motives, see Tommie Sjoberg, *The Powers and the Persecuted: The Refugee Problem and the Intergovernmental Committee on Refugees* (Lund University Press, Lund, 1991), chapter 3.

70 Allan Metz, 'Latin American Immigration Policy and the Jews, 1938–43: The Discrepancy Between Word and Deed', *Immigrants and Minorities*, 11 (July 1992), pp. 130–55; Herbert Strauss, 'Jewish Emigration from Germany – Nazi Politics and Jewish Responses (1)', *Leo Baeck Institute Year Book*, 15 (1980), pp. 354–5. In launching an appeal for the refugee Jews of Egypt and Hungary in 1957, the Association of Jewish Refugees stressed the role of Britain after the November pogrom in letting in almost half of those escaping. See *AJR Information*, 12 (Apr. 1957).

71 See Sherman, *Island Refuge*, chapter 7; Louise London, 'British Immigration Control Procedures and Jewish Refugees 1933–1939', in Werner Mosse et al. (eds), *Second Chance: Two Centuries of German-speaking Jews in the United Kingdom* (J. C. B. Mohr, Tubingen, 1991), pp. 507–15; Maga, 'Closing the Door', pp. 438–42. For France, see Caron, 'Jewish Refugees', pp. 163–8, and Abella and Troper, *None is Too Many*, chapter 2, for Canada. Also, see Paul Bartrop, '"Not A Problem for Australia": The Kristallnacht viewed from the Commonwealth, November 1938', *Journal of the Australian Jewish Historical Society*, X (1989), pp. 489–99; Moore, *Refugees from Nazi Germany*, pp. 82–8, for Holland; Feingold, *The Politics of Rescue*, pp. 41–4; and, for a more positive assessment of the United States, Breitman and Kraut, *American Refugee Policy*, pp. 56–67.

72 The most thorough account of British policy (after the earlier *Island Refuge* by Sherman) is Lousie London, 'British Immigration Control Procedures'. See chapters 4 and 5 for post-*Kristallnacht* policy.

73 Concerns about domestic antisemitism were voiced by the Home Secretary, Sir Samuel Hoare in *Hansard* (HC), vol. 341, col. 1468, 21 Nov. 1938; Chamberlain's 'neglected' role is stressed by London, 'Immigration Control Procedures', p. 507.

74 For the United States, see Dobkowski, *The Politics of Indifference*, pp. 338–90; Abella and Troper, *None is Too Many*, pp. 41–6, for Canada; Bartrop, 'The Kristallnacht', pp. 492–3, for Australia. In Britain the pressure is best seen in the response to help refugee children. See Mary Ford, 'The Arrival of Jewish Refugee Children in England, 1938–39', *Immigrants and Minorities*, 2 (July 1983), pp. 135–151.

75 For the rejection of the Wagner-Rogers Bill, see Feingold, *The Politics of Rescue*, pp. 148–55; support for it is reproduced in Dobkowski, *The Politics of Indifference*, pp. 360–89.

76 Moore, *Refugees from Nazi Germany*, pp. 84–91. Many children were brought out by Dutch schemes (although only 700 were placed with Dutch families); Turner, . . . *And The Policeman Smiled*, chapter 5 for the formulation of British child refugee policy; M-O A: D5460, July 1946 directive.

77 Turner, . . . *And The Policeman Smiled*, pp. 69–70 on the financial concerns of the Chamberlain government. Unsympathetic and even brutal treatment of the children by their British hosts is a not uncommon theme in the two collective autobiographies Karen Gershon (ed.), *We Came as Children* (Gollancz, London, 1966), esp. pp. 39 and 65, and Bertha Leverton and Shmuel Lowensohn (eds), *I Came Alone: The Stories of the Kindertransports* (Book Guild, Lewes, Sussex, 1990).

78 For the Jewish and non-Jewish refugee organizations, see the chapters by Ronald Stent and Gerhard Hirschfeld respectively in *Second Chance*, pp. 579–98 and 599–610. The specific case of the Academic Assistance Council, which rescued over 600 scholars, is documented in Ray Cooper, *Refugee Scholars: Conversations with Tess Simpson* (Moorland Books, Leeds, 1992); Turner, . . . *And The Policeman Smiled*, p. 74; Imperial War Museum, 'Britain and the Refugee Crisis 1933–1947', oral history recordings (Imperial War Museum (IWM) refugee tapes) no. 4588 for Burkill; Walter Bieringer interview, Research Foundation for Jewish Immigration, New York (Research Foundation collection).

79 Griffiths, *Fellow Travellers*, p. 159; Diamond, 'The *Kristallnacht*', p. 208.

80 Quentin Reynolds in *Collier's*, 11 Feb. 1939, quoted by Lipstadt, *Beyond Belief*, p. 38; Peter Harlow, *The Shortest Way With the Jews* (Allen & Unwin, London, 1939), p. 238.

81 J. B. C. Grundy, *Brush Up Your German: Conversations of real use* (Dent and Sons, London, 1931) and *idem, The Second Brush up Your German* (Dent and Sons, London, 1939), pp. ix, 38–40, 112. Dent themselves showed little sensitivity to Jewish concerns about another school textbook which included the information that 'Jews stink'. See their letter to the Board of Deputies of British Jews, 11 May 1943, in Board of Deputies archive (BDA) C8/2/2.

82 Diamond, 'The *Kristallnacht*', p. 209.

83 M-O A: D5291, diary entry, 5 Nov. 1939.

84 N. Rose (ed.), *Baffy: The Diaries of Blanche Dugdale 1936–1947* (Vallentine, Mitchell, London, 1973), p. 115.

85 Robert Rhodes James, *Chips: The Diaries of Sir Henry Channon* (Weidenfeld & Nicolson, London, 1967), p. 178; John Vincent (ed.), *The Crawford Papers: The Journals of David Lindsay* (Manchester University Press, Manchester, 1984), pp. 591, 596; Chamberlain, quoted by Martin Gilbert, *The Holocaust: The Jewish Tragedy* (Collins, London, 1987), p. 81.

86 M-O A: TC Antisemitism Box 1, Files C and D; FR A12.

87 *Action*, 19 and 26 Nov. 1938 and, similarly, *Anglo-German Review*, Dec. 1938; *Peace News*, July–Aug. 1939; and particularly the contributions of the novelist Ethel Mannin.

88 Taylor, *English History*, p. 419.

89 IWM refugee tapes, nos 4494 and 3967 for the Hallgartens and, similarly, no. 4645 and 'A German Jewish Scientist', *Why I Left Germany* (J. M. Dent, London, 1934), p. 1; Susan Goodman, *Spirit of Stoke Mandeville: the story of Sir Ludwig Guttmann* (Collins, London, 1986), pp. 89–90, and his IWM refugee tape no. 4596; The Earl of Birkenhead, *The Prof in Two Worlds: The Official Life of Professor F.A. Lindemann, Viscount Cherwell* (Collins, London, 1961), pp. 24–5, 101–10.

90 Myra Baram, *The Girl With Two Suitcases* (Book Guild, Lewes, Sussex, 1988), pp. 17, 29; Central Office for Refugees, 'Entertaining Our Refugee Guests' (London, 1939), p. 7; Bruno Bettelheim, 'The Ultimate Limit' in *idem, Surviving and Other Essays* (Thames and Hudson, London, 1979), pp. 14–15 (originally published in *Midway*, 9 (Autumn 1968), pp. 3–25); Bieringer interview, in the Research Foundation for Jewish Immigration archive, New York.

91 Gershon, *We Came as Children*, p. 60; Stella Bell, in Leverton and Lowensohn, *I Came Alone*, p. 32.

92 Cantril, *Public Opinion*, p. 1150. The British Union of Fascists grew slightly in the year before war but this was from a very low base. See G. C. Webber, 'Patterns of Membership and Support for the British Union of Fascists', *Journal of Contemporary History*, 19 (1984), pp. 575–606, and the British intelligence material on the British fascist and antisemitic movement in PRO HO 45 and 144 series.

93 Headlam diaries, 14 Nov. 1938; Leonard Woolf (ed.), *A Writer's Diary: Being Extracts from the Diary of Virginia Woolf* (Hogarth Press, London, 1953), p. 311.

94 See chapter 3 for the domestic servants; Judith Tydor-Baumel, 'The Kitchener Transmigration Camp at Richborough', *Yad Vashem Studies*, 14 (1981), pp. 233–46.

95 The most infamous example of British Jewry imposing its anglicizing influences on the refugees was the Bloomsbury House pamphlet, *While You Are in England* (1938 and 1940) which almost imposed second-class status on the refugees; *Kitchener Camp Review*, no. 2 (Apr. 1939), p. 4, in AJA 45/1, SUA; Professor John Grenville, quoted in Zoe Josephs, *Survivors: Jewish Refugees in Birmingham 1933–1945* (Meridian Books, Warley, West Midlands, 1988), p. 69; Peter Scheuer, IWM refugee tape no. 4624.

96 See, for example, the bitter correspondence in October 1939 concerning a refugee hostel for orthodox Jews in London run by the Chief Rabbi's Emergency Council and assimilationist Jews, in Rothschild archive (RA), 000/315C. The issue will be dealt with in greater detail in the following section on World War II.

97 Report of the *Hilfsverein*, July 1938, on emigration to the USA, reproduced in Norberte Kampe (ed.), *Jewish Immigrants of the Nazi Period in the USA*, vol. 4/1 *Jewish Emigration from Germany 1933–1942: A Documentary History* (K. G. Saur, New York, 1992), pp. 207–11; Walter Bieringer and Karl Albert interviews in the Research Foundation for Jewish Immigration archive, New York; Eduard Hermann quoted by Dobkowski, *The Politics of Indifference*, p. 461; Zosa Szajkowski, 'The Attitude of American Jews to Refugees from Germany in the 1930's', *American Jewish Historical Quarterly*, 61 (Dec. 1971), pp. 101–43; Richard Weiss, 'Ethnicity and Reform: Minorities and the Ambience of the Depression Years', *The Journal of American History*, 66 (Dec. 1979), pp. 566–85 (esp. p. 566); preface to George Mikes's *How to be an Alien* (1946), reproduced in his *How to be a Brit* (Penguin, Harmondsworth, 1987), p. 18.

98 See Adler-Rudel, 'The Evian Conference', p. 465.

99 Dorothy Thompson, 'Refugees: A World Problem', *Foreign Affairs*, 16 (Apr. 1938), pp. 375–8; Cantril, *Public Opinion*, p. 1150.

2 NAZI PERSECUTION AND THE LABOUR MOVEMENT

1 Wolfe minute, 5 Mar. 1935, and comment of R. F. Wigram, 10 July 1935, in PRO LAB 8/78.

2 Emerson, 17 Oct. 1939, in J. Mendelsohn (ed.), *The Holocaust: Selected Documents in Eighteen Volumes*, vol. 6 (Garland, New York, 1982), pp. 54–5; George Orwell, 'London Letter', *Partisan Review*, Mar.–Apr. 1942.

3 The omission is shared equally by specialists on the liberal democracies and the refugee crisis and labour historians of the period. Saul Friedman, *No Haven for the Oppressed: United States Policy Toward Jewish Refugees, 1938–1945* (Wayne State University Press, Detroit, Mich., 1973), chapter 4 provides passing treatment. For specific studies, see George Berlin, 'The Jewish Labor Committee and American Immigration Policy in the 1930s', in Charles Berlin (ed.) *Studies in Jewish Bibliography History and Literature in Honor of I. Edward Kiev* (Ktav, New York, 1971), pp. 45–73; Sidney Kelman, 'Limits of Consensus: Unions and the Holocaust', *American Jewish History*, 79 (Spring 1990), pp. 314–34; Gail Malmgreen, 'Labor and the Holocaust', *Labor's Heritage*, Oct. 1991, pp. 20–35; and David Kranzler, 'The Role in Relief and Rescue During the Holocaust by the Jewish Labor Committee', in Seymour Maxwell Finger (ed.), *American Jewry During the Holocaust* (Holmes & Meier, New York, 1984), appendix 4. There has been no consideration given to the question of Jewish immigration in the growing literature on British and American labour in the 1930s. For a perceptive analysis of the limitations of American labour historiography, see David Brody, 'Labor and the Great Depression: The Interpretative Prospects', *Labor History*, 13 (1972), pp. 231–44.

4 *New Statesman*, 6 Jan. 1940, and *Action*, 30 Nov. 1939 and 28 Mar. 1940; Paul O'Brien, Wyoming State Federation of Labor, resolution 27, *Report of the Proceedings of the Fifty-Fourth Annual Convention of the AFL* (Judd & Detweiler, Washington, DC, 1934), p.188.

5 Gillies to Dr Adler, Labour and Socialist International, Brussels, 23 Aug. 1938, in WG/REF/6/4/54, Labour Party archives, National Museum of Labour History (hereafter LPA); 70th Annual Trades Union Congress, *Report*, (TUC, London, 1938), p. 208.

6 David Feldman, 'The Importance of Being English: Jewish Immigration and the Decay of Liberal England', in David Feldman and Gareth Stedman Jones (eds), *Metropolis London: Histories and Representations Since 1800* (Routledge, London, 1989), p. 57.

7 Kenneth Lunn, 'Industrial Relations or Race Relations? Race and Labour in Britain, 1880–1950', in Kenneth Lunn (ed.), *Race and Labour in Twentieth-Century Britain* (Frank Cass, 1985), p. 2. John Higham, *Strangers in the Land: Patterns of American Nativism 1860–1925*, 2nd edn (Atheneum, New York, 1978), p. 304, has valuable comment on the same point.

8 Higham, *Strangers in the Land*, pp. 305–6, 321–2.

9 See Wedgwood in *Hansard* (HC), vol. 114, cols 2789–92, 15 Apr. 1919; Paul Foot, *Immigration and Race in British Politics* (Penguin, Harmondsworth, 1965), pp. 112–3 for Scurr; David Cesarani, 'Joynson-Hicks and the Radical Right in England After World War One', in Tony Kushner and Kenneth Lunn (eds) *Traditions of Intolerance: Historical Perspectives on Fascism and Race Discourse in British Society* (Manchester University Press, 1989), pp. 128, 132 for the use of anti-alienism in election campaigns during 1924 and 1929.

10 Labour Party Research Department, Feb. 1930, memorandum on Aliens Order, LPA.

11 The camp at Eastleigh, Hampshire, is mentioned briefly in T. W. E. Roche, *The Key in the Lock* (John Murray, London, 1969), p. 105. Its administrative history is covered in the minutes of the Union of Jewish Women, 1925–7, AJ26B,

Southampton University archive, and in Tony Kushner, 'The Eastleigh Camp in the 1920s: Changes and Continuities in Immigration Policy' (unpublished paper, Jewish Historical Society of England Centenary Conference 'Patterns of Migration', London, June 1993).

12 Michael Marrus, *The Unwanted: European Refugees in the Twentieth Century* (Oxford University Press, New York, 1985), p. 136.

13 Walter Citrine, *Men and Work: An Autobiography* (Hutchinson, London, 1964), pp. 338–347; Alan Bullock, *The Life and Times of Ernest Bevin*, vol. 1 *Trade Union Leader 1881–1940* (Heinemann, London, 1960), p. 584.

14 For the setting up of the fund, see 65th Annual Trades Union Congress, *Report*, (TUC, London, 1933), p. 84. Philip Williams, *Hugh Gaitskell: A Political Biography* (Jonathan Cape, London, 1979), pp. 53–9. See A. J. Sherman, *Island Refuge: Britain and Refugees from the Third Reich 1933–1939* (Elek, London, 1973), p. 147, for the flexibility of the British government with regard to individual refugees from the labour movement; note 26 below for the United States and note 92 for other countries.

15 For Beer, see J. S. Middleton papers, Box 13, LPA.

16 65th Annual Trades Union Congress, *Report*, pp. 83–4, does not mention Jews but see 66th Annual Trades Union Congress, *Report* (TUC, London, 1934), p. 252, for a passing reference by Citrine. In contrast, see *Report of the Proceedings of the Fifty-Third Annual Convention of the AFL* (Judd & Detweiller, Washington, DC, 1933), pp. 141–2, and subsequent reports until 1939.

17 *Report of the Proceedings of the Fifty-Third Annual Convention of the AFL*, pp. 142, 103.

18 John Garraty, 'Unemployment During the Great Depression', *Labor History*, 17 (1976), pp. 133–59; Green in *Report of the Proceedings of the Fifty-Second Annual Convention of the AFL* (Judd & Detweiller, Washington, DC, 1932), p. 464, and in *Report of the Proceedings of the Fifty-Third Annual Convention of the AFL*, p. 464. For the American Legion, see Higham, *Strangers in the Land*, p. 224.

19 Scharrenberg in *Report of the Proceedings of the Fifty-Fourth Annual Convention of the AFL*, p. 3.

20 For the importance of 'oriental exclusion' to the AFL, see Mark Starr, 'Labor Looks at Migration', *Current History*, 54 (Dec. 1943), pp. 299–300. It has been pointed out that 'At least thirty-one of the AFL's affiliates, as well as most of the independent railroad brotherhoods, barred Negroes from membership'. See Robert Zieger, *American Workers, American Unions, 1920–1985* (John Hopkins University Press, Baltimore, Md, 1986), p. 82.

21 On the split in general, see Walter Galenson, *The CIO Challenge to the AFL: A History of the American Labor Movement, 1935–1941* (Harvard University Press, Cambridge, Mass., 1960); Woll in *Report of the Proceedings of the Fifty-Sixth Annual Convention of the AFL* (Judd & Detweiller, Washington, DC, 1936), pp. 497–508. See also an allusion to this incident by the CIO's Philip Murray in *Daily Proceedings of the Fifth Constitutional Convention of the Congress of Industrial Organizations* (CIO, Washington, DC, 1942), p. 17, and a brief mention in Philip Taft, *The A.F. of L. from the Death of Gompers to the Merger* (Harper & Row, New York, 1959), p. 186.

22 William Green in *Report of the Proceedings of the Fifty-Eighth Annual Convention of the AFL* (Judd & Detweiller, Washington, DC, 1938), p. 11.

23 See resolution 206 in *Report of the Proceedings of the Fifty-Fourth Annual Convention of the AFL*, p. 279, and *Report of the Proceedings of the Fifty-Fifth*

Annual Convention of the AFL, (Judd & Detweiller, Washington, DC, 1935), pp. 268, 603. David Dubinsky, President of the ILGWU, was also Treasurer of the Jewish Labor Committee. See Berlin, 'The Jewish Labor Committee', pp. 46, 50, and, more generally, David Dubinsky and A. H. Raskin, *David Dubinsky: A Life with Labor* (Simon & Schuster, New York, 1977).

24 *Report of the Proceedings of the Fifty-Third Annual Convention of the AFL*, pp. 142, 467–71. See also Taft, *The A.F. of L.*, pp. 204–6, and Joseph Tenenbaum, 'The Anti-Nazi Boycott Movement in the United States', *Yad Vashem Studies*, 3 (1959), pp. 141–59.

25 *Report of the Proceedings of the Fifty-Fourth Annual Convention of the AFL*, pp. 173–7. Mark Starr, 'Labor Looks at Migration', p. 299, stated that 'with some exceptions, the American unions . . . have [in addition to support for immigration control] also favored tariffs to keep out foreign products'.

26 For the appeal, see Taft, *The A.F. of L.*, pp. 205–6; Berlin, 'The Jewish Labor Committee', pp. 45–73 (esp. p. 51). David Brody, 'American Jewry, The Refugees and Immigration Restriction (1932–1942)', *Publications of the American Jewish Historical Society*, 45 (June 1956), p. 231, points out that the Jewish Labor Committee had the initial aim 'to fight for the right of free immigration in all countries'. This was clearly unrealistic. What is more significant is that the Committee never challenged the restrictionism of the AFL after the 1935 convention until the war. For its close connection to the AFL, see *Report of the Proceedings of the Sixtieth Annual Convention of the AFL* (Judd & Detweiller, Washington, DC, 1940), pp. 401–2; *Report of the Proceedings of the Sixty-Second Annual Convention of the AFL* (Judd & Detweiller, Washington, DC, 1942), pp. 694–5; and, more generally, Jewish Labor Committee, *The Jewish Labor Committee: What It Does and What It Stands For* (Jewish Labor Committee, New York, 1942).

27 See *Report of the Proceedings of the Fifty-Ninth Annual Convention of the AFL* (Judd & Detweiller, Washington, DC, 1939), p. 679, and Berlin, 'The Jewish Labor Committee', pp. 60–2, for comment.

28 Charles Feinstein, *National Income, Expenditure and Output of the United Kingdom 1855–1965* (Cambridge University Press, Cambridge, 1972), T18.

29 See generally John Lovell and B. C. Roberts, *A Short History of the TUC* (Macmillan, London, 1968), and Henry Pelling, *A History of British Trade Unionism* (Macmillan, London, 1976), pp. 206–12; and, more specifically on its economic policies in the 1930s, Sidney Pollard, 'Trade Union Reactions to the Economic Crisis', in Sidney Pollard (ed.), *The Gold Standard and Employment Policies Between the Wars* (Methuen, London, 1970), and Alan Booth and Melvyn Pack, *Employment, Capital and Economic Policy: Great Britain 1918–1939* (Blackwell, Oxford, 1985), chapter 5. See Elizabeth Durbin, *New Jerusalems: The Labour Party and the Economics of Democratic Socialism* (Routledge & Kegan Paul, London, 1985), chapter 3 for the dilemmas facing the Labour party in power.

30 R. F. Wigram, 10 July 1935, in PRO LAB 8/78 and LAB 8/871 for 1938.

31 National Council of Labour, 6 Dec. 1935, in WG/REF/6/File 1, LPA.

32 Louis de Brouckere, President of the Commission of Enquiry set up by the Labour and Socialist International, Brussels, 'Political Refugees and Their Rights', WG/REF/6/File 2/13, LPA.

33 Lilli Palmer, *Change Lobsters and Dance* (W. H. Allen, London, 1976), p. 86, and, more generally, Gabrielle Tergit, 'How They Resettled', in *Britain's New Citizens* (Association of Jewish Refugees in Great Britain, London, 1951), p. 61.

34 69th Annual Trades Union Congress, *Report*, (TUC, London, 1937), pp. 388–9.

35 For the amount, see E. Parkin to Howie, 23 Sept. 1938 in WG/REF/6/File 2/61, LPA; and Taft, *The A.F. of L.*, pp. 205–6, for America. It should be added that the TUC raised £100,000 for the relief of Austrian workers in 1934 alone. See 68th Annual Trades Union Congress, *Report* (TUC, London, 1936), report of International Committee; Stephenson in *Report of the Proceedings of the Fifty-Eighth Annual Convention of the AFL*, p. 260.

36 70th Annual Trades Union Congress, *Report* (TUC, London, 1938), pp. 207–8, 409–13.

37 Lunn, 'Industrial Relations', p. 2. For unemployment figures, see Feinstein, *National Income*, T128, and *Report of the Proceedings of the Fifty-Eighth Annual Convention of the AFL*, p. 107.

38 The insecurity in the union world at this point can be seen in the the reports of the AFL, CIO and TUC in their annual conferences/conventions in summer/autumn 1938. Marrus, *The Unwanted*, p. 135.

39 Lewis in *Proceedings of the First Constitutional Convention of the Congress of Industrial Organizations* (CIO, Washington, DC, 1938), pp. 10–12.

40 *Report of the Proceedings of the Fifty-Eighth Annual Convention of the AFL*, pp. 167–8, 550; *Proceedings of the Second Constitutional Convention of the Congress of Industrial Organizations*, (CIO, Washington, DC, 1939), pp. 45, 167, 171; Steven Fraser, *Labor Will Rule: Sidney Hillman and the Rise of American Labor* (The Free Press, New York, 1991), p. 369. Ethnic divisions were not overcome totally in the CIO and emerged openly as thinly disguised antisemitism in the 1940 convention. See Fraser, loc. cit., pp. 449–50, and Melvyn Dubofsky and Warren Van Time, *John Lewis: A Biography* (Quadrangle, New York, 1977), p. 368.

41 *Report of the Proceedings of the Fifty-Ninth Annual Convention of the AFL*, pp. 133–5, 416; Scharrenberg in US Congress, Senate, Subcommittee on Immigration, *Hearings on S.407, S.408, S.409, S.410, S.411 To Restrict Immigration*, 76th Congress, First Session, 1939, p. 131, quoted by Friedman, *No Haven*, p. 99.

42 Green, quoted by David Wyman, *Paper Walls: America and the Refugee Crisis 1938–1941* (University of Massachusetts Press, Amherst, Mass., 1968), p. 45.

43 See the statements of William Green and John Lewis in *New York Times*, 9 Feb. 1939.

44 Friedman, *No Haven*, pp. 98–9.

45 Committee on Immigration and Naturalization, House of Representatives, *Hearings on Joint Resolution to Authorize the Admission of a Limited Number of Refugee Children*, 76th Congress, First session, 24–5, 31 May, 1 June 1939, pp. 3–14, 91.

46 Subcommittee of the Committee on Immigration, United States Senate, and a Subcommittee of the Committee on Immigration and Naturalization, House of Representatives, *Joint Hearings on the Admission of German Refugee Children*, 76th Congress, First Session, 20–2, 24 Apr. 1939, pp. 78, 81. For the attention given to the restrictionist lobby, see Friedman, *No Haven*, chapter 4, and Wyman, *Paper Walls*, chapter 4.

47 *Hearings on a Joint Resolution*, p. 92; and John Lewis in *Proceedings of the Second Constitutional Convention of the Congress of Industrial Organizations*, pp. 108–9 on his attempt to prove that the CIO was 'an American organization'.

48 Paul O'Brien in *Report of the Proceedings of the Fifty-Fourth Annual Convention of the AFL*, p. 188.

49   R. F. Harrod, 'Making Room for Refugees: A Strong case: Not a Cause of Unemployment: Some Economic Factors', *Manchester Guardian*, 13 July 1939. Much of the article is reproduced in Norman Angell and Dorothy Buxton, *You and the Refugee* (Penguin, Harmondsworth, 1939), pp. 200–3; for the 'Memorandum on Refugees', see WG/REF/File 4/39 vii, in LPA. Harrod's involvement in the Labour party is covered in Durbin, *New Jerusalems*, pp. 105–110 and *passim*.

50   Harrod, 'Memorandum on Refugees', WG/REF/File 4/39 vii, LPA.

51   Scott to Gillies, 13 Dec. [1939?], WG/REF/69/ii–iii.

52   WG/REF/File 4/39; Citrine in 70th Annual Trades Union Congress, *Report*, p. 413.

53   Citrine to all Secretaries of affiliated unions, 15 July (circular no. 138), in TUC archive, 910.451 (1), University of Warwick, Modern Record Centre (hereafter TUC survey); Lunn, 'Industrial Relations', p. 2.

54   'Summary of Replies to Circular 138', TUC survey. In 1939 there were 4,669,000 trade union members. The 45 unions which responded had just over three million members. See 71st Annual Trades Union Congress, *Report* (TUC, London, 1939), pp. 14–54.

55   TUC survey; Nellies to Citrine, 17 July 1939.

56   Seventeen unions responded positively and ten negatively to the first question; Welply of the MPU to Citrine, 17 July 1939. Fred Smith of the Amalgamated Engineering Union wrote to Citrine, 26 July 1939, explaining that he believed that it was the government that was insisting on rigid restrictionism (all in TUC survey).

57   Fourteen unions responded positively to the second question, 28 negatively and three provided no clear response. Thirteen responded positively to the last question, 30 negatively, and there were just two with no clear response; Kneale to Citrine, 21 July 1939, in TUC survey.

58   Bagnell of the Dyers to Citrine, 18 Aug. 1939, and A. Douglas of the Monotype Casters to Citrine, 3 Aug. 1939, all in TUC survey.

59   B. Godwin of the Association of Women Clerks to Citrine, 11 Aug. 1939; C. Dingwall of the National Laundry Workers to Citrine, 1 Aug. 1939; H. Boothman of the Cotton Spinners to Citrine, 21 July 1939; F. Smith of the Engineers to Citrine, 26 July 1939; and T. Mckenna of the Blastfurnacemen to Citrine, 25 July 1939. All in TUC survey.

60   For example the Dyers had unemployment at 5 per cent (Bagnell to Citrine, 18 Aug. 1939) and the Cine-Technicians claimed half their members were without jobs (Elvin to Citrine, 24 July 1939) – in TUC survey; D. H. Coleman of the Wheelwrights and Coachmakers, in 70th Annual Trades Union Congress, *Report*, pp. 411–12.

61   Alex Gossip of NAFTA to Citrine, 18 Aug. 1939, TUC survey; *Sixth Annual Report of the Association of Cine-Technicians* (ACT, London, 1939), p. 10; Bevin to Citrine, 14 Aug. 1939, TUC survey.

62   These were the National Union of Glovers (A. Stroud to Citrine, 8 Aug. 1939); the Society of Goldsmiths (A. Raxworthy to Citrine, 19 July 1939); the National Union of Boot and Shoe Operatives (G. Chester to Citrine, 20 July 1939); and the Association of Cine-Technicians (G. Elvin to Citrine, 24 July 1939 and their *Sixth Annual Report*).

    For past anti-alienism, see James Schmiechen, *Sweated Industries and Sweated Labour: The London Clothing Trades, 1860–1914* (Croom Helm, London, 1984), pp. 34, 104–6 and Harold Pollins, *Economic History of the Jews in England*

(Associated University Presses, East Brunswick, NJ, 1982), p. 159. For the persistence of accusations of Jewish 'sweating' in the 1930s, see *Jewish Chronicle*, 22 and 29 Jan. 1939 and all of Feb. 1937.

63 70th Annual Trades Union Congress, *Report*, pp. 275–9.

64 Citrine letter to Secretaries, 15 July 1939, and, similarly, in a report on the proposed survey in *The Times*, 27 July 1939. The 'race blind' approach was made clear in 'The Refugees', an editorial in the *Daily Herald*, 25 Aug. 1938, which although sympathetic did not mention the word 'Jew' once. Chester to Citrine, 20 July 1939, and Bevin to Citrine, 14 Aug. 1939, in TUC survey.

65 See note 62 for details. The Domestic Workers Union proposed a similar substitution scheme. See Harries to Citrine, 29 Aug. 1938, in Box 54.76 (4), TUC archive, University of Warwick.

66 Francois Lafitte, *The Internment of Aliens* (Penguin, Harmondsworth, 1940), pp. 37–9, 63, has useful statistics on gender and the refugees; Norbert Soldon, *Women in British Trade Unions 1874–1976* (Gill & Macmillan, Dublin, 1978); Sheila Lewenhak, *Women and Trade Unions* (Ernest Benn, London, 1977); and James Kennealy, *Women and American Trade Unions* (Eden Press, St Albans, Vt, 1978); for the lack of unionization in nursing, see Lewenhak, loc. cit., pp. 230–1; Smith of the Power Loom Weavers to Citrine, 26 July 1939 and, similarly, Gibson of the Mental Hospital Workers to Citrine, 11 Aug. 1939; Godwin to Citrine, 11 Aug. 1939. For the United States, see the interviews with Walter Bieringer and Freda Muhr in the Research Foundation for Jewish Immigration archive, New York.

67 Alan Armstrong, *Farmworkers: A Social and Economic History 1770–1980* (Batsford, London, 1988), pp. 184–5, and 71st Annual Trades Union Congress, *Report*, p. 49 for membership and other details; Alun Howkins, *Poor Labouring Men: Rural Radicalism in Norfolk 1870–1923* (Routledge, London, 1985), pp. 176–7; Howard Newby, *The Deferential Worker: A Study of Farm Workers in East Anglia* (Allen Lane, London, 1977), pp. 236–8, and Reg Groves, *Sharpen the Sickle! The History of the Farm Workers' Union* (Porcupine Press, London, 1949), pp. 98–9, 214, 232–4, for Holmes and Gooch.

68 Hoare in *Hansard* (HC), vol. 341, col. 1972, 24 Nov. 1938; *Jewish Chronicle*, 6 Jan. 1939; Norman Bentwich, *They Found Refuge* (Cresset Press, London, 1956), pp. 86–114; minutes of Executive meeting, 19–20 Jan. 1939, reproduced in *The Land Worker*, 20 (Feb. 1939).

69 Figure from Bentwich, *They Found Refuge*, p. 95; costs in *The Land Worker*, 20 (Aug. 1939); Holmes to Comrades, Feb. 1939, in TUC survey; Holmes to Citrine, 29 July 1939, in TUC survey, and to his Executive Committee, July 1939, in *The Land Worker*, 20 (Aug. 1939).

70 For concern, see *The Landworker*, 20 (June and Aug. 1939).

71 Dawson, quoted by Sherman, *Island Refuge*, p. 48. For more recent surprise, see Stephen Brook, *The Club: The Jews of Modern Britain* (Constable, London, 1989), pp. 30–1, and Bernard Levin in *The Sunday Times*, 16 Apr. 1989. The MPU is mentioned by Frank Honigsbaum, *The Divisions in British Medicine: A History of the Seperation of General Practice from Hospital Care 1911–1968* (Kogan Page, London, 1979), pp. 276–7, and E. Hearst, 'A Brain-Gain Rejected: Refugee Doctors in Britain', *Wiener Library Bulletin*, 19 (Apr. 1965). In Australia, the medical profession showed a similar opposition to refugee doctors (in this case to maintain a position of strength as a scarce resource). See Suzanne Rutland, 'An Example of "Intellectual Barbarism": The Story of "Alien" Jewish Medical Practitioners in Australia, 1933–1956', *Yad Vashem Studies*, 18 (1987), pp. 237–8.

For the similar opposition of the American Medical Association, see Friedman, *No Haven*, note 66, p. 247.

72 Honigsbaum, *The Divisions in British Medicine*, pp. 275–83, and Tony Kushner, *The Persistence of Prejudice: Antisemitism in British Society During the Second World War* (Manchester University Press, Manchester, 1989), pp. 40, 90, 113, 150, for its antisemitism; 70th Annual Trades Union Congress, *Report*, pp. 409–13; Sir Samuel Hoare, *Nine Troubled Years* (Collins, London, 1954), p. 240.

73 Dr L. W. Hefferman in 70th Annual Trades Union Congress, *Report*, p. 409 and p. 412, for the critique by the representative of the Wheelwrights and Coach-makers; *Medical World*, 2 December 1938 and all of August 1940 for an indication of the virulence of the antisemitism of its leadership.

74 *Medical World*, 2 Dec. 1938; see the Special Branch report, 2 Apr. 1940, in PRO HO 144/22454, on Welply and others in the 'Pro-British Association'.

75 Honigsbaum, *The Division of British Medicine*, p. 260, for the SMA; Home Office memorandum on the BMA, 8 Feb. 1939, in PRO HO 213/259; Friedman, *No Haven*, note 66, p. 247.

76 A. Chapman and R. Knight, *Wages and Salaries in the United Kingdom 1920–1938* (Cambridge University Press, Cambridge, 1953), pp. 215–7, and 71st Annual Trades Union Congress, *Report*, p. 138.

77 71st Annual Trades Union Congress, *Report*, p. 139; National Union of Domestic Workers, 'Notes for Interview with Rt. Hon. Ernest Brown', 1938, Box 54.76 (4), TUC archive, University of Warwick.

78 Bezzant, note on 'Refugees', 14 Dec. 1938, and Bezzant to Franklin, 20 Dec. 1938, Box 54.76 (4), TUC archive; *Jewish Chronicle*, 20 Jan. 1939. The *Sunday Pictorial*, 15 Jan. 1939, had a headline 'Refugees Get Jobs: Britons get Dole'; Harries to Citrine, 29 Aug. 1938, Box 54.76 (4), TUC archive; PRO HO 213/5 for orders from the Nazi government for German domestics to return home.

79 For her limited role in the Domestic Bureau, see its minutes in the *The Archive of the Central British Fund*, reel 6, file 38. Bezzant's help to individual refugee domestics was acknowledged by some Austrian servants, in undated note, Box 54.76 (4), TUC archive. The union's continued opposition to a refugee influx is made clear in its Executive Committee's minutes, 1 Mar. 1939, in Box 54.76 (7), TUC archive.

80 For pressure from the National Council of Women to let more foreign women enter as domestics and the failure of union objections on the same issue, see PRO LAB 8/77. Kenneally, *Women and American Trade Unions*, p. 162, describes the failure to unionize domestics. See chapter 3 for fuller treatment of the United States and domestic service.

81 Kneale to Citrine, 21 July 1939, TUC survey; note 51 for the Labour party response to the Harrod memorandum.

82 TUC statement, quoted by A. Sheinfield and A. Slaberdain, 'The Attitude of the Trade Union', *Manchester Guardian*, 26 Aug. 1939.

83 *Daily Herald*, 25 Aug. 1938; H. Cantril (ed.), *Public Opinion 1935–1946* (Princeton University Press, Princeton, NJ, 1951), p. 1150; *Fortune*, July 1938.

84 For responses to anti-alienism, see *Daily Herald*, 30 Aug. 1938; *Manchester Guardian*, 1 and 30 Aug. 1939; 'Unemployed Repudiate Fascist Propaganda: Refugees not our enemy', *Jewish Chronicle*, 3 Feb. 1939.

85 Taft, *The A.F. of L.*, pp. 205–6; File 'refugees', 1934–38, in the Middleton papers, Box 13, and William Gillies papers, Box 8, for help to other victims of fascism, in LPA. See also David Corkill and Stuart Rawnsley (eds), *The Road to Spain: anti-fascists at war 1936–1939* (Borderline, Dunfermline, 1981).

86 Martha Long, *The Austrian Cockney* (Centerprise, London, 1980), reveals the process of initial suspicion and ultimate acceptance. Life histories of refugees in the collections of the Imperial War Museum, Manchester Jewish Museum and Birmingham Jewish History Group (Birmingham Reference Library) indicate a similar process. The experience of the refugee domestics will be covered in the following chapter.

87 Harrod, 'Memorandum on Refugees', LPA.

88 Citrine in the 70th Annual Trades Union Congress, *Report*, p. 413.

89 For the limited impact of Keynesianism on the labour world in the inter-war period, see Durbin, *New Jerusalems*, part 2, and Patrick Renshaw, *American Labour and Consensus Capitalism 1935–1990* (Macmillan, London, 1991), pp. 13, 39–40; Sheinfield and Slaberdain in *Manchester Guardian*, 26 Aug. 1939, for 'labour nationalism' and the 'exclusiveness of labour'.

90 Citrine in *Report of the Proceedings of the Sixtieth Annual Convention of the AFL*, p. 391; Citrine to Secretaries, 15 July 1939, in TUC survey and in 70th Annual Trades Union Congress, *Report*, p. 413.

91 'The Refugees', *Daily Herald*, 25 Aug. 1938, for non-mention of Jews. For the approach of some of the groups in the Jewish Labor Committee, see David Brody, 'American Jewry', pp. 231–3, 245. The parallel approach of the very orthodox is charted in David Kranzler, *Thy Brother's Blood: The Orthodox Response During the Holocaust* (Menorah Publications, New York, 1987). See also his articles on the Jewish Labor Committee, the Vaad Hatzalah and Agudath Israel in Finger, *American Jewry During the Holocaust*, appendix 4. The willingness of the American government to rescue individual labour and religious leaders is shown in Wyman, *Paper Walls*, chapter 7. See also Malmgreen, 'Labor and the Holocaust', pp. 20–35.

92 Bob Moore, *Refugees from Nazi Germany in the Netherlands 1933–1940* (Martinus Nijhoff, Dordrecht, 1986), pp. 56–9 and chapter 4; Timothy Maga, 'Closing the Door: The French Government and Refugee Policy, 1933–1939', *French Historical Studies*, 12 (Spring 1982), pp. 432, 434, 441; Vicki Caron, 'Prelude to Vichy: France and the Jewish Refugees in the Era of Appeasement', *Journal of Contemporary History*, 20 (1985), pp. 167–8; Irving Abella and Harold Troper, *None is Too Many: Canada and the Jews of Europe 1933–1948* (Random House, New York, 1983), p. 41; Michael Blakeney, *Australia and the Jewish Refugees 1933–1948* (Croom Helm, Sydney, 1985), pp. 139, 155, 157.

93 Wedgwood, in *Manchester Guardian*, 26 May 1939.

3 DOMESTIC SERVICE AND THE JEWISH CRISIS, 1933–1939

1 The Nuremberg Laws are reproduced and translated in J. Noakes and G. Pridham (eds), *Nazism 1919–1945*, vol. 2 *State, Economy and Society 1933–39: A Documentary Reader* (University of Exeter, Exeter, 1987), pp. 535–7.

2 For psycho-histories of Hitler, see Rudolf Binion, *Hitler among the Germans* (Greenwood, Westport, Conn., 1981) and Robert Waite, *The Psychopathic God: Adolf Hitler* (Basic Books, New York, 1977). Lucy Dawidowicz, *The War against the Jews 1933–45* (Pelican Books, Harmondsworth, 1977), p. 99. Quote from David Bankier, *The Germans and the Final Solution: Public Opinion under Nazism* (Blackwell, Oxford, 1992), p. 79.

3 Pam Taylor, 'Daughters and mothers – maids and mistresses: domestic service between the wars', in John Clarke, Chas Critcher and Richard Johnson (eds), *Working Class Culture: Studies in History and Theory* (Hutchinson, London, 1980), pp. 121–39 for the persistence of the occupation. Leonore Davidoff, 'Mastered for Life: Servant and Wife in Victorian and Edwardian England', *Journal of Social History*, Summer 1974, p. 410, points out that 23 per cent of all employed women were servants in Britain as late as 1930. For the United States, see David Katzman, *Seven Days a Week: Women and Domestic Service in Industrializing America* (Oxford University Press, New York, 1978). There is little international comparative work on domestic service. See, however, Theresa McBride, *The Domestic Revolution: the modernisation of household service in England and France, 1820–1920* (Croom Helm, London, 1976).

4 Marion Kaplan, *The Jewish Feminist Movement in Germany: The Campaigns of the Jüdischer Frauenbund, 1904–1938* (Greenwood, Westport, Conn., 1979), p. 174; Pamela Horn, *The Rise and Fall of the Victorian Servant* (Gill and Macmillan, Dublin, 1975), p. 25; and Davidoff, 'Mastered for Life', p. 417, on the 400,000 who left service in Britain during World War I.

5 Violet Firth, *The Psychology of the Servant Problem* (C. W. Daniel, London, 1925), pp. 11–13; A. Chapman and R. Knight, *Wages and Salaries in the United Kingdom 1920–1938* (Cambridge University Press, Cambridge, 1953), pp. 215–17; and Pam Taylor, 'Women Domestic Servants 1919–1939' (unpublished MA thesis, Birmingham University, 1978), for the most detailed account.

6 Hundreds of thousands of male and female servants left Europe for the United States before 1914. See Katzman, *Seven Days A Week*, esp. chapter 2, and Hasia Diner, *Erin's Daughters in America: Irish Immigrant Women in the Nineteenth Century* (John Hopkins University Press, Baltimore, Md, 1983), chapter 4. After World War I, immigration restriction and the lack of opportunities in American society increased the intra-European market; for British statistics, see PRO LAB 8/871; for Holland, see Bob Moore, *Refugees from Nazi Germany in the Netherlands 1933–1940* (Martinus Nijhoff, Dordrecht, 1986), pp. 55 and 204, note 14; and Taylor, 'Women Domestic Servants', p. 55, for movement from the depressed areas.

7 Horn, *The Rise and Fall*, chapter 10, and F. Dawes, *Not in Front of the Servants* (Wayland, London, 1973), p. 112, for the improvement in wages; Taylor, 'Women Domestic Servants', for confirmation that conditions had changed little; Firth, *The Psychology of the Servant Problem*, p. 10. Status concerns were equally important in the United States: see Katzman, *Seven Days A Week*, p. vii.

8 Paul Thompson, *The Voice of the Past: Oral History* (Oxford University Press, Oxford, 1988), p. 151. On past attempts to unionize domestics, see N. Soldon, *Women in British Trade Unions 1874–1976* (Gill and Macmillan, Dublin, 1978), p. 144; James Kenneally, *Women and American Trade Unions* (Eden Press, St. Albans, Vt, 1978), p. 162; and Katzman, *Seven Days A Week*, pp. 196–7, 234–5. Moore, *Refugees from Nazi Germany*, pp. 55–58; PRO LAB 8/871 and LAB 8/77.

9 Memorandum, Nov. 1938, in PRO LAB 8/871.

10 For the reluctance of Jewish women to become servants, see Katzman, *Seven Days A Week*, pp. 11–12, 69, 172, 272, and Alice Kessler-Harris, *Out to Work: A History of Wage-Earning Women in the United States* (Oxford University Press, New York, 1982), pp. 127–8; testimony of Pauline Notkoff at the Ellis Island Immigration Museum, New York (section on 'Mental Testing'); for Germany, see Kaplan, *The Jewish Feminist Movement*, chapter 6, and Steven Ascheim,

Brothers and Strangers: The East European Jew in German and German Jewish Consciousness, 1800–1920 (University of Wisconsin Press, Madison, Wis., 1982); for the United States, see Nora Sinkoff, 'Educating for "Proper" Jewish Womanhood: A Case Study in Domesticity and Vocational Training, 1897–1926', *American Jewish History*, 77 (June 1988), pp. 572–99; Lara Marks, '"The Luckless Waifs and Strays of Humanity": Irish and Jewish Immigrant Unwed Mothers in London, 1870–1939', *Twentieth Century British History*, 3, no. 2 (1992), pp. 129–30, and Eugene Black, *The Social Politics of Anglo-Jewry, 1880–1920* (Blackwell, Oxford, 1988), pp. 117, 224, 227, for Britain.

11 Lara Marks, 'Jewish Women and Jewish Prostitution in the East End of London', *The Jewish Quarterly*, 126 (1987), pp. 6–10; E. Bristow, *Prostitution and Prejudice: The Jewish Fight against White Slavery 1870–1939* (Clarendon, Oxford, 1983); Harold Pollins, *Economic History of the Jews in England* (Associated University Presses, East Brunswick, NJ, 1982), pp. 126–8, 178.

12 Kaplan, *The Jewish Feminist Movement*, pp. 183–7.

13 See the minutes of the Union of Jewish Women, AJ 26, in Southampton University archive; Tony Kushner, 'Sex and Semitism: Jewish Women in Britain in War and Peace', in Panikos Panayi (ed.), *War and Minorities* (Berg, Oxford, 1993) pp. 118–49.

14 For domestic service and Irish labour in the United States, see Hasia Diner, *Erin's Daughters in America*; for black workers, Jacqueline Jones, *Labor of Love, Labor of Sorrow: Black Women, Work and the Family from the Civil War to the Present* (Basic Books, New York, 1985), and Katzman, *Seven Days a Week*, chapter 5.

15 PRO CAB 27/549, 6 Apr. 1933, cited by Louise London, 'British Immigration Control Procedures and Jewish Refugees, 1933–1942' (unpublished PhD thesis, University of London, 1992), pp. 86–7.

16 PRO LAB 8/78, 3 Oct. 1934, and LAB 2/1189, Aug. 1933, cited by London, 'British Immigration Control Procedures', pp. 116–18.

17 For the importance of the household, see Deborah Hertz, *Jewish High Society in Old Regime Berlin* (Yale University Press, New Haven, Conn., 1988).

18 Avraham Barkai, *From boycott to annihilation: the economic struggle of German Jews, 1933–1943* (Brandeis University Press, Hanover, NH, 1989); Kaplan, *The Jewish Feminist Movement*, pp. 173–4.

19 For the impact of Nazi legislation on non-Jewish servants, see Bankier, *The Germans and the Final Solution*, p. 80. See also Marion Kaplan, 'Sisterhood under Siege: Feminism and Antisemitism in Germany, 1904–1938', in Renate Bridenthal et al. (eds), *When Biology Became Destiny. Women in Weimar and Nazi Germany* (Monthly Review, New York, 1984), p. 191. For a more critical perspective, see Herbert Strauss, 'Jewish Emigration from Germany – Nazi Policies and Jewish Responses (II)', *Year Book of the Leo Baeck Institute*, 26 (1981), p. 400, who refers to the 'sexist nature' of these policies. For a critical insight into these schools from the recipients' point of view, see Lore Segal, *Other People's Houses* (Gollancz, London, 1965), p. 21.

20 For the earlier domination of Austrian women, see the statistics in PRO LAB 8/77 and the essays by Bentwich and Rosenkranz in Joseph Fraenkel (ed.), *The Jews of Austria: Essays on their Life, History and Destruction* (Vallentine, Mitchell, London, 1967), pp. 361–374 and 467–546.

21 Figures in PRO LAB 8/77; for the estimate of Ministry of Labour permits, see minutes of the Domestic Bureau of the Council for German Jewry, 22 Sept. 1939, in Archives of the Central British Fund (hereafter CBF), reel 6, file 38.

22 For the importance of domestic agencies, see PRO LAB 8/92; Manchester Jewish

Museum (MJM), tape J283; Julie Hoglund, letter to the author, 14 Feb. 1988; for letters, see Imperial War Museum 'Britain and the Refugee Crisis 1933–1947' (hereafter IWM), tape nos 4296, 3816; Hilde Gerrard, 'We Were Lucky', (unpublished MS, London Museum of Jewish Life, 34/84), p. 11. On the importance of relatives, see Frances Goldberg, 'Memoirs' (unpublished MS, MJM) for an individual who saved her sister then her parents, and Marion Smith in *AJR Information*, 43 (Apr. 1988), p. 13, and MJM tape J283. On information put out by the *Hilfsverein der Juden in Deutschland*, see Strauss, 'Jewish Emigration', *passim*.

23 The phrase was used by Mrs Waley Cohen, a senior figure in the refugee organizations' hierarchy, at a meeting of the Board of Deputies of British Jews and the German Jewish Aid Committee, 23 Apr. 1939, in Barash papers, M533, Manchester Central Reference Library.

24 'Memorandum on the Future of Assistance to Refugees', Refugee Co-ordinating Committee, July 1938, in William Gillies' correspondence, WG REF6/File 4/41, Labour party archives.

25 Holderness to Major General Martelli, 4 July 1938, PRO HO 213/281.

26 *Daily Mail*, 17 Oct. 1930; A. H. Lane, *The Alien Menace* (Boswell, London, 1934), pp. 32–6; *Action*, 25 Feb. and 3 June 1939.

27 See the resolution, Oct. 1937, and discussion, Dec. 1937, in PRO LAB 8/77 and, similarly, PRO HO 213/322.

28 For the transfer of authority, see PRO LAB 8/82 and PRO FO 371/22534 W12173, memorandum, 9 Sept. 1939; Domestic Bureau memorandum to the Council for German Jewry, Feb. 1939 [?], in CBF archives, reel 7.

29 Domestic Bureau memorandum, cited in note 28; Domestic Bureau Executive minutes, 24 Feb. 1939, and 'Relations with Home Office and Ministry of Labour', 15 Mar. 1939, in CBF archives, reel 6, file 38.

30 Crookenden memorandum, 28 Nov. 1945, in PRO LAB 8/92 gives statistics for the 1930s.

31 Jeffes to Ernest Cooper, 5 June 1939, in PRO HO 213/107 E409; Parkin, 8 May 1939, in PRO FO 371/24100 W7740.

32 For a full listing of the new regulations and block visas, see TUC archive, 195/910/454, Modern Record Centre, University of Warwick (hereafter TUC archives). For the relaxation of procedures, see PRO HO 213/324.

33 Domestic Bureau report, 28 Jan. 1939, in TUC archive, 54/76 (7).

34 For the Polish Jewish question, see M. Stephany, letter to the Domestic Bureau Executive, 8 Mar. 1939, in CBF archives, reel 7; for the insistence on inspection, statement by Mr Robbins in Domestic Bureau Executive minutes, 24 Feb. 1939, in CBF archives, reel 6, file 38; for the tests, see Domestic Bureau minutes, 1 May 1939, in TUC archives, 456.

35 IWM tape 3822.

36 For contemporary criticism of the chaos in Bloomsbury House, see *Jewish Chronicle*, 6 Jan. 1939. The controversy was revived in the *Sunday Times*, 23 Feb. 1986, and *Jewish Chronicle*, 28 Feb. 1986.

37 Statistics from Domestic Bureau Executive minutes, 22 Sept., CBF archives, reel 6, file 38.

38 Bentwich, 'Report on a visit to Vienna', Council for German Jewry, 17 Aug. 1939, in CBF archives, reel 25, file 1.

39 Fanny Hunter, MJM tape J277. Similarly, see Myra Baram, *The Girl with Two Suitcases* (Book Guild, Lewes, Sussex, 1988), p. 10.

40 Mrs H. Jahn, interview with the author, Feb. 1988; IWM tape 3816; Hilde Gerrard, 'We Were Lucky', p. 10.

41 MJM tape J283 and IWM tape 3790 for those not wishing to leave. See also Marion Berghahn, *German-Jewish Refugees in England: The Ambiguities of Assimilation* (Macmillan, London, 1984), p. 73. For the untaken permits, see Domestic Bureau Executive minutes, 22 Sept. 1939, in CBF archives, reel 6, file 38; IWM tape 3816.

42 Letter, 14 June 1939, reproduced in Bertha Leverton and Shmuel Lowensohn (eds), *I Came Alone: The Stories of the Kindertransports* (Book Guild, Lewes, Sussex, 1990), pp. 34–6.

43 Segal, *Other People's Houses*, p. 73; MJM tape J281.

44 Cambridge statistics in IWM tape 4588; Gerrard, 'We Were Lucky', p. 12; Goldberg, 'Memoirs', p. 7, and Anne Fields, letter to the author, 18 Aug. 1989, for various forms of last-minute preparation.

45 For these regulations, see PRO LAB 8/83 and LAB 8/84.

46 The activities of Selfhelp can be traced in the interviews of Kurt Herz, Irma Mayer and Thekla Meyerbach in the Research Foundation for Jewish Immigration archive, New York. The interview with Hertz is reproduced in Herbert Straus (ed.), *Jewish Immigrants of the Nazi Period in the USA*, vol. 5 *The Individual and Collective Experience of German-Jewish Immigrants 1933–1984: An Oral History Record* (K. G. Saur, New York, 1986), pp. 125–7.

47 Pam Taylor, 'Daughters and Mothers', p. 139.

48 Oscar Schiff, 23 Apr. 1939, in Barash papers, M533. Bloomsbury House was requested not to support refugee domestics who 'were unwilling to work in the provinces', German Jewish Aid Committee minutes, 22 Nov. 1939, Barash papers, loc. cit. The description of domestic service is by Ronald Fraser, *In Search of a Past* (Verso, London, 1984), pp. 13–14.

49 Domestic Bureau, 15 Mar. 1939, 'Relations with the Home Office and Ministry of Labour', CBF archives, reel 6, file 38.

50 Neden minute, 6 Aug. 1938, in PRO HO 213/324.

51 Domestic Bureau, 15 Mar. 1939, 'Relations with the Home Office and Ministry of Labour'; Neden minute, 6 Aug. 1938, in PRO HO 213/324.

52 Barry Turner, . . . *And the Policeman Smiled: 10,000 Children Escape from Nazi Europe* (Bloomsbury Books, London, 1990), p. 238–9, for the support of the liberal refugee organizations, such as the Refugee Childrens Movement, to avoid a ghetto-like concentration and the opposition of the Chief Rabbi's Emergency Council to what it saw as refugee girls being 'obliged to do what is euphemistically called "domestic training" and what, to put it bluntly, is domestic service'. So onerous were their duties that these girls were 'forbidden to attend synagogue'.

53 For countryside isolation, see IWM tape 3822 and Martha Lang, *The Austrian Cockney* (Centerprise, London, 1980); statistics in Domestic Bureau Executive minutes, 22 Sept. 1939; reference to card index, 2 Feb. 1940, CBF archives, reel 6, file 38.

54 Kershaw House minutes, Barash papers, M533; report on the training hostels by Ruth Tomlinson, 18 Mar. 1940, in PRO HO 213/519; cost of rescuing domestics in Domestic Bureau Executive minutes, 21 Apr. 1939, in CBF archives, reel 6, file 38.

55 The Harris House diary, MJM, kept by 15 refugee girls in Southport in 1939/1940, reveals that five of the girls were being trained for domestic service in spite of their greater ambitions. See also Turner, . . . *And the Policeman Smiled*, p. 179, and Karen Gershon (ed.), *We Came as Children: A Collective Autobiography of*

Refugees (Gollancz, London, 1966), p. 40; Domestic Bureau Executive minutes, 27 May 1940, CBF archives, reel 6, file 38; MJM tapes J283 and J282, and *Jewish Chronicle*, 6 Jan. 1939, for refugee views on Bloomsbury House.

56 *Mistress and Maid* (Bloomsbury House, London, 1939 and 1940), copies in TUC archive, and Domestic Bureau Executive minutes, 24 Feb. and 19 May 1939, CBF archives, reel 6, file 38 for discussion of its contents; IWM tape 4588.

57 MJM refugee tape J281; 'The Refugee Housekeeper: First Year', *Manchester Guardian*, 13 July 1938.

58 IWM tape 4588.

59 Segal, *Other People's Houses*, pp. 85, 83; Erica Marks, letter to the author, 17 Feb. 1988.

60 Crookenden memorandum, 28 Nov. 1945, PRO LAB 8/92; Franklin to Bezzant, 19 Dec. 1938, TUC archives, 54/76 (4); for sexual harassment in domestic service, see James Young, *Socialism and the English Working Class: A History of English Labour 1883–1939* (Harvester, Wheatsheaf, Hemel Hempstead, 1989), p. 70, and Lucy Long, 'Memoirs', p. 1 (in the author's possession); Inge Ader, letter to her mother, 22 May 1939, and letter to the author, 11 Feb. 1988, for evidence of such abuse in the experience of refugee domestics; 'Aliens', *Manchester Guardian*, 26 Sept. 1938, editorial.

61 Isabelle Beck, letter to the author, 16 Feb. 1988; Baram, *The Girl with Two Suitcases*, p. 25.

62 Charles Myers, 'The Servant Problem', *Occupational Psychology*, 30 (Apr. 1939), pp. 85–6, on small households and the treatment of servants; MJM refugee tape J281 and MJM tape J205.

63 For hostility between German Jews and the *ostjuden*, see Ascheim, *Brothers and Strangers*, and, for a different perspective, Jack Wertheimer, *Unwelcome Strangers: East European Jews in Imperial Germany* (Oxford University Press, New York, 1987). See also *Manchester Guardian*, 13 July 1938. MJM refugee tape J277, IWM tape 4296, and Fraser, *In Search of a Past*, p. 134, for further confirmation of the tensions between the refugee domestics and their Jewish employers.

64 *Jewish Chronicle*, 6 Jan. 1939.

65 Naomi Shephard, *Wilfred Israel: German Jewry's Secret Ambassador* (Weidenfeld & Nicolson, London, 1984), p. 169; letter from Ethel Yahuda, 'Refugees and Domestic Service, *Jewish Chronicle*, 13 Jan. 1939.

66 Samuel Rich diaries, 10 July 1939, AJ 217, Southampton University archives (SUA). See also correspondence in *Jewish Chronicle*, 2, 9 and 16 Dec. 1938.

67 For the regulations, see memorandum on the Domestic Bureau, TUC archives, 195, file 910.454; Bezzant meeting with Franklin, 20 Dec. 1938, in TUC archives 54.76 (7); National Union of Domestic Workers, minutes, 1 Feb. 1939, in TUC archives, 54.76 (7).

68 For domestics and the BUF, see Tony Kushner, 'Politics and Race, Gender and Class: Refugees, Fascists and Domestic Service in Britain, 1933–1940', in Tony Kushner and Kenneth Lunn (eds), *The Politics of Marginality: Race, the Radical Right and Minorities in Twentieth Century Britain* (Frank Cass, London, 1990), pp. 52–4; Union minutes, 7 Dec. 1938, in TUC archives, 54.76 (7), for the ban on refugee membership; Fraser, *In Search of a Past*, pp. 136, 138; IWM tape 3816; A. Gotthelf, letter to the author, 14 Feb. 1988, and Turner, . . . *And the Policeman Smiled*, p. 192, for evidence of servant resentment and jealousy.

69 'Our English Colleagues and Us', 1939 [?], in TUC archives, 54.76 (4).

70 Ibid. In Aug. 1941 the union received applications to join from members of a

Czech Refugee hostel which it received sympathetically in spite of the communist leanings of the women concerned. See TUC archives, 195, file 910.454.

71 Eva Freeman, letter to the author, 12 Feb. 1988; Goldberg, 'Memoirs', p. 5.

72 Goldberg, 'Memoirs', pp. 7–10; Eva Freeman, letter to the author, 12 Feb. 1988; Marianne von Kahler in *AJR Information*, 43 (Apr. 1988).

73 'The First Breakfast', TUC archives 54/76 (4); Lucy Long, 'Memoirs', p. 1.

74 Letters to the author from Julie Hoglund (14 Feb. 1988), A. Gothelf (14 Feb. 1988), Anne Fields (18 Feb. 1988) and Eva Freeman (12 Feb. 1988) all stress the importance of moving positions, not necessarily with positive results; see Taylor, 'Women Domestic Servants', pp. 54–5, for the importance of moving in improving the status of inter-war domestics; Austrian Centre, *Our Paper*, TUC archives, 54/76 (4).

75 *Our Paper*, TUC archives, 54/76 (4).

76 Gerrard, 'We Were Lucky', pp. 15–16; Segal, *Other People's Houses*, p. 80; Eva Freeman, letter to the author, 12 Feb. 1988.

77 Jillian Davidson, 'German-Jewish Women in England', in Werner Mosse et al. (eds), *Second Chance: Two Centuries of German-speaking Jews in the United Kingdom* (J. C. B. Mohr, Tubingen, 1991), pp. 533–51; Berghahn, *German-Jewish Refugees*, p. 119; IWM tape 4599; Segal, *Other People's Houses, passim*; and Maurice Davie, *Refugees in America: Report of the Committee for the Study of Recent Immigration from Europe* (Greenwood, Westport, Conn., 1974, reprint of 1947 edn), p. 125. See S. Quack, 'Everyday Life and Emigration: The Role of Women', in Hartmut Lehmann and James Sheehan (eds), *An Interrupted Past: German-Speaking Refugee Historians in the United States after 1933* (GHI and CUP, New York, 1991), p. 106, for confirmation of the greater ability of refugee women to adjust to their new situation.

78 *Our Paper*, TUC archives, 54/76 (4).

79 Ibid.; Goldberg, 'Memoirs', p. 8.

80 *AJR Information*, 20 (Apr. 1965); Francois Lafitte, *The Internment of Aliens* (Penguin, Harmondsworth, 1940), p. 87. The bias towards elite 'contributions' is very evident in Mosse et al. (eds), *Second Chance* and, similarly, the otherwise impressive study by Herbert Strauss, *Jewish Immigrants of the Nazi Period in the USA*, vol. 6 *Essays on the History, Persecution and Emigration of German Jews* (K. G. Saur, New York, 1987), section IV.

81 Bob Moore, 'Jewish Refugees in the Netherlands 1933–1940: The Structure and Pattern of Immigration from Nazi Germany', *Leo Baeck Institute Year Book*, 29 (1984), pp. 73, 77, 82, 85, 90, 92–5.

82 Vicky Caron, who is working on French responses to Jewish refugees, informs me that French newspapers in the late 1930s carried advertisements about domestic positions for refugees; see Domestic Bureau, Executive minutes, 21 July 1939, CBF archives, reel 6, file 38, for the Australian scheme.

83 For the American statistics, see Davie, *Refugees in America*, p. 40. See notes 6 and 14 for the literature on Irish and black domestics in the United States. Rochelle Gatlin, *American Women since 1945* (Macmillan, London, 1987), p. 28 and Esther Peterson, 'Working Women', *Daedalus*, 43 (Spring 1964), p. 683, confirm that, until World War II, domestic service was the largest employer of both black and white American women. After 1945, however, it ceased to be so important for white women – in 1960, only 4 per cent of white women workers were domestics. For the increasing use of day workers and the subsitution of black women, see Katzman, *Seven Days A Week*, pp. 272–3.

84 Statistics on employment levels in Katzman, *Seven Days A Week*, p. 282; for

Selfhelp generally, see Davie, *Refugees in America*, pp. 179–80; Strauss, *Jewish Immigrants of the Nazi Period*, vol. 5, pp. 128–38 and *passim*; interviews of Kurt Herz and Irma Mayer in Research Foundation for Jewish Immigration archives.

85 Barbara Schaap, 'A Study of the Vocational Adjustment of Twenty-Four Refugee Women', (unpublished masters thesis, New York School of Social Work, Columbia University, 1941), p. 38 and *passim* for the retraining of these women by the Council of Jewish Women; Rebecca Godfrey, 'Fifteen Case Studies of Refugee Women: Their Social and Economic Adjustment', (unpublished masters thesis, New York School of Social Work, Columbia University, 1941), p. 17; Davie, *Refugees in America*, pp. 55, 125. The case studies carried out by Schaap and Godfrey indicate the temporary nature of domestic employment for refugee women in the United States, as do the extensive collection of interviews in the Research Foundation for Jewish Immigration archive. For poor treatment of these women in domestic service, see the interviews with Melitta Apt, Ruth Eis and Kaethe Wurtenberg. For the maintenance of boundaries between mistress and maid see the interviews with Irma Meyer and Melitta Apt.

86 James Roose-Evans (ed.), *Joyce Grenfell. Darling Ma: letters to her Mother 1932–1944* (Hodder & Stoughton, London, 1988), pp. 231–2; Segal, *Other People's Houses*, pp. 120–1.

87 For preference, see MJM refugee tape J283 and Fraser, *In Search of a Past*, pp. 135–8; Mass-Observation Archive: D5349, 27 Oct. 1939.

88 IWM tape 4644; for status concerns in American domestic service, see Katzman, *Seven Days A Week*, *passim*.

89 The change in treatment will be covered in chapter 5; IWM tape 3816.

4   CONTEMPORARY CONFRONTATION WITH THE DESTRUCTION OF EUROPEAN JEWRY

1 Jakov Lind, 'Crossings', *The Jewish Quarterly*, 143 (Autumn 1991), p. 29; *idem*, *Crossing* (Methuen, London, 1991); Judith Doneson, *The Holocaust in American Film* (Jewish Publication Society, Philadelphia, Penn., and New York, 1987), pp. 6–7.

2 Patrick Wright, *On Living in an Old Country: The National Past in Contemporary Britain* (Verso, London, 1985), pp. 167, 245; John Bodnar, *Remaking America: Public Memory, Commemoration and Patriotism in the Twentieth Century* (Princeton University Press, Princeton, NJ, 1992); Angus Calder, *The Myth of the Blitz* (Cape, London, 1991), p. 117.

3 John Major, speech to the 109th Conservative party conference, Brighton, 9 Oct. 1992, issued by Conservative Central Office, *Conservative Party News*, pp. 8–9.

4 Calder, *The Myth of the Blitz*, p. 10; Bodnar, *Remaking America*, p. 103.

5 K. R. M. Short, 'Documents', *Historical Journal of Film, Radio and Television*, 3 (Oct. 1983), pp. 171–80; Bodnar, *Remaking America*, pp. 102–4.

6 Robert Ross, *So It Was True: The American Protestant Press and the Nazi Persecution of the Jews* (University of Minnesota Press, Minneapolis, Minn., 1980), pp. 163–4, 202; Doneson, *The Holocaust in American Film*, pp. 6–7; Charles Stember et al., *Jews in the Mind of America* (Basic Books, New York, 1966), pp. 141–2.

7 Arthur Morse, *While Six Million Died* (Secker & Warburg, London, 1968), p.

199; Andrew Sharf, *The British Press & Jews Under Nazi Rule* (Oxford University Press, Oxford, 1964), pp. 113, 194, 209.

8 Walter Laqueur, *The Terrible Secret* (Weidenfeld & Nicolson, London, 1980), pp. 3, 197; *idem*, 'Hitler's Holocaust: Who Knew What, When and How?', *Encounter*, 55 (July 1980), p. 24; Ross, *So It Was True*, p. 164.

9 Laqueur, *The Terrible Secret*, pp. 66, 99, 208; *idem*, 'Hitler's Holocaust', p. 24.

10 Cadogan minute, 16 Sept. 1939, and general discussion in PRO FO 371/23105 C16788.

11 Halifax to Weizmann, 19 Dec. 1939, in PRO FO 371/24563/273, quoted by Bernard Wasserstein, *Britain and the Jews of Europe 1939–1945* (Oxford University Press, Oxford, 1979), p. 352.

12 For public demand for the White Paper, see Robert Kee, *The World We Left Behind: A Chronicle of the Year 1939* (Weidenfeld & Nicolson, London, 1984), p. 329; Mass-Observation Archive (M-O A): D5039.9, 1 Nov. 1939, who reports that a newspaper agent told him he 'had more orders for the Concentration Camp White Paper than . . . for any other'. Sharf, *The British Press*, pp. 85–7 summarizes British responses; Deborah Lipstadt, *Beyond Belief: The American Press & the Coming of the Holocaust 1933–1945* (Free Press, New York, 1986), pp. 143–4, for the United States. See Ian McLaine, *Ministry of Morale: Home Front Morale and the Ministry of Information in World War II* (Allen & Unwin, London, 1979), p. 31, and Angus Calder, *The People's War: Britain 1939–45* (Cape, London, 1969), pp. 61–2, for the earlier propaganda campaign.

13 M-O A: D5291, 31 Oct. 1939; D5145, 31 Oct. 1939; D5173, 31 Oct. 1939; D5276, 3 Nov. 1939; D5295, 1 Nov. 1939.

14 For doubt, see particularly *Truth*, 3 Nov. 1939 and M-O A:D5416, 31 Oct. 1939; M-O A: D5145, 31 Oct. 1939, for criticism of the government's use of material as atrocity stories.

15 Sargent minute, 5 Feb. 1940, in PRO FO 371/24422 C2026, and Fraser minute, 10 Feb. 1942, in PRO INF 1/251 Pt 4.

16 Roberts to Stevens, 16 Oct. 1939, in PRO FO 371/23105 C16788; *Papers Concerning the Treatment of German Nationals in Germany 1938–9*: Cmd 6120, (HMSO, London, 1939), pp. 9–36, cases 5–11. None of the Mass-Observation diaries for this period mention references to the persecution of the Jews in the White Paper although the document itself was mentioned frequently.

17 Thus Doneson, *Beyond Belief*, pp. 143–4, comments that even *Christian Century*, one of the leading sceptics on the subject of German atrocities, 'found its doubt giving way "as report follows report"'; *Christian Century*, 30 Nov. 1939.

18 M-O A: D5291, 5 Nov. 1939. Perceptions of the concentration camp in the liberal democracies, it could be argued, reveal an acceptance that cruelty and sadism existed, and sometimes led to death. Ultimately, however, the image of the concentration camp was limited by the liberal imagination. In 1942, reporting of the extermination process was again limited to past perceptions, this time as 'pogroms' or as isolated atrocities, corresponding to the violence at the turn of the century and its East European setting.

19 Cadogan minute, 16 Sept. 1939, in PRO FO 371/23105 C16788; Michael Holroyd, *Bernard Shaw*, vol. III *The Lure of Fantasy* (Chatto, London, 1991), p. 433.

20 'Plan to Combat the Apathetic Outlook of "What Have *I* Got to Lose Even if Germany Wins"', 25 July 1941, in PRO INF/251 Pt 4; Lowell Mellett, quoted by K. R. M. Short, 'Hollywood Fights Anti-Semitism, 1940–1945', in K. R. M. Short (ed.), *Film and Radio Propaganda in World War II* (Croom Helm, London, 1983), pp. 159–60, and, more generally, A. M. Winkler, *The Politics of Propa-*

ganda, The Office of War Information, 1942–1945 (Yale University Press, New Haven, Conn., 1978).

21 'Mr Smith, I Presume', *Sunday Dispatch*, 10 Jan. 1943. For the ethnic tensions behind the veneer of Americanism, see Richard Polenberg, *One Nation Divisible: Class, Race, and Ethnicity in the United States since 1933* (Penguin, Harmondsworth, 1980) and *idem, War and Society: The United States, 1941–1945* (Greenwood, Westport, Conn., 1980).

22 Bodnar, *Remaking America*, chapter 6; Tony Kushner, *The Heimische Front: Jews in Wartime Britain* (London Museum of Jewish Life, London/Leicester, 1992); Roberts, 11 May 1944, in PRO FO 371/42790 W7937; Bryan Cheyette, 'H. G. Wells and the Jews: Antisemitism, Socialism and English Culture', *Patterns of Prejudice*, 22, no. 3 (1988), pp. 22–35; *idem*, 'Beyond Rationality: H. G. Wells and the Jewish Question', *The Wellsian*, 14 (Summer 1991), pp. 41–64. Wells was referred to with approval in debate between the Ministry of Information and the Foreign Office. See Lias of the Ministry of Information to Grubb, 30 Aug. 1942, in PRO FO 371/30917 C7839, and Dixon of Foreign Office to Martin of Prime Minister's Office, 16 May 1944, in PRO PREM 4/51/8.

23 M-O A: D5406, 31 Oct. 1939; D5291, 3 Nov. 1939.

24 *The Times*, 16 Dec. 1939. For the Lublin plan, see Philip Friedman, *Roads to Extinction: Essays on the Holocaust* (Jewish Publication Society of America, Philadelphia, Penn. and New York, 1980), chapter 2, and Christopher Browning, 'Nazi Resettlement Policy and the Search for a Solution to the Jewish Question, 1939–1941', *German Studies Review*, 9 (1986), pp. 497–519.

25 Lipstadt, *Beyond Belief*, p. 143, and *New York Times*, 1 Nov. 1939, p. 2, and 4 Nov. 1939, p. 2; American Jewish Committee, quoted by Alex Grobman, 'What Did They Know? The American Jewish Press and the Holocaust, 1 September 1939–17 December 1942', *American Jewish History*, 68 (Mar. 1979), p. 331; Goldmann, reported in *The Friend of Zion*, June 1940, quoted by Ross, *So It Was True*, p. 149.

26 Goldmann, *So It Was True*, p. 149; *Buffalo Courier Express*, 6 Apr. 1940, quoted by Lipstadt, *Beyond Belief*, p. 153; M-O A: D5349, 18 Sept. 1939.

27 'Do We Realise?', *Zionist Review*, 4 Jan. 1940.

28 See the collective diary of the refugee children, 'Our First Year in Harris House', Sept. 1939–Feb. 1940, in Manchester Jewish Museum; Werner Rosenstock, 'Twenty Years After', *AJR Information*, Sept. 1959; Esther Rosenquit (ed.), 'And Then There Were Eleven . . . A Book of Family Memories', (unpublished MS, London Museum of Jewish Life, 4/1991), p. 170, *passim*.

29 Grobman, 'What Did They Know?', p. 345, and *Jewish Advocate*, 2 Aug. 1940, quoted in the same article, p. 338.

30 See *Jewish Chronicle*, 22 Apr. 1938, for Rich's retirement after 40 years at the JYS. Rich diaries are in AJ 217, Southampton University archive (SUA): see entries of 24 and 25 Aug. 1939, 30 Oct. 1939, 17 Mar. 1940, 11 May 1940 (although it should be added that it is unclear where Rich obtained his information concerning the euthenasia programme and the use of gas), 6 and 17 June 1940, 2 July 1940, summer 1944 onwards (for the fear of flying bombs), and 7 May 1945. *Jewish Chronicle*, 11 Dec. 1942 – David Cesarani, *The Jewish Chronicle and Anglo-Jewry 1841–1991* (Cambridge University Press, Cambridge, 1994), pp. 165–83, covers this newspaper's reporting of the Holocaust throughout the war.

31 An extreme critical example is Haskel Lookstein, *Were We Our Brothers' Keeper? The Public Response of American Jews to the Holocaust, 1938–1944* (Hartmore, New York, 1985). For the pressures operating on British Jewry, see Tony Kushner,

The Persistence of Prejudice: Antisemitism in British Society During the Second World War (Manchester University Press, Manchester, 1989).

32 Hertz to Temple, 23 June 1942, papers of the Chief Rabbinate 2805/124, in Greater London Record Office.

33 The domination of liberal values within British Jewry is emphasized in Richard Bolchover, *British Jewry and the Holocaust* (Cambridge University Press, Cambridge, 1993). Chapter 6 of Bolchover's important study deals with outsider groups who provided an alternative 'fighting model'. For resistance to popular protest on behalf of Anglo-Jewry, see *Zionist Review*, 18 Dec. 1942, and Home Intelligence Report in PRO INF 1/292, 22–9 Dec. 1942. For the fights within American Jewry, see David Wyman, *The Abandonment of the Jews: America and the Holocaust 1941–1945* (Pantheon, New York, 1985), chapter 9 and *passim*.

34 Lipstadt, *Beyond Belief*, p. 140.

35 For the report, see M-O A: FR 523B; and the survey, M-O A: Directive, Oct. 1940.

36 M-O A: Directive, Oct. 1940, DR1190; D2669; for sympathy towards Nazi antisemitism DR1145; DR1563 and DR2588; for the influence of Wells, see DR2356, DR2514, and DR2502 especially; DR2042; and for the puzzlement over the role of international Jewry, see DR1226 and DR1048.

37 M-O A: Directive, Oct. 1940, DR1329, DR1056 for war tension; DR1048 for the lack of prominence given to their fate; and DR1206 and DR2486 for avoidance.

38 *Time and Tide*, 13 Apr. 1940.

39 Christopher Browning, *Fateful Months: Essays on the Emergence of the Final Solution*, 2nd edn (Holmes and Meier, New York, 1991); Yitzhak Arad et al. (eds), *The Einsatzgruppen Reports* (Holocaust Library, New York, 1989); Ilya Ehrenburg and Vasily Grossman (eds), *The Black Book* (Holocaust Library, New York, 1981); Lipstadt, *Beyond Belief*, p. 151; for Britain see the complaints aired in the Home Intelligence reports in the second half of 1941 in PRO INF 1/292.

40 See Laqueur, *The Terrible Secret*, pp. 69–70, and M-O A: D5423, 12 Jan. 1942, D5004, 17 Jan. 1942, and D5098, 7 Jan. 1942, for its limited impact. It was later published in Britain by the government as *The Molotov Notes on German Atrocities – Notes sent by V. M. Molotov, People's Commissar for Foreign Affairs, to all Governments with which the USSR has Diplomatic Relations* (HMSO, London, 1942).

41 *Daily Telegraph*, 25 June 1942; Yehuda Bauer, 'When Did They Know?', *Midstream*, 14 (Apr. 1968), pp. 51–8, reproduces the *Bund* report; see Sharf, *The British Press*, pp.92–3, and 'The Greatest Pogrom', *Zionist Review*, 3 July 1942, for press reactions in Britain, and Lipstadt, *Beyond Belief*, pp. 162–70, for American reactions. Lipstadt suggests (p. 163) that in contrast to the British press, 'The American press did not ease [the report's] path [of acceptance]'. See also Silverman, in minutes of Press Conference, 29 June 1942, who also provides an impressive list of British papers covering the story, in World Jewish Congress papers, C2/409, Central Zionist archives, Jerusalem.

42 Only one Mass-Observer commented on the 'spate of German "atrocity" stories' and he 'wonder[ed] how many [were] true' in M-O A: D5230, 20 June 1942. 'Greatest Pogrom', *Daily Mail*, 30 June 1942; *Zionist Review*, 3 July 1942, and comments of Chief Rabbi referred to in note 32; Zygmunt Bauman, 'The Homecoming of Unwelcome Strangers: Eastern European Jewry 50 Years After the War', *The Jewish Quarterly*, 135 (Autumn 1989), p. 15.

43 See the report and Allen's reaction to it, 10 Sept. 1942, in PRO FO 371/30917 C7853.

44 Allen, 27 Nov. 1942, and Roberts, 1 Dec. 1942, in PRO FO 371/30923 C11923;
    Rathbone to Crozier, 4 Dec. 1942, in Manchester Guardian archive, 223/5/47,
    University of Manchester.
45 M-O A: D5271, 10 Dec. 1942; M-O A: DR 2925, 1393 and 2804; *Catholic
    Herald*, 24 Dec. 1942; *Catholic Times*, 24 Dec. 1942; *Peace News*, 14 Aug. 1942;
    New Leader, 19 Dec. 1942; *Socialist Appeal*, Jan. 1943. For Reed, see Kushner,
    The Persistence of Prejudice, and M-O A: DR Mar. 1943 in general.
46 PRO INF 1/292, 22–9 Dec. 1942; M-O A: FR 1648, Mar. 1943.
47 Richard Lichteim, 18 Sept. 1942, quoted by Martin Gilbert, *Auschwitz and the
    Allies* (Mandarin, London, 1991 [originally published in 1981]), p. 70. For levels
    of American antisemitism, see Stember, *Jews in the Mind*, pp. 121–4, 128, and
    p. 141 for belief about the Holocaust in 1942. See Lipstadt, *Beyond Belief*, pp.
    184–5, for the doubts expressed by the *Christian Century*.
48 M-O A: D5460, Nov./Dec. 1942; for the electrician, see M-O A: D5173, 4, 5, 8,
    9, 10, 11 Dec. 1942.
49 Victor Gollancz, 13 Apr. 1943, in National Committee for Rescue from Nazi
    Terror Executive minutes, 15/057 file 1, and Nicolson to the Executive, 24 Nov.
    1943, 15/057 file 2, Parkes papers, SUA. For allegations of a lack of general
    concern in 1944, see *Jewish Chronicle*, 30 June 1944. The silence in the Mass-
    Observation diaries in the spring/summer of 1944 would tend to confirm this
    analysis although Home Intelligence did detect some limited sympathy, in PRO
    INF 1/292, 18–25 July 1944.
50 *The Times*, 12 Aug. 1944; Alexander Werth, *Russia at War 1941–1945* (Barrie
    & Rockliff, London, 1964), pp. 890–4; *Illustrated London News*, 14 Oct. 1944.
51 See PRO FO 371/51185 for official British reactions to the liberation of Auschwitz
    and, more generally, John Conway, 'The First Report About Auschwitz', *Simon
    Wiesenthal Center Annual*, 1 (1984), pp. 133–51; M-O A: D5390, 23 Apr. 1945.
52 Arthur Koestler, 'The Mixed Transport', *Horizon*, 8 (Oct. 1943), pp. 244–51,
    and correspondence in *Horizon*, Nov. 1943, p. 362, and Dec. 1943, p. 433. The
    correspondence prompted Koestler to write 'On Disbelieving Atrocities', *New
    York Times*, 9 Jan. 1944. The article also appeared in *Time and Tide*, 5 Feb. 1944.
    See also Iain Hamilton, *Koestler: A Biography* (Secker & Warburg, London,
    1982), pp. 77–9, for a rather inaccurate account of this story, and Michael Shelden,
    Friends of Promise: Cyril Connolly and the World of 'Horizon' (Hamilton,
    London, 1989), p. 84 for a more impressive version. Karski describes meeting
    Koestler and others in Britain in Brewster Chamberlin and Marcia Feldman (eds),
    *The Liberation of the Nazi Concentration Camps: Eyewitness Accounts of the
    Liberators* (United States Memorial Council, Washington, DC, 1987), p. 179.
53 M-O A: D5233, May 1943 and Sept. 1944; M-O A: D5460, 24 Oct. 1944.
54 M-O A: D5233, Jan. 1943; for their efforts in rescuing a child refugee before the
    war, see M-O A: DR 5460, July 1946.
55 Thus, Mrs W wrote 'I remember all the dreadful things that have happened to
    them, just because they were Jews and might just as well as happen to me because
    I am Welsh', in M-O A: DR5460, July 1946. The role of these leading campaigners
    will be examined in later chapters.
56 Karski quoted in 'Messenger from Poland', Channel 4, 25 May 1987; Orwell in
    Tribune, 11 Feb. 1944; MacLaren to Calder, 3 Jan. 1945, in PRO FO 898/422.
57 M-O A: DR3153, Mar. 1943.
58 Herbert Emerson, memorandum, 14 Dec. 1942, in PRO FO 371/32682 W17272;
    McNair to World Jewish Congress, 2 Dec. 1942, in WJC papers C2/459, Central
    Zionist Archives; Stember, *Jews in the Mind*, p. 141.

59 *Time and Tide*'s reviewer commented on *Mr Emmanuel* that it was 'blissfully
     unsubtle' (9 Sept. 1944), and *Tribune*, 29 Sept. 1944, that its 'message [was]
     blurred'. Ilan Avisar, *Screening the Holocaust: Cinema's Images of the Unim-
     aginable* (Indiana University Press, Bloomington and Indianapolis, Ind., 1988),
     pp. 102–5.
60 Avisar, *Screening the Holocaust*, pp. 102–4.
61 Short, 'Hollywood Fights Anti-Semitism', pp. 149,–50, 155–6; see also Avisar,
     Screening the Holocaust, pp. 94–6.
62 For *The Great Dictator*, see Avisar, *Screening the Holocaust*, chapter 4, part 2,
     Short, 'Hollywood Fights Anti-Semitism', pp. 152–4, Doneson, *The Holocaust
     in American Film*, chapter 1, and Charles Chaplin, *My Autobiography* (Penguin,
     Harmondsworth, 1976), pp. 387–8. For *None Shall Escape*, see *Jewish Chronicle*,
     2 June 1944.
63 For the image of the refugee in contemporary Britain, see Kushner, *The Persist-
     ence of Prejudice*, pp. 115–9. *Next of Kin* (England, 1942) features a refugee
     turned spy: see *Time and Tide*, 25 July 1942. For the Jew as hero, see Kushner,
     loc. cit., p. 125, and Short, 'Hollywood Fights Anti-Semitism', pp. 156–8, and
     loc. cit., pp. 164–5, for the disturbances. For violence in the East End when *Mr
     Emmanuel* was shown, see the intelligence report to Scotland Yard, 13 Oct. 1944,
     in Board of Deputies of British Jews archive, BD C6/10/29. For boredom with
     Chaplin's speech, see M-O A: FR 764 'The Great Dictator'.
64 See, for example, Low's cartoons in *Picture Post*, 20 Jan. 1940, *Evening Standard*,
     14 Dec. 1942 and 18 June 1943, and *Manchester Guardian*, 15 Dec. 1942; and
     'Vicky' in *News Chronicle*, 10 and 22 Dec. 1942. The first two Low cartoons
     are reproduced in David Low, *Years of Wrath: A Cartoon History 1932–1945*
     (Gollancz, London, 1986), pp. 98, 226. David Low, *Low's Autobiography* (Mi-
     chael Joseph, London, 1956). For *We Will Never Die*, see Wyman, *The Aban-
     donment of the Jews*, pp. 90–2, and Avisar, *Screening the Holocaust*, pp. 100–1.
65 John Gross, *Shylock: Four Hundred Years in the Life of a Legend* (Chatto &
     Windus, London, 1992), p. 178; Redfern in *The Spectator*, 26 Feb. 1943.
66 Nicolson in *The Spectator*, 25 Dec. 1942, and letter in response from Olive
     Bennett, *The Spectator*, 8 Jan. 1943; Israel Gutman, *The Jews of Warsaw,
     1939–1943* (Indiana University Press, Bloomington and Indianapolis, Ind., 1982);
     Christopher Browning, *The Path to Genocide: Essays on Launching the Final
     Solution* (Cambridge University Press, Cambridge, 1992), p. 169.

5   BRITAIN, THE UNITED STATES AND THE JEWS,
          SEPT. 1939 TO DEC. 1942

1 Saul Friedman, *No Haven for the Oppressed: United States Policy Toward Jewish
    Refugees, 1938–1945* (Wayne State University Press, Detroit, Mich., 1973), pp.
    46–7.
2 See chapters 1 and 2; Haim Genizi, 'American Non-Sectarian Refugee Relief
    Organizations (1933–1945)', *Yad Vashem Studies*, 11 (1976), pp. 205–8; William
    E. Nawyn, *American Protestantism's Response to Germany's Jews and Refugees,
    1933–1941* (UMI Research Press, Ann Arbor, Mich., 1981), pp. 23–4.
3 Thus, in a conference of Bloomsbury House organizations in Dec. 1939 there
    was unanimous 'appreciation . . . of the liberal policy of HMG towards the
    refugees' according to the Chairman, W. W. Simpson, when addressing E. N.

Cooper of the Home Office (who worked closely with the refugee bodies), 28 Dec. 1939, in PRO HO 213/455.

4   Orwell in the *Observer*, 30 Jan. 1944; Ian Kershaw, 'The Churches and the Nazi Persecution of the Jews', *Yad Vashem Studies*, 19 (1988), pp. 427, 434, reviewing Otto Dov Kulka and Paul Mendes-Flohr (eds), *Judaism and Christianity under the Impact of National Socialism* (Historical Society of Israel, Jerusalem, 1987). The major volumes, edited by Yehuda Bauer et al., *Remembering for the Future* (Pergamon Press, Oxford, 1989) have corrected this imbalance.

5   Although highly critical of British Jewry, Richard Bolchover's *British Jewry and the Holocaust* (Cambridge University Press, Cambridge, 1993) acknowledges the essential weakness of this minority. The attempt of the Board of Deputies of British Jews to control protests within its own ideological framework is high-lighted in Geoffrey Alderman, *Modern British Jewry* (Oxford University Press, Oxford, 1992), pp. 303–5. Friedman, *No Haven*, and David Wyman, *The Abandonment of the Jews: America and the Holocaust 1941–1945* (Pantheon, New York, 1984), highlight the problems caused by the divisions within the American Jewish world and the problems this created in terms of pressurizing the government. Henry Feingold, *The Politics of Rescue: The Roosevelt Administration and the Holocaust, 1938–1945* (Holocaust Library, New York, 1980), pp. 298–301, although acknowledging the divisions within American Jewry, concludes that 'The role that fell to American Jewry was difficult, perhaps impossible to fill'. A similar line is taken by Yehuda Bauer, *American Jewry and the Holocaust: The American Jewish Joint Distribution Committee, 1939–1945* (Wayne State University Press, Detroit, Mich., 1981), chapter 20. For a review of the major questions involved, see Saul Friedman, 'The Power or Powerlessness of American Jews, 1939–1945', in Seymour Finger (ed.), *American Jewry During the Holocaust* (Holmes & Meier, New York, 1984), and the volume *passim*.

6   For the role of Christians in the Wagner-Rogers Bill, see Nawyn, *American Protestantism's Response*, pp. 23–4, and Genizi, 'American Non-Sectarian Refugee Relief Organizations', pp. 204–8. Chapter 2 describes the role of American labour.

7   Parkes to Bell, 14 July 1938, in Parkes papers, 16/51, Southampton University archive (SUA); Samuel Rich diaries, 30 Mar. and 18 Apr. 1933, AJ 217, SUA. See, however, Richard Gutteridge, 'The Churches and the Jews in England, 1933–1945', in Kulka and Mendes-Flohr (eds), *Judaism and Christianity*, p. 355, for a more positive assessment of Lang.

8   Charles Raven and Henry Carter to Bell, 12 July 1938, in Parkes papers, 16/51, SUA; Nawyn, *American Protestantism's Response*, p. 47.

9   Parkes memorandum, Feb. 1940 and Brotman to Parkes, 15 Feb. 1940, in Parkes papers, 17/31; Parkes to Simpson, 12 July 1938, in Parkes papers, 16/715, SUA. See also the correspondence on Christian–Jewish relations in C15/3/17, Board of Deputies of British Jews archive (BDA).

10   'The Refugees', *Daily Herald*, 25 Aug. 1938.

11   G. J. Renier, *The English: Are They Human?* (Williams & Norgate, London, 1931), p. 21; Alfred Perles, *Alien Corn* (Allen & Unwin, London, 1944), p. 21.

12   For MI5 concern, see 16 Mar. 1939, CAB 23/93. The accusation of radicalism even emerged in the American discussion of child refugees: see Friedman, *No Haven*, p. 94.

13   Cooper to Randall, 18 Sept. 1939, in PRO FO 371/24100 W13792, on visa policy; Rathbone to Anderson, 3 Feb. 1940 and, Anderson to Rathbone, 6 Mar. 1940, in Rathbone papers, XIV/2/17, University of Liverpool archive (ULA). For Jews

amongst the Poles, Belgians, Dutch etc. arriving in May/June 1940, see B4/ROS 7 and 9, BDA, and M-O A: FR 238. Bernard Wasserstein, *Britain and the Jews of Europe 1939–1945* (Oxford University Press, London, 1979), p. 82, describes the problem of finding accurate statistics.

14 Cooper to Randall, loc. cit; Maxwell to Morrison, 11 July 1941, in PRO HO 213/298; and CAB 98/1, CRP (39) 17, memorandum from the Home Secretary, 22 Sept. 1939.

15 Home Office memorandum 'for the guidance of persons appointed by the Secretary of State to examine cases of Germans and Austrians', Sept. 1939, in PRO HO 213/231. See also the correspondence between J. L. Cohen and Miss Tomlinson of Bloomsbury House, Sept. 1939, with regard to choosing suitable liaison officers for the tribunals in Joseph Cohen papers, A 173/63, Central Zionist Archive (CZA).

16 *Kitchener Camp Review*, no. 2 (Apr. 1939), no. 8 (Oct. 1939) and no. 9 (Nov. 1939).

17 R. M. Urquhart, quoted by Peter and Leni Gillman, *'Collar the Lot!': How Britain Interned and Expelled Its Wartime Refugees* (Quartet, London, 1980), p. 65; Maxwell to Anderson, 3 Jan. 1940, in PRO HO 213/460.

18 Harris House diary, 'We Went to the Police', in Manchester Jewish Museum. The range of experiences at the tribunals is covered in the Imperial War Museum's oral history recordings 'Britain and the Refugee Crisis 1933–1947' (IWM).

19 The correspondence can be followed in RAL 000/315C, Rothschild archive, London.

20 Gerald Hurst, *Closed Chapter* (Manchester University Press, Manchester, 1942), pp. 157–8.

21 See IWM tapes 4469, 4300, 3963 on the bias of certain tribunal leaders. For further Home Office clarification of procedures in Jan. 1940 to counter such discrepancies, see PRO HO 213/547. Figures for domestic servants are from Francois Lafitte, *The Internment of Aliens* (Penguin, Harmondsworth, 1940), pp. 36–9, 62–3. Lord Reading, 15 Sept. 1939, in PRO HO 213/452, on the domestics.

22 For statistics, see PRO HO 213/459 and Lafitte, *The Internment*, pp. 36–9, 62–3; Michael Marrus and Robert Paxton, *Vichy France and the Jews* (Schocken Books, New York, 1983), p. 65.

23 See PRO HO 283/10/3A and Eugen Spier, *The Protecting Power* (Skeffington & Son, London, 1951), for the early internments of Jewish refugees by the security forces.

24 Peake to Assheton, 12 Jan. 1940, and Assheton to Peake, 29 Jan. 1940, in PRO HO 213/503.

25 M-O A: FR 84, 26 Apr. 1940, and FR 107, for the change in public mood a month later. The literature on alien internment has grown recently: see, particularly, Ronald Stent, *A Bespattered Page? The Internment of 'His Majesty's Most Loyal Enemy Aliens'* (Deutch, London, 1980); Peter and Leni Gillman, *'Collar the Lot!'*; Miriam Kochan, *Britain's Internees in the Second World War* (Macmillan, London, 1983); and David Cesarani and Tony Kushner (eds), *The Internment of Aliens in Twentieth Century Britain* (Frank Cass, London, 1993).

26 Anderson in *Hansard*, 354, col. 367, 4 Sept. 1939; Howard Brotz, 'The Position of the Jews in English Society', *Jewish Journal of Sociology*, 1, no. 1 (1959), p. 101; for the criticism of the government, probably by the British Zionist Harry Sacher, see correspondence between S. Adler-Rudel of Bloomsbury House and Anthony de Rothschild 1940, in RAL XI/35/19, and correspondence between Joseph Cohen and Sacher, in Cohen papers, A 173/63, CZA.

27 For further information on this issue, see Tony Kushner, 'Clubland, Cricket Tests and Alien Internment, 1939–1940', in Cesarani and Kushner, *The Internment of Aliens*, pp. 79–101; Nevile Bland, 14 May 1940, in PRO FO 371/25189 W7984.

28 The role of secret government was highlighted by Peter and Leni Gillman, *'Collar the Lot!'*, and is also covered extensively in Cesarani and Kushner, *The Internment of Aliens*, and in F. Hinsley and and C. Simkins, *British Intelligence in the Second World War*, vol. 4 *Security and Counter-Intelligence* (HMSO, London, 1990), chapter 3.

29 Louise Burletson, 'The State, Internment and Public Criticism in the Second World War', in Cesarani and Kushner, *The Internment of Aliens*, p. 115; Lieutenant-Colonel W. Scott's report on *The Dunera*, quoted by Peter and Leni Gillman, *'Collar the Lot!'*, p. 254.

30 For the refusal to criticize government policy, see IWM tape no. 4469 and Cohen to Sacher, 5 Aug. 1940, in Joseph Cohen papers, A 173/63, CZA.

31 *Daily Herald*, 17 May 1940; Orwell in *Partisan Review*, Mar.–Apr. 1942.

32 *Daily Herald*, 4 July 1940; International Committee minutes, 23 July 1940, in TUC archive, Box 1854, Modern Record Centre, University of Warwick.

33 For the bias against women, see the Eleanor Rathbone papers, XIV/2/17/20, ULA; domestic statistics, in minutes of the Manchester Jewish Refugee Committee, June 1943, Manchester Central Reference Library; for the decline in the fear of invasion, see Home Intelligence report of 23 July 1940, in INF 1/264; International Committee minutes, 27 May 1941, Box 1854, TUC archive; Orwell in *Partisan Review*, Mar.–Apr. 1942.

34 Bishop Bell in *Hansard* (HC) 121, col. 365, 17 Dec. 1941.

35 Home Office briefing, 1941, in PRO HO 215/21, quoted by Burletson, 'The State', p. 109.

36 Poll quoted by Deborah Lipstadt, *Beyond Belief: The American Press & the Coming of the Holocaust 1933–1945* (Free Press, New York, 1986), pp. 126–7; William Leuchtenberg, *Franklin D. Roosevelt and the New Deal 1932–1940* (Harper & Row, New York, 1963), p. 300.

37 *Sunday Dispatch*, 14 Apr. 1940. For the growth in such conspiracy theories in the United States, see Lipstadt, *Beyond Belief*, chapter 6; Friedman, *No Haven for the Oppressed*, chapter 5; and Richard Breitman and Alan Kraut, *American Refugee Policy and European Jewry, 1933–1945* (Indiana University Press, Bloomington and Indianapolis, Ind., 1987), chapter 5 and p. 126.

38 Fred Israel (ed.), *The War Diary of Breckinridge Long: Selections from the Years 1939–1944* (University of Nebraska Press, Lincoln, Nebr., 1966), p. 114; Breitman and Kraut, *American Refugee Policy*, pp. 128, 138.

39 Wyman, *The Abandonment of the Jews*, p. 191; Breitman and Kraut, *American Refugee Policy*, p. 145.

40 For his sympathy and its restraints, see Israel (ed.), *The War Diary*, p. 128 (9 Sept. 1940) and p. 283 (29 Sept. 1942).

41 Ibid., p. 307 (20 Apr. 1943) and pp. 225–6 (28 Nov. 1941) for his list of undesirables; *American Federationist*, May 1944 for Long's speech to the AFL; and, for his help to individuals, see Breitman and Kraut, *American Refugee Policy*, pp. 129–30, 138.

42 For the American labour movement and the war in general, see Robert Zieger, *American Workers, American Unions, 1920–1985* (John Hopkins University Press, Baltimore, Md, 1986), chapter 3; Executive Council report, *Report of the Proceedings of the Sixtieth Annual Convention of the AFL* (Judd & Detweiller, Washington, DC, 1940), pp. 87–8; *Proceedings of the Fourth Constitutional*

Convention of the Congress of Industrial Organizations (CIO, Washington, DC, 1941), p. 107; *Report of the Proceedings of the Sixty-First Annual Convention of the AFL* (Judd & Detweiller, Washington, DC, 1941), p. 671.

43 For immigration statistics, see Michael Marrus, *The Unwanted: European Refugees in the Twentieth Century* (Oxford University Press, New York, 1985), p. 206. For criticism of American Jewish leadership in 1942, see Wyman, *The Abandonment of the Jews*, p. 25.

44 *Report of the Proceedings of the Sixtieth Annual Convention of the AFL*, pp. 401–2; *Proceedings of the Third Constitutional Convention of the Congress of Industrial Organizations* (CIO, Washington, DC, 1940), p. 261.

45 David Dubinsky and A. H. Raskin, *David Dubinsky: A Life With Labor* (Simon and Schuster, New York, 1977), pp. 248–9; Gail Malmgreen, 'Labor and the Holocaust: The Jewish Labor Committee and the Anti-Nazi Struggle', *Labor's Heritage*, Oct. 1991, p. 24; Seymour Finger (ed.), *American Jewry During the Holocaust* (Holmes & Meier, 1984), p. 35, and David Kranzler's contribution on the Jewish Labor Committee in the same volume. See also Kenneth Waltzer, 'American Jewish Labor and Aid to Polish Jews during the Holocaust', a paper presented at United States Holocaust Memorial Council conference, March 1987, referred to by Malmgreen, loc. cit., note 13.

46 *Report of the Proceedings of the Sixtieth Annual Convention of the AFL*, pp. 9, 89.

47 There was criticism of the JLC's close relationship with the AFL in the war – see Malmgreen, 'Labour and the Holocaust', p. 25. For more general comments on American labour, see Sidney Kalman, 'Limits of Consensus: Unions and the Holocaust', *American Jewish History*, 79 (Spring 1990), pp. 314–35. *Proceedings of the Fourth Constitutional Convention of the Congress of Industrial Organizations*, p. 107.

48 Hans Eysenck, *Rebel With A Cause* (W. H. Allen, London, 1990), pp. 82–3; George Mikes, preface to *How to Be an Alien* (1946), reprinted in *idem, How to be a Brit* (Penguin, Harmondsworth, 1987), p. 18.

49 Stephen Spender, 'Waiting for the bombers', *The Weekend Guardian*, 11–12 Feb. 1989.

50 Ernst Lowenthal, 'By Our Own Efforts', *AJR Information*, Oct. 1962. In Dec. 1942, a group of Jewish refugees still interned in the Isle of Man threatened to go on hunger strike after hearing about the extermination of the Jews. They wished to be released so that they could join the war effort. H. Ralph of the Metropolitan Police wrote to Mr Kirk of the Home Office, 20 Dec. 1942, opposing their suggestion: 'Since the publication of the Polish note they have been labouring their desire to become good citizens etc but I imagine it to be an attempt to get loose. Casually looking down the names it is noticeable that some have little or no connection with continental Jewry.' See PRO HO 215/126. For Selfhelp during the war, see Genizi, 'Non-Sectarian Organizations', p. 214. Tony Kushner, *The Persistence of Prejudice: Antisemitism In British Society During the Second World War* (Manchester University Press, Manchester, 1989), pp. 119–22.

51 See the voluminous correspondence in the Rathbone papers, XIV/2/17, ULA and Schonfeld papers, 228, 240 and 593, SUA; Orwell in *Partisan Review*, Mar.–Apr. 1941.

52 Simpson to Parkes, 15 July 1941, Parkes papers, 16/715, SUA; Dean of St Paul's, correspondence on Jewish–Christian cooperation, in BDA B5/4/3.

53 Lewison to Bell, 3 Nov. 1941, in Parkes papers, 16/51, SUA; W. W. Simpson, 'History of the International Council of Christians and Jews' (unpublished MS),

chapter 3, p. 17, Simpson papers, SUA; *idem*, 'Jewish–Christian Relations since the Inception of the Council of Christians and Jews', *Transactions of the Jewish Historical Society of England*, 28 (1981–2), p. 91.

54 Minutes of the conference can be found in the Parkes papers, SUA and BDA C15/3/21.

55 See the minutes of the CCJ, 1942–1945, in CCJ papers, 2/1 and 2, SUA; Marcus Braybrooke, *Children of One God: a History of the Council of Christians and Jews* (Frank Cass, London, 1991), p. 11.

56 'Aims of the Council', 20 Mar. 1942, CCJ council minutes, CCJ papers, 2/1, SUA; 'Model Resolution', Executive Committee minutes, 13 Apr. 1942, CCJ papers, 2/1, SUA.

57 M-O A: DR 1230, 1182, June 1939; *Christian News-Letter*, 7 May and 11 June 1941.

58 *Jewish Chronicle*, 17 Dec. 1941, for the response to Simpson's broadcast; Tony Kushner, 'James Parkes, The Jews, and Conversionism: A Model for Multi-Cultural Britain?', in Diana Wood (ed.), *Christianity and Judaism* (Blackwell, Oxford, 1992), pp. 451–61 [*Studies in Church History*, 29].

59 CCJ executive minutes, 3 Dec. 1942, CCJ papers, 2/1, SUA; meeting with Foreign Office, PRO FO 371/32682 W17401; Brodetsky to Greenberg, 8 Dec. 1942, in Greenberg papers, 110/4, SUA.

60 For the Christian–Jewish delegation including Temple, see PRO FO 371/32681 W14673 and Namier to Crozier, Crozier papers, B/N8A/134, University of Manchester archive (UMA); Temple in *Hansard*, 125, cols 21–4, 11 Nov. 1942. For later Christian disgust at Morrison and others over the French children, see, for example, Sir Neill Malcolm, letter to *The Times*, 22 Dec. 1942.

61 Executive Committee of the Jewish Agency for Palestine, 3 and 7 Dec. 1942, Z4/302/26, CZA; see also memorandum of the World Jewish Congress, 1/2 Dec. 1942, in C2/460, CZA.

62 A. Walker minute, 28 Dec. 1942, PRO FO 371/32668 W17422; Law minute, 7 May 1943, PRO FO 371/42751 W6933.

63 Executive minutes, 4 Mar. 1943, in CCJ papers, 2/2, SUA; the nineteenth meeting of its Executive meeting, 6 May 1943, was devoted to the issue of domestic antisemitism, CCJ papers 2/2.

64 Thomas Moloney, *Westminster, Whitehall and The Vatican: The Role of Cardinal Hinsley, 1935–43* (Burns, Oates & Co, Tunbridge Wells, 1985), pp. 174–5. For Christian doubt, see *Catholic Herald*, 18 Sept. and 24 Dec. 1942; *Catholic Times*, 24 Dec. 1942. For similar denial of the Holocaust in the United States, see Lipstadt, *Beyond Belief*, pp. 184–5, on *The Christian Century* in 1942.

65 Silverman, 29 June 1942, C2/409, CZA.

66 Press releases in ibid. For contacts with the *Manchester Guardian*, see Manchester Guardian archive, 223/5 UMA and correspondence between Lewis Namier and W. Crozier, the editor of the *Manchester Guardian*, B/N8A, Manchester Guardian archive.

67 Riegner to Silverman and Easterman, 3 Oct. 1942, and memorandum, Dec. 1942, in C2/540, CZA.

68 Memorandum, Dec. 1942, loc. cit., and, for the assimilation of this information in Whitehall, see PRO FO 371/30923 C11923 and FO 371/30917 C7853. Parkes, undated letter (but Nov. 1942) to Greenberg, Leftwich and Helpern, in Greenberg papers, 110/2, SUA.

69 British section memorandum, 4 Dec. 1942, and memorandum, Dec. 1942, in C2/540, CZA.

70 British section, notes on Allied Declaration, 21 Jan. 1943, in C2/459, CZA.

71 For accusations of Polish army antisemitism, see *Jewish Chronicle*, 16 Aug. 1940, PRO FO 371/24481 C5143, and National Council for Civil Liberties records, 310/8, University of Hull archive.

72 These issues are dealt with thoroughly by David Engel, *In the Shadow of Auschwitz: The Polish Government-in-Exile and the Jews, 1939–1942* (University of North Carolina Press, Chapel Hill, NC, 1987), chapters 3–5 (esp. p. 113).

73 Mark Levene, *War, Jews, and the New Europe: The Diplomacy of Lucien Wolf, 1914–19* (Littman Library, Oxford, 1992) deals brilliantly with the belief in Jewish power in international politics in World War I. For the uneven coverage in the Polish government in exile's English language newspaper, see *Polish Fortnightly Review*, 15 Mar.; ibid., 1 and 15 July 1942 for an absence of Jewish victims, and 1 Dec. 1942 for emphasis on Jewish suffering. Engel, *In the Shadow of Auschwitz*, p. 183.

74 Engel, *In the Shadow of Auschwitz*, p. 200. Sir Herbert Emerson, one of the leading figures in the Inter-Governmental Committee on Refugees, wrote in a memorandum of 14 Dec. 1942, in PRO FO 371/32682 W17272, that now 'There can be no doubt that it is the policy of Germany literally to exterminate all Jews in Germany and Austria and the occupied countries in Europe, not only German and Austrians, but Jews of all nationality'.

75 Easterman to Gestetner, 29 Dec. 1942, and Gestetner to Easterman, 18 Dec. 1942, in C2/459, CZA.

76 *Hansard* (HC), 385, cols 2082–89, 17 Dec. 1942.

77 Rathbone, 'Speech Notes on the Jewish Question', Rathbone papers, XIV/3/85, ULA.

78 Randall, note of 9 Sept. 1942, in PRO FO 371/32683.

79 Randall to the Cabinet Committee on Refugee Problems, 29 Dec. 1942, PRO FO 371/36651 W2069; the minutes and correspondence of this new Cabinet Committee are in PRO CAB 95/15.

6 BRITAIN, THE UNITED STATES AND THE HOLOCAUST,
1943 TO 1945

1 Christopher Browning, *The Path to Genocide: Essays on Launching the Final Solution* (Cambridge University Press, Cambridge, 1992), p. 169; Leni Yahil, *The Holocaust: The Fate of European Jewry* (Oxford University Press, New York, 1991), chapter 15.

2 Eleanor Rathbone, 'Speech Notes on the Jewish Question', Dec. 1942, Rathbone papers, XIV/3/85, University of Liverpool archive (ULA). Raul Hilberg, *The Destruction of the European Jews*, vol. 3 (revised and definitive edition, Holmes & Meier, New York, 1985), p. 1120, provides estimates of Jewish deaths by year. Suggesting a final total of 5.1 million, Hilberg posits that 2.7 million Jews were killed in 1942, giving a cumulative figure of 3.9 million dead by 1 Jan. 1943.

3 Rathbone, 'Speech Notes on the Jewish Question'. See, for example, Sir Andrew McFadyean's letter to the *Daily Telegraph*, 6 Jan. 1943, which dismissed the possibility of antisemitism in Britain being generated if Jewish children had been admitted from Vichy France as 'a slander on the British people'.

4 The debate in the House of Commons would be delayed until 19 May 1943. A

debate in the House of Lords took place on 23 Mar. 1943. Rathbone, 'Speech Notes on the Jewish Question', and letter to *News Chronicle*, 17 Dec. 1942.

5 For a brilliant account of his career, see Ruth Dudley Edwards, *Victor Gollancz: A Biography* (Gollancz, London, 1987). Gollancz to Lord Bearsted, 4 Apr. 1938, Gollancz papers 157/3/JE/i/28i–ii, Modern Record Centre, University of Warwick (MRC).

6 Victor Gollancz, *"Nowhere to Lay Their Heads": The Jewish Tragedy in Europe and its Solution* (Gollancz, London, 1945); *idem*, *What Buchenwald really means* (Gollancz, London, 1945); and *idem*, *Leaving them to their fate: the ethics of starvation* (Gollancz, London, 1946). Karski's meeting with Gollancz and others is described in his testimony in Brewster Chamberlin and Marcia Feldman (eds), *The Liberation of the Nazi Concentration Camps; Eyewitnesses of the Liberators* (United States Memorial Council, Washington DC, 1987), p. 179. Victor Gollancz, *Let My People Go* (Gollancz, London, 1942), p. 2.

7 Gollancz, *Let My People Go*, pp. 2–33; eventually 250,000 were sold. See Edwards, *Victor Gollancz*, p. 375, PRO FO 371/36651, M-O A: D3215, 30 Jan. 1943, D5378, 4 Mar. 1943, and DR3207, Mar. 1943, for an indication of public concern generated by the pamphlet.

8 PRO CAB 95/15, Foreign Office to American Chargé d'Affaires, 19 Feb. 1943; see also PRO FO 371/36651 W2069 and FO 371/36694 W416 for Foreign Office concern. For the Committee of Rescue, see its records in Schonfeld papers, 153/1, Southampton University archive (SUA).

9 For the Burlington House meeting, see E1/74, Board of Deputies of British Jews archive (BDA); Schonfeld's letters and replies are in Schonfeld papers, 153/1, SUA. A meeting of the parliamentary group organized by Schonfeld took place on 27 Jan. 1943 – see *The Times*, 28 Jan. 1943, for a report.

10 Thus, while Eleanor Rathbone was a prominent member of the Burlington House group, she does not appear to have been involved in Schonfeld's activities until later. Schonfeld has been described by his biographer as an 'independent operator' (see the contribution of Marcus Retter in David Kranzler and Gertrude Hirschler (eds), *Solomon Schonfeld: His Page in History* (Judaica Press, New York, 1982), p. 44) and this led to conflict with those in the Board of Deputies of British Jews and mainstream Zionist organizations. See, for example, the heated exchange between Schonfeld and Brodetsky, *Jewish Chronicle*, 29 Jan. and 5 Feb. 1943. The revisionist Zionist *Jewish Standard*, 29 Jan. 1943, sided with Schonfeld. David Kranzler, *Thy Brother's Blood: The Orthodox Jewish Response During the Holocaust* (Menorah Publications, New York, 1987), pp. 182–3, provides a pro-Schonfeld account of this episode. It should be added that Schonfeld's manner of operation created many problems for Jewish organizations trying to coordinate activities in their dealings with the British government.

11 75th Trades Union Congress, *Report* (TUC, London, 1943), pp. 92–3; National Council of Labour minutes, 28 Jan. 1943, TUC archive, MRC; for Church concern at a local level, see Parkes papers, 15/22 file 3, SUA.

12 Memorandum to the American Chargé d'Affaires, 19 Feb. 1943, in PRO CAB 95/15.

13 Minutes of the meeting, 9 Mar. 1943, and Gollancz to Executive Committee, 24 Mar. 1943, in Parkes papers, 15/057 file 1.

14 Schonfeld to Eden, 7 Feb. 1943. Schonfeld wrote to Mr F. Watkins, MP, 10 Feb. 1943, explaining that the motion had been watered down and that he was concerned 'to prevent its handling being left to people who would wish to sidetrack

it into controversial lines' (presumably over entry to Palestine). Both in Schonfeld papers, 153/1, file 2, SUA.

15 Notices for the motion were, for example, given on 10 and 16 Feb. 1943. Arthur Greenwood called the Prime Minister's attention to the motion without success. See *Hansard* (HC) cols 345–6, 1 Apr. 1943; Schonfeld to *The Times*, 2 Apr. 1943. The letter was not published although *The Times* was running a correspondence on refugees *in* Britain at this point.

16 See Schonfeld, letter to Isaac Wolfson, 18 Mar. 1943, calling for financial support for those given visas, in Schonfeld papers, 153/1, file 2, SUA.

17 For the delay, see 4th meeting of the Cabinet Committee on Refugees, 19 Feb. 1943, in PRO CAB 95/15; for American delay see David Wyman, *The Abandonment of the Jews: America and the Holocaust 1941–1945* (Pantheon, New York, 1985), chapter 6, and Henry Feingold, *The Politics of Rescue: The Roosevelt Administration and the Holocaust, 1938–1945* (Holocaust Library, New York, 1980), chapter 7.

18 Gollancz to Executive Committee of the National Committee, 24 Mar. 1943, and in general meeting, 25 Mar. 1943, in Parkes papers, 15/057, file 1, SUA; for the cancelled meetings, see Wyman, *The Abandonment*, p. 87; *New York Times*, 8 and 16 Feb. 1943; M. Penkower, 'In Dramatic Dissent: The Bergson Boys', *American Jewish History*, 70 (Mar. 1981), pp. 281–309; 'Instructions for Organizing Public Meetings', Joint Emergency Committee on European Jewish Affairs, Mar. 1943, reproduced in David Wyman (ed.), *America and the Holocaust*, vol. 2 *The Struggle for Rescue Action* (Garland Press, New York, 1990), pp. 218–9.

19 Department of State Visa Department, confidential memorandum, 7 May 1943, reproduced in Wyman (ed.), *America and the Holocaust*, vol. 2, p. 266; compare Gollancz, *Let My People Go*, *passim*, with the proposals of the Joint Emergency Committee outlined in Wyman, *The Abandonment*, pp. 88–9.

20 For the British government and Bermuda, see PRO FO 371/36725 W6785 and CAB 65/34 WM (43), 10 May 1943. For the choice of Bermuda, see Wyman, *The Abandonment*, p. 108. See the diary of Major-General L. A. Hawes, 26 Feb. 1941, Imperial War Museum, 87/41/2, for Weizmann's earlier concern.

21 PRO CAB 66/34 WM (43), 10 May 1943. On the revival of the IGC, see Tommie Sjoberg, *The Powers and the Persecuted: The Refugee Problem and the Intergovernmental Committee on Refugees* (Lund University Press, Lund, 1991), chapter 4.

22 Eleanor Rathbone, *Rescue the Perishing* (National Committee for Rescue from Nazi Terror, London, 1943), p. 25; Rathbone in *Hansard* (HC) 389, cols 1137–8, 1143.

23 See particularly the comments of Sir A. Lambert Ward in *Hansard* (HC) cols 1145–9, 19 May 1943; Eden, loc. cit., col. 1202.

24 Rathbone to Executive Committee, 28 June 1943, in Parkes papers, 15/057, file 3, SUA.

25 Rathbone, *Rescue the Perishing*, pp. 5–7; meeting 7 Jan. 1943, in E1/74, BDA; Rathbone to Executive Committee, 28 June 1943, in Parkes papers, 15/057, file 3. See PRO FO 371/36662 for the government's critical response to the new pamphlet.

26 Law memorandum, 3 Sept. 1943, and Eden note, 4 Sept. 1943, in PRO FO 371/36666 W12841.

27 Law memorandum, ibid.

28 Martin Gilbert, *Auschwitz and the Allies* (Michael Joseph, London, 1981), pp. 162–8, and Dalia Ofer, *Escaping the Holocaust: Illegal Immigration to the Land*

of Israel, 1939–1944 (Oxford University Press, New York, 1990), chapter 12; for Schonfeld's success in getting visas, see the minutes of the Chief Rabbi's Emergency Council (CREC), 28 June 1943, in Schonfeld papers, 576/1, SUA; Law, 3 Sept. 1943, in PRO FO 371/36666 W12841.

29 For the growing support of church groups in the United States during 1943, see documents 103–7 in Wyman (ed.), *America and the Holocaust*, vol. 2, pp. 293–305; for labour, see *CIO News*, 8 Mar., 6 Dec. 1943; *Final Proceedings of the Sixth Constitutional Convention of the Congress of Industrial Organizations* (CIO, Washington, DC, 1943), pp. 4–5, 144–50, 338; *Report of the Proceedings of the Sixty-Third Annual Convention of the AFL* (Judd & Detweiller, Washington, DC, 1943), pp. 147–8, 358–64. See Wyman, *The Abandonment*, chapter 8 for the Emergency Committee and continuing State Department resistance.

30 Edwards, *Victor Gollancz*, pp. 378–80. Gollancz was much criticized for his opposition to the Eichmann Trial in 1961 and at this stage pointed out the effort and trauma he had suffered from trying to imagine the persecution of the Jews when campaigning in 1943. See the correspondence in Gollancz papers, 157/3/LI/AE, MRC; Rathbone, *Rescue the Perishing*, p. 8. In March 1943, the National Committee sponsored a Gallup poll to prove popular support for rescue measures – 78 per cent responded positively. See *News Chronicle*, 26 Mar. 1943.

31 Medlicott to Schonfeld, Feb. 1943, in Schonfeld papers, 153/1, file 2, SUA.

32 Memorandum, 23 Nov. 1943, on campaign against antisemitism, Parkes papers, 15/057, file 3, SUA. Pamphlets produced included Sir Norman Angell, *Have We Room for the Refugees?* (National Committee, London, 1944) and Eleanor Rathbone, *Falsehoods and Facts about the Jews* (National Committee, London, 1944). Gollancz believed that the latter was so apologetic that it would actually generate antisemitism itself. See Edwards, *Victor Gollancz*, pp. 390–1.

For the revival of their public campaign, see General Meeting, 10 Feb. 1944, in Parkes papers, 15/057, file 2, and *News from Hitler's Europe*, 22 Feb. 1944. Their frustration with the government is recorded in a Rathbone memorandum, 9 Aug. 1943, in PRO FO 371/36665.

33 Schwartzbart in National Council Minutes of the World Jewish Congress, British Section, 13 Dec. 1943, C2/279, Central Zionist archives; *Continuing Terror* (National Committee, London, 1944); for its lack of impact, see 10 May 1944 report in C11/7/3d/6, BDA.

34 Meeting with Rogers, 1 Sept. 1943, in Parkes papers 15/057, file 3, and decision not to exchange, 4 Nov. 1943, 15/057, file 2, SUA. See PRO CAB 95/15 throughout 1943 for British unease concerning the American government.

35 Charles Stember et al., *Jews in the Mind of America* (Basic Books, New York, 1966), pp. 79–80, 121. M-O A: FR 1948 summarizes British findings in 1941 and 1943. See *Sydney Jewish News*, 5 May 1944, for its last war survey on this topic. The analysis of the 1943 material is from M-O A: DR Mar. 1943, 'Foreigners'. PRO INF 1/292, 18–25 July 1944. *Time*, 10 Jan. 1944, for anti-Jewish violence in the United States.

36 For the restrictionist lobby in Congress, see Sjoberg, *The Powers and the Persecuted*, chapter 3. Many MPs were away by 1943, thus Schonfeld managed to obtain the support of the vast majority of the House of Commons. See the correspondence in Schonfeld papers, 153/1, SUA. The blatancy of the stalling tactics of the State Department enabled the successful Treasury revolt in late 1943/early 1944.

37 This campaign is dealt with by Wyman, *The Abandonment*, chapter 11. The two versions of the document are reproduced by Michael Mashberg, 'Documents

Concerning the American State Department and the Stateless European Jews, 1942–1944', *Jewish Social Studies*, 39 (1977), pp. 163–179. Morgenthau's diary entries for this period are also reproduced in Seymour Maxwell Finger (ed.), *American Jewry During the Holocaust* (Holmes & Meier, New York, 1984), appendix 6, item 5.

38 The Presidential order is reproduced by Mashberg, 'Documents', pp. 179–80. For a highly critical assessment of the WRB, see M. Penkower, *The Jews Were Expendable: Free World Diplomacy and the Holocaust* (University of Illinois Press, Urbana and Chicago, Ill., 1983), chapter 5. Wyman, *The Abandonment*, part IV, and Feingold, *The Politics of Rescue*, chapter 9, see its limited success as reinforcing the wasted opportunities before 1944. The most positive account of the WRB is that by Richard Breitman and Alan Kraut, *American Refugee Policy and European Jewry, 1933–1945* (Indiana University Press, Bloomington and Indianapolis, Ind., 1987), chapters 9 and 10.

39 Yehuda Bauer, *American Jewry and the Holocaust: The American Jewish Joint Distribution Committee, 1939–1945* (Wayne State University Press, Detroit, Mich., 1981), chapter 17 (esp. p. 407).

40 For its tiny budget, see memorandum, Nov. 1943, in E3/536, file 1, BDA; CREC minutes, 20 June 1944, in Schonfeld papers, 576/1, SUA.

41 Rosette to Greenberg, 23 Feb. 1944, in Greenberg papers, 110/2, SUA.

42 For Palestinian Jewish attacks on British Jewry, see Dina Porat, *The Blue and the Yellow Stars of David: The Zionist Leadership in Palestine and the Holocaust, 1939–1945* (Harvard University Press, Cambridge, Mass., 1990), pp. 105–6. The impact of the earlier commitment is stressed in the memorandum of Nov. 1943 referred to in note 40. For the government's descriptions of the Board of Deputies, see comments of Frank Roberts, 24 Apr. 1943, in PRO FO 371/36658 W5550, and 12 Oct. 1944, in FO 371/39454 C14201.

43 CCJ Executive Minutes, 28 Oct. 1943, CCJ 2/2, SUA. The support of American labour and church groups is covered in note 29 above. There is no indication of support for rescue measures from British labour after Jan. 1943.

44 Eden to the Cabinet Committee, 7 Feb. 1944, JR (44) 1, and 10 Mar. 1944, JR (44) 4, in PRO CAB 95/15.

45 Randolph Braham, 'The Uniqueness of the Holocaust in Hungary', in Randolph Braham and Bela Vago (eds), *The Holocaust in Hungary Forty Years Later* (City University of New York Press, New York, 1985), pp. 177, 187.

46 Eden, 10 Mar. 1944, JR (44) 4, in PRO CAB 95/15.

47 For the credit scheme, see 9th meeting of the Cabinet Committee, 14 Mar. 1944, in PRO CAB 95/15. For Saly Mayer's operations in Switzerland, see Yehuda Bauer, 'The Negotiations Between Saly Mayer and the Representatives of the SS in 1944–1945', in Y. Gutman and E. Zuroff (eds), *Rescue Attempts During the Holocaust* (Yad Vashem, Jerusalem, 1977), pp. 5–45.

48 See letter from Washington to the Ministry of Economic Warfare, 12 Mar. 1944, highlighting American concern, in JR 44 (7), 15 Mar. 1944. Eden, in JR 44 (16), 29 June 1944, in PRO CAB 95/15. Sir Herbert Emerson referred to the Board's 'extravagant hopes' in JR 44 (12), 16 May 1944. For the government reports stressing British action, see JR 44 (16), 16 June 1944, JR 44 (23), 29 Sept. 1944, and JR 45 (1), 16 Jan. 1945, all in PRO CAB 95/15.

49 Randall on Brandt proposal, in 2nd meeting of Cabinet Committee, PRO CAB 95/15. Foreign Office telegram to Washington, in PRO PREM 4/51/10/1394–5. Emerson reported that given the pressure on the American government he was 'surprised that the Board had been able to agree to our proposal to refuse direct

negotiations through the agency of Brandt', in 3rd meeting of the Cabinet Committee, 13 July 1944, in PRO CAB 95/15.

50 Eden memorandum on the Horthy offer, JR 44 (21), 3 Aug. 1944. For fears of a German-inspired flood of Jewish refugees, see Eden to Churchill, 14 Aug. 1944, in PRO FO 371/42814 WR 682 and CAB 65/43 WM 44 (104), 9 Aug. 1944. For the American response, see Wyman, *The Abandonment*, pp. 238–9. Rathbone to Eden, 9 Aug. 1944, in PRO FO 371/42815 WR 752 and notes of the meeting of the National Committee, 2 Aug. 1944, in E3/536, file 1, BDA, where their immense frustration at government inaction on the Horthy offer was expressed. For the resumption of deportations, see Randolph Braham, *The Politics of Genocide: The Holocaust in Hungary*, vol. 2 (Columbia University Press, New York, 1981), pp. 791–7.

51 Mason, 20 Sept., and Hall, 21 Sept. 1944, in PRO FO 371/42852.

52 Eden note on the WRB, JR 44 (1), 7 Feb. 1944, in PRO CAB 95/15; *Hansard* (HC) 396, cols 1740–2, 9 Feb. 1944.

53 *Hansard* (HC) 397, cols 1458–70, 1492–4, 1 Mar. 1944; Mashberg, 'Documents', pp. 165–7.

54 *Hansard* (HC) 397, cols 1458–70, 1492–4, 1 Mar. 1944; *News from Hitler's Europe*, 20 June 1944. See also the General Meeting of the National Committee, 10 Feb. 1944, where it was acknowledged that 'it was impossible to exaggerate the importance of the step taken by President Roosevelt, and of the very wide powers vested in the Board', in Parkes papers, 15/057, file 2. *The Times*, 10 Apr. 1944.

55 Emerson memorandum on the Board, JR 44 (12), 16 May 1944, in PRO CAB 95/15; Treasury official, 1 May 1944, quoted by Louise London, 'British Immigration Control Procedures and Jewish Refugees, 1933–1949' (unpublished paper, University of Bristol History Research Seminar, Feb. 1990). I am grateful to Dr London for permission to use this quote. For the activists' sense of impotence, see Nigel Nicolson (ed.), *Harold Nicolson: Diaries and Letters 1939–1945* (Collins, London, 1967), p. 344; Mary Stocks, *Eleanor Rathbone* (Gollancz, London, 1949), p. 300; and James Parkes, *Voyage of Discoveries* (Gollancz, London, 1969), p. 180. For government irritation, see Dew memorandum, 1 Sept. 1944, in PRO FO 371/42817 WR 993.

56 Archbishop of Canterbury in delegation of 26 July 1944, in PRO 371/42817 WR 993; PRO INF 1/292 18–25 July 1944; for deflection of the delegation, see PRO FO 371/42814 WR 680; Gilbert, *Auschwitz and the Allies*, pp. 295, 327 and 333, and Ofer, *Escaping the Holocaust*, chapters 14 and 15, for small-scale rescue to Palestine in 1944.

57 For the US Treasury revolt, see Breitman and Kraut, *The Politics of Rescue*, chapter 9. Louise London is presently working on an account of British immigration control procedures which will cover the Treasury Department in the 1930s and World War II.

58 R. Braham, *The Politics of Genocide*, vol. 2, p. 1096; Breitman and Kraut, *The Politics of Rescue*, introduction and p. 181; Bernard Wasserstein, *Britain and the Jews of Europe, 1939–1945* (Oxford University Press, Oxford, 1979), conclusion, for the stress on indifference; for the accusation of antisemitism, see Bela Vago, 'The British Government and the Fate of Hungarian Jewry in 1944', in *Rescue Attempts During the Holocaust*, p. 233.

59 Foreign Office telegram to Washington, 3 June 1944, in PRO PREM 4/51/10/1394–5. It must be suggested that for both British and American officials, the Nazi persecution of the Jews was unwelcome, not just for humanitarian

reasons but because it created difficulties that made already complex issues even harder.

60 L. Lochner (ed.), *The Goebbel's Diaries* (Hamish Hamilton, London, 1948), p. 181; R. Ainsztein, 'The Failure of the West', *The Jewish Quarterly*, 14 (Winter 1966/1967), p. 20. Thus, even J. S. Bennett, an undoubted antisemite in the Foreign Office, was not incapable of sympathy to the Jewish plight – see Wasserstein, *Britain and the Jews*, p. 291.

61 Memorandum on Jews and propaganda, 10 Aug. 1939, in PRO INF 1/770; Butler minute, 19 Feb. 1943, in PRO FO 371/34362 C1741; Chief Rabbi's request and response to it, in PRO FO 371/42811 WR 457.

62 For the change of title in the Cabinet Committee, see Eden note, in JR 43 (4), 9 Jan. 1943; for opposition to Jewish representation at Bermuda, see Eden, 15 Apr. 1943, in PRO FO 371/36659 W 5962; for Winterton, see *Jewish Chronicle*, 27 Nov. 1946, and K. Young (ed.), *The Diaries of Sir Robert Bruce Lockhart 1939–65* (Macmillan, London, 1980), p. 373, entry of 4 Dec. 1944.

63 For the 'Jewish goals' of the WRB, see 2nd meeting of the Cabinet Committee, 31 May 1944, in PRO CAB 95/15; Law in *Hansard* (HC) 397, cols 1493–4, 1 Mar. 1944.

64 Sharon Lowenstein, *Token Refuge: The Story of the Jewish Refugee Shelter at Oswego, 1944–1946* (Indiana University Press, Bloomington, Ind., 1986); for concern in 1944/1945 to remove the refugees in Britain after the war, see PRO HO 213/1009.

65 Schwartzbart diaries, 29 Jan. 1945, in M2/775, Yad Vashem Institute archives; for the high death rate of the National Committee, see its *News from Hitler's Europe*, 3 July 1945; Stocks, *Eleanor Rathbone, passim*.

7 LIBERAL CULTURE AND THE POST-WAR CONFRONTATION WITH THE HOLOCAUST

1 British and other medical teams tried valiantly to save the lives of many who were beyond rescue. The Imperial War Museum and the Wellcome Institute, London, have materials relating to the medical relief of the camps. This subject will form part of a PhD study by Joanne Reilly, 'Britain and Belsen', at the University of Southampton. For a summary of literature on survivors and its bias towards psychiatry and psychology, see William Helmreich, 'The Impact of Holocaust Survivors on American Society: A Socio-Cultural Portrait', *Judaism*, 39 (Winter 1990), pp. 14–16, and, more generally, Anton Gill, *The Journey Back From Hell: Conversations With Concentration Camp Survivors* (Grafton Books, London, 1988). Rosensaft's testimony, in Brewster Chamberlin and Maria Feldman (eds), *The Liberation of the Nazi Concentration Camps 1945: Eyewitness Accounts of the Liberators* (United States Memorial Council, Washington, DC, 1987), pp. 152–4. Primo Levi, *The Drowned and the Saved* (Michael Joseph, London, 1988), p. 53, rejects any attempt to portray the camp liberations in a triumphalist manner.

2 James Parkes, *Voyage of Discoveries* (Gollancz, London, 1969), p. 180.

3 *Chronology of Principal Events, Consolidated Edition: Munich Agreement to*

Dec. 31, 1942 (Royal Institute of International Affairs, London, 1944), pp. 92, 115; *Chronology of Principal Events*, no. 18 (1 Apr.–30 June 1945), p. 7; *Chronology and Index of the Second World War, 1938–1945* (Royal Institute of International Affairs, London, 1947), pp. 48, 132, 159, 178, 276, 279, 322, 343, 345, 346, 350.

4 Henry Rousso, *The Vichy Syndrome: History and Memory in France Since 1944* (Harvard University Press, Cambridge, Mass., 1991 [originally published in French in 1987]), p. 1.

5 Ilan Avisar, *Screening the Holocaust: Cinema's Images of the Unimaginable* (Indiana University Press, Bloomington and Indianapolis, Ind., 1988), pp. 105–6.

6 For an overview of this subject, see Jon Bridgman, *The End of the Holocaust: The Liberation of the Camps* (Batsford, London, 1990); Eberhard Kolb, 'Bergen-Belsen, 1943–1945', in Yisrael Gutman and Avital Saf (eds), *The Nazi Concentration Camps* (Yad Vashem, Jerusalem, 1984), pp. 331–42.

7 *Buchenwald: The Report of a Parliamentary Delegation*, Cmd 6626 (HMSO, London, 1945), p. 7; *The Victory Book* (Odhams Press, London, 1945), pp. 308–9.

8 For Foreign Office discussion of Auschwitz in 1944, see PRO FO 371/42809 WR 218 and FO 371/39454 C 13824; for 1945, see PRO FO 371/51134 WR 89; Henderson minute, 28 May 1945, and Mason minute, 10 Feb. 1945, in PRO FO 371/51185.

9 'Buchenwald Camp', *Hansard* (HL), vol. 186, cols 61–97; general index to Nov. 1944–June 1945, *Hansard* (HC), vol. 412, p. 162; *Hansard* (HC), vol. 410, cols 2481–2, 16 May 1945.

10 M-O A: D 5390, 23 Apr. 1945; for explicit mention of the White Paper in connection to the spring 1945 liberations, see M-O A: TC 'Victory Celebrations', Box 1, File A.

11 For belief and disbelief during the war, see chapter 4 of this study; George Gallup, *The Gallup Poll: Public Opinion 1935–1971*, vol. 1 *1935–1948* (Random House, New York, 1972), pp. 472, 504.

12 M-O A: FR 2228, Apr. 1945.

13 M-O A: D 5110, 18 and 23 Apr. 1945; D 5205, 24 Apr. 1945; D 5261, 18 Apr. 1945.

14 Nicholas Pronay, 'Defeated Germany in British Newsreels: 1944–45', in *Hitler's Fall: The Newsreel Witness* (Croom Helm, London, 1988), pp. 42–44. Most of the liberation newsreels are kept by the Imperial War Museum.

15 M-O A: TC 'Victory Celebrations', Box 1, File A; M-O A: D 5110, 27 Apr. 1945.

16 M-O A: D 5270, 21 Apr. 1945; D 5275, 18 Apr. 1945.

17 M-O A: TC 'Victory Celebrations', Box 1, File A; M-O A: D 5358, 20 Apr. 1945.

18 M-O A: TC 'Politics', Box 15, File C has interviews with those visiting the *Daily Express* exhibition; M-O A: D 5270, 5 May 1945; M-O A: FR 2248; M-O A: D 5337, 21 Apr. 1945.

19 Churchill, in *Hansard* (HC), vol. 410, cols 389–90, 19 Apr. 1945; *Buchenwald: The Report of a Parliamentary Delegation*, p. 3.

20 Chuter Ede diaries, 19 and 20 Apr. 1945, in ms 59700, British Library, Department of Manuscripts; *Hansard* (HC) vol. 410, cols 392–3; *Buchenwald: The Report of a Parliamentary Delegation*, pp. 3, 7. For Mavis Tate, see *The Times*, 6 and 11 June 1947.

21 Bridgman, *The End of the Holocaust*, pp. 34, 111; Levi, *The Drowned and the Saved*, p. 52.

22 See PRO INF 1/636 for the official British liberation film; Pronay, 'Defeated Germany', pp. 42–4 for newsreels; and for radio reports and the absence of Jews as specific victims, see Desmond Hawkins and Donald Boyd (eds), *War Report: A Record of Dispatches Broadcast By the BBC's War Correspondents With the Allied Expeditionary Force 6 June 1944–5 May 1945* (Oxford University Press, London, 1946), pp. 394–404. The Rosensaft papers contain British newspaper cuttings relating to Belsen which have almost no references to Jews, in Yad Vashem archives, 070/83. For the United States, see K. R. M. Short, 'American Newsreels and the Collapse of Nazi Germany', in *Hitler's Fall*, pp. 11–12; *The Liberation of the Nazi Concentration Camps*, chapter 3, for American war correspondents; and Deborah Lipstadt, *The American Press & the Coming of the Holocaust 1933–1945* (Free Press, New York, 1986), chapter 11. For details on the population make-up of Belsen, see Bridgman, *The End of the Holocaust*, chapter 2.

23 Mitchell testimony, in *The Liberation of the Nazi Concentration Camps*, pp. 46–8; Dixey testimony, in Paul Kemp (ed.), *The Relief of Belsen: April 1945 Eye Witness Accounts* (Imperial War Museum, London, 1991), pp. 19–20; Joy Trindles, 'Until Belsen', in *More Poems of the Second World War: The Oasis Selection* (Dent & Sons, London, 1989), pp. 265–6.

24 Jonathan Dimbleby, *Richard Dimbleby: A Biography* (Hodder & Stoughton, London, 1975), chapter 5 (esp. pp. 188–94) which reproduces the text of the broadcast; Leonard Miall (ed.), *Richard Dimbleby Broadcaster, By His Colleagues* (BBC, London, 1966), pp. 41–44; Murrow broadcast, reproduced in *The Liberation of the Nazi Concentration Camps*, pp. 42–5. See also Lipstadt, *Beyond Belief*, p. 244, and Alexander Kendrick, *Prime Time: The Life of Edward R. Murrow* (Little, Brown, Boston, Mass., 1969).

25 *Buchenwald: The Report of a Parliamentary Delegation*, p. 7.

26 Archibald note, 21 Apr. 1945, and undated note from the Psychological Warfare Department of SHAEF, in PRO INF 1/636. For the film, see also the *Sunday Times*, 19 Feb. 1984; *Observer*, 8 Sept. 1985, and *Jewish Chronicle*, 13 Sept. 1985 and 14 Mar. 1986.

27 Pronay, 'Defeated Germany', pp. 44–5, refers to the change in attitude during the autumn of 1945. The film was eventually shown as part of a general documentary on the liberation of Belsen, 'A Painful Reminder', on Granada Television, 8 Sept. 1985; Hodson in *Time and Tide*, 19 May 1945; *Socialist Appeal*, Jan. 1943, Mid-Apr. 1945, Mid-May 1945.

28 Susan Sontag, *On Photography* (Penguin, Harmondsworth, 1979), pp. 19–20.

29 M-O A: FR 2228 and 2248; Dorothy Sheridan (ed.), *Among You Taking Notes . . . The Wartime Diary of Naomi Mitchison* (Gollancz, London, 1985), p. 319, diary entry for 23 Apr. 1945.

30 For suspicion of the government's motives, see the material in M-O A: FR 2248.

31 M-O A: TC 'Politics', Box 15, File C.

32 M-O A: D 5390, 23 Apr. 1945; M-O A: FR 2228.

33 M-O A: D 5447, 1 Aug. 1945; D 5239, 2 Sept. 1945.

34 M-O A: FR 2248.

35 Victor Gollancz, *What Buchenwald Really Means* (Gollancz, London, 1945); Low, in *Evening Standard*, 19 Apr. 1945.

36 M-O A: FR 2248; M-O A: D 5098, 22 May 1945; D 5205, 20 Apr. 1945, who reports a conversation in which there is agreement that the only solution was to exterminate the Germans. See also M-O A: FR 2263 and 2248.

37 K. Alexander to Rathbone, 30 Apr. 1945, in Rathbone papers, XIV/2/17/65, University of Liverpool archive (ULA).

38 Executive minutes of National Committee, 5 June 1945, in Parkes papers, 15/057, Southampton University archive (SUA) and *News From Hitler's Europe*, 15 May 1945. Lord Ailwyn in *Hansard* (HL), vol. 136, cols 102–16, 130, 136, 2 May 1945 – he was supported by other members of the Lords. See also Mr Hopkinson, MP, in *Hansard* (HC), vol. 410, cols 2266–7, 15 May 1945.

39 Alfred Perles, *Alien Corn* (Allen & Unwin, London, 1944), p. 241, refers to such refugee anxieties; E. G. to Gollancz, 5 July 1945, in Gollancz papers, 157/3/LI/NT/1/89, Modern Records Centre, University of Warwick.

40 *News From Europe*, 11 Sept. and 13 Nov. 1945; *Hampstead and Highgate Express*, 12 Oct. 1985; Hampstead Borough Council minutes, 25 Oct. 1945, Swiss Cottage Library, London; report, 30 Nov. 1945, on fascist involvement in the petition movement, in Board of Deputies of British Jews archive (BDA), C6/3/2/6; Rathbone, notes on speech, 22 Oct. 1945, in Rathbone papers, XIV/3/80, ULA.

41 For objections to the showing of the Donald Duck cartoon and other reactions to the liberation newsreels, see M-O A: TC 'Victory Celebrations', Box 1, File A; comments of Alan Borg, director of the Imperial War Museum, in *The Relief of Belsen*, p. 3, and autobiographical comments of Colin Richmond, in 'Diary', *London Review of Books*, 13 Feb. 1992.

42 Neal Ascherson, 'The film Britain hid from Germany', *Observer*, 8 Sept. 1985.

43 Reverend Isaac Levy, conversation with the author, 22 Feb. 1989; Gill, *The Journey Back From Hell*, p. 285, and, similarly, Dorothy Rabinowitz, *New Lives: Survivors of the Holocaust Living in America* (Knopf, New York, 1976), pp. 89, 193, 196, for evidence of American Jewish ignorance of the Holocaust.

44 *Opinion*, quoted by Robert Ross, *So It Was True: The American Protestant Press and the Nazi Persecution of the Jews* (University of Minnesota Press, Minneapolis, Minn., 1980), p. 293; Anglo-Jewish Association memorandum on British Jews, June 1950, in Anglo-Jewish Association papers, AJ 37/13/7, SUA, and, similarly, Basil Henriques, in *Jewish Outlook*, Sept./Oct. 1947.

45 Yehuda Bauer, *Out of the Ashes: The Impact of American Jews on Post-Holocaust European Jewry* (Pergamon Press, Oxford, 1989), p. xviii; David Nathan, 'The Agony of Anglo-Jewry', *Jewish Chronicle*, 26 Aug. 1977, and Tony Kushner, 'Antisemitism and austerity: the August 1947 riots in Britain', in Panikos Panayi (ed.), *Racial Violence in Britain* (Leicester University Press, Leicester, 1993), pp. 149–68. Differences between British and American Jewry in their post-war confrontation with the Holocaust were underlined in a symposium held by the Spiro Institute in 1985 – see *Jewish Chronicle*, 17 May 1985. For the limitations of Anglo-Jewish relief efforts after 1945, see the constant complaints in the minutes of the Jewish Committee for Relief Abroad, Jan. 1945–Oct. 1948, MF 2838, Manchester Central Reference Library, and Richard Bolchover, *British Jewry and the Holocaust* (Cambridge University Press, Cambridge, 1993), pp. 72–3.

46 Victor Gollancz, *"Nowhere to Lay Their Heads": The Jewish Tragedy in Europe and its Solution* (Gollancz, London, 1945), p. 4; D. H. to Gollancz, 5 July 1945, and E. B. to Gollancz, 7 Aug. 1945, in Gollancz papers, 157/3/LI/NT 1/ 55, 173.

47 *Talking Picture News*, 2 May 1945; Oswald Mosley, 28 Nov. 1947, reproduced in Lionel Rose, *Fascism in Britain* (no publisher, London, 1948), p. 15; for their war detentions, see PRO HO 283/13–18 for Mosley and HO 45/25729 for Bowman; *Truth*, 4 May 1945; Douglas Reed, *Far and Wide*, (Jonathan Cape,

London, 1951), p. 308; M-O A: D 5303, 29 Sept. 1945; M-O A: DR July 1946, Was 1, for Reed's influence.

48 Gollancz, *"Nowhere to Lay Their Heads"*, p. 2; R. A. to Gollancz, 5 July 1945, in Gollancz papers, 157/3/LI/NT/1/95.

49 *Zionist Review*, 21 Sept. 1945; Michael Marrus, *The Holocaust in History* (Weidenfeld & Nicolson, London, 1988), p. 4; for boredom with the Nuremberg trials in Britain, see M-O A: FR 2428A and M-O A: TC 'Politics', Box 15, File E, and 'Nuremberg', Box 104.

50 For example, Frederic Raphael recalls the term 'Belsen' being used to describe skinny boys at his public school. See his *The Necessity of Anti-Semitism* (University of Southampton, Southampton, 1989), p. 17, and, similarly, *Jewish Chronicle*, 4 May 1990. Miles Lloyd, *Six Million Died! Stark – Factual: Nazi Germany's Extermination Programme* (Brown, Watson, London, 1961), p. 5. For the lack of interest and attention given to the Auschwitz trial, see *Jewish Chronicle*, 11 Apr. 1947.

51 M-O A: DR Jam 11, Pin 1, Cle 2, July 1946.

52 M-O A: DR Pea 2, Thu 1, Bam 1, Cap 1, Coo 15, July 1946.

53 M-O A: D 5270, 2 May 1945; M-O A: DR Gar 115, Bec 1, July 1946; poll quoted by Leonard Dinnerstein, *America and the Survivors of the Holocaust* (Columbia University Press, New York, 1982), p. 56.

54 M-O A: DR Tow 1, July 1946; Charity Blackstock, *Wednesday's Children* (Hutchinson, London, 1967), p. 161; *Jewish Chronicle*, 12 and 26 Oct. 1945, on the trial, and *Truth*, 19 Oct. 1945. The papers of Major Winwood, who defended Kramer, are in the Imperial War Museum; for Patton, see Dinnerstein, *America and the Survivors of the Holocaust*, pp. 17, 47 and chapter 1 *passim*; and Mark Wyman, *DP: Europe's Displaced Persons, 1945–1951* (Balch Institute Press, Philadelphia, Pen., 1989) describes army treatment of the displaced persons.

55 No definitive figures are available on the number of Jewish survivors who came to Britain after the war. By the end of 1949, of some 365,000 post-war immigrants to Britain, some 5,600 had come under the Distressed Relatives scheme. By no means of all of these were Jewish – see *AJR Information*, Dec. 1949. For the post-war immigration into Britain in general, see J. Isaac, *British Post-War Migration* (Cambridge University Press, Cambirdge, 1954); J. Tannahill, *European Voluntary Workers in Britain* (Manchester University Press, Manchester, 1958); Diana Kay and Robert Miles, *Refugees or Migrant Workers? European Volunteer Workers in Britain, 1946–51* (Routledge, London, 1992); Dinnerstein, *America and the Survivors of the Holocaust*, p. 251.

56 The Harrison report is reproduced in full in appendix B of Dinnerstein's *America and the Survivors of the Holocaust*, pp. 291–305 (see esp. pp. 294–5, 298). Memorandum, Mar. 1946, in PRO FO 372/57689 WR 850, quoted by Dinnerstein, loc. cit., p. 47.

57 W. M. Louis, *The British Empire in the Middle East, 1945–1951* (Clarendon Press, Oxford, 1984); Richie Ovendale, *Britain, the United States, and the End of the Palestine Mandate, 1942–1948* (Boydell Press, Woodbridge, Suffolk, 1989); Dinnerstein, *America and the Survivors of the Holocaust*, pp. 113–16; PRO FO 371/51606, Logan minute, 8 Jan. 1946.

58 Leonard Dinnerstein, *Uneasy at Home: Antisemitism and the American Jewish Experience* (Columbia University Press, New York, 1987), chapter 9, for post-war antisemitism; *idem, America and the Survivors of the Holocaust*, chapter 5, on the Citizens Committee.

59 Dinnerstein, *America and the Survivors of the Holocaust*, pp. 123, 126; resolution

from the International Ladies' Garment Workers' Union, in *Report of the Proceedings of the Sixty-Fifth Convention of the American Federation of Labor* (Judd & Detweiller, Washington, DC, 1946), pp. 520–1; and resolution from the same union, in *Report of the Proceedings of the Sixty-Sixth Congress of the American Federation of Labor* (Judd & Detweiller, Washington, DC, 1947), pp. 611–17.

60 See the Executive Committee minutes of the CCJ, 1945–50, in 2/2 and 3, SUA; James Parkes, 'The Jewish World Since 1939', *International Affairs*, 21 (Jan. 1945), pp. 87–105; *idem*, 'Life is With People', *Common Ground*, 6 (Aug.–Oct. 1952), pp. 16–21; *idem*, 'The German Treatment of the Jews', in Arnold Toynbee and Veronica Toynbee (eds), *Survey of International Affairs, 1939–1946* (Oxford University Press, London, 1954), pp. 153–64; CCJ Middle East Group, CCJ papers, 15/034, SUA.

61 Joseph Gorny, *The British Labour Movement and Zionism 1917–1948* (Cass, London, 1983); H. Child of the National Union of Tailors and Garment Workers to the Secretary of the National Council of Labour, 23 May 1947, in TUC archive, Box 324; union membership details in *Jewish Chronicle*, 14 Oct. 1949; for union perspectives on unemployment, see Kenneth Lunn, 'Race Relations or Industrial Relations? Race and Labour in Britain, 1880–1950', in Kenneth Lunn (ed.), *Race and Labour in Twentieth-Century Britain* (Frank Cass, London, 1985), pp. 19–20; immigration figures in *AJR Information*, Aug. 1950.

62 Memorandum by Chuter Ede, Oct. 1945, and Dennys to Ince, 18 Oct. 1945, in PRO LAB 8/99; for further inter-departmental discussion, see PRO FO 1071/2 and HO 213/1360 E409; testimony of the two sisters is in Gill, *The Journey Back From Hell*, chapter 17 (esp. pp. 405–6 for British immigration procedures).

63 Gee to Dennys, 16 Oct. 1945, and Dennys to Ince, 18 Oct. 1945, in PRO LAB 8/99.

64 The most sympathetic portrayal of Bevin and the Jews can be found in Alan Bullock, *Ernest Bevin: Foreign Secretary* (Heinemann, London, 1984), pp. 164–9 while the introduction of Louis, *The British Empire in the Middle East*, gives a balanced critique of his role in Palestine after 1945. See David Holly, *Exodus 1947* (Little, Brown, Boston, 1969), 'Exodus', *Sunday Times Magazine*, 15 May 1988, and the diaries of Captain A. C. Barclay (who was in charge of the British naval operation) in SUA, for this dramatic post-war episode. Bullock, loc. cit., p. 449, and PRO CAB 128/10, 66th meeting, 31 July 1947, describe the decision not to send the Jews on the ships to Britain and thus avoid 'more anti-Jewish demonstrations'. See also Ariel Joseph Kochavi, 'Britain and the Jewish Exodus from Poland Following the Second World War, *Polin*, 7 (1992), pp. 161–75.

65 Chuter Ede to Dennys, 19 Nov. 1945, and Bevin to Isaacs, 21 Feb. 1946, in PRO LAB 8/99; see chapter 2 for Bevin's earlier policies as a trade union leader; *Zionist Review*, 21 June 1946.

66 *Sunday Express*, 6 Jan. 1946; Tilling to Markham, 25 Mar. 1946, in PRO HO 213/695 E409.

67 Judge memorandum, 21 May 1946, and Oliver to Arthur Salter, 23 May 1946, in PRO HO 213/695 E409; the administration of the Care of Children from the Camps can be found in the Archives of the Central British Fund for World Jewish Relief, reel 37; see also Rothschild archives 000/315 C for local reports in 1945. Ben Helfgott and Hugo Gryn, two of those who came on the scheme, comment on the inability to find enough eligible children – see their testimony in Gill, *The Journey Back From Hell*, p. 165. Home Office policy with regard to these children can be followed in PRO HO 213/618, 781 and 782.

68 Gee to Dennys, 7 Dec. 1945, in PRO LAB 8/99; Dennys to Evans, 5 July 1946, in PRO LAB 8/92; and Dennys to Alice Bacon in the Home Office, 2 Aug. 1946,

in PRO HO 213/1360 E409. For Ministry of Labour pressure to relax procedure with regard to domestics, see PRO LAB 8/92, 1170 and 1171, and Home Office response, in PRO HO 213/696, 865, 1360. Russell Davies and Liz Ottoway, *Vicky* (Secker & Warburg, London, 1987), p. 79. See also Vicky Weisz's correspondence in DX 166, University of Hull archive. Vicky wrote to his wife on 12 Feb. 1946: 'My sister wrote another desperate letter to me saying that even if she gets the visa from the Home Office here she won't get the exit permit from Hungary – so there's deadlock again – she's absolutely destitute now and there's no way of getting money or food to her.' Correspondence in PRO HO 213/1360 E409 refers to a Mrs E. Weisz in Budapest.

69 These desirability 'lists' can be found in PRO FO 945/500 and 501 and FO 371/66709 and 66711. See David Cesarani, *Justice Delayed: How Britain Became A Refuge for Nazi War Criminals* (Heinemann, London, 1992), chapter 4, and Louise London, 'British Attitudes Towards Jews in the Post War Period' (unpublished MS), pp. 35–6; for the obsession of Home Office fears with regard to domestic antisemitism (including reference to the Hampstead petition movement), see Dennys to Ince, 18 Oct. 1945, in PRO LAB 8/99. Herbert Morrison was at the forefront of promoting such concern and kept the issue of domestic antisemitism alive in the Cabinet until the very end of his period as Home Secretary – see his comments in PRO CAB 95/15 JR (45), 16 May 1945. His successor, Chuter Ede, maintained this paranoia– see his similar comments in PRO CAB 129/2, 6 Nov. 1945.

70 For Australia, even W. D. Rubinstein (who has provided a revisionist critique of those who have attacked government policy on Jewish refugee policy) acknowledges that of 170,000 Displaced Persons coming to Australia from 1947 to 1954 only 500 at most were Jews. He suggests that it seems 'undeniable that Jews were covertly excluded from the programme'. W. D. Rubinstein, 'Australia and the Refugee Jews of Europe, 1933–1954: A Dissenting View', *Journal of the Australian Jewish Historical Society*, 10 (1989), p. 507; Irving Abella and Harold Troper, *None is Too Many: Canada and the Jews of Europe 1933–1948* (Random House, New York, 1982), chapters 7 and 8; Dinnerstein, *America and the Survivors of the Holocaust*, chapters 6–9.

71 For specific recruitment of Nazis, see Tom Boyer, *Blind Eye to Murder* (Deutsch, London, 1981) and *idem, Paperclip Conspiracy* (Grafton, London, 1988); Mayhew, quoted in 'Special Assignment', BBC Radio 4, 17 Nov. 1989; *AJR Information*, July 1946 and Oct. 1948.

72 Gee to Dennys, 16 Oct. 1945, in PRO LAB 8/99.

73 Kitty Hart, *Return to Auschwitz* (Atheneum, New York, 1985), pp. 11–12; testimony in Gill, *The Journey Back From Hell*, pp. 152–4, 75–6, for the second survivor.

74 Gena Turgel, *I Light a Candle* (Grafton, London, 1988), p. 177.

75 Blackstock, *Wednesday's Children*, pp. 54–5 and chapter 'Baruch, Nathan and Franz'; for patterns of dispersement across the United States, see Rabinowitz, *New Lives, passim*, and Gill, *The Journey Back From Hell*, chapter 13; for the '45 Aid Society, see Helfgott in Gill, loc. cit., p. 186. Martin Gilbert has been commissioned to write the history of the '45 Aid Society. Most of the children from the camps were boys – reflecting the gender of those who survived the Terezin camp where most of those sent to the UK were liberated from. Material relating to the earlier Primrose Club, which served as an informal meeting place (especially for meeting girls), is in Archives of the Central British Fund, reel 37, file 203.

76 Blackstock, *Wednesday's Children*, p. 57; Turgel, *I Light a Candle*, p. 172. See

also *Jewish Chronicle*, 11 Sept. 1987. For Kramer and Grese, see Lord Russell of Liverpool, *The Scourge of the Swastika: A Short History of Nazi War Crimes* (Cassell, London, 1954), pp. 177, 180, 207.

77 Rabinowitz, *New Lives*, pp. 93, 196–7; Foxman, quoted by Judith Miller, *One, By One, By One*, pp. 220–1.

78 Michel testimony in Gill, *The Journey Back From Hell*, pp. 288–9; John Hersey, *The Wall* (Knopf, New York, 1950); James Young, 'Holocaust Memorials in America: The Politics of Identity', in William Frankel (ed.), *Survey of Jewish Affairs: 1991* (Blackwell, Oxford, 1991), pp. 163–4.

79 Diary entries 1 Feb., 28 Apr., 25 Sept. and 6 Oct. 1945, in Schwartzbart papers, M2/775 and 776, Yad Vashem archives; Reuven Dafni (ed.), *Yad Vashem* (Yad Vashem, Jerusalem, 1990), p. 3.

80 For the Memorial Committee, see correspondence in BDA, C10/5/3; Louis Golding, *The Glory of Elsie Silver* (London, Hutchinson, 1945) dealt with the ghetto in a continuation of his 'Mr Emmanuel' series; for the commemoration of the Holocaust in refugee circles see *AJR Information, The Jewish Quarterly* and *The Wiener Library Bulletin*.

81 Helmreich, 'The Impact of Holocaust Survivors', p. 23; for the aim of the Wiener Library to achieve a 'great narrative' of the Jewish war experience, see Eva Reichmann in *AJR Information*, Nov. 1954.

82 Helmreich, 'The Impact of Holocaust Survivors', pp. 22–4, suggests that they were not so isolated from the power structures of American Jewry as has often been assumed. See Miller, *One, By One, By One*, pp. 220–2, for an alternative view. *AJR Information*, Apr. 1956.

83 Review of Reitlinger's book in the *Manchester Guardian*. For a summary of the responses to this book, see *Wiener Library Bulletin*, May–Aug. 1953 and Jewish Chronicle archive 225/5/25 and 225/6/13, SUA, for its British and overseas marketing. See publisher's comments in 1958 edition of Lord Liverpool, *The Scourge of the Swastika*.

84 Gollancz, *"Nowhere to Lay Their Heads"*, p. 3; E. L. to Gollancz, 20 July 1945, and Capt. H. to Gollancz, 16 Sept. 1945, in Gollancz papers, 157/3/LI/NT/1/149 and 211; Blackstock, *Wednesday's Children*, p. 150.

85 The *Daily Telegraph* debate is summarized in *AJR Information*, Aug. 1956; the Manchester Jewish Museum has material on Fred Kirkby, whose experience of the liberation of Belsen made a deep psychological impact on the rest of his life, especially due to the sense of isolation he later felt – see MJM 1905/502; Rabinowitz, *New Lives*, p. 196.

86 Golding quoted by Alan Sinfield, *Literature, Politics and Culture in Postwar Britain* (Blackwell, Oxford, 1989), p. 140; William Golding, *Lord of the Flies* (Faber & Faber, London, 1954); *Jewish Chronicle*, 4 Oct. 1991, for the Amis family. Sinfield, loc. cit., pp. 139–47 argues persuasively for the implicit racism of authors such as Golding and Plath when confronting the horrors of European society, who explain its existence by the 'savage within'. For a critique of British writers' silence on the Holocaust, see George Steiner's comments in Stephen Brook, *The Club* (Constable, London, 1989), p. 421. One artist deeply influenced by the images from Belsen and the other western camps in spring 1945 was Francis Bacon, but even he did not refer directly to the suffering of the victims in his work. For Bacon and other British-based artists' reluctance to confront the horror directly, see Andrew Sinclair, *War Like a Wasp: the Lost Decade of the 'Forties* (Hamish Hamilton, London, 1989), chapter 13.

87 Ephraim Sicher, *Beyond Marginality: Anglo-Jewish Literature After the*

Holocaust (State University of New York Press, Albany, NY, 1985), chapters 3–6; M-O A: DR Den 6, Oct. 1946; Mel Calman, 'In the Psychiatrist's Chair', BBC Radio 4, 28 Aug. 1991; this indirect impact is covered with much subtlety by Howard Cooper and John Morrison, *A Sense of Belonging: Dilemmas of British Jewish Identity* (Weidenfeld & Nicolson, London, 1991), *passim* (esp. pp. 88–94, 'In the Shadow of the Holocaust'). Transcripts of the interviews and films from Cooper and Morrison's research are now deposited at the University of Southampton.

88 K. R. M. Short, 'Hollywood Fights Anti-Semitism, 1945–1947', in K. R. M. Short (ed.), *Feature Films as History* (Croom Helm, London, 1981), chapter 8; Avisar, *Screening the Holocaust*, pp. 110–11; Terry Lovell, 'Frieda'; Andy Medhurst, '1950s War Films' and Christine Geraghty, 'Masculinity' in Geoff Hurd (ed.), *National Fictions: World War Two in British films and television* (British Film Institute, London, 1984), pp. 30–34, 35–38, 63–65.

89 The diary was first published in English in 1952 by Vallentine, Mitchell. For the marketing of this book in Britain and beyond, see Jewish Chronicle archives, 225/5/25, SUA. By 1959 the diary was in its tenth printing with Pan Books. Judith Doneson, *The Holocaust in American Film* (Jewish Publication Society, Philadelphia, Penn., 1987), chapter 2. The book continues to be the leading non-fiction work in libraries. See *The Guardian*, 7 Jan. 1993; the denial of its authenticity prompted the publication of a definitive edition: Netherlands State Institute for War Documentation, *The diary of Anne Frank: the critical edition* (Viking, London, 1989).

90 Doneson, *The Holocaust in American Film*, pp. 61, 66, 73 and chapter 2, *passim*.

91 Frith Banbury, quoted by *AJR Information*, Nov. 1956, and review, loc. cit., Jan. 1957; Jill Tweedie, 'The silent byways of the righteous gentiles', *The Guardian*, 17 Dec. 1990; Shulman in the *Evening Standard*, 30 Nov. 1956. I am grateful to David Cesarani for this last reference. There are other reviews of the play from Britain during 1956 in the Charles Landstone papers, A311 (2), Central Zionist Archives.

92 Delargy's comments reported in *AJR Information*, June 1958; sales figures from the 1958 edition; John Gross, 'Is Anti-Semitism Dying Out?', *20th Century*, 172 (Spring 1963), p. 21; for comparative comments on Britain and the United States with regard to the twenty-fifth anniversary, see Schwartzbart to Barnett Janner, MP, 15 Apr. 1958, in C11/13/34, BDA.

93 Gideon Hausner, *Justice in Jerusalem* (Harper & Row, New York, 1966) provides a good summary of the trial; Raul Hilberg, *The Destruction of the European Jews* (Quadrangle Books, Chicago, Mich., 1961).

94 James Young, *Writing and Rewriting the Holocaust: Narrative and the Consequences of Interpretation* (Indiana University Press, Bloomington and Indianapolis, Ind., 1988), chapter 7 and esp. p. 132; M. B. to Gollancz, 11 June 1961, in Gollancz papers, 157/3/LI/AE/2/83.

95 Hannah Arendt, *Eichmann in Jerusalem* (Viking, New York, 1963). One of the first comprehensive responses was Reuben Ainsztein, *Jewish Resistance in Nazi-Occupied Eastern Europe* (Elek, London, 1974). Ainsztein's papers are now deposited at the University of Southampton.

96 George Gallup, *The Gallup Poll: Public Opinion 1935–1971*, vol. 3 *1959–1971* (Random House, New York, 1972), p. 1719; T. S. to Gollancz, 15 June 1961, and E. C. to Gollancz, 16 Aug. 1961, in Gollancz papers, 157/3/LI/AE/2/313 and 550; *Parish Magazine of All Saints' Church, Otley*, June 1961, for an attack on Old Testament 'revenge'; M. H. to Gollancz, 14 June 1961, in Gollancz papers,

157/3/LI/AE/2/139 and Rabinowitz, *New Lives*, pp. 191–2, for evidence of equating Eichmann's trial with that of Jesus.

97 F. W. to Gollancz, 28 Mar. 1961, D. W. to Gollancz, no date, and S. W. to Gollancz, 17 July 1961, in Gollancz papers, 157/3/LI/AE/2/2,167 and 175 for Holocaust denial; J. V. to Gollancz, 9 June 1961, Gollancz papers, loc. cit., 2/62 for a more typical insistence on the need to forget; George Gallup, *The Gallup International Public Opinion Polls: Great Britain 1937–1975*, vol. 1 *1937–1964* (Random House, New York, 1976), p. 595.

98 Doneson, *The Holocaust in American Film*, chapter 3 (esp. p. 139); Avisar, *Screening the Holocaust*, chapter 4; for Wiesel, see the comments of Rabbi Irving Greenberg, quoted in Miller, *One, By One, By One*, p. 222.

99 Blackstock, *Wednesday's Children*, p. 150; see the document *Lifeline Cavalcade* produced in 1965 by those connected to the Association of Nazi Camp Survivors, in CCJ papers, 9/21, SUA; for later limited facilities for survivors in Britain, see *Jewish Chronicle*, 27 Dec. 1985 and 13 July 1990.

100 Warsaw Ghetto Memorial Committee, 'Aims and Objects' (1960?) in BDA, C11/13/34; John Alldridge, 'Letters to My Daughter', *Manchester Evening News*, 23 Jan. 1960, reprinted as a pamphlet in 1963 (no publisher).

101 Warsaw Ghetto Memorial Committee, 'Aims and Objects'; Robert Miles and Annie Phizacklea, *White Man's Country: racism in British politics* (Pluto, London, 1984).

102 N. C. Williams (Provost) to Bill Simpson, 8 May 1961, in BDA E1/41; *Coventry Cathedral Review*, May 1961; *The Times*, 2 May 1961; for a review of the exhibition and the controversy surrounding it, see *AJR Information*, July 1961.

103 The ghetto film ban is referred to in *AJR Information*, Jan. 1961; for the exhibition, see B6/2/43 and C10/5/3 in BDA; Lloyd, *Six Million Died!*, p. 5.

104 G. Ringrosse to Simpson, 24 Jan. 1960, and ANCCS, *Newsletter*, June 1964, both in CCJ papers, 9/21, SUA.

105 Hanauer to Simpson, July 1964 and 27 Jan. 1965, Simpson to Hanauer, 3 Feb. 1965, and Hanauer to Simpson, 5 Feb. 1965, in CCJ papers, 9/21, SUA.

106 Jewish Aid Committee of Britain, *With a Strong Hand*, (JACOB, London, 1966) for an account of fascist activities in the 1960s in London. Government papers for 1962 have recently been released on this topic. See *Jewish Chronicle*, 8 Jan. 1993; J. E. S. to W. W. S. memorandum, 1 Apr. 1965, summarizes Christian and Jewish objections to the proposed survivors' event within the CCJ, in CCJ papers, 9/21, SUA.

107 Alan Bullock, *Hitler: A Study in Tyranny* (Pelican, Harmondsworth, 1962 [revised edition], first published 1952); A. J. P. Taylor, *The Origins of the Second World War* (Hamilton, London, 1961); Norman Cohn, *Warrant for Genocide: The Myth of the Jewish World Conspiracy and the "Protocols of the Elders of Zion"* (Eyre and Spottiswoode, London, 1967) – Cohn has been described by Anthony Storr as 'the historian of important parts of history that other historians do not reach: the collective myths that underpin the assumptions, prejudices and beliefs which shake and shape human societies' in the *Independent on Sunday*, 14 Nov. 1993; Lucy Dawidowicz, *The Holocaust and the Historians* (Harvard University Press, Cambridge, Mass., 1981), chapter 2 (esp. pp. 31–2); Gerd Korman, 'Silence in the American Textbooks', *Yad Vashem Studies*, 8 (1970), pp. 183–202, and Randolph Braham (ed.), *The Treatment of the Holocaust in Textbooks* (Columbia University Press, New York, 1987), part 3; comments of Gideon Hausner, Chair of Yad Vashem, to the British Yad Vashem Committee, 30 Apr. 1980, minutes of the National Yad Vashem Committee in the United Kingdom (YVCUK archives).

108 Egon Larsen, 'What Every Child Should Know . . .', *AJR Information*, June 1962; Kenneth Ambrose, *The Story of Peter Cronheim* (Constable, London, 1962); Anne Holm, *I am David* (Methuen, London, 1965); Judith Kerr, *When Hitler Stole Pink Rabbit* (Collins, London, 1971). Kerr was born in Germany in 1923 but had emigrated to Britain by the outbreak of the war. For an overview of such books, see Caroline Marcus, 'Holocaust Literature for Children', *New Moon*, Nov. 1991.

109 Lucy Dawidowicz, 'Visualising the Warsaw Ghetto: Nazi Images of the Jews refiltered by the BBC', *Shoah*, 1/1 (1978), p. 6; Judith Doneson, 'Teaching the Holocaust with Film', *The Jewish Quarterly*, no. 141 (Spring 1991), pp. 59–60.

110 Young, 'Holocaust Memorials in America', pp. 163–5; Doneson, *One, By One, By One*, pp. 220–303; Michael Berenbaum, 'On the Politics of Public Commemoration of the Holocaust', *Shoah*, 2/3 (Fall/Winter 1981–2), pp. 6–11; Steiner in the *Sunday Times*, 10 Apr. 1988.

111 For these writers, see Sicher, *Beyond Marginality*, chapters 7 and 8; Naomi Jacob's 'Gollantz Saga' and Louis Golding's 'Mr Emmanuel' dealt with the persecution of the Jews in books published in the late 1930s and 1940s; Martin Gilbert, *Atlas of the Holocaust* (Joseph, London, 1982); *idem, Auschwitz and the Allies* (Michael Joseph, London, 1981) and *The Holocaust: The Jewish Tragedy* (Collins, London, 1986); for Martin Gilbert's background, see *New Moon*, Mar. 1992.

112 Jon Harris, 'An Elegy for Myself: British Poetry and the Holocaust', *English*, 41 (Autumn 1992), pp. 213–33, comments on the general absence of attention given to the subject; Philip Norman, 'A cosy British dose of the same old anti-Semitic poison', *The Independent on Sunday*, 25 Aug. 1991.

113 James Young, 'The Counter-Monument: Memory against Itself in Germany Today', *Critical Inquiry*, 18 (Winter 1992), pp. 267–96 (esp. p. 270); *idem*, 'Holocaust Memorials in America', p. 162; the recent release of documentation indicating the involvement of local officials in the deportation of Jews in Guernsey prompted *The Guardian*, 7 Jan. 1993, to comment 'Guernsey warns us that we ought not to be so cocooned in national complacency as to think that sleeping with the enemy is a continental disease'.

114 Carter in *Reform*, Feb. 1974; Lawrence to Simpson, 13 Feb. 1973 and Feb. 1974, Archbishop of Westminster to Carter, 13 Feb. 1973, Archbishop of Canterbury to Carter, 13 Feb. 1973, and Carter to Simpson, 5 Apr. 1973, in CCJ papers, 9/84, SUA.

115 Warsaw Ghetto Memorial Committee, 'A Permanent Memorial', in CCJ papers, 9/84, SUA.

116 Carter approached the newly created Community Relations Council in 1975/6 – it decided it could not help. See *Harpenden Advertiser*, 2 Nov. 1979, and Carter to Baroness Birk, 25 Oct. 1979, in CCJ papers, 9/84, SUA.

117 Minutes of the National Yad Vashem Committee, 24 July 1979, in YVCUK archives.

118 Doneson, *The Holocaust in American Film*, chapter 4; Miller, *One, By One, By One*, pp. 255–8; Berenbaum, 'On the Politics of Public Commemoration', pp. 6–11; Yehuda Bauer, 'Holocaust Questions', *AJC Monthly*, May 1980, on the President's Commission and the issue of uniqueness. Ironically, given the unresolved problems in the United States, Reverend Jennings of the CCJ in Britain wrote to Rabbi Irving Greenberg, President of the President's Commission, 3 June 1980, asking advice on whether a Holocaust monument should cover all victims of the Nazis, in CCJ papers, 9/85 file 2.

119 See the minutes of 15 Feb. 1977 for a chronology of development since June 1976, in YVCUK archive; loc. cit., 21 May 1979 for an unveiling of a Holocaust memorial at Bushey cemetery, London, and 25 June 1979 for discussion of a national monument; *AJR Information* for the 1970s and 1980s for similar, private memorials; Jennings to Webster, 25 Apr. 1980, in CCJ papers, 9/86.

120 Janner's Presidential statement in CCJ papers, 9/85; 'Cenotaph for Jewish war dead', *The Guardian*, 23 Oct. 1979. In contrast, see the *Daily Telegraph*, 22 Oct. 1979; T. Chadwick (Manchester CCJ) to Jennings, 1 Nov. 1979, and E. Rothschild to Jennings, in CCJ papers, 9/85 file 2. Greville Janner later reported in the *Jewish Chronicle*, 8 Sept. 1989, that the promised Whitehall site 'was withdrawn, allegedly under pressure from Arab embassies, transmitted via the Foreign and Commonwealth Office'.

121 Harry O'Morton (British Council of Churches) to CCJ, 4 Mar. 1980, and Moshe Davis to Jennings, 15 Oct. 1980, in CCJ papers, 9/85; Immanuel Jakobovits, *The Holocaust, Contemporary Jewry, Zionism Today, Spiritual Leadership – A Call for Reappraisal* (Office of the Chief Rabbi, London, 1979), p. 2; for the Memorial Garden, see 'Forgetting to Remember', *New Moon*, June 1992, and minutes 3 Sept. 1986, 31 Oct. 1988 and 21 May 1992, YVCUK archive.

122 See the minutes of the Yad Vashem Committee through the 1980s and early 1990s. In 1980 a scheme was put forward to create a Holocaust museum in the Roundhouse, north London (YVCUK minutes, 20 Oct. and 8 Dec. 1980). Like many exciting but speculative ventures at the Roundhouse it came to nothing. For grafitti at the Hyde Park memorial, see *Jewish Chronicle*, 18 Aug. 1989. For recent gatherings at the memorial before *Yom Hashoah*, see *Jewish Chronicle*, 28 Apr. 1989 and 27 Apr. 1990. For a sceptical view of the American Holocaust museum 'business', see Miller, *One, By One, By One*, pp. 255–75.

123 East London Auschwitz Exhibition Committee, *Auschwitz: An Exhibition* (no publisher, London, 1983) and YVCUK minutes, 12 July 1982 and 24 Feb. 1983; *Anne Frank in the World: 1929–1945* (Anne Frank Centre, Amsterdam, 1985); for the ILEA pack, see *Jewish Chronicle*, 4 Nov. 1988; schoolteacher interest, with a small minority opposed, is confirmed in Carrie Supple, 'The teaching of the Nazi Holocaust in North Tyneside, Newcastle and Northumberland secondary schools' (unpublished research report, Newcastle University, 1990); the Yad Vashem Charitable Trust in its 1990 report stressed the connection between 'the growing interest in anti-racist education' and concern about the Holocaust in Britain, in YVCUK archives.

124 The life stories of Hart, Gryn and Helfgott feature in Gill, *The Journey Back From Hell*, chapters 8 and 9. Ben Helfgott's increasing role in the Yad Vashem Committee in the 1980s indicated the greater prominence of survivors in the Board of Deputies of British Jews; see also *Chasing Shadows*, Naomi Gryn's moving film of her father's background (1990).

125 John Hamshire, 'How little we know today about the war', *Daily Mail*, 26 Aug. 1989, and *Jewish Chronicle*, 1 Sept. 1989, for comment. A 1993 poll carried out by the American Jewish Committee in the United States and Britain confirms this age profile. Partial details of the poll are reported in *Jewish Chronicle*, 23 Apr. 1993.

126 For lobbying over the National curriculum, see *Jewish Chronicle*, 13 Apr. 1990 and 29 Mar. 1991, and Philip Rubenstein and Warren Taylor, 'Teaching about the Holocaust in the National Curriculum', *The British Journal of Holocaust Education*, 1 (Summer 1992), pp. 47–54; National Curriculum History Working Group, *Final Report* (Department of Education and Science and the Welsh Office,

1990), p. 99; for the absence of Holocaust education, even in Jewish schools, see the minutes of the Yad Vashem Committee, 21 May 1979, in YVCUK archive; Melanie Philips in *The Guardian*, 21 Aug. 1990, on changing attitudes to Holocaust education in Britain; Carrie Supple, *From Prejudice to Genocide – Learning about the Holocaust* (Trentham, London, 1992) is an excellent example of the new material available.

127 John Fox, *Teaching the Holocaust: The Report of a Survey in the United Kingdom (1987)* (National Yad Vashem Charitable Trust, Leicester, 1989), p. 6; Juliet Gardiner, *The History Debate* (Collins & Brown, London, 1990). In contrast, see the important student reader by two leading scholars of Nazi Germany: Jeremy Noakes and Geoffrey Pridham (eds), *Nazism: 1919–1945: A Documentary Reader*, vol. 3 *Foreign Policy, War and Racial Extermination* (Exeter University Press, Exeter, 1987), esp. chapters 38 and 39. The *British Journal of Holocaust Education* is edited by John Fox and published by Frank Cass for the Yad Vashem Charitable Trust and the Holocaust Educational Trust.

128 For a brief history of the IWM, see its catalogue *The* New *Imperial War Museum* (1992?), pp. 1, 44, and comments of its director, Alan Borg, in *The Relief of Belsen*, p. 3; for the Buchenwald exhibition, see *Jewish Chronicle*, 6 Apr. and 18 May 1990, and Borg, quoted in Yad Vashem Committee minutes, 25 Sept. 1990, YVCUK archives; *The* New *Imperial War Museum*, p. 40; for early American proposals and the link to the liberation of the camps, see Young, 'Holocaust Memorials in America', pp. 167–8; for the proposed Warsaw ghetto uprising exhibition, see Yad Vashem Committee minutes, 15 Sept. 1992, YVCUK archives.

129 The 1950/1 reports are still to be released by the British government. See *Observer*, 5, 12 May and 9 June 1991, and *Jewish Chronicle*, 10 May 1991. For the lack of screening in the United States and the later setting up of the OSI, see Allan Ryan, *Quiet Neighbours: Prosecuting Nazi War Criminals in America* (Harcourt Brace Jovanovich, Orlando, Fla, 1984), chapters 1–3 and 8; for earlier accusations in Britain, see the All-Party Parliamentary War Crimes Group, *Report on the Entry of Nazi War Criminals and Collaborators into the UK, 1945–1950* (HMSO, London, 1988); Mavis Hill and L. Norman Williams, *Auschwitz in England: A Record of a Libel Action* (MacGibbon and Kee, London, 1965) for the Dering case; a history of the development of the issue in the 1970s and 1980s is provided in Eli Rosenbaum, 'The Investigation and Prosecution of Suspected Nazi War Criminals: a Comparative Overview', *Patterns of Prejudice*, 21 (Summer 1987), pp. 17–24; Cesarani, *Justice Delayed*, p. 190.

130 The campaign for legislation is dealt with thoroughly in Cesarani, *Justice Delayed*, chapter 9; *Searchlight*, 192 (June 1991) for its own role in the campaign.

131 All-Party Parliamentary War Crimes Group, *Report on the Entry of Nazi War Criminals*; see also the *Jewish Chronicle*, 27 Oct. 1989, for the Group's conference in Oct. 1989, 'Time for Justice'; Sir Thomas Hetherington and William Chalmers, *War Crimes: Report of the War Crimes Inquiry* (Cmd. 744, HMSO, London, 1989); Commons debates on 12 Dec. 1989, 19 Mar. 1990, 25 Apr. 1990; for an overview, see Joseph Finklestone, 'Suspected Nazi War Criminals in the United Kingdom: Aspects of the Controversy in Parliament', *British Journal of Holocaust Education*, 1 (Summer 1992), pp. 25–46 and Cesarani, *Justice Delayed*, chapter 10.

132 Bishop of St Albans in *Hansard* (HL), vol. 518, cols 621–4, 4 Dec. 1989; Bishop of Southwark in *Hansard* (HL), vol. 519, col. 1097, 4 June 1990, and Lord Dacre and Lord Monkswell in *Hansard* (HL), vol. 528, cols 634–7, 663–4, 30 Apr.

1991, on the danger of stimulating antisemitism; Lady Soulton and Lord Hankey in *Hansard* (HL), vol. 518, cols 644, 672, 4 Dec. 1989; Lord Mayhew and Earl of Longford in *Hansard* (HL), vol. 519, cols 1092–3, 1177–78, 4 June 1990, and Bishop of Southwark and Earl of Longford in *Hansard* (HL), vol. 528, cols 634–7, 663–4, 30 Apr. 1991, on the Jews as 'alien' and 'un-British' demanding Old Testament revenge; for the leading campaigner against war crimes legislation in the House of Commons, Ivor Stanbrook, see *Jewish Chronicle*, 19 Feb. 1988, and *New Moon*, Mar. 1991, and generally on the 'antipathy to minority voices', David Cesarani, 'Conditional Tolerance', *Times Higher Educational Supplement*, 26 May 1989. See *Jewish Chronicle*, 18 June 1993 and 1 July 1994 for the continued delay in bringing prosecutions.

133   Alexander Ratcliffe, *The Truth about the Jews* (Scottish Protestant League, Glasgow, 1943), pp. 15–16; Newsam minute, June 1943, and Morrison reply, 28 June 1943, in PRO HO 45/25398/278–9.

134   Gill Seidel, *The Holocaust Denial* (Beyond the Pale Collective, Leeds, 1986); for anecdotal evidence of its influence, see *Jewish Socialist*, 8 (Winter 1986/7); Supple, 'The teaching of the Nazi Holocaust', p. 44 for its lack of impact based on a small survey of local schoolchildren in the north-east of England; the state's continuing reluctance to take action is highlighted in *Jewish Chronicle*, 5 Feb. 1988, 17 Aug. and 12 Oct. 1990, and 19 Apr. 1991; Lady Mosley appeared on the prestigious 'Desert Island Discs' (see *The Times*, 27 Nov. 1989); for Irving, see *Searchlight*, 170 (Aug. 1989), *Daily Mail*, 26 Apr. 1983, *The Guardian*, 17 Jan. 1992, *Observer*, 19 Jan. and 12 July 1992. Irving was used by the *Sunday Times* in July 1992 to translate unpublished material from the Goebbels diaries; for the use of Irving, see David Cesarani in *New Statesmen & Society*, 10 July 1992, and *New Moon*, Oct. 1992. Lady Birdwood, a leading supporter of Holocaust denial, appeared on the 'James Whale Radio Show' (Yorkshire Television) in Nov. 1990 along with a Holocaust survivor. For Buchanan, see *The Guardian*, 14 Jan. and 9 Mar. 1992, and Douglas Rose (ed.), *The Emergence of David Duke and the Politics of Race* (University of North Carolina Press, Chapel Hill, NC, 1992) on Duke. For Le Pen, see *Jewish Chronicle*, 13 Nov. 1987, 23 Sept. 1988 and 25 Aug. 1989, and James Shields, 'Antisemitism in France: the spectre of Vichy', *Patterns of Prejudice*, 24 (Winter 1990), pp. 5–17. The results of the American Jewish Committee poll on British and American attitudes towards the Holocaust are reproduced in Jennifer Golub and Renae Cohen, *What Do the British Know About the Holocaust?* (American Jewish Committee, New York, 1993). Gallup have queried the figure of 22 per cent and have revised it to 13 per cent – see *Jewish Chronicle*, 27 May 1994.

135   Doneson, *The Holocaust in American Film*, p. 139. Michael Berenbaum, *The World Must Know: The History of the Holocaust As Told in the United States Holocaust Memorial Museum* (Little, Brown and Company, Boston, Toronto and London). For a critique of the Americanization of the Holocaust in this museum, see Philip Gourevitch, 'In the Holocaust Theme Park', *Observer*, 30 Jan. 1994. Claude Lanzmann has criticized Spielberg's film for its Hollywood happy ending, in *Evening Standard*, 10 Feb. 1994. Nevertheless, its partially redemptive ending hardly compares with the earlier and equally important Hollywood version of *The Diary of Anne Frank*. Mark Steyn, in *The Independent*, 15 Oct. 1990.

136   Thus Joshua Sobol's 'Ghetto' won the *Evening Standard* 'Best Play of 1989' award; for the 1991 Booker Prize and Holocaust literature, see Bryan Cheyette in the *Jewish Chronicle*, 18 Oct. 1991; Jennifer Wingate, 'The National Life Story Collection', *British Journal of Holocaust Education*, 1 (Winter 1992), pp.

127–55. The 'Testimony' project, sponsored by the Union of Jewish Students, is videoing survivors and is linked to a larger scheme being carried out at Yale University. For the first major use of the Yale tapes, see Lawrence Langer, *Holocaust Testimony: Ruins of Memory* (Yale University Press, New Haven, Conn., 1991). Bertha Leverton, 'Heritage or survival?', *Jewish Chronicle*, 25 Dec. 1992, on public demand for talks by a former *Kindertransporte* child. Marcus Braybrooke, *Time to Meet* (SCM, London, 1990) for Christian interest in the Holocaust.

137 For a crude and notorious example of Trotskyite distortion of the Holocaust, see Jim Allen, *Perdition: A Play in Two Acts* (Ithaca Press, Exeter, 1987); Young, *Writing and Rewriting the Holocaust*, p. 133.

CONCLUSION

1 Rathbone, notes for speech, 19 May 1943, in Rathbone papers, XIV/3/74, University of Liverpool archive and in *Hansard* (HC), vol. 389, col. 1142, 19 May 1943.

2 For numbers, see Roger Smith's foreword to Israel Charny (ed.), *Genocide: A Critical Bibliographic Review* (Mansell, London, 1988), p. v; Primo Levi, *The Drowned and the Saved* (Michael Joseph, London, 1988), pp. 66, 135, 167.

3 Joint letter to *The Guardian*, 4 August 1992; David Hawk, 'The Cambodian Genocide', in *Genocide: A Critical Bibliographic Review*, pp. 137–54, summarizes the debate and existing literature. For the revival of Pol Pot's fortunes, see John Pilger, 'The holocaust game', *Weekend Guardian*, 28–9 Oct. 1989. For the Kurds in Iraq, see Helga Graham, 'Hitler-Style genocide threatens the Kurds', *Observer*, 7 May 1989; 'Genocide', *Jewish Chronicle*, 16 June 1989. See Mark Huband, Donatella Lorch and Kieth Richberg, 'Blood Brothers', *The Guardian*, 3 May 1994, on Rwanda.

4 For international diplomacy and genocide, see Leo Kuper, *Genocide: Its Political Use in the Twentieth Century* (Yale University Press, New Haven, Conn., 1981), chapters 2 and 9; *idem, The Prevention of Genocide* (Yale University Press, New Haven, Conn., 1985); Frank Chalk, *The History and Sociology of Genocide: Analyses and Case Studies* (Yale University Press, New Haven, Conn., 1990), p. xvii.

5 Zygmunt Bauman, *Modernity and the Holocaust* (Polity Press, Oxford, 1989); Levi, *The Drowned and the Saved*, p. 5.

6 Monty Penkower, *The Jews Were Expendable: Free World Diplomacy and the Holocaust* (University of Illinois Press, Urbana and Chicago, Ill., 1983); A. J. Sherman, *Island Refuge: Britain and the Refugees from the Third Reich 1933–1939* (Elek, London, 1973), chapter 9, 'A Balance Sheet'; Helen Fein, *Accounting For Genocide: National Responses and Jewish Victimization during the Holocaust* (The Free Press, New York, 1980), pp. 82, 185; chapter 6 of this study for the War Refugee Board.

7 Nigel Nicolson (ed.), *Harold Nicolson: Diaries and Letters 1939–1945* (Collins, London, 1967), p. 469, diary entry for 13 June 1945.

8 Otto Dov Kulka and Aron Rodrigue, 'The German Population and the Jews in the Third Reich: Recent Publication and Trends in Research on German Society and the "Jewish Question"', *Yad Vashem Studies*, 16 (1984), p. 430, argue powerfully that 'it becomes apparent that the term "indifference" may be more

confusing than helpful'. Their comments can be applied outside the specific area of public opinion in Nazi Germany and the Jews.

9 Raul Hilberg, 'The Significance of the Holocaust', in Henry Friedlander and Sybil Milton (eds), *The Holocaust: Ideology, Bureaucracy, and Genocide* (Kraus International, New York, 1980), p. 96.

10 See Levi, *The Drowned and the Saved*, p. 52, on the desire to construct a positive memory of the liberation process; Feingold, 'The Government Response', in *The Holocaust: Ideology, Bureaucracy and Genocide*, p. 257; chapters 1 and 4 of this study.

11 Levi, *The Drowned and the Saved*, p. 5.

12 Fein, *Accounting For Genocide*, p. 92; Ervin Staub, *The Roots of Evil: The Origins of Genocide and Other Group Violence* (Cambridge University Press, Cambridge, 1989), p. 80.

13 The responses of Nicolson and Rathbone appear throughout this volume; Storm Jameson, *Journey From The North*, vol. 1 and vol. 2 (Collins, London, 1969, 1970); Staub, *The Roots of Evil*, p. 77.

14 Samuel and Pearl Oliner, *The Altruistic Personality: Rescuers of Jews in Nazi Europe* (Free Press, New York, 1988); Levi, *The Drowned and the Saved*, chapter 2 (esp. p. 39).

15 See chapters 5 and 6 of this study. The British government's Home Intelligence unit emphasized only the existence of antisemitism among the public – see its reports, particularly for the end of 1942 and the start of 1943, in PRO INF 1/292. The National Committee for Rescue from Nazi Terror's *News From Hitler's Germany* for 1944 and 1945 reveals the detailed knowledge of the Holocaust available in the last stages of the war as well as the deep frustrations and angers of these activists.

16 For the newly independent East European countries and the Holocaust, see generally *The Guardian*, 22 Feb. 1990, and Jonathan Webber (ed.), *Jewish Identities in the New Europe*, (Littman Library, Oxford, 1994); *New York Times*, 17 Nov. 1991, on Lithuania; *The Guardian*, 18 Aug. 1990, and *Jewish Chronicle*, 7 July 1989, for Czechoslavakia (now itself split); *The Guardian*, 29 Sept. 1988, for Hungary; the change in atmosphere in Eastern Europe has been illustrated by the fact that the 'Anne Frank in the World Exhibition' has been shown successfully in Moscow and Kiev; James Young, 'The Future of Auschwitz', *Tikkun*, 7 (Nov./Dec. 1992), pp. 31–4, 77; Antony Polonsky (ed.), *My Brother's Keeper: Recent Polish Debates on the Holocaust* (Routledge, London, 1990) and Jonathan Webber, 'A day to heal and hope', *Jewish Chronicle*, 20 Apr. 1990, on Poland; John Bunzl, 'Austrian Identity and Antisemitism', *Patterns of Prejudice*, 21, no. 1 (1987), pp. 3–8, and Judith Miller, *One, By One, By One: Facing the Holocaust* (Weidenfeld & Nicolson, London, 1990), pp. 61–92, on Austria; Henry Rousso, *The Vichy Syndrome: History and Memory in France since 1944* (Harvard University Press, Cambridge, Mass., 1991), esp. chapter 4, and Paul Webster in *The Guardian*, 14 and 15 Apr., 16 June and 30 Nov. 1992, on recent developments in France; and *Jewish Chronicle*, 22 and 29 Apr. 1994, for the Touvier verdict.

17 The comments of the Archbishop of Westminster, 1973, cited in MS 65 9/85, Southampton University archive; see my comments and those of David Cesarani in *Patterns of Prejudice*, 25 (Winter 1991), pp.13–16, 37–9, on the dangers of ignoring racism from *within* the liberal tradition in the modern world. Britain especially has attempted to appease the far right by implementing racist and draconian immigration controls. France and Germany are increasingly following the British example.

18 Y. Yerushalmi, *Zakhor: Jewish History and Jewish Memory* (Schocken, New York, 1989), pp. 105–17, and Jonathan Boyarin, *Storm from Paradise: The Politics of Jewish Memory* (University of Minnesota Press, Minneapolis, MN, 1992), pp 1–8, on the issue of 'forgetting'; Antony Polonsky, 'Introduction', in John Fox, *Teaching the Holocaust: The Report of a Survey in the United Kingdom* (Yad Vashem Charitable Trust, Leicester, 1989), p. 1.

19 Fein, *Accounting For Genocide*, p. 92; Staub, *The Roots of Evil*, p. 87, suggests 'Bystanders can exert powerful influence. They can define the meaning of events and move others toward empathy or indifference.' Staub is right to stress the importance of individual responsibility in this area. It should be added, however, that governments in the twentieth century have been reluctant to believe the best of their peoples. They have therefore made the task of the non-violent, humanitarian bystander immensely difficult.

Sources and Bibliography

Full details of all secondary literature referred to in this work are provided in the notes to each chapter. The bibliography is therefore limited to primary sources (archival and printed).

Manuscript sources

PUBLIC COLLECTIONS

British Library, London	Chuter Ede papers
Central Zionist Archives, Jerusalem	Joseph Cohen papers Jewish Agency for Palestine papers Charles Landstone papers World Jewish Congress papers
Greater London Record Office	Board of Deputies of British Jews archives Office of the Chief Rabbis papers
Imperial War Museum, London	'Britain and the Refugee Crisis 1933–1947', oral history recordings Major-General L. A. Hawes' diaries
Jabotinsky Institute, Tel Aviv	Abraham Abrahams papers Ivan Greenberg papers
London Museum of Jewish Life	Unpublished memoirs
Manchester Central Reference Library	Barash papers Jean Gafan papers

	Jewish Committee for Relief Abroad papers Manchester Jewish Refugee Committee papers
Manchester Jewish Museum	Harris House diary and papers Fred Kirkby Belsen Liberation papers Refugee oral history recordings Unpublished memoirs
National Labour Museum, Manchester	William Gillies papers Labour party archives J. S. Middleton papers National Council of Labour papers
Public Record Office, Kew	CAB 24, 27, 66, 95, 98, 128 and 129 FO 371, 1071 and 945 HO 45, 144, 213 and 215 INF 1 LAB 2, 8, 24 PREM 4
Research Foundation for Jewish Immigration, New York	Refugee oral history recordings
Rothschild archives, London	Anthony de Rothschild papers
Swiss Cottage Library	Hampstead Borough Council minutes
University of Hull	National Council for Civil Liberties archive Vicky Weisz papers
University of Liverpool	Eleanor Rathbone papers
University of Manchester	Manchester Guardian archive W. Crozier papers
University of Southampton	Anglo-Jewish Association papers W. W. Ashley papers Captain A. C. Barclay papers Central British Fund for World Jewish Relief papers Council of Christians and Jews papers Ivan Greenberg papers Jewish Association for the Protection of Children and Women papers Jewish Chronicle archive Phineas May papers J. H. Hertz papers

	National Committee for Rescue from Nazi Terror papers
	James Parkes papers
	Samuel Rich papers
	W. W. Simpson papers
	Solomon Schonfeld papers
	Union of Jewish Women papers
University of Sussex	Mass-Observation archive:
	Diaries (1939–50)
	File Reports (1938–50)
	Directives (1939–50)
	Topic Collections (1938–50)
University of Warwick	Trades Union Congress archive
	Victor Gollancz papers
Yad Vashem Institute, Jerusalem	Joseph Rosensaft papers
	Ignacy Schwartzbart papers

PRIVATE COLLECTIONS

Letters, memoirs and oral history material relating to refugee domestic servants (held by Tony Kushner)

National Yad Vashem Committee minutes (held by the Board of Deputies of British Jews)

Oral history material of refugees settling in the Midlands (held by Birmingham Jewish History Group)

Printed sources

DOCUMENT COLLECTIONS

Yitzhak Arad et al. (eds), *The Einsatzgruppen Reports* (Holocaust Library, New York, 1989)

Hadley Cantril (ed.), *Public Opinion 1935–1946* (Princeton University Press, Princeton, NJ, 1951)

Michael Dobkowski (ed.), *The Politics of Indifference: A Documentary History of Holocaust Victims in America* (University Press of America, Washington, DC, 1982)

Ilya Ehrenburg and Vasily Grossman (eds), *The Black Book* (Holocaust Library, New York, 1981)

George Gallup (ed.), *The Gallup Poll: Public Opinion 1935–1971*, vol. 1 *1935–1948* and vol. 3 *1959–1971* (Random House, New York, 1972)

George Gallup (ed.), *The Gallup International Public Opinion Polls: Great Britain 1937–1975*, vol. 1 *1937–1964* (Random House, New York, 1976)

Jeffrey Gurock and Robert Hirt (eds), *Kidush Hashem: Jewish Religious and*

Cultural Life in Poland During the Holocaust (Yeshiva University Press, New York, 1987)

Desmond Hawkins and Donald Boyd (eds), *War Report: A Record of Dispatches Broadcast by the BBC's War Correspondents with the Allied Expeditionary Forces, 6 June 1944–5 May 1945* (Oxford University Press, London, 1946)

Norberte Kampe (ed.), *Jewish Immigrants of the Nazi Period*, vol. 4/1 *Jewish Emigration from Germany 1933–1942: A Documentary History* (K. G. Saur, New York, 1992)

Joseph Kermish (ed.), *To Live with Honor and Die with Honor: selected documents from the Warsaw Ghetto underground archives 'O.S.' (Oneg Shabbath)* (Yad Vashem, Jerusalem, 1986)

Ernst Klee et al. (eds), *'Those Were the Days': The Holocaust through the Eyes of the Perpetrators and Bystanders* (Hamish Hamliton, London, 1991)

David Low, *Years of Wrath: A Cartoon History: 1932–1945* (Gollancz, London, 1986)

Michael Mashburg, 'Documents Concerning the American State Department and the Stateless European Jews, 1942–1944', *Jewish Social Studies*, 39 (1977), pp. 163–79

J. Mendelsohn (ed.), *The Holocaust: Selected Documents in Eighteen Volumes* (Garland, New York, 1982)

J. Noakes and G. Pridham (eds), *Nazism 1919–1945*, vol. 2 *State, Economy and Society 1933–39: A Documentary Reader* (University of Exeter, Exeter, 1987)

J. Noakes and G. Pridham (eds), ibid., vol. 3 *Foreign Policy, War and Racial Extermination* (Exeter University Press, Exeter, 1987)

R.Phillips (ed.), *Trial of Joseph Kramer and Forty-Four Others: The Belsen Trial* (William Hodge & Co, London, 1949)

Antony Polonsky (ed.), *My Brother's Keeper: Recent Polish Debates on the Holocaust* (Routledge, London, 1990)

Jacob Robinson and Henry Sachs, *The Holocaust: The Nuremberg Evidence*, Part 1: *Documents, Digest, Index and Chronological Tables* (Yad Vashem, Jerusalem, 1976)

Charles Stember et al. (eds), *Jews in the Mind of America* (Basic Books, New York, 1966)

David Wyman (ed.), *America and the Holocaust* [13 volumes] (Garland Press, New York, 1990)

OFFICIAL

Hansard:
  House of Commons Debates, 1919–1992
  House of Lords Debates, 1933–1992

All-Party Parliamentary War Crimes Group, *Report on the Entry of Nazi War Criminals and Collaborators into the United Kingdom, 1945–1950)* (HMSO, London, 1988)

Buchenwald: The Report of a Parliamentary Delegation (Cmd 6626, HMSO, London, 1945)

Hearings Before the Committee on Immigration and Naturalization, House of Representatives, *Admission of German Refugee Children*, 76th Congress, 1st Session on H.J. Res. 165 and H.J. Res. 168, 24–5 and 31 May, and 1 June 1939 (US Government Printing Office, Washington, DC, 1939)

Joint Hearings Before a Subcommittee of the Committee on Immigration, United States Senate and A Subcommittee of the Committee on Immigration and Naturalization, House of Representatives, *Admission of German Refugee Children*, 76th Congress, 1st Session on S.J. Res. 64 and H.J. Res. 168, 20–2 and 24 April 1939 (US Government Printing Office, Washington, DC, 1939)

The Molotov Notes on German Atrocities: Notes Sent by V. M. Molotov, People's Commisar For Foreign Affairs, to all Governments with which the USSR has Diplomatic Relations (HMSO, London, 1942)

National Curriculum History Working Group, *Final Report* (Department of Education and Science and the Welsh Office, London, 1990)

Papers Concerning the Treatment of German Nationals in Germany 1938–9 (Cmd 6120, HMSO, London, 1939)

Sir Thomas Hetherington and William Chalmers, *War Crimes: Report of the War Crimes Inquiry* (Cmd 744, HMSO, London, 1989)

E. Woodward and R. Butler (eds), *Documents on British Foreign Policy 1919–1919*, vol. 4 (HMSO, London, 1950) and vol. 5 (HMSO, London, 1956)

PRINTED REPORTS

Daily Proceedings of the Constitutional Conventions of the Congress of Industrial Organizations

Reports of the Annual Conventions of the American Federation of Labor

Reports of the Annual Trades Union Congress

NEWSPAPERS AND JOURNALS

National

Daily Herald	*Daily Mail*
Daily Telegraph	*Evening Standard*
Fortune	*Illustrated London News*
The Guardian	*Manchester Guardian*
New Statesman	*New York Times*
Observer	*Partisan Review*
Picture Post	*The Spectator*
Sunday Dispatch	*Sunday Times*
Time	*Time and Tide*
The Times	*Tribune*
Truth	

Jewish

AJR Information	*Jewish Chronicle*
The Jewish Quarterly	*Jewish Standard*
Zionist Review	

Other

Action	American Federationist
Anglo-German Review	Catholic Herald
Christian Newsletter	Chronology of Principal Events
CIO News	Common Ground
Horizon	Kitchener Camp Review
Labour	The Land Worker
Medical World	News from Hitler's Europe
Now & Then	Peace News
Polish Fortnightly Review	Talking Picture News
Wiener Library Bulletin	

BOOKS, PAMPHLETS AND ARTICLES

Louis Adamic, *America and the Refugees* (Public Affairs Committee, New York, 1939)

John Alldridge, *Letters to My Daughter* (publisher unknown, Manchester, 1963)

Norman Angell, *Have We Room for the Refugees?* (National Committee for the Rescue of Victims from Nazi Terror, London, 1944)

Norman Angell and Dorothy Buxton, *You and the Refugee* (Penguin, Harmondsworth, 1939)

Anne Frank Stichting, *Anne Frank in the World 1929–1945* (AFS, Amsterdam, 1985)

Anon., *The Victory Book* (Odhams Press, London, 1945)

Hannah Arendt, *Eichmann in Jerusalem: A Report on the Banality of Evil* (Viking Press, New York, 1963)

Michael Berenbaum, *The World Must Know: The History of the Holocaust as told in the United States Holocaust Memorial Museum* (Little, Brown and Company, Boston, 1993)

Board of Deputies of British Jews, *Germany and the Jews* (Board of Deputies, London, 1937 and 1939)

Marcus Braybrooke, *Time to Meet* (SCM, London, 1990)

Central Coordinating Committee for Refugees, *Mistress & Maid* (CCCR, London, 1939 and 1940)

Israel Cohen, *The Jews in Germany* (Murray, London, 1933)

Maurice Davie, *Refugees in America: Report of the Committee for the Study of Recent Immigrants from Europe* (Greenwood Press, Westport, Conn., 1974 [first published in 1947])

East London Auschwitz Exhibition Committee, *Auschwitz: An Exhibition* (publisher unknown, London, 1983)

B. J. Elliot, *Hitler and Germany* (Longman, London, 1966)

Violet Firth, *The Psychology of the Servant Problem* (C. W. Daniel, London, 1925)

John Fox, *Teaching the Holocaust: The Report of a Survey in the United Kingdom (1987)* (National Yad Vashem Charitable Trust, Leicester, 1989)

Juliet Gardiner, *The History Debate* (Collins and Brown, London, 1990)

Victor Gollancz, *Let my People Go* (Gollancz, London, 1942)

Victor Gollancz, *"Nowhere to Lay Their Heads": The Jewish Tragedy in Europe and its Solution* (Gollancz, London, 1945)

Victor Gollancz, *What Buchenwald Really Means* (Gollancz, London, 1945)

Victor Gollancz, *Leaving Them to Their Fate: the ethics of starvation* (Gollancz, London, 1946)

J. B. C. Grundy, *Brush Up Your German: Conversations of real use* (Dent and Sons, London, 1931)

J. B. C. Grundy, *The Second Brush Up Your German* (Dent and Sons, London, 1939)

Peter Harlow, *The Shortest Way With the Jews* (Allen & Unwin, London, 1939)

Immanuel Jakobovits, *The Holocaust: Contemporary Jewry, Zionism Today, Spiritual Leadership – A Call for Reappraisal* (Office of the Chief Rabbi, London, 1979)

Jewish Aid Committee of Britain, *With A Strong Hand* (JACOB, London, 1966)

Jewish Labor Committee, *The Jewish Labor Committee: What It Does and What It Stands For* (JLC, New York, 1942)

Joint Foreign Committee of the Board of Deputies and the Anglo-Jewish Association, *The Persecution of the Jews in Germany* (JFC/AJA, London, 1933)

G. E. O. Knight, *In Defence of Germany* (Golden Vista Press, London, 1933)

Arthur Koestler, 'The Mixed Transport', *Horizon*, 8 (Oct. 1943), pp.244–51

A. H. Lane, *The Alien Menace* (Boswell, London, 1934)

Miles Lloyd, *Six Million Died! Stark – Factual: Nazi Germany's Extermination Programme* (Brown, Watson, London, 1961)

Lord Londonderry, *Ourselves and Germany* (Robert Hale, London, 1938)

Lord Russell of Liverpool, *The Scourge of the Swastika: A Short History of Nazi War Crimes* (Cassell, London, 1954)

Charles Myers, 'The Servant Problem', *Occupational Psychology*, 30 (Apr. 1939), pp.85–6

National Committee for Rescue from Nazi Terror, *Continuing Terror* (National Committee, London, 1944)

Beverley Nichols, *News of England* (Jonathan Cape, London, 1938)

James Parkes, 'The Jewish World Since 1939', *International Affairs*, 21 (Jan. 1945), pp. 87–105

James Parkes, 'Life Is With the People', *Common Ground*, 6 (Aug.–Oct. 1952), pp. 16–21

James Parkes, 'The German Treatment of the Jews', in Arnold Toynbee and Veronica Toynbee (eds), *Survey of International Affairs, 1939–1946* (Oxford University Press, London, 1954), pp. 153–64

Geoffrey Ward Price, *I Know These Dictators* (Right Book Club, London, 1937)

Alexander Ratcliffe, *The Truth about the Jews* (Scottish Protestant League, Glasgow, 1943)

Eleanor Rathbone, *Rescue the Perishing* (National Committee for Rescue from Nazi Terror, London, 1943)

Eleanor Rathbone, *Falsehoods and Facts about the Jews* (National Committee, London, 1944)

Douglas Reed, *Insanity Fair* (Jonathan Cape, London, 1938)

Douglas Reed, *Far and Wide* (Jonathan Cape, London, 1951)

Royal Institute of International Affairs, *Chronology of Principal Events: Consolidated Edition: Munich Agreement to December 31, 1942* (Royal Institute, London, 1944)

Royal Institute of International Affairs, *Chronology and Index of the Second World War* (Royal Institute, London, 1947)

Mark Starr, 'Labor Looks at Migration', *Current History*, 54 (Dec. 1943), pp. 299–304

Dorothy Thompson, 'Refugees: A World Problem', *Foreign Affairs*, 16 (Apr. 1938), pp.375–8

DIARIES, ORAL TESTIMONY, AUTOBIOGRAPHIES AND BIOGRAPHIES

Myra Baram, *The Girl With Two Suitcases* (Book Guild, Lewes, Sussex, 1988)

Bruno Bettelheim, *Surviving and Other Essays* (Thames and Hudson, London, 1979)

Earl of Birkenhead, *The Prof in Two Worlds: The Official Life of Professor F. A. Lindemann, Viscount Cherwell* (Collins, London, 1961)

Charity Blackstock, *Wednesday's Children* (Hutchinson, London, 1967)

Elaine Blonde with Barry Turner, *Marks of Distinction: The Memoirs of Elaine Blond* (Vallentine, Mitchell, London, 1988)

Meirion Bowen, *Michael Tippett* (Robson, London, 1982)

Alan Bullock, *The Life and Times of Ernest Bevin*, vol. 1 *Trade Union Leader 1881–1940* (Heinemann, London, 1960)

Alan Bullock, *Ernest Bevin: Foreign Secretary* (London, 1984)

Thomas Campbell and George Herring (eds), *The Diaries of Edward R. Stettinus Jr. 1943–1946* (Franklin Watts, New York, 1975)

Brewster Chamberlin and Marcia Feldman (eds), *The Liberation of the Nazi Concentration Camps: Eyewitness Accounts of the Liberators* (United States Memorial Council, Washington, DC, 1987)

Charles Chaplin, *My Autobiography* (Penguin, Harmondsworth, 1976)

Winston Churchill, *The Second World War*, vol. 1 *The Gathering Storm* (Cassell, London, 1948)

Walter Citrine, *Men and Work: An Autobiography* (Hutchinson, London, 1964)

Mark Cocker, *Richard Meinertzhagen: Soldier, Scientist and Spy* (Mandarin, Gilmour, London, 1990)

Ray Cooper, *Refugee Scholars: Conversations with Tess Simpson* (Moorland Books, Leeds, 1992)

J. Cross, *Sir Samuel Hoare: A Political Biography* (Jonathan Cape, London, 1977)

Russell Davies and Liz Ottoway, *Vicky* (Secker & Warburg, London, 1987)

Lucy Dawidowitz, *From That Place and Time: A Memoir 1938–1947* (Norton, New York, 1989)

Jonathan Dimbleby, *Richard Dimbleby: A Biography* (Hodder & Stoughton, London, 1975)

David Dubinsky and A. H. Raskin, *David Dubinsky: A Life with Labor* (Simon & Schuster, New York, 1977)

Melvyn Dubofsky and Warren Van Time, *John Lewis: A Biography* (Quadrangle, New York, 1977)

Ruth Dudley Edwards, *Victor Gollancz: A Biography* (Gollancz, London, 1987)

Hans Eysenck, *Rebel With A Cause* (W. H. Allen, London, 1990)

Ronald Fraser, *In Search of a Past* (Verso, London, 1984)

Steven Fraser, *Labor will Rule: Sidney Hillman and the Rise of American Labor* (The Free Press, New York, 1991)

'A German Jewish Scientist', *Why I Left Nazi Germany* (J. M. Dent, London, 1934)

Karen Gershon (ed.), *We Came as Children* (Gollancz, London, 1966)

Miep Gies, *Anne Frank Remembered* (Bantam, London, 1987)

Martin Gilbert, *Sir Horace Rumbold: Portrait of a Diplomat 1869–1941* (Heinemann, London, 1973)

Susan Goodman, *Spirit of Stoke Mandeville: the story of Sir Ludwig Guttmann* (Collins, London, 1986)

Iain Hamilton, *Koestler: A Biography* (Secker & Warburg, London, 1982)

Kitty Hart, *Return to Auschwitz* (Atheneum, New York, 1985)

H. Henson, *Retrospect of an Unimportant Life*, vol. 1 *1920–1939* (Oxford University Press, London, 1943)

Samuel Hoare, *Nine Troubled Years* (Collins, London, 1954)

Michael Holroyd, *Bernard Shaw*, vol. 3 *The Lure of Fantasy* (Chatto, London, 1991)

Gerald Hurst, *Closed Chapter* (Manchester University Press, Manchester, 1942)

Fred Israel (ed.), *The War Diary of Breckinridge Long: Selections from the Years 1939–1944* (University of Nebraska Press, Lincoln, Nebr., 1966)

Robert Rhodes James (ed.), *Chips: The Diaries of Sir Henry Channon* (Weidenfeld & Nicolson, London, 1967)

Storm Jameson, *Journey From the North: Autobiography*, vol. 1 (Collins, London, 1969) vol. 2 (Collins, London, 1970)

R.Jasper, *George Bell* (Oxford University Press, London, 1967)

Alfred Kazin, *Starting Out in the Thirties* (Secker & Warburg, London, 1966)

Paul Kemp (ed.), *The Relief of Belsen: April 1945 Eye Witness Accounts* (Imperial War Museum, London, 1991)

Ian Kemp (ed.), *Michael Tippett: A Symposium on his 60th Birthday* (Faber, London, 1965)

Alexander Kendrick, *Prime Time: The Life of Edward R. Murrow* (Little, Brown, Boston, Mass., 1969)

David Kranzler and Gertrude Hirschler (eds), *Solomon Schonfeld: His Page in History* (Judaica Press, New York, 1982)

Claude Lanzmann, *Shoah: An Oral History of the Holocaust* (Pantheon, New York, 1985)

Vera Laska (ed.), *Women in the Resistance and in the Holocaust: The Voices of Eyewitnesses* (Greenwood Press, Westport, Conn., 1983)

Bertha Leverton and Shmuel Lowenson (eds), *I Came Alone: The Stories of the Kindertransports* (Book Guild, Lewes, Sussex, 1990)

Primo Levi, *The Drowned and the Saved* (Michael Joseph, London, 1988)

Rhoda Lewin (ed.), *Witnesses to the Holocaust: An Oral History* (Twayne, Boston, Mass., 1990)

Jakov Lind, *Crossing* (Methuen, London, 1991)

L. Lochner (ed.), *The Goebbels Diaries* (Hamish Hamilton, London, 1948)

Martha Long, *The Austrian Cockney* (Centerprise, London, 1980)

David Low, *Low's Autobiography* (Michael Joseph, London, 1956)

David Matthews, *Michael Tippett: An Introductory Study* (Faber, London, 1980)

Richard Meinertzhagen, *Middle East Diary 1917 to 1956* (Cresset Press, London, 1959)

Leonard Miall (ed.), *Richard Dimbleby: Broadcaster, By His Colleagues* (BBC, London, 1966)

George Mikes, *How to be a Brit* (Penguin, Harmondsworth, 1987)

Thomas Moloney, *Westminster, Whitehall and the Vatican: The Role of Cardinal Hinsley 1935–43* (Burns, Oates & Co, Tunbridge Wells, Kent, 1985)

Netherlands State Institute for War Documentation (ed.), *The Diary of Anne Frank: the critical edition* (Viking, London, 1989)

Nigel Nicolson (ed.), *Harold Nicolson: Diaries and Letters*, vol. 1 *1930–39* (Weidenfeld & Nicolson, London, 1966) vol. 2 *1939–1945* (Collins, London, 1967)

Lilli Palmer, *Change Lobsters and Dance* (W. H. Allen, London, 1976)

James Parkes, *Voyage of Discoveries* (Gollancz, London, 1969)

Alfred Perles, *Alien Corn* (Unwin, London, 1944)

G. J. Renier, *The English: Are They Human?* (Williams & Norgate, London, 1931)

James Roose-Evans (ed.), *Joyce Grenfell: Darling Ma: Letters to her Mother 1932–1944* (Hodder & Stoughton, London, 1988)

Douglas Rose (ed.), *The Emergence of David Duke and the Politics of Race* (University of North Carolina Press, Chapel Hill, NC, 1992)

N. Rose (ed.), *Baffy: the Diaries of Blanche Dugdale 1936–1947* (Vallentine, Mitchell, London, 1973)

Lore Segal, *Other People's Houses* (Gollancz, London, 1965)

Michael Sheldon, *Friends of Promise: Cyril Connolly and the World of 'Horizon'* (Hamilton, London, 1989)

Naomi Shephard, *Wilfred Israel: German Jewry's Secret Ambassador* (Weidenfeld & Nicolson, London, 1984)

Dorothy Sheridan (ed.), *Among You Taking Notes . . . The Wartime Diary of Naomi Mitchison* (Gollancz, London, 1985)

Susan Sontag, *On Photography* (Penguin, Harmondsworth, 1979)

Eugen Spier, *The Protecting Power* (Skeffington & Son, London, 1951)

Mary Stocks, *Eleanor Rathbone: A Biography* (Gollancz, London, 1949)

Herbert Strauss (ed.), *Jewish Immigrants of the Nazi Period in the USA*, vol. 5 *The Individual and Collective Experience of German-Jewish Immigrants 1933–1984: An Oral History Record* (K. G. Saur, New York, 1986)

Ernest Tennant, *True Account* (Max Parrish, London, 1957)

Gena Turgel, *I Light A Candle* (Grafton, London, 1988)

John Vincent (ed.), *The Crawford Papers: The Journals of David Linsay* (Manchester University Press, Manchester, 1984)

F. Watson, *Dawson of Penn* (Chatto & Windus, London, 1950)

Philip Williams, *Hugh Gaitskell: A Political Biography* (Jonathan Cape, London, 1979)

Leonard Woolf (ed.), *A Writer's Diary: Being Extracts from the Diary of Virginia Woolf* (Hogarth Press, London, 1953)

K. Young (ed.), *The Diaries of Sir Robert Bruce Lockhart 1939–65* (Macmillan, London, 1980)

FICTION

Jim Allen, *Perdition: A Play in Two Acts* (Ithica Press, Exeter, 1987)

Kenneth Ambrose, *The Story of Peter Cronheim* (Constable, London, 1962)

Kingsley Amis, *Lucky Jim* (Gollancz, London, 1953)

Martin Amis, *Time's Arrow* (Jonathan Cape, London, 1991)

Louis Golding, *Mr Emmanuel* (Rich & Cowan, London, 1939)

Louis Golding, *The Glory of Elsie Silver* (Hutchinson, London, 1945)

William Golding, *Lord of the Flies* (Faber & Faber, London, 1954)

John Hersey, *The Wall* (Knopf, New York, 1950)

Anne Holm, *I Am David* (Methuen, London, 1969)

Ted Hughes (ed.), *Sylvia Plath: collected poems* (Faber, London, 1981)

Naomi Jacob, *The Gollantz Saga* (Hutchinson, London, 1952)

Judith Kerr, *When Hitler Stole Pink Rabbit* (Collins, London, 1970)

Joshua Sobol, *Ghetto* (Hern, London, 1990)

Michael Tippett, *A Child of Our Time* (Schott & Co, London, 1944)

Miscellaneous

UNPUBLISHED DISSERTATIONS, THESES AND PAPERS

Stephen Glassock, 'Early Interpretations of Nazism: The British Press and Hitler, 1922–1928' (BA Dissertation, Department of History, University of Southampton, 1985)

Rebecca Godfrey, 'Fifteen Case Studies of Refugee Women: Their Social and Economic Adjustment' (Masters thesis, Columbia University, 1941)

Tony Kushner, 'The Eastleigh Camp in the 1920s: Changes and Continuities in Immigration Policy' (Jewish Historical Society of England, Conference, Patterns of Migration, London, 1993)

Louise London, 'British Immigration Control Procedures and Jewish Refugees, 1933–1942' (PhD thesis, University of London, 1992)

John Major, speech to the 109th Conservative party conference, 9 Oct. 1992, Brighton (Conservative Central Office)

William Parsons and William Ferkekes, 'Days of Remembrance: 1992 Lesson Plans' (United States Holocaust Memorial Museum, 1992)

Barbara Schaap, 'A Study of the Vocational Adjustment of Twenty-Four Refugee Women' (Masters thesis, Columbia University, 1941)

Carrie Supple, 'The teaching of the Nazi Holocaust in North Tyneside, Newcastle and Northumberland secondary schools' (Research report, Newcastle University, 1990)

Pam Taylor, 'Women Domestic Servants 1919–1939' (Masters thesis, Birmingham University, 1978)

MUSEUM EXHIBITIONS

Ellis Island Museum, New York

'Before the Holocaust', Manchester Jewish Museum, 1987

'Kristallnacht', Wiener Library, 1988

'Refugee from Nazism', London Museum of Jewish Life, 1988

FILM AND TELEVISION

Auschwitz and the Allies (BBC, 1982)

Chasing Shadows (Channel 4, 1990)

Crossfire (USA, 1947)

The Cruel Sea (UK, 1952)

The Dam Busters (UK, 1959)

The Desert Fox (USA, 1951)

The Diary of Anne Frank (USA, 1959)

Frieda (UK, 1947)

The Gathering (BBC, 1982)

Genocide (ITV, 1985)

Gentleman's Agreement (USA, 1947)

The Great Dictator (USA, 1940)

Heimat (West Germany, 1984)

Holocaust (USA, 1978)

The House of Rothschild (USA, 1934)

Judgment at Nuremberg (USA, 1961)

The Mortal Storm (USA, 1940)

Mr Emmanuel (UK, 1944)

Next of Kin (UK, 1942)

None Shall Escape (USA, 1943)

A Painful Reminder (ITV, 1985)

The Pawnbroker (USA, 1965)

Return to Auschwitz (ITV, 1979)

Roots (USA, 1977)

Shoah (France, 1985)

So Ends Our Night (USA, 1941)

The Warsaw Ghetto (BBC, 1968)

Index